Author
Sunghoon Kim, Ed.M.

Contributing author
Josh Goreczny, MAT

Printed in the United States of America

First Printing, July 2018
Second Printing, March 2019

ISBN-13: 978-1090339676

All inquiries should be directed to:

Pittsburgh Prep
134 S. Highland Ave 2nd Floor
Pittsburgh PA 15206

info@pittsburghprep.com
www.PittsburghPrep.com

Dedicated to you,
the student who never gives up

Preface

When I myself took the SATs over two decades ago, I wished I had a book like the one you're holding right now. A clear, easy-to-follow, versatile and authoritative study guide proven to increase your test score. This book contains our **powerful SAT essentials study program** that we administer to our students at Pittsburgh Prep.

This book was written over a 18-month period: each lesson tested on over 1000 students in our live class settings, every page created with a tremendous amount of thought in the wording and presentation of concepts so that YOU can benefit from our expertise.

In this study guide, you will review every single concept to improve your SAT score, and to give you an academic advantage in college and beyond. This textbook has undergone many revisions to create the best study guide possible as you embark on this very important task.

Your first three weeks of study will be tough and will require diligent effort: this study guide covers 3 years-worth of high school Math, Reading and Writing intensively during this initial time period. Go to our YouTube page at Pittsburgh Prep and **watch our Preview Lessons before you begin any lesson in this book,** as directed. This will help you get in the right mindset, stay motivated, and remain focused. Type and search for "Pittsburgh Prep SAT Preview *Writing Lesson* 4," for example.

Also, follow us on f/insta @thepittsburghprep and on facebook.com/pittsburghprep. We'll post videos, motivational content, memes, and even Q&A's to help you perform your best.

Do work on this textbook DAILY. No rest days. Strengthen your resolve and make the next six weeks count. No one can take away your accomplishments. Your SAT score stays with you forever. Ask anybody and they all remember their SAT score and how it affected their college admissions. Make this a point of pride for yourself. At the end of the road, make sure that you've studied hard, given your best effort, and utilized this book to its fullest.

The axioms that you must follow:

- Set aside a minimum of 1 hour of study time **every day** for SAT prep using this study guide
- **Register** for the actual exam on collegeboard.com (Pick a date! Mark it on your calendar!)
- Reserve a minimum of **6 weeks of study time** from beginning of test prep to actual test date
- Make sure to take at least **6 full length SAT exams** on the weekends – downloaded from collegeboard.com

And finally, never, ever give up.

Sunghoon Kim, Ed.M

Acknowledgments

I'd like to thank all our students and instructors who have come through the doors of Pittsburgh Prep who've helped solidify the curriculum contained within this textbook. Through each and every one of you, I have learned so much and will always remain grateful.

In particular, I'd like to thank Josh Goreczny, my right-hand man and co-conspirator for just about everything, for his contributions and immense support in creating many of the problems, lessons and proofreading. Special thanks to Valeria Antúnez for editing and formatting the textbook.

My entire family, my two beautiful children, and my wife, who has stayed with me through thick and thin, and has always believed in me far more than anyone ever could. I love you.

Sunghoon Kim
Ed.M 2011
Harvard Graduate School of Education

I'd like to thank all my students over the years – teaching is not a one-way street, and I have learned far more from you than I could ever have imparted to you.

I'd like to thank my wife Rachel, the most genuine person I have ever met, and my family, who give me strength that cannot be described.

Finally, I'd like to thank Hoon for believing in me more than I believed in myself. We've fought through hardships and savored successes; we've built a school, a textbook, and a friendship. Best boss since sliced bread.

Josh Goreczny
MAT 2008
University of Pittsburgh
Graduate School of Education

Table of Contents

Your Study Schedule
Week 1

**"Preview" & "Deepdive" videos can be found under Pittsburgh Prep on Youtube*

Day	Writing	Math	Reading	Exam	Homework
1				Take exam #1 from collegeboard.com	Self-grade exam results
2	Watch Youtube Writing lesson 1 preview video + read lesson 1 (p.17) + complete application exercises (p.27)				Writing (WR) 1 HW exercises (p.29) + review
3		Watch Youtube preview Math lesson 1 (M1) video + read lesson 1 (p.101) + application exercises (p.109)			Math 1 HW exercises (p.112) + review
4			Watch Youtube preview Reading 1 video + RC lesson 1 (p.277)		RC 1 HW exercise (p.286) + review
5		Preview M2 video + lesson 2 (p.123) + application exercises (p.137)			Math 2 HW exercises (p.141) + review
6			Preview RC2 video + RC lesson 2 (p.293) + application exercises (p.297)		RC 2 HW exercise (p.299) + review
7	Preview WR2 video + WR lesson 2 (p.33) + application exercises (p.39)				WR 2 HW exercises (p.41) + review

Your Study Schedule
Week 2

Day	Writing	Math	Reading	Exams	Homework
8				Take exam #2 from collegeboard.com	Self-grade + review
9		Preview M3 video + lesson 3 (p.153) + application exercises (p.163)			Math 3 HW exercises (p.166) + review
10			Preview RC3 video + RC lesson 3 (p.313) + application exercises (p.317)		RC 3 HW exercise (p.321) + review
11		Preview M4 video + lesson 4 (p.179) + application exercises (p.189)			Math 4 HW exercises (p.192) + review
12	Preview WR3 video + WR lesson 3 (p.47) + application exercises (p.53)				WR 3 HW exercises (p.54) + review
13		Preview M5 video + lesson 5 (p.205) + application exercises (p.215)			Math 5 HW exercises (p.218) + review
14				Take exam #3 from collegeboard.com	Self-grade + review

Your Study Schedule
Week 3

Day	Writing	Math	Reading	Exams	Homework
15	Preview WR4 video + WR lesson 4 (p.59) + application exercises (p.65)				WR 4 HW exercises (pg.67) + review
16			Preview RC4 video + RC lesson 4 (p.331) + application exercises (p.335)		RC 4 HW exercise (p.340) + review
17				Take exam #4 from collegeboard.com	Self-grade + review
18		Preview M6 video + lesson 6 (p.233) + application exercises (p.241)			Math 6 HW exercises (p.244) + review
19	Preview WR5 video + WR lesson 5 (p.73) + application exercises (p.79)				WR 5 HW exercises (p.81) + review
20			Preview RC5 video + RC lesson 5 (p.349) + application exercises (p.353)		RC 5 HW exercise (p.355) + review
21		Preview M7 video + lesson 7 (p.257) + application exercises (p.263)			Math 7 HW exercises (p.266) + review
22	Preview WR6 video + WR lesson 6 (p.87) + application exercises (p.93)				WR 6 HW exercises (p.95) + review

Your Study Schedule
Weeks 4-6

Days				Exams	Homework
23-26				Take Pittsburgh Prep Exam #1 (p.361)	Self-grade + review
26-30				Take exam #5 from collegeboard.com	Self-grade + review
31-36				Take exam #6 from collegeboard.com	Self-grade + review
37-42				Take exam #7 from collegeboard.com	Self-grade + review

- **You have video preview lessons available to you at Youtube.com/pittsburghprep**
- **Contact us at info@pittsburgprep.com for online tutoring options**
- **Follow us on social media @thepittsburghprep (f/insta) @pittsburghprep (tweet)**
- **Recommend this study guide to your friends and family!**
- **Don't even *think* about quitting!**

Writing
Lesson 1

Clauses and Phrases

Goals

We will develop our grammatical fluency and gain meaningful understanding by learning to:

1) Distinguish between clauses and phrases
2) Explain the purpose of independent and dependent clauses, and their combined usage
3) Identify common types of phrases in English usage
4) Explain the proper usage for commas, semicolons, colons and other punctuations

Contents

- Clauses and Predicates
- Phrases
- Punctuation
- Application Exercises
- Homework Exercises

Lesson 1
Clauses and Phrases

Sentence Essentials

Sentences can have a variety of structure, but correct sentences will always have **at least one independent clause** containing a subject and predicate.

Independent clause
A complete idea that contains a subject and predicate

Predicate
The part of a sentence or clause that contains a verb and states something about the subject

The best way to analyze the structure of a sentence is to find the verb first, then the subject next. Not every complete sentence will have an object, but it will always have a subject and verb in the predicate.

'I am happy.'

The first thing we should look for in determining an independent clause is the verb**. A verb can be either an action or a linking verb (or both)**. In this instance, a form of the verb "to be" is the verb here. Once we determine the verb, we should ask what is doing or fulfilling this verb. Here, "I" is the subject that is being happy. **Subjects are nouns, pronouns or noun phrases that perform the action or links the subject to the part of the predicate**.

Verbs: Action verbs like "to play" conveys an action, while linking verbs like "to be" links the subject to words that describe it, or helps the main verb

Subjects: A person, place, thing or idea that is doing the action (action verb) or is being described in some way (linking verb)

eg 1. Determine the type of subject and verb that is used in the following independent clauses:

A) Reindeers pulled the sleigh.
B) Rucker Park, a desolate place in a desolate city, is designated as historically relevant.
C) Despite all odds, my truck driver, a lonely shell of a man, called in sick today.

Types of Clauses

There are two distinct types of clauses:

Independent clause
A complete idea that contains a subject and predicate.

Dependent clause
An idea that contains a subject and predicate, but it is not independent. Must be accompanied by a subordinating conjunction and an independent clause.

Every sentence is made up of at least one independent clause, consisting of a subject and a predicate. Dependent clauses, on the other hand, cannot stand alone.

Conjoining Clauses

There are a variety of options that we can take when trying to convey information by utilizing different clauses in a sentence. However, specific rules dictate how we can combine them. If we have two independent clauses, modern convention of English state that we should use a specific category of words called *coordinating conjunctions*, aptly described as FANBOYS. This mnemonic device stands for:

Coordinating Conjunctions	For	And	Nor	But	Or	Yet	So

Some example sentences are:

- John went to the theater, ***but*** his sister went to ballet.
- The camping trip was so boring, ***and*** the food was terrible.
- Permission was granted, ***or*** it wasn't.

Note that whenever two independent clauses are conjoined, we must have a comma that precedes the coordinating conjunction. Later, we will see other uses for punctuations when combining two independent clauses together.

eg. 2 In the following sentences, conjoin the two given independent clauses correctly and logically:

A) Marco took a long time to study for the test, ______ he still didn't do well on the exam.
B) You can buy the cake, ______ you can eat the cake.
C) She doesn't like adults, ______ does she like children for that matter.
D) It was terribly hot outside, ______ everyone decided to shed their sweaters in unison.
E) The dogs like cookies, ______ they also like butter.
F) Marcella did not partake in the conversation, ______ she was quite tired.

To combine an *independent clause* and a *dependent clause* we must utilize a subordinating conjunction. Fifty common subordinating conjunctions are listed in the chart below.

Let's take a sentence as follows:

Before she went to the movie, Shawna checked her email.

The first clause '*before she went to the movie'* is not a complete idea – the subordinating conjunction '*before'* indicates there is more information needed and, therefore, is a dependent clause.

The second clause, '*Shawna checked her email'*, has a subject and a verb, but unlike the dependent clause, it **can** stand as a complete idea. Therefore, it is an independent clause.

eg. 3 Combine the following sentences with proper subordinate conjunctions chosen from the list below:

A) My father yawned ______ he had finally managed to complete his long workday.

B) ______ the snake slithered across the room, it left a trail of disgusting slime in its wake.

C) ______ we get together, it seems as though we always get in trouble.

50 Subordinating Conjunctions

after	once
although	provided
as	provided that
as if	rather than
as long as	since
as much as	so that
as soon as	supposing
as though	than
because	that
before	though
even	till
even if	unless
even though	until
if	when
if only	whenever
if when	where
if then	whereas
inasmuch	where if
in order that	wherever
just as	whether
lest	which
now	while
now since	who
now that	whoever
now when	why

Phrases

Phrases add more information, and meaning, about the subject, verb or the object of the sentence. Phrases can have either a subject or a verb (or neither), but cannot have both, otherwise they would be considered a clause. There are seven different types of phrases that we will learn together:

Noun, Verb, Infinitive, Appositive, Prepositional, Gerund, Participial

Learning to recognize each of these phrases will not only improve your own knowledge of English grammar construction, but also make other errors more noticeable.

Noun phrases are nouns in a group acting as a single subject or object. A typical example of this would be in titles, such as fictional works or bands. The band Tom Petty and the Heartbreakers may be composed of two separate nouns but would be considered a singular noun phrase. Other noun phrasal type:

- <u>The surprised elephant</u> suddenly woke up.
- Sunday always turns out to be a <u>warm, sunny day</u>.

Verb phrases contain the main verb of a sentence and all of their modifiers. Many of us don't really think of these phrases as phrases, per se, since they are usually just the entirety of the predicate of any independent clause. Some verb phrases:

- Jenny <u>took herself up the hill</u>.
- Unfortunately, my homie never <u>bothered to look back</u>.

Infinitive phrases are constructed from the infinitive, or the unconjugated, form of a verb and accompanying modifiers. They can function as a noun, adjective, or adverb, depending on the position in the sentence. Recognizing an infinitive is relatively quick since they always begin with '*to + verb*'. Some infinitive phrases at work:

- <u>To have a satisfying career while helping and improving people</u> is his goal.
- Maiden voyages on sailboats have <u>to be scary</u>.

Appositive phrases are used to describe or restate a noun and exist almost exclusively between commas. Titles are a typical use of appositive phrases. Some appositive phrases:

- Mark Jackson, <u>Princeton's Dean of Student Affairs</u>, spoke to the class.
- The Mugunghwa, <u>a light-pink hibiscus</u>, is the national flower of South Korea.

Appositive phrases can be thought of as adjectives, or descriptor, that are not essential parts of a clause.

Prepositional phrases are constructed with three possible parts: a <u>preposition</u>, an <u>object</u> of the preposition and <u>modifiers</u>. A preposition is a word that indicates a relationship between two objects in space or time. Some common prepositions are listed below:

Above	After	At	Before	But	By	Despite	For	From	In
Of	**Onto**	**Over**	**Towards**	**Under**	**Until**	**Upon**	**Via**	**With**	**Without**

Prepositional phrases are modifiers, and function as either adjectives or adverbs. The object of the preposition can be a noun, pronoun, gerund, or even a phrase. Some prepositional phrases:

- His work <u>in the scientific community</u> garnered respect <u>from his colleagues and peers</u>.
- <u>Under the bridge</u> are dozens of massive stones.
- I never liked his cookies, <u>between you and me</u>.

Prepositional phrases can be ignored! Ignoring them will also help you to clarify the subject and verb of the clause correctly.

Gerund phrases can also be constructed with three parts: a gerund, the object of the gerund, and a modifier. A gerund is a present participle form of a verb that acts as a noun ('I *run*' vs. '*Running* is a great hobby.'). A gerund phrase acting as a subject is always considered singular. Look at the following sentences, where the gerund is underlined:

- <u>Excelling</u> in sports **is** an important aspect of every growing student.
- <u>Saving</u> endangered birds **leads** to happiness.
- <u>Creating</u> havoc in meetings **is** not recommended for one looking for promotion.

No matter how many objects exist in the gerund phrase, there is still only one controlling gerund. Therefore, the phrase is always considered singular so long as it acts as the subject.

Participial Phrases are constructed by utilizing past or present participles functioning as adjectives. With regular verbs, participial phrases use either an *–ed* or *–ing* verbal construction. With irregular verbs, past participial forms are unique to the verb. Note that they are different than the past tense form.

Infinitive	**Past Tense**	**Past Participle**	**Present Participle**
To wash	Washed	Washed	Washing
To run	Ran	Run	Running
To smile	Smiled	Smiled	Smiling
To eat	Ate	Eaten	Eating

Participial phrases must be near the noun/pronoun that they modify. Some participial phrases at work are:

- A student <u>trying to achieve a perfect score</u> must study constantly.
- His sister, <u>tired from her efforts</u>, continued to run in the marathon.
- <u>Marked for demolition</u>, the old office building was no longer viable.

eg. 4 Match and identify the types of phrases with the correct clauses (logically):

Phrase	←→	Clause
In the loose outfit,		Jamie stood out from the crowd.
Standing over 7 foot tall,		the eggs were ready for the frying pan.
Beaten with a whisk,		the new karate instructor looked rather ridiculous.
To buy a car,		the struggling middle class almost always must take out a loan.

Punctuation

There are many punctuations that come into play when constructing sentences. These are the four most common:

The comma (,) is used in lists, (like this one), separation of a clause from a phrase, and separation of two or more independent clauses with a FANBOYS conjunction. Some examples:

- To make this infinitive phrase work, we need this independent clause.
- Merck was hindered only by its ambition, for its coffers were aplenty.

The semicolon (;) is mainly used to separate two topically related independent clauses. An example:

- Focusing on improvement matters; therefore, every minute of practice makes us better.
- Cindy retired from the music industry; however, she kept her public profile fairly prominent.

The colon (:) is used to introduce a list. It is also used to provide a definition, example, or explanation after an independent clause.

- Pizza should never have the following toppings: anchovies, pineapple and mushrooms.
- I can only do one thing at a time: multitasking is a nightmare for me.

The dash (-) is used to separate parenthetical, or extra, information in a sentence, or to highlight some bonus info, almost like a comma would in an appositive phrase. Dash placements usually also end with a dash:

- If you use dashes - like this - in a sentence, be sure to place them properly.

Common Clausal and Phrasal Errors

1) **No independent clause.** Every sentence must contain a subject and predicate that forms an independent clause. A lack of one or the other is a common error. For example, in this example "*Running for their lives, scared out of their minds,*" two predicates without subjects exist on both sides of the comma. Therefore, it is not an independent clause.

2) **Incorrect use of participial, infinitive and gerund phrases.** Remember to distinguish among the various different types of phrases grammatically, logically and stylistically.

3) **A comma conjoining two independent clauses.** Otherwise known as a comma splice, this type of run-on is a common violation of grammatical rules.

4) **Semicolons separating dependent clauses**. A semicolon's primary use is to separate two independent and related clauses. If a clause on one side or the other of a semicolon is a dependent clause or a phrase, then the sentence is grammatically incorrect.

A Note on Recognizing Sentence Construction

Every time we read a sentence, it is imperative that we always look for how a sentence is constructed. This involves looking for active or passive voice, and/or inverted construction. Typically, sentences tend to be written in the active voice.

Examples of ***active voice***: subject + predicate (verb)

- I like pizza.
- Mahoney owns a bar.
- My 1991 Toyota Supra has no air conditioning.

Passive voice occurs when the subject acts as the object, and the object acts as the subject. Generally, passive voice should be avoided. It is a stylistic error, rather than a grammatical one, but an important detail to consider when reflecting on how the intent of the author is conveyed. It is not necessarily wrong, per se, to utilize the passive voice, but when there is a more clear, concise alternative, always default to the active voice. Most passive constructions have the word "by" in the sentence, but not always.

Examples of ***passive voice***: subject/object role reversal

- My sneaker was made by Nike.
- This tea was made by a British Company in India.
- Last runner of the race was whom?

Note that we can always construe the passive voice into a (better) active voice. Circle the subject and objects in the following, and note how their roles are reversed in each pair:

- My sneaker was made by Nike. → Nike made my sneaker.
- This tea was made by a British Company in India. → A British Company in India made this tea.
- The last runner of the race was whom? → Who was the last runner of the race?

In most cases, active voice is much more concise, and, therefore, preferable.

Inverted construction, unlike passive voice, is stylistically correct, but may contain grammatical errors. An inverted construction occurs when the verb comes before the subject. The good news is that you are already familiar with inverted sentences.

Circle the subject and verb in the following examples of ***inverted construction***: Verb → Subject

- Rarely has my mother loved me.
- Never have I understood Lil Uzi's lyrics.
- Little did she know the truth behind the relationship.

Writing Lesson 1
Clauses and Phrases
Application Exercises

Time – 15 Minutes

Answer the questions in this worksheet within the time allotted. No answer sheets needed.

Directions: This is an identification exercise set. Break up the following sentences into their particular types of various phrases and clauses. Remember that phrases and clauses can be embedded within other phrases and clauses. There are **no errors** in the following sentences.

1) Standing on the diving board, Jack wanted to jump into the pool.

2) To ensure that you are not overwhelmed by the external environment, homeostatic mechanisms are present in your body.

3) Having been introduced to North America by the Spanish, horses have become common in the contiguous United States.

4) Swimming in a pool during a lightning storm, a dangerous activity, can be lethal because the ions present in the water are able to conduct electricity.

5) In his red outfit, Santa Claus flew over the roofs of the houses and under the long bridges.

6) John always hated doing his nightly homework, but when he himself became a teacher, he invariably assigned plenty of it.

7) "To be or not to be" is the question.

8) In the United States Supreme Court case *Engel v. Vitale* (1962), the Court ruled that government-directed prayer in public schools violates the Establishment Clause of the First Amendment, even if the prayer is voluntary.

9) He studied so hard to become a doctor, and he achieved his goal after four years of college, four years of medical school, and three years of residency.

10) Demonstrating courage in a legislative culture so often lacking it, a group of lawmakers has decided to introduce a controversial bill, which would increase funding for unpopular but effective programs.

11) Under the Second Amendment, the right to bear arms is an essential right of every citizen of the United States; however, this and other rights can be taken away if said citizen violates them.

12) This pair of old sneakers was originally made by NIKE, a profitable Oregonian company.

13) Questioning the decisions of the proletariat is not the intent of this council.

14) Isha created her proprietary curriculum last year, but Chen found plenty of mistakes; therefore, making your own problems, even easy ones, is generally not recommended.

Writing Lesson 1
Clauses and Phrases
Homework Exercises

Time – 10 Minutes

Answer the questions in this worksheet within the time allotted. No answer sheets needed.

Directions: Identify the different parts of the provided sentences into their various phrases and clauses. Then, choose the correct answer choice.

1) Mosaic, the first internet browser, <u>with its ability to make</u> privileged information available to the public.

   A) NO CHANGE
   B) had an ability to make
   C) having had an ability, which was to make
   D) that had an ability to make

2) Because many cities use volunteer <u>firefighters, and so</u> the community must rely on extensive donations and support to maintain public safety.

   A) NO CHANGE
   B) firefighters: plus
   C) firefighters,
   D) firefighters; and so

3) <u>Austin, Texas is one of the most unique cities in the United States, its</u> history reveals that it has been part of three countries.

   A) NO CHANGE
   B) Austin, Texas is one of the most unique cities in the United States, moreover
   C) Austin, Texas is one of the most unique cities in the United States: its
   D) Austin, Texas is one of the most unique cities in the United States – its

4) <u>While women were not allowed</u> to apply for credits cards on their own until 1974; many banks until then required a male co-signer.

   A) NO CHANGE
   B) Even though women were not allowed
   C) Women were not allowed
   D) They did not allow women

5) <u>In believing that</u> much of the flora and fauna of the rainforest is undiscovered, many researchers look to the vanishing habitat for possible medical discoveries.

   A) NO CHANGE
   B) Believing that
   C) He believed that
   D) By believing that

6) Francis Scott Key was a captive of the British when he wrote "The Star-Spangled Banner," <u>it was chosen to be</u> the national anthem of the United States in 1931.

   A) NO CHANGE
   B) choosing it to be
   C) which they had chose for
   D) which was chosen as

7) Numismatics, or coin collecting, <u>and becoming</u> popular in the United States around 1857, when the replacement of the large cent by the new flying-eagle cent led enthusiasts to start collecting the earlier coin.

A) NO CHANGE
B) becoming
C) it became
D) became

8) Paradoxically pungent and aromatic, the <u>Durian being</u> a fruit of Singaporean origin.

A) NO CHANGE
B) Durian being what it is
C) Durian is
D) Durian was being

9) Many Eastern European countries have curbed the proliferation of nuclear arsenal <u>over the past decade, however, North America</u> – specifically the United States – has not followed suit.

A) NO CHANGE
B) over the past decade, moreover, North America
C) over the past decade: however, North America
D) over the past decade; however, North America

10) Because the landscaper refused to work under the guidelines of the homeowner, <u>so he was</u> fired.

A) NO CHANGE
B) therefore he was
C) and he was
D) he was

11) Jackson Pollock was able to create an innovative painting style called "drip <u>painting," yet he was</u> able to shed prior conceptions of accepted art that had bound other artists.

A) NO CHANGE
B) "drip painting" because he was
C) "drip painting," because he was
D) "drip paining" yet he was

12) Except in mathematics, absolute proof is difficult to find, <u>a fact that the courts recognize by setting</u> varying standards of proof for various kinds of cases.

A) NO CHANGE
B) consequently, the courts recognize and set
C) and this is recognized when the courts are setting
D) and the courts recognize this fact by setting

Writing Lesson 1
Clauses and Phrases
Answer Key

Homework Exercises

1) B
2) C
3) C
4) C
5) B
6) D
7) D
8) C
9) D
10) D
11) B
12) A

Application Exercises

1) Participial phrase (Standing...) + prepositional phrase (on the...) → Independent Clause (Jack wanted ...)

2) Infinitive phrase (To ensure...) + dependent clause (that you are...) + prepositional phrase (by the external...) → Independent clause (homeostatic mechanisms are present...) + prepositional phrase (in your...)

3) Participial phrase (Having been...) + prepositional phrase (to North America) + prepositional phrase (by the Spanish) → independent clause (horses have become...) + prepositional phrase (in the contiguous...)

4) Gerund/independent clause (Swimming... can be...) + prepositional (in a pool) + prepositional (during a lightning storm) + appositive phrase (a dangerous activity) → dependent clause (because the ions...) + prepositional phrase (in the water)

5) Prepositional (In his...) → independent clause (Santa Claus flew...) + prepositional (over the roofs...) + prepositional (of the houses...) + prepositional (under the long...)

6) Independent clause (John always hated...) + gerund (doing his homework...) → dependent clause (when he became...) → independent clause (he invariably assigned...) + prepositional phrase (of it)

7) Infinitive phrase (To be or not to be) + inverted independent clause (is + the question).

8) Prepositional/appositive phrase (In the United States...) → independent clause (the Court ruled...) + dependent relative clause (that government prayer...violates) + prepositional phrase (in public schools) + prepositional (of the First Amendment) → dependent clause (even if the prayer is voluntary)

9) Independent clause (He studied...) + infinitive phrase (to become...) → independent clause (he achieved...) + prepositional (after four years) + prepositional (of college) + prepositional (of medical...) + prepositional (of residency)

10) Participial phrase (Demonstrating courage...) + prepositional (in a legislative...) → independent clause (a group of lawmakers has decided...) + infinitive phrase (to introduce...) → relative dependent clause (which would increase...) + prepositional (for unpopular but effective programs)

11) Prepositional phrase (Under the...) → independent clause (the right to bear arms is) prepositional (of every citizen) + prepositional (of the United States) → independent clause (however, this and other rights can...) + dependent clause (if said citizen violates...)

12) Passive voice independent clause (This pair... were...) + prepositional (by Nike) → appositive phrase (a profitable...)

13) Independent gerund clause (Questioning... is...) + prepositional (of the proletariat) + prepositional (of this council)

14) Independent clause (Isha created...) + independent clause (Chen found...) + prepositional phrase (of mistakes) → Gerund independent clause (making your own problems is...) + appositive phrase (even easy ones)

Homework Exercises

1) **Choice B is correct.**
This is a sentence fragment. The subject "mosaic" does not have a verb. Inserting the verb "had" in Choice B creates an acceptable independent clause. Choice C creates an awkward sentence fragment. Choice D introduce the verb "had," but also introduce "that", which makes the entire sentence into a sentence fragment as well.

2) **Choice C is correct.**
The sentence contains a dependent clause incorrectly conjoining with an independent clause. We correct this mistake in Choice A by dropping the needless conjunctions "and so". Choice B incorrectly uses a colon to introduce a dependent clause. Choice D uses a semicolon with a dependent clause incorrectly.

3) **Choice C is correct.**
This is a run-on sentence. More specifically, run-on sentences that utilize a comma is called a comma-splice. To correct this, we use a colon to connect the two independent clauses together. Choice B's use of moreover doesn't properly link the clauses since "moreover" is not a proper conjunction. Choice D's use of a dash is just as incorrect since dashes do not act as conjunctions.

4) **Choice C is correct.**
A dependent clause cannot be conjoined with an independent clause with a semi-colon. Choice B is incorrect for the same reason. Choice D seems like it should work, but the pronoun "they" is ambiguous.

5) **Choice B is correct.**
The prepositional phrase "in believing" illogically modifies "many researchers." Instead, a participial phrase works better to modify the subject "many researchers." Choice C creates a comma splice or run-on. Choice D contains a similar incorrect logic as choice A.

6) **Choice D is correct.**
This is two independent clauses linked solely by a comma, a classic run-on sentence aka. comma splice. Choice D corrects this mistake by creating a dependent clause. Choice B creates an odd participial phrase, where an ambiguous person chooses the Star-Spangled Banner. Choice C is incorrect due to improper tense and incorrect use of "which".

7) **Choice D is correct.**
This is a sentence fragment. We need a verb to pair with a subject here to create a complete sentence. Choice B is incorrect for the same reason. Choice C creates two appositive phrases unnecessarily ("Numismatics" and "or coin collecting").

8) **Choice C is correct.**
This is a sentence fragment. Choice B and D are both incorrect because they utilize the verb "being" incorrectly.

9) **Choice D is correct.**
Conjunctive adverbs like "therefore, moreover, however" cannot be used to join two independent clauses. Choice B is incorrect for the same reason. Choice C is incorrect because a colon should be used to exemplify or describe the prior sentence's topic. It also utilizes "however" incorrectly.

10) **Choice D is correct.**
This sentence is a dependent clause conjoined with an independent clause by using a coordinating conjunction incorrectly. We correct this mistake by dropping the conjunction "so".

11) **Choice B is correct.**
This sentence utilizes a coordinating conjunction illogically. To correct this mistake, we convert the second clause into a dependent one. Since a dependent clause that follows an independent clause does not usually require a comma, choice C can be eliminated.

12) **Choice A is correct.**
There are no errors in this sentence.

Writing
Lesson 2

Verb Tenses and Aspects

Goals

We will develop our grammatical fluency and gain meaningful understanding by learning to:

1) Distinguish the construction among all different verb tenses & aspects
2) Understand the function of all tenses & aspects
3) Identify common errors on sentence constructions involving tenses & aspects

Contents

- Tenses & Aspects
- Common Errors
- Application Exercises
- Homework Exercises

Lesson 2
Verb Tenses and Aspects

The basics of tenses and aspects involve a thorough understanding of their construction and function. First, let's look into how these different combinations are created. Second, we'll explore their proper uses. And finally, we will see examples of common errors.

Verb *tenses*, in every language, comes in three forms: The past, present and future.

Verb *aspects*, on the other hand, indicates time of completion of action, and in English, it comes in four forms: simple, perfect, progressive and perfect progressive.

Colloquially, we always state the tense first, then aspect second. (ie. "Past simple", or "Present perfect progressive") The following matrices provide a more thorough understanding of the various concepts.

Simple Aspect

Verb Tense	Aspect	Function	Example
Past	Simple	Indicates an action that occurred	It *rained* last night.
Present	Simple	Denotes things that occur, but not necessarily occurring now	It *rains* in Seattle.
Future	Simple	Indicates an action that will occur at a later time	It *will rain* when we reach the theater.

Perfect Aspect: Conjugate "to have" + past participle

Verb Tense	Aspect	Function	Example
Past	Perfect	Usually indicates an action that occurred prior to another completed action	Mohammed *had licked* his lollipop before eating lunch.
Present	Perfect	Denotes an action that is either completed and/or continues to the present	Mohammed *has studied* calculus.
Future	Perfect	Indicates an action that will have been completed at a later point in time	Mohammed *will have eaten* cake by the time his Dad arrives.

Progressive Aspect: Conjugate "to be" + present participle

Verb Tense	Aspect	Function	Example
Past	Progressive	Indicates continuing action at some point in the past	The horse *was running* in the rain.
Present	Progressive	Denotes continuing action, going on now	The horse *is running* in the rain.
Future	Progressive	Indicates an action will be continuing at a later time	The horse *will be running* in the rain.

Perfect Progressive Aspect: Conjugate "to have" + past participle of "to be" (been) + present participle

Verb Tense	Aspect	Function	Example
Past	Perfect Progressive	Indicates a continuous action that was completed	Jerry *had been preparing* dinner all day, up until the guests showed up.
Present	Perfect Progressive	Denotes recently completed event, often using the adverb "just"	Jerry *has just been preparing* dinner.
Future	Perfect Progressive	Indicates continuous action that will be completed at a later time	Jerry *will have been preparing* dinner for seven hours.

Progressive aspects are fairly rare and are not used often in composition.

Regular vs. Irregular verbs

A regular verb such as "to jump" conjugates differently than an irregular verb such as "to eat". We can see the difference when the verb forms are used in their different uses. Note these differences between tenses and participles, and their respective uses as outlined prior.

Verb	Past tense	Present tense	Future tense	Past participle	Present participle
To jump (regular)	He jumped	He jumps	He will jump	He had jumped	He is jumping
To eat (irregular)	She ate	She eats	She will eat	She had eaten	She is eating

Practice Exercises

Determine the proper tense and aspect of the main verb in the following sentences. Note that there are no errors:

eg 1. Ashwin has been to five of the seven continents.

eg 2. I will try to solve the problem.

eg 3. Are you attempting to break the school record?

eg 4. Despite the weather, we will be camping over the weekend.

eg 5. Writers often devise innovative ways to express old truths.

eg 6. Since public outcry over the size of the deficit, the government has been attempting to encourage growth without incurring debt.

eg 7. My boss had fired his employee before he took his vacation.

Common Tense Errors

The following lists the most common tense errors in written passages:

1) Inconsistent tense.

   As a rule, unless there is a reason to change verb tense, keep the tense consistent between all clauses. For example:

   Although he spent several years as a prominent local lawyer, John Adams <u>becomes</u> a revolutionary politician several years into the American Revolution.

   Since the dependent clause initiates the sentence with a past simple tense, the independent clause that follows should do the same. The corrected sentence should read "*John Adams <u>became</u> a revolutionary politician.*"

2) Incorrect tense.

   During Prohibition, women <u>have experienced</u> more social freedom because of the clandestine nature of speakeasies.

   This sentence uses the present perfect form needlessly. A past simple form of "women *experienced* more social freedom" would suffice.

3) Incorrect use of *would* and *will*.

   The verb "would" is a past-tense form of "will", and it indicates something that was in the future at the moment it was said in the past.

   Babe Ruth <u>would become</u> a famous baseball player, even though he grew up in an orphanage.

   Note that it would be incorrect to say "Babe Ruth will become a famous baseball player" because it would seem to indicate that he is still alive and will become one sometime in the future.

Lesson 2
Verb Tenses and Aspects
Application Exercises

Time – 10 Minutes

Answer the questions in this worksheet within the time allotted.
No answer sheets needed.

Directions: The following sentences ask you to identify the proper verb tense. There are no errors in the sentences. Refer to your notes as needed.

1) The two corporate CEOs were very excited because they **had been negotiating** a big business plan.

2) You **had not been waiting** there for more than two hours when she finally arrived.

3) He **had caught** the ball before he ran out of bounds.

4) She **will be repairing** her car if she continues to drive like that.

5) Jackson **took** command of the defenses, including militia from several western states and territories.

6) He **has studied** mathematics for 10 years.

7) He **had studied** mathematics for 10 years before he earned his doctorate.

8) I **have been worrying** about you all night.

9) He **is trying** to make a difference in the world.

10) He **was striving** to jump over the hurdle.

11) She thinks that he **will win** the lottery next month.

12) By the time your laptop finishes loading, it **will have run** out of battery.

13) The sun having set, the villagers **went** inside their huts.

14) Though a special prosecutor **had been assigned** to the case, no one was found guilty of the crime.

15) When he **finishes** his job at the company, he **will have worked** there for forty years.

16) Mary **had written** the lectures notes, but she found compiling the notes into a coherent book to be a challenging task.

17) They **had been sleeping** when the messenger arrived to deliver the wonderful news.

18) The ethics committee **has determined** that there was little, if any, wrongdoing.

19) In 1940, no one **guessed** that a haberdasher would become President of the United States.

20) The 18th Amendment **had instituted** Prohibition before the 21st Amendment **repealed** it.

21) The general **is** currently in command of the 3rd Division.

22) We **had never sought** to disparage anyone's character.

Lesson 2
Verb Tenses and Aspects
Homework Exercises

Time – 10 Minutes

Answer the questions in this worksheet within the time allotted. No answer sheets needed.

Directions: Break up the following sentences into their various phrases and clauses, then find the error, if any exists. Correct the error. And finally, choose the best answer choice.

1) First run in 1984 in the month of May, the Pittsburgh Marathon, which has acted as an Olympic qualifier, <u>was</u> one of the most popular races in America.

A) NO CHANGE
B) is
C) were
D) has been

2) If people refused to purchase a particular product, then the price for it <u>will be</u> lowered solely by the economics of supply and demand.

A) NO CHANGE
B) would have been
C) was to be
D) would be

3) Henry Ford was by no means the first person to build an automobile, but he <u>has been the first who conceived</u> the assembly line that made it affordable.

A) NO CHANGE
B) had been the first who conceived
C) was the first having conceived
D) was the first to conceive

4) Hermann Hesse's *Siddhartha* <u>begins with his childhood in the elite caste and culminates</u> with his achievement of inner peace.

A) NO CHANGE
B) have begun with his childhood in the elite caste and culminates
C) have begun with his childhood in the elite caste and culminating
D) began with his childhood in the elite caste and are culminated

5) The class only wanted to study the steps necessary to solve the example problems, so it <u>having</u> no understanding of the theory.

A) NO CHANGE
B) have
C) had
D) had had

6) By next year the gentrification of the decrepit block <u>had been</u> complete, with two offices built specifically for startup companies.

A) NO CHANGE
B) has been
C) will be
D) will have been

7) Now that Killian finished his prerequisites, he feels reasonably confident about completing his thesis paper on the assembly of nation-states.

A) NO CHANGE
B) will finish
C) finishes
D) has finished

8) From 1911 until 1913, the Mona Lisa, famously located in the Louvre museum, was stolen by a museum employee; however, the painting had not been placed in a secure case until 2005.

A) NO CHANGE
B) have not been
C) was not
D) will not have been

9) At first, we panicked when we discovered we had forgotten Sofia's birthday, but then we took a trip to the mall, where there were several items that seemed like perfect gifts.

A) NO CHANGE
B) had been forgetting
C) have forgot
D) are forgetting

10) Only after interest in the movie had raised substantially was the studio willing to order the release of the film to more theatres.

A) NO CHANGE
B) has rose
C) had risen
D) has been raising

11) Film producers discovered that ticket sales are considerably decreased whenever film critics panned early screenings of their films before their release.

A) NO CHANGE
B) will be panning
C) have panned
D) pan

12) Boston College is an important center of professional hockey because its alumni included players from most of the professional teams.

A) NO CHANGE
B) include
C) includes
D) has included

13) Whereas the pollen of most plants is harmless, ragweed is causing much suffering by exacerbating many people's pollen allergies.

A) NO CHANGE
B) will cause
C) caused
D) has caused

14) Jerry Brown elected to office twice, where he served as one of the youngest and the oldest governors in Californian history.

A) NO CHANGE
B) was elected
C) is elected
D) was electing

15) The Earth's molten core was cooling at a rate of 100 degrees Celsius per billion years but has sufficient heat in its core to continue this cooling.

A) NO CHANGE
B) is cooling
C) has been cooling
D) cooled

16) Because they are tuned for optimum performance, hybrid vehicles could maintain incredible fuel efficiency for many miles, making the most of their gasoline consumption.

A) could maintain
B) can maintain
C) had maintained
D) have been maintaining

17) After disparaging the restaurant's cooking as unpalatable, the food critic has criticized for giving a crass opinion of so highly regarded a restaurant.

A) has criticized
B) has been criticized
C) is criticized
D) was criticized

18) If you harness the energy in molecular bonds, you would be able to power an entire house for a full year with only one fireplace log.

A) harness
B) have harnessed
C) could harness
D) would harness

Lesson 2
Verb Tenses and Aspects
Answer Key

Homework Exercises

1) D
2) D
3) D
4) A
5) C
6) C
7) D
8) C
9) A
10) C
11) D
12) B
13) D
14) B
15) B
16) B
17) D
18) C

Practice Exercises

1) **Present perfect.**
The action '*has been*' indicates that Ashwin's travels started at some point in the past, and up to the present, he has been to five continents.

2) **Future simple.**
An action that will occur at some later point in time.

3) **Present Progressive.**
This sentence is in question form, so the best course of action would be to restate it as a declarative sentence as: *you are attempting to break the school record*. Here, we can see that the action is currently happening and will progress into the future, therefore it is in the present progressive tense.

4) **Future progressive.**
The camping has not happened yet, but at a later point in time they will do so for some duration of time.

5) **Present simple.**
This is happening currently.

6) **Past perfect progressive.**
The verb phrase *has been attempting* indicates both a timeframe (after the outcry) and progress.

7) **Past perfect.**
Note that the action of firing occurs before another action, in this case, the boss taking his vacation. (What a terrible boss!)

Application Exercises

1) Past perfect progressive
2) Past perfect progressive
3) Past perfect
4) Future progressive
5) Past simple
6) Present perfect
7) Past perfect
8) Present perfect progressive
9) Present progressive
10) Past progressive
11) Future simple
12) Future perfect
13) Past simple
14) Past perfect (note the lack of present participial form in assigned vs. assigning)
15) Present simple; future perfect
16) Past perfect
17) Past perfect progressive
18) Present perfect
19) Past simple
20) Past perfect; past simple
21) Present simple
22) Past perfect

Homework Exercises

1) **Choice D is correct.**
This action has started in the past but continues to happen in the present, so it requires a present perfect tense.

2) **Choice D is correct.**
This sentence happens hypothetically ("If people..."), so "will be" is inappropriate. "Would be" shows that the event may or may not happen in the future.

3) **Choice D is correct.**
We only need to indicate that this action happened in the past; the present perfect is unnecessary and past perfect implies that some time traveler has now beat him to the punch.

4) **Choice A is correct.**
Works of fiction are regarded in the present – if we said Harry Potter *was* in seven books, it would mean that he's not in them now, oddly.

5) **Choice C is correct.**
Use the previous verb "wanted," past simple tense, as a guide, because verb tense generally stays consistent between two clauses.

6) **Choice C is correct.**
The proper tense to use here is the future simple. The prepositional phrase "by next year" gives us a clue that the action will be in the future tense as well.

7) **Choice D is correct.**
We want to emphasize the fac that Killian has put in some time to complete his work from some point in the past. Therefore, a more correct choice here is to utilize the present perfect tense, rather than the past simple.

8) **Choice C is correct.**
Simple past should work here since there is no need for the past perfect tense.

9) **Choice A is correct.**
Since Sofia's birthday was forgotten but is no longer a concern, the best tense to use here is the past perfect form.

10) **Choice C is correct.**
Because the past perfect form is used appropriately. Choice B pairs a perfect tense with a simple past form of the verb incorrectly. Choice D uses the present perfect progressive form incorrectly since the "interest" was completed already.

11) **Choice D is correct.**
Ignore the "discovered" in the past tense. Since the verb in "ticket sales ARE panned" is in the present, we should keep the following verb "pan" in the present also.

12) **Choice B is correct.**
Since the players are *still* graduates, the alumni list should include players currently.

13) **Choice D is correct.**
Don't be fooled by the "has" in the choice: "has caused" is present perfect, and the only option in the present tense to describe the terror of allergies in the present.

14) **Choice B is correct.**
Jerry Brown was elected indicates a completed past simple action, corresponding with the past simple tense of the verb "served" in the second clause of the sentence.

15) **Choice B is correct.**
Since we are describing the Earth's current rate of cooling, the present progressive tense is the preferred form of the verb.

16) **Choice B is correct.**
When tackling problems involving can vs. could, consider whether the action is actually happening. "Could" is to be used in hypothetical situations only, and since hybrids *are* tuned for optimum performance, they *can* maintain efficiency correctly utilizes the present simple tense.

17) **Choice D is correct.**
All other choices utilize the present verb tense incorrectly. Since the action described occurred after writing a critical review, the "food critic was criticized" using the past simple is the most appropriate form here.

18) **Choice C is correct.**
This sentence gives us a hypothetical scenario to test the concept of "can vs. could." Because the context of the sentence indicates that we *would* be able to run a house hypothetically, we must use the hypothetical form "could harness."

Writing
Lesson 3

Subject-Verb Agreement

Goals

We will develop our grammatical fluency and gain meaningful understanding by:

1) Learning all relevant subject-verb agreement rules
2) Recognizing when to apply the strict rules of subject-verb agreement
3) Resolving errors contained in practice problems

Contents

- Subject Verb Rules
- Application Exercises
- Homework Exercises

Lesson 3
Subject-Verb Agreement

Subject verb agreement issues can be summarized by a set of rules that gives guidance on the proper corrections. The following are Pittsburgh Prep's rules to abide by:

Rule #1: Collective nouns are always singular

A distinct category of nouns, called collective nouns, represent a large number of things but are always considered singular nouns. Words such as *group, academy, flock*, and *army* are good examples.

A class of students is heading our way tonight.

In the above example, the subject that conjugates the verb is "a class", a collective noun. Therefore, the singular verbal conjugation of "is" is correct as written. List some other collective nouns here:

__________ __________ __________ __________

__________ __________ __________ __________

Rule #2: Ignore prepositional phrases in the subject

Many subjects contain prepositional phrases attached to the proper noun. To determine which noun conjugates the verb properly, ignore the prepositional phrase.

The Thanksgiving floats from Wisconsin State University has had a big impact on our family tradition.

In the above sentence, we can readily cross out the prepositional phrase in the subject from Wisconsin State University to read:

The Thanksgiving floats ~~from Wisconsin State University~~ has had a big impact on our family tradition.

Since "Thanksgiving floats" is plural, we need to correct the verb to "have" to read:

The Thanksgiving floats ~~from Wisconsin State University~~ *have* had a big impact on our family tradition.

Rule #3: Imperatives contain an implied "you" as the subject

Remember that any sentence that is a command has an implied second person as the subject. Therefore, all verbs should be conjugated accordingly. We would not give a command using the third person voice, such as:

Hey, gets out of here! (Um, no. HE gets out of here is just terrible construction.)

Instead, the correct imperative would be:

Hey, get out of here! (YOU is implied here.)

Rule #4: Gerund phrases as subjects are always singular

Since gerunds are present participle forms acting as nouns, if they are used as subjects of a clause, they are always considered singular. Remember to ignore prepositional phrases and identify the gerund correctly to avoid any errors here. For example:

Closing the bank too early on the weekends and holidays <u>are</u> generally to be avoided.

Note that (1) we identify the subject proper as the gerund "closing" and (2) we ignore the phrase "the bank too early on the weekends and holidays," allowing us to conjugate the verb correctly with the third person conjugation of "is". The corrected sentence should read:

Closing ~~the bank too early on the weekends and holidays~~ ~~are~~ *is* generally to be avoided.

Rule #5: The conjunction AND can create a plural subject

When the conjunction AND is used in the subject with two singular subject nouns, it creates a plural subject. No other conjunctions do this. For example:

Marcus and Hajimi *take* the bus to school.

Marcus, alongside Hajimi, *takes* the bus to school.

Rule #6: The conjunction OR requires the closest subject to conjugate the verb

When the conjunction OR is used in the subject, the subject that is closest to the verb conjugates the verb. For example:

Either my mom or <u>my sisters *have*</u> interest in my new project at school.

If we have an inverted sentence, the closest subject is the first subject we encounter:

So manipulative <u>*is* my nephew</u> or my nieces that I simply cannot afford to trust either.

Whereas in a normally constructed sentence, the subject that is closest is usually the second one, changing the original verbal conjugation:

My nephew or <u>my nieces *are*</u> so manipulative that I simply cannot afford to trust either.

Rule #7: Either/neither alone is always a singular subject

When used alone, the subjects either/neither are considered singular. For example:

<u>Neither</u> of my kids <u>*is*</u> talented enough to participate in the Olympics.

Rule #8: Subjunctive mood uses "were" for all subjects

Subjunctive mood tenses in English indicate a desire or a wish. In these situations, the verb "were" is used for all pronouns. Note that in the following sentence, we would normally use "I was" were it not for its subjunctive mood:

If I <u>were</u> a rich man, I wouldn't have to work hard.

Rule #9: A number vs. The number

The way to determine the difference between the two values is to just memorize that "the number" is always singular, while "a number" is always plural. That's it!

The number on the car lot <u>says</u> a lot about the place.

A number of kids <u>decide</u> to take a joyride on the Fantastico Rollercoaster ride.

Note: As you encounter more grammatical rules through your practice and review, list them in your notes alongside the ones you've learned in this section.

Rule #10: Indefinite pronouns are usually singular

Almost always, pronouns with the four indefinite prefixes (every- , any-, some-, no-) indicate a singular entity. For example:

Someone <u>is</u> out in the backyard, Larry.

Anybody <u>has</u> potential to succeed, so long as the willpower exists.

The only exception is when indefinite pronouns are used in command form:

Everybody take only one apple from this pile!

Lesson 3
Subject-Verb Agreement
Application Exercises

Time – 10 Minutes

Answer the questions in this worksheet within the time allotted – no answer sheets are needed.

Directions: Determine whether the subject and verb agree. Circle the verb at issue, underline the agreeing subject, and correct as necessary. Good luck!

1) A group of us wants to head over to the tent.

2) The discovery of the loophole existent across college recruitment policies, on top of the recent finding of corruption of the NCAA board that oversees college sports, have influenced the method of college student-athlete recruitment this year.

3) Mustafa, in addition to the rest of his Russian speaking team, is preparing for the trip tomorrow.

4) The initial tally of the entire gathered crowd's raised hands were rather impressive.

5) In all, there are, as told to me by my deans, only one option for me: to go to college.

6) Over past the hill is a barn and a field of corn.

7) Somebody, anybody, please help me!

8) Eating with close compatriots are always fun for me.

9) The valet, as well as the chef, were smiling happily when the long evening was finally over.

10) Making and baking dough are actually very tough tasks for a novice in the kitchen.

11) A number of us wants to go head over to the tent.

12) None of the glass shards ever was found inside the laboratory.

13) None in the group were ever close to becoming the President of the Arboreal Society.

14) The boys were so crass that neither of them pique my interest.

15) The music instructor was happy to learn that either his students or his peer were going to attend the recital.

Lesson 3
Subject-Verb Agreement
Homework Exercises

Time – 10 Minutes

1) Neil Gaiman, a famous author, whose role as a visionary in the field of literature equals that of Jules Verne.

A) Neil Gaiman, a famous author, whose role as a visionary
B) Neil Gaiman, who was a famous author and whose role as a visionary
C) A famous author with a role as visionary, Neil Gaiman,
D) Neil Gaiman was a famous author whose role as a visionary

2) Any one of the several thousand students taking the exam are capable of telling you that preparation is absolutely necessary.

A) are capable of
B) are capable to
C) is capable of
D) being capable of

3) Arya and Anna will compete in the debate finals, their work in this having been outstanding this season.

A) finals, their work in this having been outstanding this season
B) finals, they have done outstanding work this season in this
C) finals, for this season they have done outstanding work in this
D) finals, for their performance has been outstanding this season

4) A plethora of self-help videos online nowadays are causing people to fix their own problems.

A) are causing people to fix their own problems
B) are causing people about fixing their own problems
C) is causing people into fixing of their own problems
D) is causing people to fix their own problems

5) A license and bloodwork is required for a valid marriage in many states.

A) is required
B) are required
C) to be requiring
D) has been requiring

6) Nikola Tesla, commonly regarded as the inventor of many key theories, including alternating current.

A) Tesla, commonly
B) Tesla, he is commonly
C) Tesla who is commonly
D) Tesla is commonly

7) Most students concede that building good study habits rather than cramming for brief periods are the solution to ensure learning.

A) are the solution
B) is the solution
C) are the solutions
D) have been the solutions

8) Despite the multiple options available for choosing the ideal school, there are but one decision to be made.

A) school, there are
B) school, there is
C) school, which is
D) school which are

9) If string theory explains the link between relativity and quantum physics, the credit for finding the explanation belong to numerous scientists.

A) belong to
B) belong with
C) belongs from
D) belongs to

10) Almost every baking recipe calls for a liquid, usually either milk or water, which are used to homogenize the mixture to ensure even baking.

A) are used
B) are using
C) is used
D) have been used

11) The Environmental Protection Agency continues to note that the effects of the Deepwater Horizon explosion, known as the BP oil spill, is still being observed in the environment today.

A) is still being
B) are still being
C) have still been
D) will still have been

12) Creative use of technology in schools allows teachers to approach education in a way that helps them to be both effective and efficient.

A) that helps
B) that help
C) which helps
D) to help

13) Meredith, an entrenched deep state politician, or other political hacks, such as Marcus Hammerman from the Olive Tree Party, has nary a shot at winning the election come October.

A) has
B) has had
C) have
D) would has

14) Almost half of incoming students who responded to the University of Pittsburgh's survey were interested in becoming a doctor or medical professional.

A) were interested in becoming a doctor or medical professional
B) were interested in becoming doctors or medical professionals
C) was interested in becoming a doctor or medical professional
D) was interested in becoming doctors or medical professionals

Lesson 3
Subject-Verb Agreement
Answer Key

Homework Exercises

1) D
2) C
3) D
4) D
5) B
6) D
7) B
8) B
9) D
10) C
11) B
12) A
13) C
14) B

Application Exercises

1) **Correctly Written**
Group words, known as **Collective Nouns** are always singular, regardless of any modification.

2) **...discovery... <u>has</u>...**
Here, the subject is a **singular** "loophole" separated by a modifier between the commas. Sometimes a singular subject is modified by an "of *something plural*" such as "The discovery of sharks or "a group of Neanderthals" but these are still singular subjects that need to correspond to singular verbs.

3) **Correctly Written**
Mustafa is the singular subject here. Don't be fooled by "in addition to" or "along with" construction that try to simulate a conjunctive phrase. Remember that **only** a conjunction using the word "AND" forms plural subjects for two singular subjects.

4) **...the tally... <u>was</u>...**
It's not that the "raised hands were impressive", the "tally was." **Identify** the **subject** correctly, and you'll surely have an easier time corresponding the verb.

5) **...there <u>is</u>... one option...**
No matter how many deans give you advice, there still "is" only one option. Hence, **singular subject** with singular verb is necessary in this construction.

6) **...hill <u>are</u>...**
Conjunctions with the word "and" creates a plural subject. A "barn and field" make up a plural subject. The verb form "are" is correct here, not "is".

7) **Correctly Written**
This is idiomatically and grammatically correct. This **declarative** sentence asks for someone to help "me".

8) **Eating...<u>is</u>...**
The act of "eating" requires further modification to be considered a subject. In this instance, the actual subject is "eating with good friends" (it is also a **subject phrase)**. In subject phrases, the verb agreement is always **singular**.

9) **...valet...<u>was</u>...**
The singular subject "valet" is modified with a phrase that doesn't create a plural subject. Thus, the verb "was" is correct, not "were".

10) **Correctly Written**
The **conjunction** "and" is used correctly here.

11) **A number of us...<u>want</u>...**
The subject phrase "A NUMBER OF US" is **not** a collective noun. "**A** number" is always plural, while "**the** number" is always singular.

12) **...none <u>were</u>...**
(See explanation for #13 below)

13) **...none <u>was</u>...**
Subjective **phrases** utilizing **numerical values**, like SOME, ALL, MOST, ANY and NONE (SAMAN), requires contextual agreement with the verb. Therefore, in Q#12 "none of the shards" is a plural subject, while in Q#13 "none in the group" is a singular subject.

14) **...<u>neither</u>...of them <u>piques</u>...**
The subject here is an **Indefinite Pronoun**, such as "neither" or "someone" or "anyone" or "whoever". Indefinite Pronouns are always singular, and therefore require a singular verb agreement.

15) **...<u>either</u>...<u>or</u> his peer <u>was</u>...**
This is a **Compound Subject** where the subject is "peer" and the verb "was" must agree with the closest subject following the "either...or" construction. In this case, a singular "peer".

Homework Exercises

1) **Choice D is correct.**
The major subject-verb error here is that there is no verb, creating a sentence fragment or incomplete sentence. Choice D introduces "was," the only likely verb for Jules Verne, creating a complete sentence.

2) **Choice C is correct.**
"Any" is both an indefinite pronoun and a SAMAN (see Application Q#13 explanation in previous page) pronoun, therefore the controlling subject is determined by the following singular quantifier "one", requiring the verb to be conjugated singularly as well.

3) **Choice D is correct.**
When connecting two independent clauses, a FANBOYS conjunction must be used. In this instance, we use FOR as the proper conjunction. Choice C utilizes a FANBOYS but is just ew awkward.

4) **Choice D is correct.**
"A plethora" is the subject of the sentence and is a collective noun. Since there is only one plethora, "is" would be the correct verb. We have two choices with a singular verb, but choice C is idiomatically incorrect (we don't *cause* people *into* fixing things, we *cause* people *to* fix things).

5) **Choice B is correct.**
Because license and bloodwork are linked with AND, they count as a united plural subject, requiring a plural verbal conjugation.

6) **Choice D is correct.**
To correct this sentence fragment, we must add a verb to the subject to create an independent clause.

7) **Choice B is correct.**
The controlling gerund subject here is "building," which is always singular.

8) **Choice B is correct.**
This inverted sentence must show agreement between the subject and verb. In this clause, "one option" serves as a singular subject to the verb "is".

9) **Choice D is correct.**
The "credit" is the singular subject of this conditional sentence, requiring a singular verbal conjugation. Also, "belongs to" is the correct idiomatic pair.

10) **Choice C is correct.**
The underlined verb "are used" must agree with the pronoun "which", a relative pronoun (a concept we will tackle in Writing Lesson 4). Since "which" refers to the singular object of the independent clause "liquid", the verbal conjugation must also use the singular "is used" form.

11) **Choice B is correct.**
We should ask ourselves what is still being observed? The explosion or oil spill? It's actually neither, because the subject is "the effects", a plural noun. Since the sentence indicates that the event is ongoing, we must use the present progressive tense.

12) **Choice A is correct.**
The relative pronoun "that" is singular because it refers to a singular "way" (more on relative pronoun "that" later).

13) **Choice C is correct.**
The rule of OR dictates that the closest subject "other political hacks" conjugates the verb. Here, the verb is incorrectly conjugated singularly so we must change it to the plural form "have".

14) **Choice B is correct.**
This is an error in subject-object agreement: a rare event but very important to recognize. Multiple students are involved in the sentence, so we should use the plural forms of "doctors or medical professionals." Furthermore, the subject "half" must take into account the plural quantity "students", which dictates a plural verbal conjugation.

Writing
Lesson 4

Pronouns

Goals

We will develop our grammatical fluency and gain meaningful understanding by learning to:

1) Apply Pittsburgh Prep's method of Triple A's to recognize correct pronoun usage
2) Correct any errors through exercises

Contents

- Pronoun Types
- Triple A's Method of Error Correction
- A Note on Relative Pronouns
- Application Exercises
- Homework Exercises

Lesson 4
Pronouns

Pronoun Fundamentals

A pronoun is a word that replaces a noun. Pronouns come in various shapes and sizes: they change by person, gender, case, and number as follows:

(Subject Pronouns)	Singular	Plural
1st person	**I**	**We**
2nd person	**You**	**You**
3rd person	**He/She/It**	**They**

Since it is quite easy to mistake pronouns in one form or another, the following chart will help you to understand the different pronoun types:

Pronoun Types	Example	Usage
Subjective	I, you, he/she/it, we, they	Used as subjects in clauses & phrases
Objective	Me, you, him/her/it, us, them	Used as objects in clauses & phrases
Reflexive	Myself, yourself, herself, themselves	Used to denote an emphasis on the noun preceding/proceeding
Possessive	My, your, his/her/its, our, their	Used to denote possession of a noun
Indefinite	Anyone, somebody, everywhere, nothing	Used to refer to things without specificity
Demonstrative	This, that, these, those	Used to denote specific items or as adjectives
Relative*	This, which, who, whom, where	A special pronoun that relates on idea to another as a dependent-type clause

**Pay special attention to the "Note on relative pronouns" at the end of this lecture*

Pittsburgh Prep's Method of Finding Pronouns Errors

Whenever we encounter pronouns in a given sentence, Pittsburgh Prep's method of testing for correct usage involves the Triple A's approach. They are as follows:

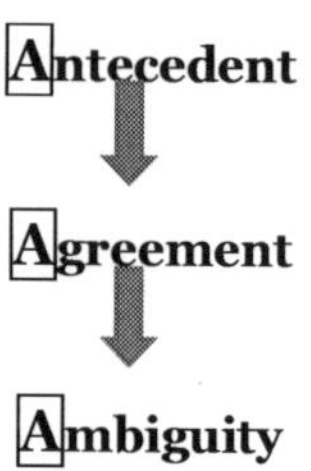

The "Triple A Method" is straightforward to apply towards any pronoun.

Antecedent refers to the noun that the pronoun replaces. This noun can come before or after the pronoun, and it can also come in another sentence altogether. However, in a single clause, it is entirely possible to think that the antecedent exists when in fact it does not.

For example, identify the antecedent in the following sentence:

The testimony was lengthy, but they didn't mind the time at all.

In the above sentence, the pronoun "they" has no referring noun at all. In other words, no antecedent exists. Always make sure to check for the existence of the antecedent whenever a pronoun is used. The sentence should be corrected with a proper noun "...***but ~~they~~ the witnesses didn't mind the time at all.***"

Find the error below:

eg 1. Carl's hair flowed luxuriously as he walked down the street.

Agreement issues occur mainly between pronoun and noun, or pronoun and verb. Note that pronouns must agree in number, gender, and case. For example:

Each person must remember to punch their own ticket at the show.

The issue above reflects a common agreement error between the singular subject "each person" and the plural pronoun "their". The corrected sentence should state, "***Each person must remember to punch ~~their~~ his/her own ticket at the show.***"

eg 2. The crowd entertained themselves by bouncing a massive beach ball.

Finally, **Ambiguity** errors occur when it's unclear to exactly what the pronoun refers to. Many times, this happens due to haphazard noun and pronoun placement in an awkward sentence construction. Take the following example:

Madeline and Jessie took a long hike in the forest, then decided to go back to her house.

The pronoun issue exhibited here can be resolved by replacing the ambiguous pronoun "her" with one of the antecedent nouns to make clear to who's home they are going back to. The corrected sentence should read: "...**then decided to go back to ~~her~~ Jessie's house**."

eg 3. Jenny dabbled in science and sports in high school, but she took to it the best.

A Note on Relative Pronouns

Relative pronouns can best be thought of as pronoun that relate one idea to another. Relative pronouns are a distinct category of pronouns that function as dependent clauses, but do not follow the conventions of either a clause or a pronoun. Common relative pronouns are *that, which, who, whom,* and *where*. They are also a special kind of dependent clauses. They all have the following characteristics:

- They MUST refer to the immediately preceding noun
- They can often be mistaken for demonstrative pronouns

Relative pronouns can be found at the start, middle, or end of a sentence, and are normally part of a *relative clause* that relates another idea to a topic introduced in the sentence. At first, learn to identify relative pronouns when they occur. (Remember: Relative pronouns are different from demonstrative pronouns.) Some examples of relative clauses embedded in a sentence are:

> The interesting part of the story **that allowed me to understand it better was at the** very end of the plotline.
>
> My uncle's great escape from Riker's Island**, which was supposed to be the toughest prison in the world at the time,** was reported all over the news.
>
> I am going to hug this boy **who was quite nice to me during the reception.**
>
> The guardian, **whom I considered my very best friend,** quietly passed away last month.

eg 4. Remind the man, that has been waiting, that his order is ready.

eg 5. There was a horse who could pick up its trainer's cues so well that it fooled crowds into thinking that it could perform basic math.

Relative Pronouns	**Usage**	**Punctuation?**	**Essential/Nonessential?**
That			
Which			
Who			
Whom			
Where			

Relative pronoun errors consist of either misplacement of the relative clause or improper usage of the relative pronoun. When these errors occur, make sure to decide on the proper resolution. If the error involves a misplaced relative clause, we can look to move the entire clause. If the error improperly uses a relative pronoun, we can look to drop the relative pronoun altogether, and replace it with either a phrase or make it into a dependent clause utilizing a subordinating conjunction.

Lesson 4
Pronouns
Application Exercises

Time – 10 Minutes

Answer the questions in this worksheet within the time allotted – no answer sheets are needed.

Directions: For each sentence in this section, determine whether pronouns agree with their referents. Circle the pronoun at issue, underline the agreeing referent and correct *as necessary*. Good luck!

1) Only pack the clothes that you are planning to wear.

2) The artist who presented the paintings must bring their portfolio with them.

3) Sometimes the lawyer intentionally brings her case to the courtroom, even though the rules specifically prohibit her from bringing them.

4) Ashna cannot be promoted as First Lieutenant in the Army because she fails to meet their strict qualifications.

5) We cooked seventeen pounds of turkey for our annual family gathering, which we all ate heartily.

6) Mike's eyelashes twitched in the sunlight, and it was apparent that he needed sunglasses.

7) Did no one here make a mistake on their exam?

8) When the opera was over, the actors made sure to confer with their director, who were very concerned with the horrible reviews that they were sure to receive.

9) The musicians decided to skip Montana in its tour, which had a very low popularity rating for the band.

10) I definitely think the nutrients in broccoli are better than that in cabbage.

11) Kelsey, would you like to go to the movies with Jeremy, Abdulla, and me tonight at eight o'clock?

12) The head of the Animal League is always shocked by how fast Marsha and I can sign up 50 volunteers every weekend.

13) Even though they had committed crimes in their past, the prisoner's work inside the prison actually produces beneficial results for society now.

14) Quincy's stomach was so full that he decided to go on a diet for the next two weeks.

15) My doctor told me that I should not live with my dog, with whom I have an allergy to.

Lesson 4
Pronouns
Homework Exercises

1) The American musical tradition known as jazz is one of the greatest American contributions to music because of their songs that use unique time signatures and keys.

   A) NO CHANGE
   B) its songs use
   C) the songs that used
   D) of how it uses their

2) Mike cherished the memory of the day when him and his son were presented with awards in recognition of meritorious service to the community.

   A) NO CHANGE
   B) when he
   C) that him
   D) which he

3) Although their culture and people are separate from English tradition, Scotland is generally considered part of Britain, which includes Wales, England, and Scotland.

   A) NO CHANGE
   B) it has a culture and people, that are
   C) they have cultures and people
   D) its culture and people are

4) Zebras have never been domesticated, unlike horses and donkeys, most of whom working for humans in some form since prehistoric domestication.

   A) NO CHANGE
   B) of which have worked
   C) of them have worked
   D) have worked

5) Astronomers dispute the existence of a hypothetical planet on the edge of our solar system, which would have ten times the mass of Earth.

   A) NO CHANGE
   B) which has
   C) that has
   D) predicted to have

6) After Nick, the hero of Fitzgerald's *The Great Gatsby*, is exposed to the decadence of East Egg, he realizes that one's social class matters less than your character.

   A) NO CHANGE
   B) he realizes that one's social class matters less than one's
   C) then realizing that one's social class matters less than their
   D) there is his realization about how social class matters less than

7) The computers in the order were assembled too haphazardly, without enough care behind it.

   A) NO CHANGE
   B) too haphazard, and there is not enough care behind them.
   C) too haphazardly, without enough care behind them
   D) too haphazardly, and there is not enough care behind it

8) The principles of calculus revolve around derivation, a principal whereby it becomes possible to find the change of a rate over time.

   A) NO CHANGE
   B) that
   C) which
   D) when

9) A whistle-blower is <u>when an employee reports fraud or mismanagement</u> in a company.

A) NO CHANGE
B) an employee who reports fraud or mismanagement
C) reporting by an employee of fraud or mismanagement
D) if an employee reports fraud or mismanagement

10) In 1961, a hydrogen bomb was accidentally dropped in Eureka, North Carolina by a crashing B-52, <u>there</u> it was left buried until 2013.

A) NO CHANGE
B) then
C) where
D) so

11) The historic council, angered at seeing a block of Victorian houses scheduled to be demolished, vowed to use every legal means to fight <u>it</u>.

A) NO CHANGE
B) them
C) this
D) the council's scheduled demolition

12) A skilled kitchen of chefs show their talent in the creativity of their dishes, their ability to work as an ensemble, and <u>how he or she react</u> to the tensions of mercurial customers.

A) NO CHANGE
B) how to react
C) they react
D) their reactions

13) Despite inclement weather and technological setbacks during Apollo 11's lunar landing, 600 million people on Earth used their televisions <u>to spectate that</u>.

A) NO CHANGE
B) for its spectating
C) to spectate
D) in spectating

14) To truly understand computer programming, <u>we must be familiar with Boolean logic and mathematics, whether one is well-versed in them</u> or not.

A) NO CHANGE
B) we must be familiar with Boolean logic and mathematics, whether one is well-versed in it
C) one must be familiar with Boolean logic and mathematics, whether one is well-versed in it
D) one must be familiar with Boolean logic and mathematics, whether one is well-versed in them

15) When Jonathan Franzen published *The Corrections* in 1962, <u>it established himself</u> as one of the most important writers in contemporary fiction.

A) NO CHANGE
B) it established him
C) they established him
D) he established it

Lesson 4
Pronouns
Answer Key

Homework Exercises

1) B
2) B
3) D
4) B
5) D
6) B
7) C
8) A
9) B
10) C
11) D
12) D
13) C
14) D
15) B

Example Exercises

1) ...as Carl walked...
The issue here with the antecedent is that Carl's hair ≠ Carl. Since Carl himself is not in the sentence, "he" would not be appropriate without an antecedent.

2) ...entertained itself by...
Consider the gender, case, and number of

the original "themselves." Gender isn't an issue (all neutral), the case works (reflexive is OK

3) ... master these subjects before...
The use of a singular "it" here is confusing to the reader. Is science or sports the antecedent? If we are unsure, it would be best to not use a pronoun at all and replace "it" with "sports".

4) Remind the man that has been waiting that his order ...
Relative pronouns using that will not use a comma, as the comma creates a run-on. We can say "the man that has been waiting" without any pause or hesitation

5) "a horse who could pick up its trainer's cues"
The issue here is the use of the pronoun 'who' with regards to a horse. The pronoun 'who' only works with known animals. It's OK to tell your dog "who's a good boy" because that is a known animal, but you wouldn't refer to a dog across the street as "the dog who is across the street" when "a dog that is across the street" is more grammatically appropriate.

Relative Pronouns	**Usage**	**Punctuation**	**Essential/Nonessential**
That	Universal	Never	Essential – adds meaning to the sentence.
Which	Objects only	Comma	Nonessential – gives additional information not necessary to the sentence's understanding.
Who	People and known animals as a SUBJECT	Depends	Depends on usage (is there a comma or not?)
Whom	People and known animals as an OBJECT	Depends	Depends on usage (is there a comma or not?)
Where	Places and instances	Depends	Depends on usage (is there a comma or not?)

Application Exercises

1) **Correctly Written**

2) **Artist...his/her portfolio...with him/her.** Here, the subject is a singular "artist." Therefore, the referential pronoun must agree with the singular subject. Using "them" or "their" is incorrect.

3) **...bring her case... from bringing it.** The "case" is the singular referent here. Since "case" is singular, the pronoun "them" must also be changed to singular "it."

4) **...fails to meet its strict qualifications...** The failure of meeting the qualifications is by the Army, a singular referent collective noun. Therefore, the pronoun must also be singular.

5) **... seventeen pounds of turkey, which we all ate heartily, for our family gathering.** Original construction implies the family is eating the family gathering. Move the relative clause closer to the object eaten to correct this mistake.

6) **... apparent that Mike needed sunglasses ...** Pronouns must have a clear antecedent – here, the referent is not Mike, but Mike's eyelashes. Therefore, the pronoun "he" cannot be used in the second clause.

7) **... make a mistake on his/her exam?...** The antecedent "no one" is singular, therefore the possessive pronoun must either be singular: "his" or "her."

8) **... the actors, who were very concerned with the horrible reviews that they were sure to receive, made sure to confer with their director...** The subject here is "actors", and the corresponding pronoun is "who". It is ambiguous. By placing the modifier closer to the subject, we prevent this clarity issue.

9) **...decided to skip Montana, because the musicians thought they had low popularity there.** This is a tough question to correct – pronouns were misused all over the place, and the contextual meaning of the sentence was lost throughout. The only way to correct this sentence is to keep the second clause ACTIVE, and clearly demonstrate the referent-pronoun relationship.

10) **...nutrients in broccoli are better than those in cabbage...** Make sure that the referent agrees in proper number! "Nutrients" is plural, whereas the pronoun "that" indicates a singular referent. Therefore, "those" is the correct pronoun to use here.

11) **Correctly Written**

12) **Correctly Written**

13) **... the prisoners had committed crimes in their past, the prisoners' work ...** The referent here is not "prisoner's work", but the prisoners themselves. Therefore, the pronoun "they" cannot be used, as it lacks a referent altogether. Using the subject, "prisoner", resolves this problem.

14) **... Quincy's stomach was so full that Quincy...** The subject here is Quincy, and use of the pronoun "he" cannot work due to a lack of proper referent. Remember that "he" is a subject pronoun, and therefore, requires a subject as its referent. "Quincy's stomach" is not a subject in the second clause.

15) **... I should not live with my dog, because I have an allergy to it.** Using who/whom here is improper. The definitive word "because" is better suited to connect the relative clause, clearly showing that you have an allergy to your dog.

Homework Exercises

1) **Choice B is correct.**
The antecedent for "their" is jazz, which is singular, so we should use the possessive pronoun "its". Choice D has a singular "it," but contains a plural "their" with no antecedent.

2) **Choice B is correct.**
The "him" given in the original sentence has an antecedent in Mike, but it is used as the subject of the verb "were presented." "Him" is the objective form of "he," which should be more correct. Choice D is a bit misleading since it has "he," but notice that this choice also uses the relative pronoun "which" without a comma incorrectly.

3) **Choice D is correct.**
Think about the pronoun "their": what does it refer to? The Scottish people? That might seem logical, but that antecedent is nowhere in our sentence. The only appropriate antecedent is Scotland, a singular country, and it acts like a collective noun.

4) **Choice B is correct.**
The pronoun that we must deal with here is "whom," and it incorrectly refers to zebras. Pronouns like "who" and "whom" can only refer to *specific* animals, like your dog Chewy, or Smokey the Bear. Since these are general zebras, this won't work. Choice B contains "which," a suitable replacement. Choices C and D may have appropriate pronouns, but they create independent clauses and comma splices.

5) **Choice D is correct.**
It may seem like B would work because of the change in the verb tense but notice that the relative pronoun "which" follows "the solar system," which could not serve as the correct antecedent. We should instead use the participial phrase in choice D to refer to the hypothetical passage.

6) **Choice B is correct.**
Our issue here is agreement of pronouns. The pronouns "he" and "one" in the initial sentence match case and number, but still do not fit each other: we should exclusively use "he" or "one."

7) **Choice C is correct.**
The computers are the focus of the pronoun, so we should use a plural pronoun. Just pay attention to the use of "haphazard" in Choice B (more on that later).

8) **Choice A is correct.**
Whereby is rare, but that does not make it incorrect. The other choices should all be eliminated from the bad pronouns used to substitute for the conjunction whereby.

9) **Choice B is correct.**
Whistle-blowers are people, not time, so "when" is used incorrectly here as a relative pronoun.

10) **Choice C is correct.**
Using "there" instead of a relative pronoun creates a comma splice, the same problem as choice B. Choice D may seem grammatically sound, but it is not logically sound: the conjunction "so" requires a cause-effect relationship.

11) **Choice D is correct.**
Looking at the three pronouns in choices A, B, C, we should notice that *none of the pronouns have clear antecedents!* Are we fighting the council? The houses? Choice D may seem roundabout, but often when we don't have a clear antecedent for a pronoun, the best solution is to substitute the antecedent instead and use no pronoun at all.

12) **Choice D is correct.**
Keep your pronouns consistent and parallel with the rest of the sentence. Since we already have plural chefs and other phrases to go off of ("their talent ... their dishes").

13) **Choice C is correct.**
This is another case of an ambiguous pronoun. It does not need to be there. The infinitive phrase "to spectate" suffices.

14) **Choice D is correct.**
This is another case of pronoun agreement, where we have competing pronouns in the third person (singular "one" vs plural "we"). Choice C gives two cases of "one," but also has the pronoun "it," which does not match the antecedents "Boolean logic and mathematics."

15) **Choice B is correct.**
The issue with the reflexive pronoun "himself" is that for a reflexive pronoun to work, the subject and object must be the same. The subject "it" will not work with the object "himself" even with Jonathan Franzen already in the sentence

Writing Lesson 5

Modifiers

Goals

We will develop our grammatical fluency and gain meaningful understanding by learning to:

1) Differentiate between the three types of modifiers: adjective, adverbs, and phrases
2) Correct the three most common error types

Contents

- Essential Modifier Usage
- Application Exercises
- Homework Exercises

Lesson 5
Modifiers

What is a modifier? A modifier changes, clarifies or qualifies a particular word to add and explain in detail. Modifying words add color to sentences, and they can be powerful in the way a narrator expresses an idea. There are generally three types to consider, and three common errors.

Modifier Types	Common Errors
Adjectives	Incorrect Usage
Adverbs	Misplaced Modifier
Phrases	Dangling Modifier

Adjectives

We define **adjectives** as modifiers that describe nouns or pronouns, whereas **adverbs** are modifiers that describe verbs, other adverbs and adjectives. We have already discussed **modifying phrases** in our Clauses & Phrases (Lesson 1) together, so we can define modifying phrases as a group of words that acts to describe a concept further.

Adjectives tend to be placed in front of the nouns they describe, though not always so. Adjectives that describe the subject can be placed after the verb if the verb is a linking verb. Examples of adjectives for both types are underlined in the following sentences:

> The **flat-footed** gentleman spoke gently to the crowd.
> A mile through the forest leads to the **vile** caves.
> Amidst the row house, only one structure was **yellow**. ("was" is a linking verb here)

Note that in the first sentence, the gentleman is modified as "flat-footed". In the second, the caves are described as "vile".

However, in the third sentence, the subject "structure" is modified by the adjective "yellow". This modifier "yellow" comes at the end of the sentence, not in front of the noun "structure" linking verbs (such as "to be, to look, to smell, to taste") almost always require an adjective that describes the subject noun of the sentence after the verb. The less complicated reason involves logic: it just makes sense. In the following sentence, identify the adjective and what it's modifying:

> Jamie Harrison looked **inconsolable**.

Here, the adjective "inconsolable" describes "Jamie Harrison," because the verb "looked" is a linking verb.

Another type of adjectives are **participles**, verbs in the present or past participle that describe an object further. Example of participles acting as adjectives are:

> The **seasoned** turkey tasted great.
> The rookie accidentally kicked the goal keeper in his **gaping** mouth.

Collective adjectives are adjectival phrases that are always plural and preceded by the article "the". Examples of collective adjectives are:

> **The rich** are always in need of something.
> I have heard **the young** are never satisfied with what they've got.

Adverbs

Adverbs, unlike adjectives, can be placed almost anywhere in the sentence, so long as it does not confuse the reader. Most adverbs end in an *-ly*, but not all. To confuse the matter more, some words that do end in an *-ly* are not adverbs, but adjectives.

Adverbs that DO end in *-ly*	*helpfully, thoroughly, fearfully*
Adverbs that do NOT end in *-ly*	*quite, very, hard, fast*
ADJECTIVES that end in *-ly*	*lovely, motherly, friendly, lonely*

Specific relative clauses (special dependent clauses, see pronouns lesson in this study guide) also act as adverbial clauses. Some examples:

> **When I took the car**, my mother declared war.
> We are making cake, **when your Royal Highness asks for it**.

Yet the most common use of adverbs are the ones that modify adjectives, or other adverbs. They are:

> These lads are **really** terrible at chess.
> Who let the **very** hungry dogs out?

As a general rule of thumb, if the modifier answers "how?" it is most likely an adverb.

Comparatives using adverbs are commonly mistaken in colloquial usage. Countable nouns utilize the comparative adverb "fewer", whereas uncountable mass nouns use the adverb "less". Comparative adverbs can have degrees notated by the suffix *–er* (two) or *–est* (three or more).

> This lane is for ten items or ~~less~~ **fewer**.
> There is **less** air in this room.
> My sister is the **strongest** person in the entire team.

Phrases

Most prepositional phrases and infinitive phrases act as adverbial phrases, or phrases that serve to modify the verb of the clause. Some examples are:

> Marylinne went **to the cinema**.
> Congenital defects affect the heart **in the most terrible way.**
> The President never hesitated **to deny his previous statement.**

Phrases such as participial phrases and appositive phrases act as adjectives, or phrases that serve to modify nouns:

> Batman, **munching on his granola bar**, asked Alfred for some more milk.
> The University hospital, **overrun with debt for years**, finally declared bankruptcy.
> The pigeon climbed as high as it could into the night sky, **a desolate place**.

Gerundive phrases or subjective phrases serve to help the subject or object with a modifier:

> T**hrowing dirty baseballs into the wind** creates havoc in the space-time continuum.
> I am not happy with the task of **finding your long-lost father**, Luke.

Common Modifier Errors

The first common type of error occurs from incorrect usage of the various forms of modifiers. Often, we may say things a certain way, but they would be incorrect grammatically. For example:

That movie is **real** scary!

The sentence above may sound correct to many of us, but since "real" is an adjective that is modifying another adjective "scary", which modifies "that movie, the correct form would be to use the adverbial form "really':

That movie is ~~real~~ **really** scary!

The second common type of error is a misplaced modifier. Just as it states, any modifier in the wrong place of a sentence will create confusion and sometimes unintended humor. In the following examples, correct the error by moving the entire modifying phrase, and properly determine the fallacy within each sentence:

The kindergarten teacher passed out cookies to all of her kids **in small plastic bags**.

Correction: ____

My sassy uncle Renatch saw a dead moose **driving on the highway**.

Correction: ____

Crusted and old, my grandmother inadvertently ate the bread.

Correction: ____

The third common type of error is a dangling modifier. Unlike misplaced modifiers, dangling modifiers lack the proper noun that they are supposed to modify. In these instances, a proper referent must be inserted into the sentence to make the proper correction. This can happen often when a possessive is used with a subject: for instance, smiling can describe Jesse, but not Jesse's car. As examples:

Leaving the butcher, the dry aged sirloin steak fell out of the bag and plopped unto the sidewalk.

Correction: ____

Flying over the countryside, the cows looked so tiny grazing on the grass fields.

Correction: ____

Amazed at his luck, Robert's lottery ticket had the winning numbers printed in stark black font.

Correction: ____

Final Note on Modifiers

Utilizing a systems approach as taught to you by Pittsburgh Prep, you must remember to attune your senses to be able to recognize modifier errors as they occur. This will take time. Since errors will never be as humorous or apparent as they are exemplified in this session, make careful considerations of all of the parts of sentence construction. This, again, will take time.

So be patient, be thorough, and utilize the comprehensive approach of review for the following exercises.

Lesson 5
Modifiers
Application Exercises

Time – 10 Minutes

Directions: For each sentence in this section, determine whether modifiers are at issue. Underline the modifier at issue, circle the thing being modified and correct as necessary.

1) My shoes, my favorite pair, were originally colored red, my favorite color.

2) The bird became hungry, like the rest of the flock, when the lunch bell was rung by the farmer every afternoon.

3) Are you feeling good? Or, are you feeling well?

4) Revered by millions of people, all of the TV channels aired the Pope's last speech.

5) Macon, who was shivering from the frigid air, eventually caught pneumonia.

6) The wolf's cries at night are real scary.

7) Both charismatic and captivating, the incumbent's speech was inspiring and motivating.

8) That's fantastic news!

9) Obviously, this car drives fantastic.

10) Who's cheese is this which is making all this stink?

11) Joshua aced the final exam, which made his summer much more enjoyable.

12) The Cleveland Browns, which has not won the Superbowl for the past 20 years, finally acquired a strong Quarterback.

13) I drank tons of grapefruit juice yesterday, that was supposed to help with my digestive problems.

14) A complete novice, Melody's method of dancing was surprisingly fluid and graceful.

15) Boy, this Apple Pie is real good!

Lesson 5
Modifiers
Homework Exercises

1) A writer who well understood the plight of the underprivileged, <u>many acclaim Richard Wright as</u> the novelist of the downtrodden.

   A) many acclaim Richard Wright as
   B) many have acclaimed Richard Wright as
   C) Richard Wright is being acclaimed by many as
   D) Richard Wright has been widely acclaimed as

2) <u>Arthur, perpetual devoted to the Mitchell family,</u> made time for regular family outings between business trips.

   A) Arthur, perpetual devoted to the Mitchell family,
   B) Arthur, perpetually devoted to the Mitchell family,
   C) Arthur's perpetual devotion to the Mitchell family
   D) Arthur, perpetually devoted by the Mitchell family

3) Looking down through the boat's glass bottom, <u>a school of yellow fish was seen</u> swimming along with the turtles.

   A) a school of yellow fish was seen
   B) a school of yellow fish were seen
   C) we saw a school of yellow fish
   D) we had seen a school of yellow fish

4) The <u>surprisingly sweet concoction</u> had given Edna a headache.

   A) surprisingly sweet concoction
   B) surprising sweet concoction
   C) concoction, surprisingly sweet,
   D) surprisingly, sweet concoction

5) <u>No matter how cautious</u> snowmobiles are driven, they can damage the land over which they travel.

   A) No matter how cautious
   B) No matter how cautious,
   C) No matter how cautiously
   D) No matter how cautiously,

6) The movie Jurassic Park was critiqued by some scientists for making a <u>true laudable</u> attempt at plausibility.

   A) true laudable attempt
   B) truly laudably attempt
   C) true laudably attempt
   D) truly laudable attempt

7) Although fascinated by chance and coincidence, <u>Jim Butcher's novels are written</u> with careful attention to continuity and accuracy.

   A) Jim Butcher's novels are written
   B) Jim Butcher's novels were written
   C) Jim Butcher writes his novels
   D) Jim Butcher has wrote

8) <u>The Avengers tried valiantly without Iron Man, to save the world in the newest film.</u>

   A) The Avengers tried valiantly without Iron Man, to save the world in the newest film.
   B) The Avengers, without Iron Man, tried valiantly, to save the world in the newest film.
   C) Without Iron Man, the Avengers tried valiantly to save the world in the newest film.
   D) The Avengers tried valiantly, to save the world in the newest film without Iron Man.

9) At the meeting of the board, Councilman Doakes assured his constituents that he was actively seeking a long-term solution to the city's parking problem.

   A) At the meeting of the board, Councilman Doakes
   B) At the meeting of the board Councilman Doakes
   C) Councilman Doakes at the meeting of the board
   D) Councilman Doakes, on the meeting of the board,

10) Ambassador Batista was entertained lavish by Dexter, whose company has an interest in the development of the new country.

   A) lavish by Dexter, whose
   B) lavish by Dexter, who's
   C) lavishly by Dexter, which
   D) lavishly by Dexter, whose

11) The professor assured the students that they had done good on the deviously tricky exam, despite constantly missing the open-ended questions.

   A) done good on the deviously tricky
   B) done good on the devious tricky
   C) done well on the devious tricky
   D) done well on the deviously tricky

12) A deep, long recession is a fear of many economists after times of crisis or social unrest.

   A) deep, long recession
   B) deep, long, recession
   C) deep long recession
   D) deeply long recession

13) A concern with legal repercussions in patent law is common for much of the companies in Silicon Valley.

   A) much of the companies
   B) much of the company's
   C) many of the companies
   D) many of the company's

14) One of the most influential thinkers in ancient Greece, musical, scientific, and mathematical breakthroughs are attributed to Pythagoras, making him the subject of legends even during his own lifetime.

   A) musical, scientific, and mathematical breakthroughs are attributed to Pythagoras, making him
   B) Pythagoras is attributed with musical, scientific, and mathematical breakthroughs, making him
   C) musical, scientific, and mathematical breakthroughs, attributed to Pythagoras, making him
   D) Pythagoras's musical, scientific, and mathematical breakthroughs make him

15) Far less people have diabetes symptoms after careful dieting and maintenance.

   A) Far less
   B) Far fewer
   C) Much fewer
   D) Much less

Lesson 5
Modifiers
Answer Key

Homework Exercises

1) D
2) B
3) C
4) A
5) C
6) D
7) C
8) C
9) A
10) D
11) D
12) A
13) C
14) B
15) B

Application Exercises

1) **Correctly Written**
Sort of an odd sentence that seems awkward in colloquial speech, but correctly written in formal sentence construction. Both modifiers unambiguously are placed correctly right after the nouns, "shoes" and "red", respectively.

2) **...The bird, <u>like the rest of the flock</u>, became hungry when...**
The rest of the flock cannot modify "hungry;" therefore, it must logically modify the "bird".

3) **...feeling <u>well</u>...**
You can't "feel" "good", despite the song by James Brown. "Good" is used only as an adjective that modifies a person, not a verb. However, "well" is used as both an adverb (in this case) or as an adjective when it means "physically fit".

4) **...people, <u>the Pope made his last speech that was aired by all TV channels</u>...**
The "Pope" was revered, not the *TV channels* or *the speech*! The TV channels airing the speech must take a passive stance due to the nature of the modifier and the author's logic.

5) **Correctly Written**
Good in placement, use, and modification.

6) **... <u>really</u> scary ...**
Remember: if a noun is modified, then use an adjective. All else should be adverbs. In this case, since "scary" is not a noun, use the adverb form of "real".

7) **...captivating, the <u>incumbent</u> gave a speech that was...**
What's being modified here? The incumbent or the speech? Right. The incumbent.

8) **Correctly Written**
"News" is the noun, "fantastic" is the adjective modifying it. Correct.

9) **...drives <u>fantastically</u>.**
"Fantastic" is the modifier here, and since it's an adjective, it should correspond to the car – but that's not the case here. The act of driving is being modified, hence, the adverb "fantastically" must be used. (We know, it sounds weird, but it's correct!)

10) **...<u>Whose</u> cheese is this <u>that</u> is** Classic pronoun issue in this modifying clause. For one, the possessive "whose" must be used to indicate the owner of the cheese, and since the stink is essentially tied to the cheese, the relative pronoun "that" must be used as well

11) **...final exam, <u>making</u> his summer...**
When using "which", the modifying clause isn't modifying the final exam, it's modifying Joshua acing the final exam. Therefore, the pronoun "which" must be taken out of the sentence altogether.

12) **...Browns, <u>who</u> <u>have</u> not...**
Utilize "who" for relative pronouns with people, "which" for non-essential things, and "that" for essential things. Note the pronoun agreement here as well, since the Cleveland Browns are plural.

13) **... <u>Yesterday</u>, I drank tons of grapefruit juice, <u>which</u> was supposed to help...**
For one, the essential relative pronoun "that" and the non-essential pronoun "which" are incorrectly used here. Two, the relative pronoun "which" must be kept close as possible to the noun being modified. And three, logically the time frame "yesterday" must be placed elsewhere in the sentence to make it unambiguous.

14) **... novice, <u>Melody danced</u> surprisingly fluid...**
Remember the possessive issue in pronouns? The modifier here is not Melody's method of dancing, it's actually Melody herself. The sentence must reflect this sentiment.

15) **... is <u>really</u> good.**
Remember: Adverbs modify adjectives, other adverbs, and verbs. Adjectives only modify nouns. In this case, "really" is modifying the adjective "good" which in turn is modifying the noun "Apple Pie."

Homework Exercises

1) **Choice D is correct.**
This is a test of dangling modifiers. Since the initial appositive phrase "A writer..." describes a writer, then a writer should be directly proceeding the phrase.

2) **Choice B is correct.**
Notice the modifier types: we want the adjective "devoted" to modify Arthur, and the adverb "perpetually" to modify devoted. Choice C is incorrect because the "devotion" doesn't make time for family – Arthur does.

3) **Choice C is correct.**
This is a classic misplaced modifier error, and the most straightforward method of correction is turning our modifier phrase into a question: who or what was "[l]ooking down through the boat's glass bottom"? The logical answer would not be the fish. Between C and D, the best choice would be the present tense of C

4) **Choice A is correct.**
This structure has the most straightforward approach, with the adverb, adjective, and noun in a row. Other choices violate our goal of having our modifiers as close to their targets as possible.

5) **Choice C is correct.**
Cautious is an adjective, so it can only describe a noun or pronoun. Can a snowmobile be cautious? Modify the driving with an adverb (cautiously). Choice D may seem good, but not with the comma after the adverb: a comma would be appropriate between two adjectives, but not here.

6) **Choice D is correct.**
Since an "attempt" is the controlling noun, the adjective form "laudable" should be used here. Further, the adverbial form "truly" is needed to modify the adjective "laudable".

7) **Choice C is correct.**
This is a dangling modifier error: it is likely that Jim Butcher is fascinated by chance and coincidence, as novels are inanimate objects and cannot be fascinated. We can also rule out D as it corrects the modifier error but uses an incorrect verb tense.

8) **Choice C is correct.**
In this question, think of modifier placement. Choice A places the prepositional phrase "without Iron Man" before a single comma, which is clearly incorrect. Choice B introduces far too many commas to be functional, and Choice D places the preposition phrase too far from the topic.

9) **Choice A is correct.**
This modifier placement question demonstrates that it is acceptable to begin a sentence with an introductory phrase separated by a comma.

10) **Choice D is correct.**
Notice the incorrect modifier between lavish (adj) and lavishly (adv), and notice the incorrect version of "whose."

11) **Choice D is correct.**
The adverb "well" is more appropriate here than the adjective "good," and "devious" is incorrect since we are modifying the adjective "tricky."

12) **Choice A is correct.**
This is an example of separating two adjectives modifying the same noun with a comma.

13) **Choice C is correct.**
For the adjectives "many" and "much," remember that "many" is for things that are countable and "much" is for abstract amounts. Since companies are countable, we should use many, and mind the plural version of compan*ies*.

14) **Choice B is correct.**
This is a classic dangling modifier error: since the first clause is describing Pythagoras, Pythagoras should follow the first clause.

15) **Choice B is correct.**
"Less" and "fewer" work as "many" and "much", where "fewer" is used for countable items while "less" is used for uncountable mass nouns.

Writing
Lesson 6

Parallel Structure

Goals

We will develop our grammatical fluency and gain meaningful understanding in grammar by learning to:

1) Differentiate between the three major types of parallel construction
2) Identify the possible errors that may arise in sentence construction as it relates to parallels
3) Understand idioms and their role in parallel construction
4) Resolve errors properly and logically

Contents

- Parallel Types: Comparatives, Lists and Structure
- Note on Parallel Construction
- Application Exercises
- Homework Exercises

Lesson 6
Parallel Structure

Parallel Types

There are three types of sentence structure where parallelism becomes an important consideration. They are:

I. Comparatives
II. Lists
III. Sentence Structure

I. Comparatives

In **comparatives**, always compare A to A, not A to B. Learn to recognize words used in comparatives such as "like", "than", "as", or "fewer" as they arise in sentences. Once you've identified the sentence as a comparison of things, identify those exact things being compared. For example:

> The **hallowed grounds of St. Regis** were much larger than the **value of the cemetery at the Episcopalian church**.

First, we note that the comparative words "larger than" is used here.

Second, what are the two things compared here? If we look closely, they are (1) the hallowed grounds of St. Regis versus (2) the value of the cemetery at the Episcopalian church. The error that we encounter here is an illogical comparison between the hallowed grounds and the value of another.

We can, however, compare the grounds of one to the grounds of another, or, the value of one thing to the value of another. A good correction would be:

> The **hallowed grounds of St. Regis** were much larger than ~~the **value of**~~ **the cemetery at the Episcopalian church**.

A common mistake with comparatives is the contrast of an object with the quality of another object.

For example, it may make sense to say that one song is better than another, or that the lyrics for one song are more moving than the lyrics of another, but it would make no sense to say that the lyrics of one song are better than an entirely different song. For example:

> The diets of scavenging animals like hyenas and wild dogs tends to be far more diverse than herd animals like gazelles and lions.

We should note what items are compared here: we are comparing the *diets* of scavenging animals to *herd animals* like gazelles and lions. We can compare two diets, or two animals, but not diets to animals.

A good correction would be:

> The diets of scavenging animals like hyenas and wild dogs tends to be far more diverse than **the diets of** herd animals like gazelles and lions.

Comparisons can be between two or more nouns, prepositional phrases, infinitives, or even clauses.

Comparative nouns	**The** orange **is as heavy as the** potato.
Comparative prepositional phrases	He would rather drive **to the park** than **to the fair**.
Comparative infinitives	There is much **to eat**, but not at all **to drink**.
Comparative clauses	**People have much more knowledge about eating correctly** than **they did in the 1800's**.

II. Lists

In **lists**, we want to be consistent with the type of words or phrases used. Lists can be prefaced with or without a colon. Identify the errors in the following examples:

> (i) The Constitutional laws are fairly clear for all citizens of the United States: freedom of speech, ownership of guns, and having a right to a trial by jury.
>
> (ii) The maudlin Marauder liked to maim, pillage and eating his raids.

In sentence (i) the list should be in the same form of regular nouns ("freedom", "ownership") and not a gerund ("having"). In sentence (ii) the list should continue with the infinitive phrases ("to maim", "to pillage") and not end with the gerund phrase ("eating"). The corrected versions should read:

> (i) The Constitutional laws are fairly clear for all citizens of the United States: freedom of speech, ownership of guns, and ~~having a~~ right to a trial by jury.
>
> (ii) The maudlin Marauder liked to maim, pillage and ~~eating~~ eat his raids.

To be clear, if a list starts with nouns, then it should end with nouns.

Likewise, if a list starts with phrases, then it should end with phrases. The root of parallelism is such that the forms of all things listed should be consistent with each other.

III. Sentence Structure

As it pertains to sentences containing two or more clauses, the **structural integrity** of the clauses should be kept consistent. For example:

> Public policy strongly dictates that <u>healthcare for all citizens be funded by tax dollars</u>.

It may not be clear at first, but the two clauses in the sentence above changes from an active voice to a passive voice construction. Remember, active voice dictates that the subject acts as the subject. Whereas in passive voice construction the object acts as the subject and vice versa. The relative clause “that healthcare... be funded by tax dollars” flips the role of subject/object nouns, creating a passive construction in the second clause.

Therefore, the corrected sentence should read:

> Public policy strongly dictates that ~~healthcare for all citizens be funded by tax dollars~~ **<u>tax dollars fund healthcare for all citizens</u>.**

Lastly, look for the component integrity of a sentence between clauses to compare its parallel structure. If the independent clause starts with, let’s say, a “*subject-verb-adverb-object*” structure, we should keep this structure intact in all subsequent clauses as well.

Note on Parallel Structure

Parallel structure in sentence composition concern both grammatical and stylistic elements. Sentences may be *grammatically* correct, but *illogical* or *awkward* in their construction.

Be careful when using correlative conjunctions such as "not only... but also", and "n/either...n/or", since these tend to house common errors between the comparatives.

For example:

> The Muay Thai fighters <u>not only</u> **look completely fresh** <u>but also</u> **they are quite healthy**.

Since the phrases "look completely fresh" is quite different from the clause "they are healthy" we need to correct the sentence by making it parallel. The correct version, using two phrases with the parallel construction "verb-adverb-adjective" should read:

> The Muay Thai fighters <u>not only</u> **look completely fresh** <u>but also</u> **~~they~~ are quite healthy**.

Idiomatic phrases also dictate parallel construction in a sentence. Syntax idioms are phrases with a strict way of constructing a relationship between ideas. Semantic idioms are phrases that convey a specific meaning. Changes in the very wording of these idioms can create errors in the sentence.

For example, the sentence "*He fell* ***~~down~~***" conveys a redundancy with the superfluous addition of the word "down", even though we talk this way in our everyday speech.

Some of the more common idioms that follow standard parallel construction in either syntax or semantics are as follows:

Syntax Idioms	Semantics Idioms
Prefer... to...	Agreed on ...
Not only ... but also ...	Complies with ...
Either ... or ...	Discriminate against ...
Neither ... nor ...	Composed of ...
Both ... and ...	Based on ...
Considered ~~by~~ ...	Raised by ...
	On the one/other hand ...

The best way to learn idiomatic phrases is to *read as much as possible*. Even if you are not an avid reader, we can always seek to increase our language fluency by noting various pairings of words as we come across them.

Lesson 6
Parallel Structure
Application Exercises

Time - 10 Minutes

Directions: For each sentence in this section, determine the parallel structure at issue. Underline the issue and correct *as necessary*. Good luck!

1) The Court Jester howled angrily out of the courtroom, even though the procession laughed with fright throughout the entire performance.

2) My mom prefers driving to taking the bus.

3) "Neither rain or the sky hailing will slow me down!" he declared.

4) In complete adulation, the trainers were applauded loudly by the members of the club and the audience in attendance also.

5) Your mistakes that you made as a student will haunt you when you are a professional too.

6) The corporate discount will allow hundreds of employees to sustain their standard of living, families, and happiness.

7) My fashion advisor agrees that my closet is filled with too much clothes, too much shoes, and too many of everything.

8) Watching videos are a thing of the past because they are old, inferior, and use tape.

9) The florist told me that these dandelions are as like bringing roses.

10) The criminal decided to shoplift the items at the supermarket rather than paying for them.

11) Sleeping well is not only a prerequisite for purposeful training, but truly yet one more determinant for a healthy lifestyle.

12) Jamie considered walking to the bus, rather than run to work.

13) At the end of the 1980's, the insouciant workers eventually had a choice between keeping their longtime jobs at the factory or to leave the job altogether.

Lesson 6
Parallel Structure
Homework Exercises

1) The students expected a video with answers about their major and gaining information about career prospects in their field.

   A) NO CHANGE
   B) as well as information
   C) and also being informed
   D) in addition, they expect to gain information

2) For most professionals, being free to manage themselves is more important than being well paid.

   A) NO CHANGE
   B) having freedom of management is more important than
   C) there is more importance in the freedom to manage themselves than
   D) freedom to manage themselves has more importance than

3) After teaching, patenting major inventions, and after he founded General Electric, Edison engaged in the "War of the Currents" with George Westinghouse.

   A) NO CHANGE
   B) founding
   C) he had founded
   D) having founded

4) Phone frequencies must be allocated so that one transmission will not interfere with another.

   A) NO CHANGE
   B) each transmission cannot interfere with another's
   C) transmitting them will not interfere with one another
   D) no transmission is interfered with by another

5) Wi-Fi signals are made by transforming data into electromagnetic waves and of transmitting those waves through space; after this those waves must be transformed back into data.

   A) NO CHANGE
   B) waves, transmitting the waves through space, and transforming them
   C) waves, of transmitting them through space, and then the translation of them
   D) waves, of the transmitting of those waves through space and of translating same

6) The focus on running for office on personality and likeability was less important than the gold standard in the 1896 presidential elections.

   A) on running for office on personality and likeability was less important than the gold standard
   B) on running on personality and likeability for office was less important than the gold standard
   C) on running for office on personality and likeability was less important than on the gold standard
   D) on the gold standard was more important than personality and likeability during

7) The psychologist states that most people want the same things: interesting work, respect, and to have them be loved for themselves alone.

   A) NO CHANGE
   B) to have interesting work, respect, and be loved for themselves alone
   C) to have interesting work, to be respected, and to be loved for themselves alone
   D) work that has interest, to have respect, and to be beloved for themselves alone

8) The amount of nuclear waste produced in the United States could be reduced by curbing energy usage, finding better storage, and developing new technology for reactors.

A) NO CHANGE
B) and if they develop new technology
C) and new technology being developed
D) and if there was new technology

9) In the early songs of the Beatles, the Blues-inspired melodies seem to be more of a product of rural southern America than an English industrial city.

A) NO CHANGE
B) a product from rural southern America than that of an English industrial city
C) produced in rural southern America than by an English industrial city
D) a product of rural southern America than of an English industrial city

10) Eating food that has a high concentration of fat causes essentially the same reaction in the stomach than if you eat too fast.

A) than if you eat
B) as if one eats
C) as eating
D) as it does when eating

11) Someone living in a technological, consumption-oriented culture probably taxes the environment at a rate many times that of a country such as Myanmar.

A) that of a country such as Myanmar
B) that of someone living in a country like Myanmar
C) the rate in a country such as Myanmar
D) someone from Myanmar, for instance

12) Unlike the hollow body of an acoustic guitar, which acts as a sound box to project sound, the electric guitar's solid-body is almost soundless without the aid of an amplification system.

A) the hollow body of an acoustic guitar, which acts
B) an acoustic guitar's hollow body, acting
C) an acoustic guitar, which has a hollow body that acts
D) an acoustic guitar and its hollow body, acting

13) Homing pigeons can navigate over long distances, employing their sense of smell to ascertain their initial location and using the position of the Sun determining the direction in which they must fly.

A) using the position of the Sun determining
B) using the position of the Sun and determining
C) using the position of the Sun to determine
D) use the position of the Sun to determine

14) In many parts of the world where grasses cover vast expanses of land, periodic, controlled burning is practiced to keep woody brush from gaining a foothold and it stimulates continuing grass growth.

A) gaining a foothold and it stimulates
B) gaining a foothold and stimulating
C) to gaining a foothold and it stimulates
D) gaining a foothold and to stimulate

15) His love of politics led him to volunteer in local campaigns and a job in a government office in the state capital.

A) and a job in a government office
B) and take a job in a government office
C) and taking job in a government office
D) and taking a government job

Lesson 6
Parallel Structure
Answer Key

Homework Exercises

1) B
2) A
3) B
4) A
5) B
6) D
7) C
8) A
9) D
10) C
11) B
12) A
13) C
14) D
15) B

Application Exercises

1) **...howled <u>angrily</u> out of the courtroom, even though the procession laughed <u>frightfully</u>...**

Remember that adjectives must be parallel in the sentence. In this instance, the jester "angrily" storming out of the room must be parallel to the procession "frightfully" laughing at the jester.

2) **Correctly Written**

The idiom "Prefer...to..." is used correctly with perfect parallel here.

3) **... rain nor <u>hail</u>...**

In idiomatic structures with "neither...nor..." the nouns within must be parallel. In this case, "rain" and "hail" are the nouns that the speaker declares to be her deterrents, not "sky hailing".

4) **... and the audience in <u>attendance</u>.**

The use of "also" is redundant here since we already know that both the members and the audience were in adulation.

5) **...as a student ... as a professional too**

This sentence puts into place the idiomatic parallel structure of **as...as...** Also, the "too" at the end of the sentence is retained here (unlike in question #4's "also") because the intent of the author is that the mistake will haunt the person as a student AND as a professional.

6) **Correctly Written**

All looks good on this parallel front.

7) **...too <u>many</u> shoes, too <u>many</u> clothes, and too <u>much everything</u>...**

Remember "many" is used for countable things, while "much" is used to uncountable things. **Shoes** and **clothes** are countable, whereas **everything** is not.

8) **... because <u>videos</u> are old, inferior, and <u>taped</u>.**

Proper pronouns usage here requires use of the noun "video" since the referent is "watching videos"; furthermore, the video must parallel "old" and "inferior". The word "taped" accomplishes this.

9) **... that <u>bringing</u> these dandelions are <u>like bringing</u> roses ...**

"Bringing" dandelions and "bringing" roses is compared here. Remember to use "like" when you compare items or things, and use "as" when you attempt to convey the idea that the two things being compared are identical in character.

10) **...decided <u>to shoplift</u> the items at the supermarket rather than <u>pay</u>...**

The infinitive "to shoplift" is compared to "to pay"; the corrected sentence reflects this (the "to" is implied in "pay"). Also, **rather than** is used to compare actions, whereas **instead of** is used to compare items.

11) **... not only "a prerequisite"...but also "a determinant"...**

"Not only... but also..." is an idiomatic structure that requires parallel structure.

12) **... considered walking...running...**

The parallel must exist between the two gerunds 'walking" and "running" in this sentence.

13) **... between "keeping" ... and "leaving"...**

Many idiomatic expressions have an inherent parallel structure. "Between...and..." is one such example.

Homework Exercises

1. **Choice B is correct**.
   This is a case of parallel structure. Students are expecting "answers" (a noun) and should get a second noun as well. Choice B accomplishes this while using "as well as" to complete the comparison.
2. **Choice A is correct.**
   Consider what is compared to "being well paid." We are comparing two gerunds, so the comparison is fine. Choice B compares two gerunds but is also less of a direct comparison than being vs. being.
3. **Choice B is correct.**
   This is a parallel list, so we should keep the gerund spree going with teaching, patenting, and *founding*.
4. **Choice A is correct.**
   It is fine to compare "one transmission" with "another," since the transmission is implied. Choice C may be tempting because it ends by mentioning a transmission, but here we compare the verb "transmitting" with transmissions, which is incorrect.
5. **Choice B is correct.**
   We want another list of parallel items, which means they should all be of the same type. Since "transforming" is a gerund not part of the answer choice, we should align our list to be gerunds. The other choices may contain gerunds, but the odd prepositions make the list inconsistent.
6. **Choice D is correct.**
   In the other options, the comparison between the focus on the gold standard and "personality and likeability" is muddled by "running" and other ideas.
7. **Choice C is correct.**
   In this example of parallelism gone wrong, we need something in triplicate. Choice A gives us two nouns and ends in an infinitive. Choice B breaks the pattern of infinitives with the noun "respect." Choice D has a noun and two infinitives. Only Choice C gives us three infinitives.
8. **Choice A is correct.**
   Our list of triplicate gerunds will work here!
9. **Choice D is correct.**
   What are we comparing? We can use the preposition *of* to guide us. The "product" portion is implied and does not need repeated. We have the product of a rural southern American city and the product of an English industrial city. In Choice A, we are comparing a product and a city. In Choice B, notice the change in "a product from rural southern America" that changes the parallel structure. Choice C gives us the awkward structure "more of produced".
10. **Choice C is correct.**
    This is a parallel construction that happens when English demands certain idiomatic pairings (as ... as, not only ... but also, etc.). The "same" should be paired with "as," and the comparison should be between "eating" and "eating"
11. **Choice B is correct.**
    We are comparing the rates, so the rate of someone living in a technological culture should be compared to the rate of someone living in a country. Choice B accomplishes this nicely. Choice C appears to be the rate of the whole country, so it's incorrect.
12. **Choice A is correct.**
    We are comparing bodies and bodies correctly here.
13. **Choice C is correct.**
    Notice that we have several parallel structures here. First, "employing" is parallel with "using," and then "to ascertain" is parallel with "to determine." Each of the other choices fails to meet one of the parallel pieces.

14. **Choice D is correct.**
    The "gaining" must work with "from," and the "stimulates" must be parallel with it in the infinitive form.

15. **Choice B is correct.**
    Since we already have the infinitive "to volunteer," our next portion of the list should be parallel with that. The "to" is implied between "volunteer" and "take," giving us a proper parallel construction.

PITTSBURGH
PREP

Mathematics Lesson 1

Arithmetic 1

Goals

We will develop our mathematical fluency and gain meaningful understanding by learning to:

1) Recognize absolute value as a distance from zero
2) Memorize and apply exponential and radical relationships
3) Understand all component factors in exponential functions and variants including linear growth
4) Apply basic statistical analysis from given data using the concepts of mean, median, and mode
5) Meaningfully apply these concepts to solve problems based on words, data, charts, and formulas
6) Measure personal weaknesses and rectify any errors from problem sets

Contents

- Absolute Value
  - Definition
  - Application
- Exponents
  - Rules
  - Application
- Radicals
  - Applications
  - Factoring
  - Prime Factorization
  - Rationalization
- Exponential Functions
  - Calculating Interest
- Statistics
  - Mean, Median, Mode

Lesson 1
Arithmetic 1

Absolute Value

Think of absolute value as the distance from the number to zero on the number line. They are always symbolized by two bars surrounding a number:

$$|9| \text{ is } +9$$

$$|-9| \text{ is also } +9$$

Another way of thinking about absolute values is to draw a number line:

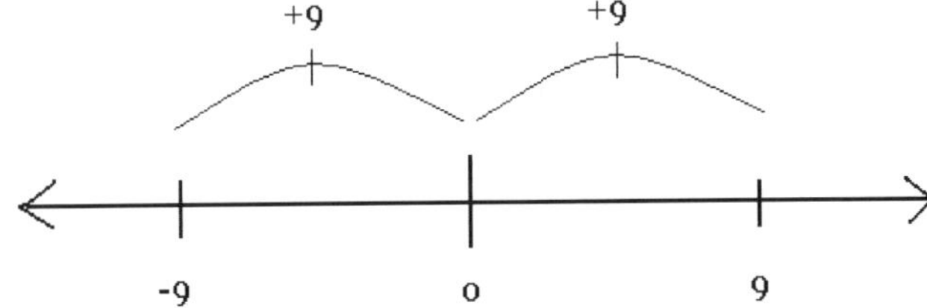

The distance between –9 and 0 on the left side of the number line is the same absolute distance between 9 and 0 on the right side of the number line. Therefore, if $|x|=9$, we know that $x = 9$ or $x = -9$.

If the absolute value is a full expression, like $|2x + 5| = 8$, then we know that $2x + 5$ is 8 units away from 0 on the number line; we can now solve $2x + 5 = 8$ and $2x + 5 = -8$ to find $x = \frac{3}{2}$ and $x = -\frac{13}{2}$.

Finally, all absolute values are positive, except for one integer: the absolute value of 0 ($|0| = 0$), which is neither positive nor negative.

Remember, the lowest value of an absolute value is 0, since an absolute value cannot be negative.

Exponents

An exponent is defined as a power taken to a base. Given 3^2, the exponential value of 2 here tells us to multiply the base 3 twice. So, $3^2 = (3)(3) = 9$.

Exponent

$$3^2 = \underbrace{3 \times 3}_{\text{2 threes}} = 9$$

Base

In the same vain, $3^3 = (3)(3)(3) = 27$. And $3^4 = (3)(3)(3)(3) = 81$. (We could do this all day.)

eg 1. If $2x^3+6 = -10$, what is x?

We solve this equation by subtracting six from both sides of the equation to give us $2x^3 = -16$. Then, divide both sides by 2 to obtain $x^3 = -8$. Since we know that $(-2)(-2)(-2) = -8$, the value of x must be x. Note the following:

- A negative base to an *even* exponent always yields positive results. For example, $(-3)^2 = 9$.
- A negative base to an *odd* exponent will always yield a negative result. For example, $(-3)^3 = -27$.

Furthermore, memorize and understand the following exponential rules:

Rule	Example
$\boldsymbol{x^1 = x}$	$4^1 = 4$
$\boldsymbol{x^0 = 1}$	$8^0 = 1$
$\boldsymbol{(x^a)(x^b) = x^{a+b}}$	$(3^2)(3^3) = 3^{2+3} = 3^5$
$\boldsymbol{\frac{x^a}{x^b} = x^{a-b}}$	$\frac{3^5}{3^2} = 3^{5-2} = 3^3$
$\boldsymbol{(x^a)^b = x^{ab}}$	$(2^3)^2 = 2^{(3)(2)} = 2^6$
$\boldsymbol{x^{-a} = \frac{1}{x^a}}$	$3^{-2} = \frac{1}{3^2}$
$\boldsymbol{x^{\frac{a}{b}} = \sqrt[b]{x^a}}$	$3^{\frac{2}{3}} = \sqrt[3]{3^2}$

The challenge here is twofold: We must first understand the rules, then learn to apply them effectively. Take a look at the following example:

eg 2. If $(9^x)(3^x) = 27$, what does x equal?

Note that all three terms share a base of 3. This allows us to convert every term into a base of 3 so that we can apply the exponential rules. Here are the steps to solve the example problem:

$(9^x)(3^x) = 27$	**Given problem**
$(3^{2x})(3^x) = 27$	Convert $9^x = 3^{2x}$
$(3^{2x})(3^x) = 3^3$	Convert $27 = 3^3$
$(3^{2x+x}) = 3^3$	Combine the left side of our equation
$3x = 3$	Drop the bases, and set exponential values equal to each other
$x = 1$	Divide both sides by 3 to obtain x

Radicals

A radical or a root can be understood as the opposite or inverse of an exponent. Note that all radicals can be defined as follows:

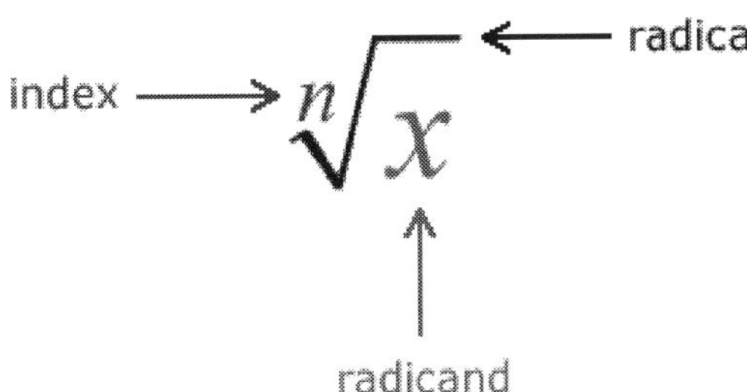

A radical expression above is asking for what value when multiplied by itself n number of times, will obtain the quantity of x. For example:

$\sqrt[3]{8}$	This is expressed as "Cubed root of 8"
$\sqrt[3]{(2)(2)(2)}$	Substitute 8 = (2)(2)(2)
2	Since the base 2 multiplied by itself 3 times gives us the value of 8

Furthermore, we also can express all radicals into exponential equivalents as follows:

$$\sqrt[n]{x} = x^{\frac{1}{n}}$$

All radicals with the same index can be multiplied together as follows:

$$\sqrt[3]{x}\sqrt[3]{y} = \sqrt[3]{xy}$$

Let's try an example problem together:

eg 3. What is $\sqrt[3]{81x^6}$?

A) $27x^2$
B) $27x^3$
C) $3\sqrt[3]{3x^6}$
D) $3x^2\sqrt[3]{3}$

This problem asks for a cubed root. Options A and B incorrectly divide 81 by 3. While 81 is a perfect square and is divisible by three, that doesn't make it a perfect cube. We can use its factors, though, to find a perfect cube. A factor tree, like shown, is a good tool to use, and shows us that $81 = 3^4$, or $3^3 \times 3$. We can substitute that for 81 in the original expression to get $\sqrt[3]{3^3 3x^6}$. The cube root of 3^3 is 3, so we will move that 3 outside of our radical to get $3\sqrt[3]{3x^6}$ (three times the cube root of $3x^6$).

81
9 9
3 3 3 3

To simplify the variable x, we can use our exponent rules to convert x^6 to x^3x^3, giving us two cubed roots, and an expression of $(3)(x)(x)\sqrt[3]{3}$, or choice D.

Exponential Functions

What are the differences between linear and exponential growth?

- *Linear growth: a constant rate or slope*
- *Exponential growth: a rate or slope that increases or decreases*

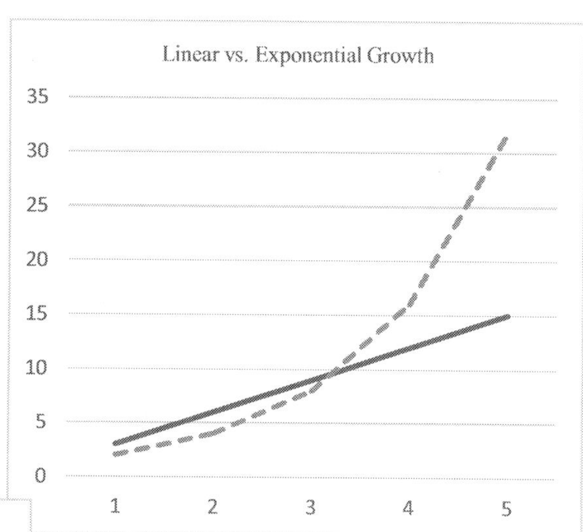

In the graph on the right, for instance, linear growth is represented as a straight line while exponential growth is represented as the dotted line that increases in slope.

Since problems will ask you to interpret exponential functions graphically, note the general trend of the lines.

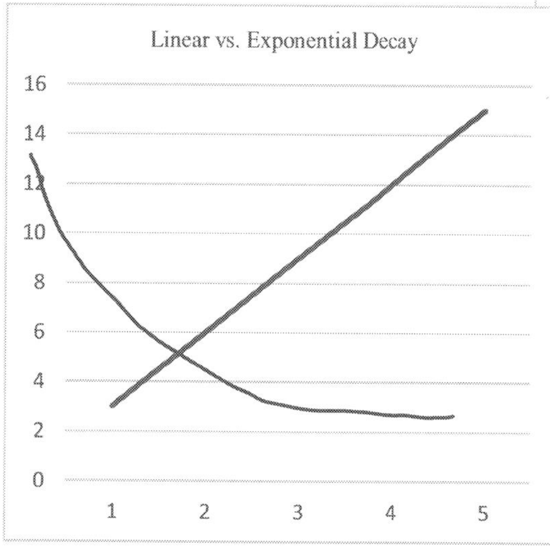

Exponential decay, on the other hand, is denoted by the graph on the left. Note that as an item or material decays, it will never quite go to zero by touching the x-axis.

Let's try a typical problem involving linear growth models on the next page:

eg 4. The table below shows the number of text messages, t, received by Ana over w weeks. What relationship exists between $t(w)$ and w?.

w	1	2	4	8	16
$t(w)$	5	10	20	40	80

A) Ana's text messages grew linearly by a rate of 5 texts per week.
B) Ana's text messages grew linearly by a rate of 100% per week.
C) Ana's text messages grew exponentially by a rate of 5 texts per week.
D) Ana's text messages grew exponentially by a rate of 100% per week.

The increase in calls seems to be an additional 5 calls per week ($\frac{5}{1} = 5, \frac{10}{2} = 5, \frac{20}{4} = 5$, etc.), which also fits the linear function $t(w) = 5w$. Notice that there is NOT an even progression of weeks: we increase by one week, then two, then four, then eight. Because the rate of increase never changes, we have linear growth: that means that choices C and D should be eliminated. Choice B may look correct, but it is flawed: only the first week increases by 100%. By week 3, where can determine a corresponding 15 texts, is only 50% larger than week 2. Each subsequent week will increase in smaller percentages. The correct answer choice is, therefore, A.

We also need to know how to work with exponential growth algebraically. Exponential growth or decay is based on a general simple interest formula:

<u>Simple Interest Formula</u>

$$Principal\ (1 + interest\ rate)^{time\ in\ years}$$

For example, let's say that a herd of deer starts with a size of 100 and grows by 30% each year. While the first yearly increase is easy to predict (30), the second year's growth is based on the new size (130). The formula to use here would look like: $100(1 + 0.3)^y$. The rate of change is given as 1.3 (or 130%) because we are dealing with growth; if we only used $.3$ (or 30%), we would multiply our population by 30% and our value would be decreasing, not increasing.

Since things like deer and money can compound more than once per year, we have a corresponding compound interest formula:

<u>Compound Interest Formula</u>

$$Principal\left(1 + \frac{interest\ rate}{\#\ of\ times\ interest\ compounds\ per\ year}\right)^{(number\ of\ compound)(time\ in\ years)}$$

eg 5. A savings account grows 8% annually with interest compounded monthly. Which of the following formulas will correctly calculate the size of an initial investment of n dollars after y years?

A) $n(.08)^y$
B) $n(1.08)^y$
C) $n(1.08)^{12y}$
D) $n(1 + \frac{.08}{12})^{12y}$

Since it's an annual interest problem with a monthly compound, this means that for the 12 months in the year, one-twelfth of the yearly interest is applied to the principal. Therefore, we use $\frac{.08}{12}$ as the corresponding interest rate. And since y is the total number of years, but interest is compounded monthly, we multiply the number of years with the months to obtain $12y$. Choice D is the correct answer.

Statistics

Basic statistics entails an understanding of the concepts of mean, median and mode. They are defined as follows:

- **Mean**: Average number
- **Median**: The "middle" number
- **Mode**: The most frequent number

Hint: *the median is the average of two middle terms in a set containing an even number of terms. Further, there may be two or more modes, so long as the term occurs more frequently than another.*

Try the following example problems:

eg 6. Given an odd number of terms in the following set, determine the mean, median and mode:

$$\{2, 4, 6, 7, 9, 9, 11\}$$

Mean:
Median:
Mode:

eg 7. Given an even number of terms in the following set, determine the mean, median and mode:

$$\{2, 2, 6, 7, 9, 9\}$$

Mean:
Median:
Mode:

Another somewhat commonly (perhaps uncommonly?) tested concept in statistics is based on the graphical representation of a statistical distribution, otherwise known as the bell curve. In stats, the standard deviation represents a measure of variation or dispersion of a set of data values. A normal distribution would look like the figure on the right.

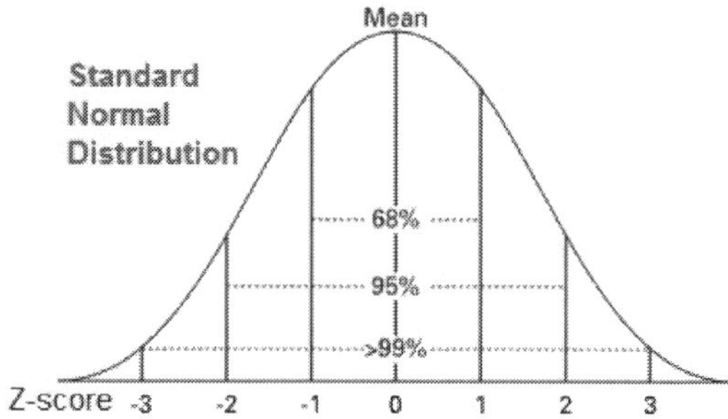

A way to interpret the bell curve is to understand that 68% of all data will fit within one standard deviation. 95% of all data will fit within 2 standard deviations, and 99% of all data will fit within three standard deviations.

PITTSBURGH PREP

Lesson 1
Arithmetic 1
Application Exercises

NO CALCULATOR SECTION
Questions 1-5

Time - 20 Minutes

1) Which of the following functions has a real value of $f(n) = 0$, where n is an integer?

A) $f(n) = 2|n + 2| + 2$
B) $f(n) = 2|n - 2| - 2$
C) $f(n) = 2|n - 2| + 2$
D) $f(n) = 2|2 - n| + 2$

2) Which of the following values is equivalent to $n^{\frac{1}{2}}n^{\frac{2}{3}}$ for all values of n?

A) n
B) $\sqrt[3]{n}$
C) $2n^{\frac{7}{6}}$
D) $\sqrt[6]{n^7}$

3) Which of the following descriptions would be considered exponential growth?

A) Carlos deposits twenty dollars into a savings account each month.
B) An overdue book fine at a library is one dollar for each day the book is overdue.
C) The sales chart for a company has a best-fit line of $y = \frac{2}{3}x - 5$
D) A bacteria population doubles every ten days

4) Alex observes that a colony of mold grows 20% each week. Which function below best models the growth of the colony?

A) B)
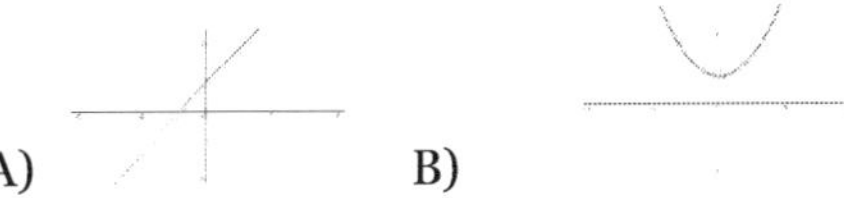

C) D)
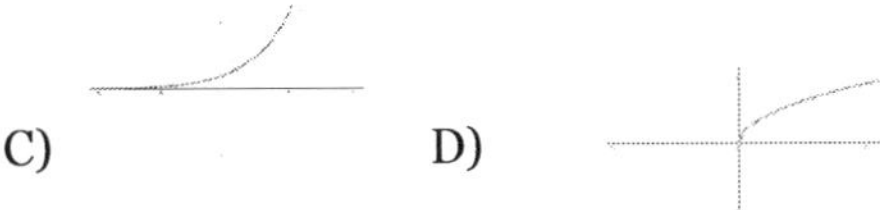

5) The area and circumference of a circle are found with $A = \pi r^2$ and $C = 2\pi r$, respectively. If r is quadrupled, the area of the new circle grows by what percent of the old circle?

A) 25%
B) 400%
C) 800%
D) 1600%

PITTSBURGH PREP

CALCULATOR SECTION
Questions 6-10

6) $x^{\frac{1}{3}}y^{\frac{2}{3}}z^{-3}$

A) $\frac{\sqrt[2]{xy^2}}{z^3}$

B) $\frac{\sqrt[3]{xy^2}}{z^3}$

C) $\frac{\sqrt[2]{x^2y^2}}{z^3}$

D) $\frac{\sqrt[3]{x^2y^2}}{z^3}$

7) If $4x = 8 + 6y$, what is the value of $\frac{3^{2x}}{27^y}$?

A) 81

B) 3

C) $\frac{1}{9}$

D) The answer cannot be determined

8) Which of the following expressions has the largest value?

A) $\sqrt{49}$

B) $\sqrt[3]{64}$

C) $\sqrt[4]{256}$

D) $\sqrt[3]{128}$

9) A population of 7,000 timber wolves in a wildlife preserve is theorized to decrease by 15% every twelve years. Assuming no change in the pattern, which of the following equations best models the population of the wolves in t years?

A) $7{,}000(.15)^{\frac{t}{12}}$

B) $7{,}000(.85)^{\frac{12}{t}}$

C) $7{,}000(.85)^{12t}$

D) $7{,}000(.85)^{\frac{t}{12}}$

10) Ayaan and Charles find accounts with 3% annual interest. Ayaan's account compounds annually, but Charles's account compounds monthly. They both invest \$1,000 for ten years. Who will have a larger balance by the end of the ten years, and by how much?

A) Ayaan, by \$5.43
B) Charles, by \$5.43
C) Charles, by \$6.16
D) Ayaan, by \$6.16

GRID-IN SECTION
Questions 11-14

11) If $x = 3$, what is the value of $(\frac{x^{-3}x^2}{x^2})^{-\frac{2}{3}}$?

12) If $\frac{(n^a)^4}{(n^a)^5} = n^{12}$, where $n > 1$, what is the value of $-2a$?

13) The average mass of 4 mineral samples from a mining site is 7.6 grams. How large would a 5th sample need to be to raise the average sample size to 9 grams?

14) An economist pours samples of a cereal to measure the number of berries in each bowl, with the results shown below. What is the average number of berries in each bowl, rounded to the nearest tenth?

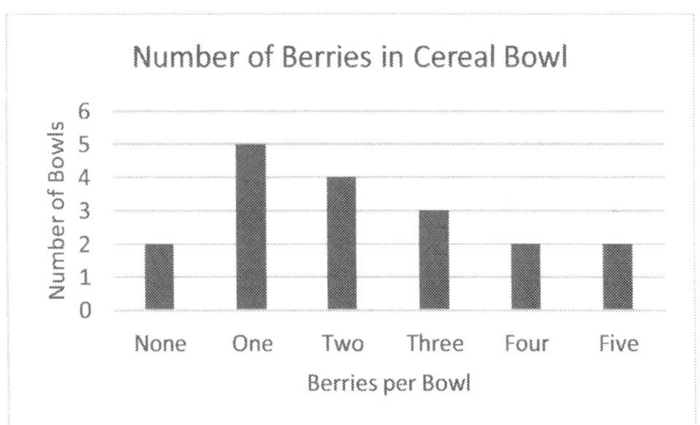

PITTSBURGH PREP

Lesson 1
Arithmetic 1
Homework Exercises

NO CALCULATOR SECTION
Questions 1-8

Time - 25 Minutes

1) Simplify $(\sqrt[4]{x^5})(\sqrt[3]{x^2})$

A) $(x)\sqrt[12]{x^{11}}$

B) $(x)\sqrt[12]{x^7}$

C) $\sqrt[12]{x^{10}}$

D) $\sqrt[4]{x^3}$

2) Simplify $\sqrt[3]{2160}$

A) $(6)\sqrt[3]{10}$

B) $(6)\sqrt[3]{20}$

C) $(36)\sqrt[3]{10}$

D) $(6)\sqrt[2]{10}$

3) If $n = x^{4n}$, which of the following is equivalent to n^2?

A) x^{4n+2}

B) x^{8n}

C) x^{16n}

D) x^{16n^2}

4) Karrin invests $8,000 with a company that promises a 6% annual return, and pays dividends every six months. Which of the expressions below best models Karrin's return after t years?

A) $8000(1.06)^{2t}$

B) $8000(1.06)^{\frac{t}{2}}$

C) $8000\left(1+\frac{.06}{2}\right)^{\frac{t}{2}}$

D) $8000(1+\frac{.06}{2})^{2t}$

5) What is the minimum value of the expression $|x^2 - 3| + 4$?

A) 0
B) $\sqrt{3}$
C) 4
D) $\sqrt{25}$

6) If the function $h(x) = \sqrt{x^3}$, which of the following values of x will not provide a real solution?

A) -5
B) 0
C) 3
D) 8.2

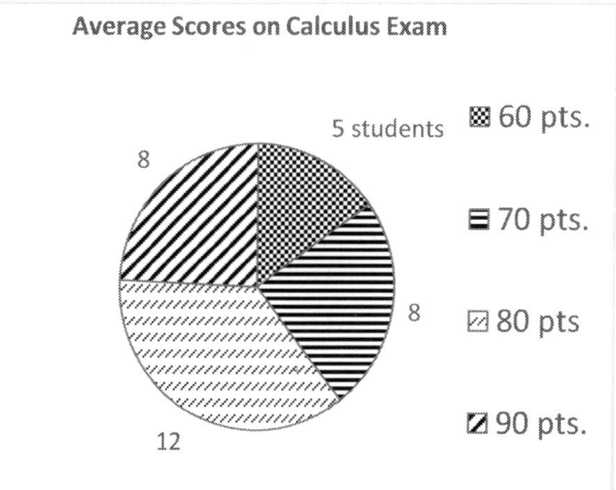

7) The figure above shows the number of students achieving particular scores on a calculus exam. What is the minimum number of additional students that would need to be polled to create a mode of a score of 60?

A) 3
B) 4
C) 7
D) 8

8) An astronomer detects a spherical planetoid that he believes has a diameter of 750 miles. A second astronomer corrects his work and believes that the planetoid has twice the initially predicted diameter. If the volume of a sphere can be found with the formula $V = \frac{4}{3}\pi r^3$, what is the ratio of the planet's newly predicted volume to the previously predicted volume?

A) $2:1$
B) $3:2$
C) $4:1$
D) $8:1$

CALCULATOR SECTION
Questions 9-16

9) Scientists are trying to model the population of 250 Asian Carp, an invasive species in Lake Erie. Scientist A claims the fish is on track to increase 10% each year, whereas Scientist B claims the fish will add 50 carp each year. After six years, what will be the approximate difference in their predictions?

A) Scientist A predicts 107 more carp
B) Scientist A predicts 88 more carp
C) Scientist B predicts 107 more carp
D) Scientist B predicts 88 more carp

10) The pay for the nine employees of a small business is shown in thousands of dollars in the table below. Assuming no pay raises occur this year, what is the minimum number of employees that could be hired to change the median employee income to $60,000?

Employee	A	B	C	D	E	F	G	H	I
Income	100	80	75	70	50	45	45	40	30

A) 1
B) 2
C) 3
D) The answer cannot be determined

11) Simplify $\sqrt[3]{0.000125}$

A) 5
B) 0.5
C) 0.05
D) 0.005

12) The expression $\sqrt{72x^3}$ can be factored to $n\sqrt{2x}$. If x is a positive integer, what is the value of n?

A) $6x^2$
B) $6x$
C) $3x^2$
D) 6

13) Traditional GPA is calculated with the following scale:

A	B	C	D
4.0	3.0	2.0	1.0

Ryan took 5 classes, and earned three As and one B. If Ryan is required to maintain a 3.3 GPA, what is the minimum grade he can get in his last class and maintain a 3.3 GPA?

A) A
B) B
C) C
D) D

14) Which of the following situations demonstrates exponential decay?

A) A stock drops by $5 each day
B) A movie doubles its income for six weeks
C) A game loses 10% of its subscribers every year
D) The weight that Ryu can lift increases by seven pounds every week

15) A certain value r is squared as part of an engineering formula $F = 3m + r^2$. If m is a constant, the value of r is the only value in the formula that changes, and it increases by five, what will the value of the formula increase by?

A) 25
B) $10r + 25$
C) $r^2 + 5$
D) $5r + 12.5$

16) Which of the following simplifies the expression $\sqrt{9x^8}$?

A) $9x^4$
B) $9x^6$
C) $3x^4$
D) $3x^6$

PITTSBURGH PREP

GRID-IN SECTION
Questions 17-20

17) A solution is known to evaporate at a rate of 10% each hour. After how many hours will the solution have less than half of its original volume?

18) In the function $f(x) = -4|-x + 5| + 3$, what value of x will yield the greatest value of $f(x)$?

19) In the function $f(x) = 2^{\frac{3x}{2}}$, $x < 8$ and x is a positive integer. If $f(x)$ is a positive integer, what is a possible value of x?

20) In a survey, six participants rated a product from $1 - 10$ as shown below. If a 7th rating is added to the data, the new mean rating will be equal to the new median. What is a possible integer value for the new rating?

A	B	C	D	E	F	G
6	9	5	9	9	4	

Lesson 1
Arithmetic 1
Answer Key

Example Exercises

1) −2
2) 1
3) D
4) A
5) D
6) Mean: 6.86
   Median: 7
   Mode: 9
7) Mean: 5.83
   Median: 6.5
   Mode: 2 and 9

Application Exercises

1) B
2) D
3) D
4) C
5) D
6) B
7) A
8) A
9) D
10) B
11) 9
12) 24
13) 14.6
14) 2.2

Homework Exercises

1) A
2) A
3) B
4) D
5) C
6) A
7) C
8) D
9) C
10) A
11) C
12) B
13) C
14) C
15) B
16) C
17) 7
18) 5
19) 2,4,6
20) 7

Application Exercises

1) **Choice B is correct.**
The smallest value an absolute value can be is 0. No positive value can be added to an absolute value and get $f(n)$to equal 0. In this problem, the lowest value that $2|2-n|$ can equal is 0. Therefore, anything added to it must be positive. This leaves Choice B as the only feasible answer. (Note that the lowest value that Choice B can be is -2.)

2) **Choice D is correct.**
First, reexpress the exponents with a lowest common denominator:

$$n^{\frac{1}{2}}n^{\frac{2}{3}} = n^{\frac{1}{2}(\frac{3}{3})}n^{\frac{2}{3}(\frac{2}{2})} = n^{\frac{3}{6}}n^{\frac{4}{6}}$$

Next, add the exponents together:

$$n^{\frac{3}{6}}n^{\frac{4}{6}} = n^{\frac{3}{6}+\frac{4}{6}} = n^{\frac{7}{6}}$$

Finally, move the denominator of the exponent to form a root:

$$\sqrt[6]{n^7}$$

3) **Choice D is correct.**
Exponential growth occurs when an amount that changes is not a constant rate of change. Choices A, B, and C demonstrate linear growth whereas choice D describes exponential growth.

4) **Choice C is correct.**
If Alex observes a pattern of growth based on a weekly percentage increase, he is observing an exponential pattern. Choice C depicts this graphically. Choice A shows a linear graph, Choice B depicts a quadratic, and Choice D show the inverse of an exponential graph.

5) **Choice D is correct.**
Start with the initial area formula:

$$A_1 = \pi r^2$$

Then quadruple the radius of the circle:

$$A_2 = \pi(4r)^2$$

In this case, when the radius quadruples, the area increases 16x.

$$\frac{16\pi r^2}{\pi r^2} = \frac{16}{1}$$

$$16 \times 100\% = 1600\%$$

6) **Choice B is correct.**

$$x^{\frac{1}{3}}y^{\frac{2}{3}}z^{-3} = \frac{x^{\frac{1}{3}}y^{\frac{2}{3}}}{z^3}$$

$x^{\frac{1}{3}} = \sqrt[3]{x}$ and $y^{\frac{2}{3}} = \sqrt[3]{y^2}$ so...

$$\frac{x^{\frac{1}{3}}y^{\frac{2}{3}}}{z^3} = \frac{\sqrt[3]{xy^2}}{z^3}$$

7) **Choice A is correct.**
Divide $4x = 8 + 6y$ by 2 to get $2x = 4 + 3y$, then substitute $4 + 3y$ for $2x$.

$$\frac{3^{4+3y}}{27^y}$$

From here, use exponent rules to simplify:

$$\frac{3^{4+3y}}{27^y} = \frac{3^4(3^{3y})}{3^{3y}} = 3^4 = 81$$

8) **Choice A is correct.**
Factor the given values or use a calculator if necessary:

$$\sqrt{49} = 7$$
$$\sqrt[3]{64} = 4$$
$$\sqrt[4]{256} = 4$$
$$\sqrt[3]{128} = 4\sqrt{2} \text{ or } 5.04$$

9) **Choice D is correct.**
Start with the formula to find a value with exponential growth:

$$Original \times (Rate)^{Period\ of\ Time}$$

With a given population decrease of 15% every 12 years, find the population remaining by subtracting 15% from 100%:

$$100\% - 15\% = 85\% = .85$$

Now, model the population change on a year-to-year basis. Given change that occurs every 12 years, set the period as $\frac{t}{12}$ to calculate the change in a single year. This leaves a formula of:

$$7{,}000(.85)^{\frac{t}{12}}$$

10) **Choice B is correct.**
Ayaan's account requires simple interest and Charles's account requires compound:

Ayaan: $1{,}000(1.03)^{10} = 1{,}343.92$

Charles: $1{,}000(1 + \frac{.03}{12})^{120} = 1{,}349.35$

$$1{,}349.35 - 1{,}343.92 = 5.43$$

Charles has a higher balance by $5.43.

11) **The correct answer is 9**
Use exponential rules to simplify:

$$= \left(\frac{x^{-3}x^2}{x^2}\right)^{-\frac{2}{3}}$$
$$= (x^{-3})^{-\frac{2}{3}}$$
$$= x^{\frac{-6}{-3}}$$
$$= x^2$$
$$= 3^2$$
$$= 9$$

12) **The correct answer is 24**
Use exponential rules to simplify:

$$n^{12} = \frac{(n^a)^4}{(n^a)^5}$$
$$n^{12} = \frac{n^{4a}}{n^{5a}}$$
$$n^{12} = n^{4a-5a}$$

Therefore,

$$12 = 4a - 5a$$
$$12 = -a$$
$$24 = -2a$$

13) **The correct answer is 14.6**
Since 4 mineral samples average to 7.6 grams, set up an equation:

$$\frac{Sum}{Amount} = Average$$
$$\frac{x}{4} = 7.6$$
$$x = 30.4$$

Use the same formula to determine the 5th mineral sample's weight:

$$\frac{30.4 + y}{5} = 9$$
$$30.4 + y = 45$$
$$y = 14.6$$

14) **The correct answer is 2.2**
Pay attention to what each axis of the chart represents! Note that there are 18 total bowls, which requires dividing the final tally of berries by 18. The setup should look like:

$$\frac{Total\ \#\ of\ berries}{Total\ \#\ of\ bowls}$$

Since total # of berries can be found by:

$$Total\ berries = (\#\ of\ bowls)(berries\ per\ bowl)$$

The final setup should look like:

$$= \frac{2(0)+5(1)+4(2)+3(3)+2(4)+2(5)}{18}$$
$$2.2 = \frac{40}{18}$$

Homework Exercises

1) **Choice A is correct.**

$$\left(\sqrt[4]{x^5}\right)\left(\sqrt[3]{x^2}\right) = x^{\frac{5}{4}}(x^{\frac{2}{3}})$$
$$x^{\frac{5}{4}} \times x^{\frac{2}{3}} = x^{\frac{15}{12}} \times x^{\frac{8}{12}}$$
$$x^{\frac{15}{12}} \times x^{\frac{8}{12}} = x^{\frac{23}{12}}$$
$$x^{\frac{23}{12}} = x(x^{\frac{11}{12}})$$
$$x\left(x^{\frac{11}{12}}\right) = (x)\sqrt[12]{x^{11}}$$

2) **Choice A is correct.**
Factor 2160, looking for a perfect cube:

$$\sqrt[3]{2160} = \sqrt[3]{216}\sqrt[3]{10}$$

Since,

$$\sqrt[3]{216} = 6$$

We get:

$$(6)\sqrt[3]{10}$$

3) **Choice B is correct.**

$$n^2 = (x^{4n})^2$$
$$(x^{4n})^2 = x^{8n}$$

4) **Choice D is correct.**
Since the annual return is 6% and a payment is made twice per year, divide 6% by two in the formula and multiply the rate of change by 2 (since there will be twice as many payments as years):

$$8000(1+\frac{.06}{2})^{2t}$$

5) **Choice C is correct.**
To find the minimum value, the absolute value must be 0. This occurs when x = $\sqrt{3}$.

$$\left|\sqrt{3}^2 - 3\right| + 4 = 4$$

6) **Choice A is correct.**
Understand that x^3 should yield a negative value since the square root of a negative is imaginary.

$$\sqrt{-5^3} = \sqrt{-125}$$

7) **Choice C is correct.**
Adding 3 more students to the 5 students who scored a 60 would yield 8 students, but not enough students to meet or exceed the 12 students with scores of 80. To do this, we would need to add 7 students. Adding 8 students is unnecessary, since data can be bimodal.

8) **Choice D is correct.**

$$r\ of\ P_1 = 375$$
$$r\ of\ P_2 = 750$$

$$\frac{750}{375} = \frac{2}{1}$$

Therefore,

$$= \frac{Volume\ P_2}{Volume\ P_1}$$
$$= \frac{\frac{4}{3}\pi(2r)^3}{\frac{4}{3}\pi r^3}$$

$$= \frac{8}{1}$$

9) **Choice C is correct.**
Scientist A:
$$250(1.10)^6 = 442.89$$
Scientist B:
$$250 + 50(6) = 550$$
$$550 - 442.89 = 107.11$$

Scientist B predicts about 107 carp more than scientist A.

10) **Choice A is correct.**
Adding just one more employee starting from \$70,000 to any other higher amount will yield a median income of \$60,000.

11) **Choice C is correct.**
The takeaway from this problem is that a number with 2 decimal places will yield 6 decimal places when raised by a power of 3.

$$(.0x)(.0x)(.0x) = 6\ decimal\ places$$

12) **Choice B is correct.**
$$\sqrt{72x^3}$$
$$= 6\sqrt{2x^3}$$
$$= 6x\sqrt{2x}$$

13) **Choice C is correct.**

$$\frac{(3)(4.0) + (3.0) + x}{5} = 3.3$$
$$\frac{15 + x}{5} = 3.3$$
$$15 + x = 16.5$$
$$x = 1.5$$

Since only whole grades are possible in the answer choices, the minimum grade Ryan must earn is a C.

14) **Choice C is correct.**
Exponential decay occurs when something decreases in value by a consistent percentage amount over some time period.

15) **Choice B is correct.**
Find the new value of F by substituting (r+5) for r and FOILing:

$$F = 3m + (r + 5)^2$$
$$F = 3m + r^2 + 10r + 25$$

Since the original formula was $3m + r^2$, subtract to find the difference:

$$(3m + r^2 + 10r + 25) - (3m + r^2)$$
$$10r + 25$$

16) **Choice C is correct.**

$$\sqrt{9x^8}$$
$$= 3\sqrt{x^8}$$
$$= 3x\sqrt{x^6}$$
$$= 3x^2\sqrt{x^4}$$
$$= 3x^3\sqrt{x^2}$$
$$= 3x^4$$

17) **The correct answer is 7**

$$100(.9)^x = 50$$
$$(.9)^x = \frac{50}{100}$$
$$(.9)^x = \frac{1}{2}$$

Using a calculator, either graph and table the function or use a logarithm to determine:
$$x = 6.74$$

Round up to the nearest whole hour to obtain 7 hours.

18) **The correct answer is 5**
The greatest value for $f(x)$ occurs when the absolute value expression $-4|-x+5| = 0$. Any other value will yield a lower value.

Solve for x:

$$-4|-x + 5| = 0$$
$$|-x + 5| = 0$$
$$-x + 5 = 0\ or\ x - 5 = 0$$
$$-x = -5\ or\ x = 5$$

19) **The correct answers are 2, 4, or 6**
Remember, an integer is a whole number. Therefore, $\frac{3x}{2}$ must be an integer for $f(x)$ to be a positive integer. Only even values of x in the domain of $\{0 < x < 8\}$ will accomplish this.

20) **The correct answer is 7**
First, rearrange the values in ascending order:

$$4, 5, 6, 9, 9, 9$$

Now find a seventh term that will cause the new mean to be equal to the new median.

For a new term to become the new median, its value must be an integer between 6 and 9, so our choices are either 7 or 8, leaving 7 as our answer since 8 does not produce an equal mean and median value.

PITTSBURGH
PREP

Mathematics
Lesson 2

Arithmetic 2

Goals

We will develop our mathematical fluency and gain meaningful understanding by learning to:

1) Create percentages from known and unknown percentages
2) Evaluate situations with multiple percentages and changing totals
3) Manipulate complex fractions
4) Create probability from a given set of data
5) Convert a rate between units
6) Manipulate an equation to create a desired rate
7) Identify a ratio inside of a scenario

Contents

- Fractions
  - Addition/Subtraction
  - Multiplication/Division/Complex Fractions/Decimal Conversion
  - Proportions/Cross-Multiplication
  - Variation
  - Eyeballing/Guesstimation
  - Probability
- Rates
  - Formula
  - Unit Conversion
  - Single Rate of Completion
  - Average Rates
- Ratios
  - Distinct Properties of Ratios
  - "Super" Ratios
  - Two or More Ratios
- Percentages
  - Conversions
  - Word Translation
  - Data Analysis

Lesson 2
Arithmetic 2

We all use fractions every day. A half of this and a quarter of that, or something is on sale of one third the price of the original sticker price. These are all common terms that we frequently hear and understand in our daily lives. As we look to translate these life occurrences into math, let's look deeper into how fractions work.

Adding or Subtracting Fractions

You can only add fractions if the denominators are the same (Or, alternatively, look for the lowest common denominator - LCD). What exactly happens when we try to add fractions with different denominators?

eg 1. $\frac{1}{2}+\frac{3}{4}=?$

For us to solve the above example, we must find the LCD. What is LCD? It is related to the idea of LCM: Lowest Common Multiple. An LCM is defined as the lowest number that each of the integers will go into together without a remainder. Therefore, the LCM of 3 *and* 5 is 15. Note that each number has many multiples, but the lowest common multiple (LCM) between these two numbers is in fact 15, as shown below:

Number	Factors
3	3, 6, 9, 12, ***15***, 18, 21 ... etc.
5	5, 10, ***15***, 20, 25, 30 ... etc.

The LCM of 2, 4 *and* 6? 12. The LCM of 6 and 11? 66. Finding the lowest common denominator (LCD) requires us to find the LCM between the denominators of the fractions that we are adding or subtracting.

For us to add the two fractions from above, we need to find the LCD, which is 4. Convert the first fraction by multiplying $\frac{1}{2}$ *by* $\frac{2}{2}$, then add as follows:

$$\frac{1}{2}+\frac{3}{4}=\left(\frac{1}{2}\times\frac{2}{2}\right)+\frac{3}{4}=\frac{2}{4}+\frac{3}{4}=\frac{2+3}{4}=\frac{5}{4}$$

The LCD must be found whenever you add or subtract two or more fractions with distinct (different) denominators. Related to the idea of LCD is the GCF: Greatest Common Factor. GCF is usually not tested as often as LCM or LCD; however, the concept is easy enough to understand. Between two integers, the GCF can be found by listing the factors of integers and determining the largest factor that both integers share.

eg 2. What is the GCF between 27 and 81?

List the factors of each integer as follows:

Number	Factor
27	1, 3, 9, ***27***
81	1, 3, 9, ***27***, 81

We can determine that the GCF here is 27. Note that a number is always a factor of itself, as well as its own multiple.

Multiplying Fractions

When multiplying fractions, note that we multiply across.

eg 3. What is $(\frac{3}{4})(\frac{3}{4})$?

$\frac{3}{4}\left(\frac{3}{4}\right) = \frac{(3)(3)}{(4)(4)} = \frac{9}{16}$, which cannot be reduced.

Dividing Fractions or Complex Fractions

In complex fractions, we multiply the reciprocal of the

bottom fraction to the top fraction. Memorize the following: $\frac{(\frac{a}{b})}{(\frac{d}{c})} = (\frac{a}{b})(\frac{c}{d}) = \frac{ac}{bd}$. Alternatively, note that

for complex fractions such as $\frac{(\frac{2}{3})}{4}$, the denominator can be expressed as $\frac{4}{1}$, so that the complex fraction

becomes $\frac{(\frac{2}{3})}{(\frac{4}{1})} = (\frac{2}{3})(\frac{1}{4}) = \frac{2}{12}$, or $\frac{1}{6}$.

Fractions and Exponents

Generally, we think of exponents as an operation that increases a value. And this is true when raising a positive integer by any exponent. For example, $2^4 = (2)(2)(2)(2) = 16$. However, raising a fraction between 0 and 1 by an exponent gets us a smaller value. For example, $(\frac{1}{2})^4 = (\frac{1}{2})(\frac{1}{2})(\frac{1}{2})(\frac{1}{2}) = \frac{1}{16}$, which is a lesser value than what we started with.

eg 4. Which is greater, $\frac{1}{4}$ raised to the power of 15 or $\frac{1}{3}$ raised to the power of 10?

Fractions with Operations in the Numerator or Denominator

In fractions with addition or subtraction operators in the numerator or denominator, note that we can only separate the fractions as separate entities when the operation occurs in the numerator. For example:

eg 5. $\frac{7}{5+3} \neq \frac{7}{5} + \frac{7}{3}$, but, $\frac{5+3}{7} = \frac{5}{7} + \frac{3}{7}$

So, what happens if the numerator and the denominator both involve two or more terms with operators? Remember that we cannot split the denominator. However, we can split the numerator by keeping the denominator intact, as follows:

eg 6. $\frac{x+y}{a+b} = \frac{x}{a+b} + \frac{y}{a+b}$

eg 7. $\frac{x+y}{a+b} \neq \frac{x+y}{a} + \frac{x+y}{b}$

Fraction to Decimal Conversion

When converting a fraction to a decimal, divide the numerator by the denominator via long division. It's old school but effective, especially if the test does not allow you to use a calculator.

eg 8. What is $\frac{3}{4}$ in decimal form?

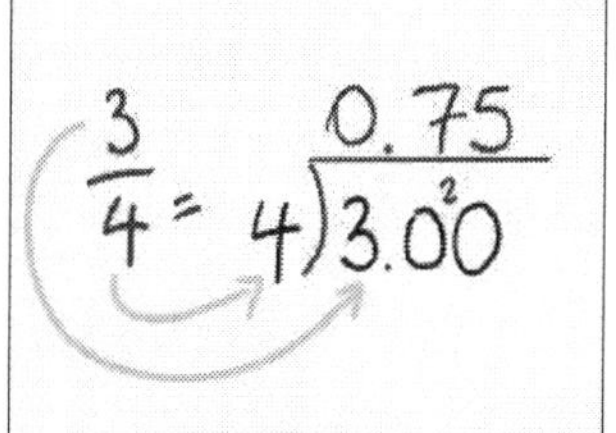

The answer is $\frac{3}{4} = 3\sqrt{4} = 0.75$. Long division isn't tested directly on any of your college entrance exams, and do not perform conversions from fractions to decimals needlessly. This skillset will come in handy in percentage and other related problems, however.

Decimal to Fraction Conversion

When converting a decimal to a fraction, count the digit's place as a measure for the denominator.

eg 9. $0.5 = \frac{5}{10};\ 0.72 = \frac{72}{100};\ 0.638 = \frac{638}{1000}$

0.5	0.72	0.638
↓↑	↓↑	↓↑
$\frac{5}{10}$	$\frac{72}{100}$	$\frac{638}{1000}$

Remember that all decimals can be converted into fractions this way.

Eyeballing and "Guesstimating"

Eyeballing or guesstimating an answer is a useful way to gauge your understanding of a question and will serve you well when you are double checking your answer to see if the answer is in the right range. Look at the following no calculator question:

eg 10. Which of the following is closest to $\frac{0.08 \times 0.12 \times 0.009}{0.02 \times 0.48}$?

A) 0.1
B) 0.01
C) 0.001
D) 0.0001

Without a calculator, it's difficult to keep every decimal place correctly and computations would be prone to a lot of potential mistakes. However, "guesstimating" an answer here will allow us to home in closer to the correct result:

$$\frac{0.08 \times 0.12 \times 0.009}{0.02 \times 0.48} \approx \frac{0.1 \times 0.1 \times 0.01}{0.02 \times 0.5} \approx \frac{0.0001}{0.01} \approx 0.01$$

In fact, there is virtually no need to perform large computations on your exam.

Always look to simplify first, compute last.

If you find yourself multiplying numbers and fractions with *large, convoluted and involved computations*, then you are probably headed in the wrong direction. Stop your work immediately, and double check that you've understood the question correctly and you're engaged in the proper methodology for that question.

Probability with Fractions

We can define probability as the likelihood of an event occurring, where 0 indicates no likelihood and 1 indicates absolute certainty. *Most probable events will be denoted somewhere between* 0 *and* 1. It is important to understand what the desired outcome is, and what the domain is.

eg 11. In the table below, Natives and Islanders are separated by their height allocations. Which of the following shows the probability of choosing an Islander from a pool of people who are below 5′5″?

Height

Origin	**Below 5′5″**	**Above 5′5″**
Islander	12	6
Native	111	210
Total	123	216

A) .035
B) .097
C) .108
D) .123

Note that in the problem above, the domain is all people who are below a certain height, and the probable outcome is a subset of people within that specified domain.

Rates

A rate (r) is determined by the relation between distance (d) and time (t). The rate formula is as follows:

$$r = \frac{d}{t} \text{ or, alternatively, } d = rt$$

We use rate concepts in our daily activities, such as:

- How fast were you driving on the highway? (miles per hour)
- How many gallons does your car use? (miles per gallon)
- What is your salary? (dollars per hour)

Keeping a consistent unit of measurement is a challenge, but careful note-taking will absolve your confusion. Questions involving rates can be categorized in three broad sub-topics that we will investigate further in the proceeding pages.

Unit Conversion

All rates are measured by some unit (miles, dollars, widgets). Some questions will give you information with one unit, yet others will ask you to translate it into another related unit. Remember to keep your units consistent!

eg 12. If a wheel on a ceramic bowl rotates 13 times per second, how many hours will it need to make 93,600 rotations?

The best way to solve this question is to linearly write down each unit of measurement on your notepad.

$$\frac{13 \text{ rotations}}{\text{second}} \times \frac{60 \text{ seconds}}{1 \text{ minute}} \times \frac{60 \text{ minutes}}{1 \text{ hour}} = \frac{13 \times 60 \times 60 \text{ rotations}}{\text{hour}}$$

The seconds and minutes cancel out to leave us with "rotations per hour" as our result. Solving the equation above, we get 46,800 rotations per hour.

$$\frac{13 \times 60 \times 60 \text{ rotations}}{\text{hour}} = 46{,}800 \frac{\text{rotations}}{\text{hour}}$$

Our 46,800 rotations per hour goes into 93,600 rotations exactly twice.

$$\frac{93{,}600\ rotations}{\frac{46{,}800\ rotations}{1\ hour}} = \frac{93{,}600\ rotations\ \times 1\ hour}{46{,}800\ rotations} = 2\ hours$$

Remember, just as we had done in our physics classes, keep your units consistent throughout, clearly marked on your scratch paper, and compute only as necessary.

Single Rate of Completion

A more advanced rate question gives you a partial completion of a task involving rate, and asks for a completion time or distance/work produced.

eg 13. If a gasoline pump fills $\frac{5}{8}$ of a gas tank in 17 minutes, approximately how many ***hours*** will it take to complete the fill-up?

A) $\frac{1}{10}$

B) $\frac{1}{8}$

C) $\frac{1}{6}$

D) $\frac{1}{2}$

Keep your units of measurement consistent! Set up a ratio equation with variable x representing the rate (minutes per fill-up). Remember, $rate = \frac{fill\text{-}up}{time}$. Another way to represent this is $time = \frac{fill\text{-}up}{rate}$. Since we already know that it takes 17 minutes to fill up $\frac{5}{8}$ of a gas tank, we can determine the rate. Substitute to

obtain 17 $Minutes = \frac{\frac{5}{8}}{x}$, where x represents the rate. Solve for x then $x = \frac{\frac{5}{8} Fill{-}up}{17\ Minutes} = \frac{5}{17 \times 8} = \frac{5}{136} = \frac{1\ fill{-}Up}{27.2\ minutes}$. Therefore, we get one fill-up every 27.2 minutes. Subtract 27.2 minutes from 17 minutes to obtain 10.2 minutes, representing about $\frac{1}{6}$ of an hour. Therefore, the correct answer choice is C).

Note that if we did not understand the question, we would've most likely chosen answer choice D) thinking 27.2 total minutes is needed to fill up the gas tank. But since the question asks for how many hours we need to complete the fill up, the correct answer remains at 10.2 minutes. Always make sure to understand and answer the question first.

Finding Averages Involving Rates (or, Identifying Variables in Rates Problems)

The type of rates problem involves finding average rates while regarding actual values. Or when data sets are plotted on a chart or a graph, and we are asked to determine the average rate. Or recognizing and defining the role of variables when given a specific rate. All of these sorts of problems involve a thorough understanding of how rates function.

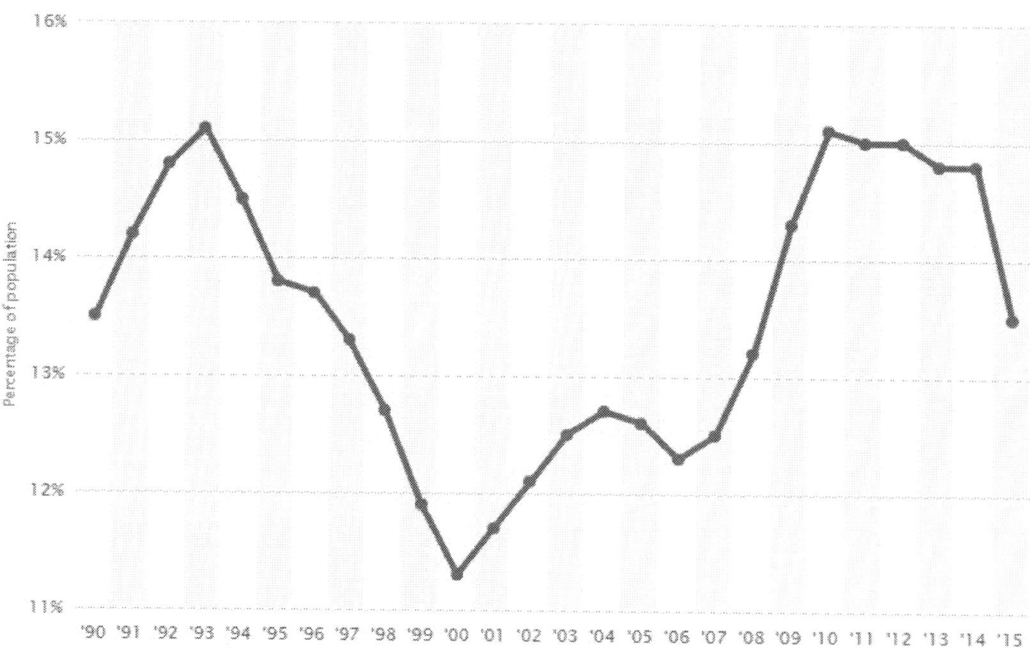

eg 14. According to the chart shown above, what is the average rate of poverty in terms of percentage of the population in the United States from 2000 to 2009? Fill your answer in the grid provided below, rounded to the nearest tenth of a percent:

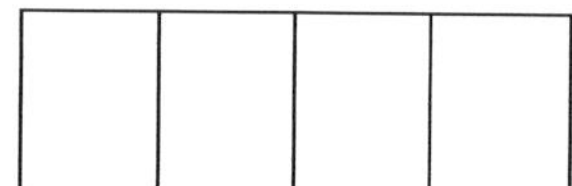

eg 15. A farmer uses 20 sacks of chicken feed, mostly organic, to sufficiently feed his chickens weekly. Each sack weighs a total of 4 kg. and costs \$19. He would like to lower his total cost by \$6 a week. Which of the following equations can the farmer refer to determine how many sacks of organic feed, s, he needs to not purchase to save money?

A) $\frac{1}{5}S = 19$

B) $\frac{19}{20}S = 6$

C) $\frac{20}{4}S = 19$

D) $\frac{19}{4}S = 6$

Ratios

Topics such as ratios, fractions and percentages are inter-related concepts, but should not be thrown together willy-nilly. We need to understand these nuanced differences to better develop our methods to solve them individually. A ratio, by definition, compares two or more terms together. Ratios are expressed by a colon, as a fraction, or by using the words "to," "out of," or "over". A ratio comparing "x to y" can be expressed as $x{:}\,y$, or, as $\frac{x}{y}$, which can be expressed as "x over y".

Imagine for a moment that at a cocktail party, there are 30 men and 40 women.

eg 16.

i. What is the ratio of men to women at this party?
ii. What is the ratio of women to men at this party?
iii. What is the ratio of men to everyone at this party?
iv. What is the ratio of women to everyone at this party?

The answers to the above questions are not only straightforward but also best obtained by determining the proper ratio:

i. To answer this question, take the number of men (30) *and women* (40), *and use a colon to express the two as* $30{:}\,40$ (*or* $\frac{30}{40}$).
ii. Women to men is expressed as $40{:}\,30$
iii. Men to total is $30{:}\,70$
iv. *Women to total is* $40{:}\,70$

All ratios may be simplified. How? By finding the Greatest Common Factor (GCF) between the numbers and dividing it into each of the terms. Taking the ratio between men and women, we have $30{:}\,40$. The GCF between 30 and 40 is 10, so we divide 10 from the men, and women, and we now have a simplified ratio of $3{:}\,4$ or $\frac{3}{4}$.

eg 17. What is the simplified ratio of women to men, men to total, and women to total?

Answers: Women to Men $= 4{:}\,3$, Men to Total $= 3{:}\,7$, Women to Total $= 4{:}\,7$. A quick way to simplify here was to eliminate the 0s. Most ratios will not be this simple.

Ratios compare values between two or more terms, but do not tell us the actual numbers of those terms.

Ratios are still valuable in determining the multiple of the actual value.

eg 18. If Oberlin College has a 3: 4 male-to-female ratio, how many males and females *could* exist in the student body?

A) 61
B) 62
C) 63
D) 64

Given the above information, there is no way of knowing how many actual students exist unless we look at the available answer choices. Ratios are useful because we know that at the very least the actual values of men must be a multiple of 3, women must be a multiple of 4, and therefore the total must be a multiple of 7. Hence, the correct answer choice is answer choice (C).

eg 19. At Oberlin College, the total student body is 14 students. What is the actual number of male students at Oberlin College, if the ratio of male to female is 3: 4?

We know that the ratio of men to total is 3: 7, or $\frac{3}{7}$, so the proportion that we set up is $\frac{3}{7} = \frac{x}{14}$, where x represents the total number of men, and 14 represents the total number of students at Oberlin. We find x by cross multiplying or multiplying the numerator and the denominator from each of the ratios to get: $(3)(14) = (7)(x)$. We divide both sides by 7 to get $x = \frac{3\times14}{7} = \frac{3\times2}{1} = 6$.

Try the following at Oberlin, with the same ratio as above.

eg 20. If the total number of students at Oberlin is 84, what is the total number of females at Oberlin?

eg 21. If the number of males at Oberlin is 12, what is the number of females?

"Super" Ratios

In a ratio that involves three comparatives, find the common comparative, then equate it between the ratios to solve for the values. Take the following example:

eg 22. A ratio of olive oil to canola oil is 2 to 10. The ratio of canola oil to peanut oil is 5 to 10. What is the ratio of olive oil to peanut oil?

Note that canola oil is the common comparative between the two given ratios, so find the lowest common multiple (LCM) for canola oil. Canola oil to peanut oil can be increased by a multiple of 2 to get 10: 20. Olive oil to canola oil is 2: 10. We are now able to create a "super" ratio of Olive oil to canola oil to peanut oil as 2: 10: 20. As a result, we can now see that olive oil to peanut oil is 2: 20. We can simplify the expression as 1: 10, which is the correct answer.

Percent

A percent is defined by its roots – "per" and "cent" – or, in conventional speak, we translate the word "per-cent" as "out of 100." You'll need to be fluent in the concept of percentages for your exam (and for life, generally). It's just an important concept overall. Let's take a look at several iterations of the concept together.

Converting Percentages from Decimals

A percent is a conversion from a decimal. Multiply the decimal by 100 and stick a % sign on the number.

eg 23. $0.43 = 0.43 \times 100\% = 43\%$
$1.98 = 1.98 \times 100\% = 198\%$
0.173 = ____ %
0.0031 = ____ %

eg 24. If Taniq ate some portion of a cake that represented 0.33 of the total, what is the total percent of cake that is remaining?

Since Taniq ate $0.33 \times 100\% = 33\%$ of the cake, there is $100\% - 33\%$ remaining. Therefore, 67% of the cake remains. (*Note that a whole cake represents* 100% *of the cake*)

Converting Percentages from Fractions

To convert percentages from fractions, convert the fraction into a decimal, then follow the methods to convert percentages from decimals.

eg 25. What is $\frac{3}{8}$ as a percentage?

$$\frac{3}{8} \times 100\% = 0.375 \times 100\% = 37.5\%$$

"Is over Of equals Percent"

Word translation is a necessary skill for percentage questions. A typical percent question consists of three components indicated by the words "is", "of" and "percent". Recognizing what values and variables make up these components is key to understanding the nature of percentage questions.

eg 26. What is 35% of 80?

In this question, we place the components in our handy dandy formula of "is over of equals percent". In math terms, this looks like "$\frac{is}{of} = \%$". Note that we're looking for "what is," so let's call this variable x. We know the % is 35% and "of 80" gives us: "$\frac{x}{80} = 35\%$". We can isolate the variable x by multiplying both sides by 80 to get $x = (0.35)(80) = 28$.

$$\frac{is}{of} = \%$$

Finding the Percent of an Original Amount

We utilize percentages in our lives every day. Let's apply this concept to typical situations that you may encounter in your activities:

eg 27. What is the final price of a \$120 skirt on sale at 40% off?

eg 28. What is the original price of the shirt that ended up costing \$450 from a discount of 60%?

Advanced Word Problems/Data Analysis

Once you have gained a solid understanding of percentages, you will then be required to work through more advanced concepts that will ask you to find multiple percentages. Take a look at the following problems and give it your best shot. There problems simulate tougher problems that you'll most likely encounter in your exams:

eg 29. Josephine wants to purchase a new phone at the store. It was originally priced at \$230. Last week, the store decided to have a storewide sale where everything was discounted by 10%. This week, Josephine decided to buy the phone after the store owner gave her a special by reducing the price further by another 20%. What was the final percentage discount that Josephine received for the phone?

eg 30. If the sum of three values is 460, what is the value of m if it is 30% greater than the value of the sum of the other two numbers?

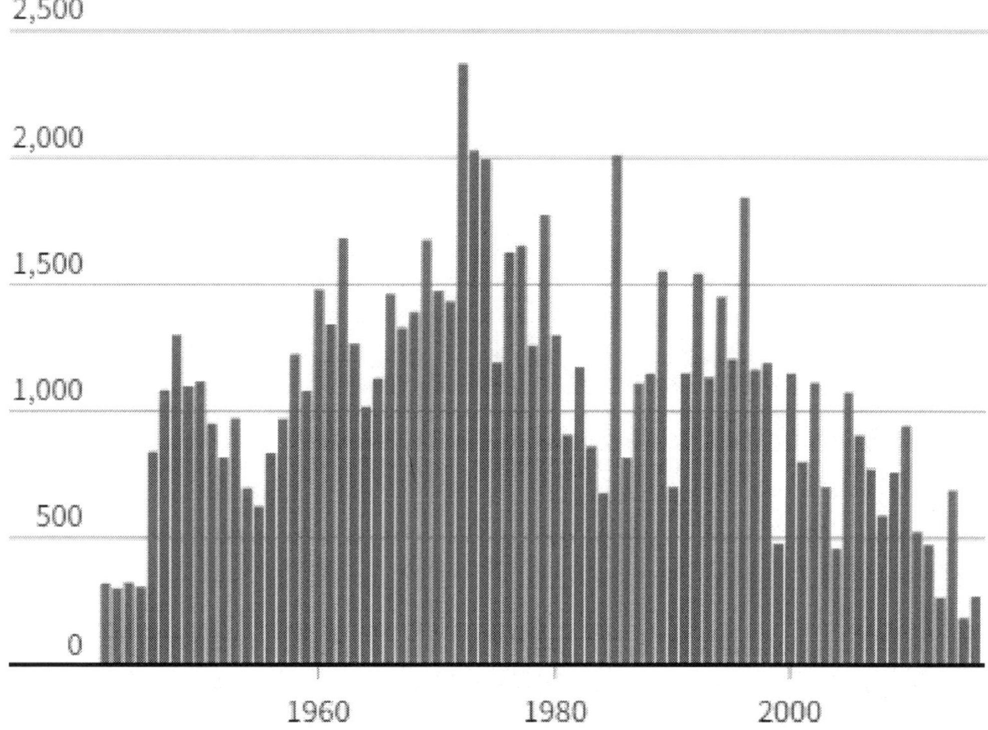

eg 31. The chart above outlines the number of fatalities of all airlines allocated by year. Which of the following is the closest approximate percent decrease of fatalities from year 1980 to 1981?

A) 15%
B) 20%
C) 31%
D) 44%

Lesson 2
Arithmetic 2
Application Exercises

NO CALCULATOR SECTION
Questions 1-5

Time - 20 Minutes

1) 80% of m is equivalent to 20% of 100% of n. Therefore, m is what percent of n?

A) 20%
B) 25%
C) 45%
D) 50%

2) An inspector at a phone factory found that, on average, 5 phones out of every 550 produced are defective. If there are no changes in manufacturing, how many phones must be produced for the inspector to find 45 defective devices?

A) 1100
B) 4500
C) 4950
D) 5500

3) A class is composed of 25% seniors, 35% juniors, 20% sophomores, and 20% freshmen. Twelve additional freshmen are enrolled in the class, dropping the percentage of seniors to approximately 20%. What is the number of seniors enrolled in the class?

A) 48
B) 28
C) 12
D) 10

4) If three-eighths of your paycheck is \$120, what is the total value of your total paycheck?

A) \$320
B) \$360
C) \$480
D) \$600

5) The table below shows the distribution of several students' political affiliations on a debate team. If p represents the final numerical value of students after 50% of all female students from non-Green party, and 25% of all males have quit the team, which of the following represents the original value in terms of p?

	Dem.	Rep.	Green	Other
Male	7	22	3	8
Female	12	6	12	12

A) $p + 35$
B) $p + 31$
C) $p + 25$
D) $p + 14$

CALCULATOR SECTION
Questions 6-10

6) If an item in a store was discounted 20% and a week later is discounted another 40%, what is the *final percentage discount*?

A) 60%
B) 52%
C) 50%
D) 48%

7) The data below shows the percentages of undergraduate enrollees at a University's four major schools. If 1650 students are enrolled in the School of Arts & Sciences, how many students are enrolled at the Business School?

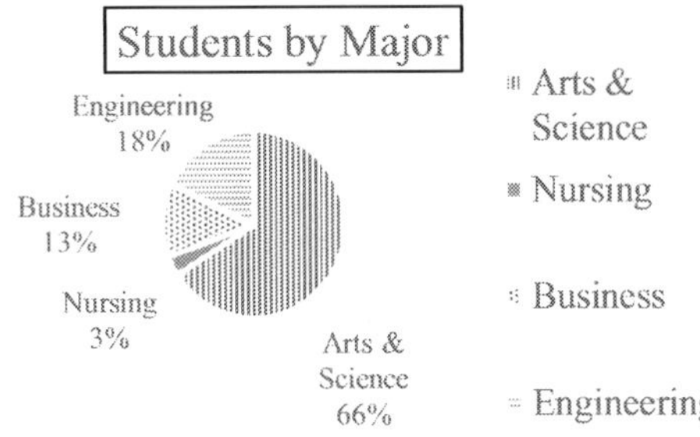

A) 2500
B) 450
C) 375
D) 325

8) At the Wakka Wakka Nut Factory, their best product, the Trail Mix, consists of Peanuts and Walnuts and Cashews. If the ratio of Peanuts to Walnuts is 3 to 5, and the ratio of Cashews to Walnuts is 2 to 3, then how many peanuts must there be in the Wakka Wakka Trail Mix if there are 600 cashews?

A) 540
B) 600
C) 900
D) 1200

9) If $\frac{5}{5r} = \frac{3+x}{9r}$ what is the value of x?

A) 5
B) 6
C) 7
D) 8

10) The amount of ground a herd of cattle can cover, in kilometers, can be calculated with the expression $1.08rt$, where t is the number of hours the herd is moving. Which of the following is the most likely value of r?

A) The speed of the herd.
B) The number of cattle.
C) Acceleration of the herd.
D) The distance covered.

GRID-IN SECTION
Questions 11-14

11) A chemist dilutes pure tungsten carbide into two solutions, one with a 35% concentration and one with a 65% concentration. If 1.5 liters of the 35% solution is mixed with an unknown amount of the 65% solution, a new solution with a 60% concentration of tungsten carbide is made. How many liters of the 65% solution must be added to the mix?

12) The table below shows the number of conference attendees from three different States broken into groups according to their highest level of education. If a random person was chosen from NY, what is the probability that the person has either a Bachelor or a PhD?

	Diploma	Bachelor	PhD
NY	18	6	2
PA	21	11	3
OH	5	8	12
Total	44	25	17

13) When changing phase from water to ice, the ice will expand to take up $\frac{180}{1}th$ the volume of the water. Steam will, at atmospheric pressure, take up 1700 times the volume of liquid water. How many cubic centimeters of steam can be made from 9 cubic centimeters of ice?

14) A model company builds model ships on a 1: 144 scale to the actual vessels. If they are looking to reproduce the USS Missouri, which has a running length of 864 feet, what will be the length of the model in inches (assume 12 inches per 1 foot)?

PITTSBURGH PREP

Lesson 2
Arithmetic 2
Homework Exercises

NO CALCULATOR SECTION
Questions 1-8

Time - 25 Minutes

Questions 1 and 2 refer to the table below:

	Smith	Chang
Chocolate	13	12
Vanilla	7	n

1) The table shows the ice cream preference for two families. If 40% of the Chang family prefers vanilla, how many Chang family members were surveyed?

A) 8
B) 12
C) 16
D) 20

2) What percentage of both families prefer vanilla, based on the value from question #1?

A) 20
B) 32
C) 37.5
D) 40

3) Which of the following expressions is an expression of the fraction $\frac{4x+3}{x-2}$?

A) $\frac{8x+6}{x-2}$
B) $\frac{4x}{x-2}+\frac{3}{x-2}$
C) $4+\frac{11}{x-2}$
D) $4-\frac{3}{2}$

4) The data below shows the number of college students in several majors. Out of all women, what is the probability of finding a business major?

	Math	Business	CS.	History
Male	327	529	125	619
Female	235	240	88	237

A) 10%
B) 20%
C) 30%
D) 35%

5) A set of 1,600 students are polled on the credibility of each news agency seen below. If the indicated percentages show the credibility indicated by each student, how many more students find WSJ credible or very credible than ABC?

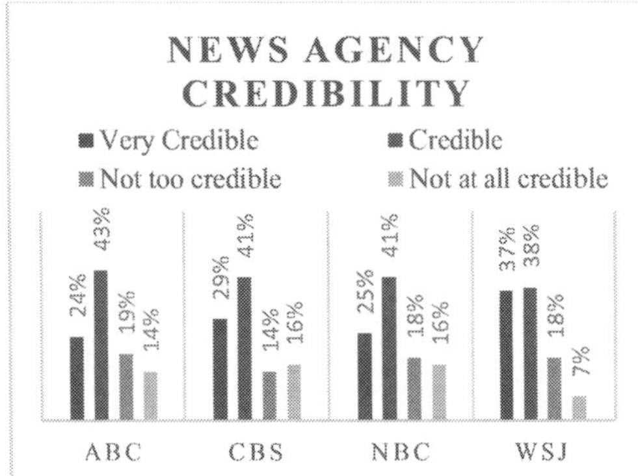

A) 80
B) 128
C) 144
D) 208

6) A student council meeting has 16 students vote today on a measure, with 12 students voting for it. Tomorrow, nine absent students will add their votes to the originals. What could be the largest % difference between the initial vote with 16 students and the full vote with 25 students?

A) 5
B) 9
C) 12
D) 27

Questions 7 and 8 are based on continuing data

7) Forty percent of the income from a new company's shirt sales goes to new investors. Another 50% of the remaining income goes toward production costs. Each shirt sells for $200. If the company is looking to make $1,000 profit this month, how many shirts must they sell?

A) 8
B) 9
C) 16
D) 17

8) Based on the information in question 7, what percentage of the shirt sales goes toward production costs?

A) 30%
B) 40%
C) 50%
D) 60%

CALCULATOR SECTION
Questions 9-16

9) To smelt an ingot of tungsten carbide, a small amount of cobalt is used. If 3.5 ounces of cobalt go into a single ingot, and 2 pounds of cobalt are sold in a pack, how many packs of cobalt are needed to smelt 25 ingots of tungsten carbide? (One pound is equivalent to 16 ounces)

A) 2
B) 3
C) 4
D) 5

10) About $\frac{7}{10}$ of all glass bottles in Kentucky are recycled, compared to other states that average a recycling rate of $\frac{1}{3}$. If 4.2 million bottles are sold in each state, how many more bottles were recycled in Kentucky than other states on average?

A) 1.54 million
B) 2.94 million
C) 3.6 million
D) 4.4 million

11) In Manhattan, approximately 30% of households are homeowners. Of that group, about 20% of homeowners spent over 50% of income on housing costs. If 8.4 million people live in Manhattan total, how many Manhattan homeowners spend over 50% of their income on housing?

A) 504,000
B) 1,176,000
C) 2,350,000
D) 4,704,000

12) An industrial recipe calls for 162 kilograms of calcium citrate, which is sold in 25 pound bundles. Assuming one pound is 0.45 kilograms, how many bundles must be purchased to complete the recipe?

A) 3
B) 13
C) 14
D) 15

13) A generator is slowed by 30%, then increased by 15%. If the generator initially turned at a rate of 37 rpm (revolution per minute), which of the following matches the speed of the generator, rounded to the nearest rpm, after the changes?

A) 5 rpm
B) 13 rpm
C) 30 rpm
D) 31 rpm

14) Store X sells appliances for 20% off, with an additional 20% off for members. Store Y has a sale for 30% off each appliance. If Tar is a member of Store X and looking to buy a new refrigerator with an initial cost of $499, which store will have the lower price, and by how much?

A) Store X, by $29.94
B) Store X, by $49.90
C) Store Y, by $29.94
D) Store Y, by $49.90

15) If $\frac{n}{8} = \frac{5}{28}$, what is the value of $\frac{3n}{5}$?

A) .40
B) .42
C) .52
D) .86

16) The formula for kinetic energy is given as $KE = \frac{mv^2}{2}$, where KE is measured in terms of joules. If a ball with 16 joules of kinetic energy has its velocity doubled, the total kinetic energy is increased by what percent?

A) 100%
B) 200%
C) 300%
D) 400%

GRID-IN SECTION
Questions 17-20

17) A high school band is comprised of $\frac{1}{6}$ sophomores. After the addition of 9 new sophomores to the band, the fraction of sophomores rose to $\frac{1}{3}$. How many sophomores were originally in the band?

18) If Marcy drives at an average of 65 miles per hour, and can drive a maximum of eight hours per day, how many days will Marcy need to set aside to drive the 2,427 miles from Pittsburgh to Los Angeles?

19) Three hundred and fifty students at a local high school report college acceptance and 120 report no acceptance. A new group of students that were not part of the original number are added to the data. What is the minimum number of new students that must report college acceptance for the school to have a 75% acceptance rate?

20) A recipe has a garlic-to-pepper ratio of 4: 3, and a pepper-to-cumin ratio of 5: 2. If a recipe calls for 10 oz. of garlic, how many ounces of cumin are needed?

PITTSBURGH PREP

Lesson 2
Arithmetic 2
Answer Key

Example Exercises

1) $\frac{5}{4}$
2) 27
3) $\frac{9}{16}$
4) $(\frac{1}{3})^{10}$
5) N/A
6) N/A
7) N/A
8) .75
9) N/A
10) B
11) B
12) 2
13) C
14) 12.5
15) N/A
16) $\frac{30}{40}$, 40: 30, 30: 70, 40: 70
17) 4: 3, 3: 7, 4: 7
18) C
19) 6
20) 48
21) 16
22) 1:10
23) 17.3% 0.31%
24) 77%
25) 37.5%
26) 28
27) 72
28) 1,125
29) 28%
30) 260
31) C

Application Exercises

1) B
2) C
3) C
4) A
5) C
6) B
7) D
8) A
9) B
10) A
11) 7.5
12) $\frac{8}{26}$ or $\frac{4}{13}$
13) 85 cm^3
14) 72

Homework Exercises

1) D
2) C
3) B
4) C
5) B
6) D
7) D
8) A
9) B
10) A
11) A
12) D
13) C
14) A
15) D
16) C
17) 6
18) 5
19) 10
20) 3

Application Exercises

1) **Choice B is correct.**
Don't be thrown off by the wording of this question. Translate the given "80% of m is equal to 20% of n". (*We can ignore 100% of n since 100% of anything is that thing itself*)

$$.8m = .2n$$
$$m = \frac{.2}{.8}n$$
$$m = \frac{1}{4}n$$
$$m = 25\%\ (n)$$

2) **Choice C is correct.**
Set up a proportion showing 5 defective phones for every 550 phones and cross-multiply:

$$\frac{5\ defective\ phones}{550\ total\ phones} = \frac{45}{x}$$
$$5x = 24750$$
$$x = \frac{24750}{5}$$
$$x = 4950$$

3) **Choice C is correct.**
Note that the number of seniors does not change, but that the percentage of seniors in the class does. Since the percentage drops from 25% to 20% as 12 new freshmen are added, set up an equation:

Let t = total number of students

$$(\#\ of\ seniors) = (\#\ of\ seniors)$$
$$(25\%)t = 20\%(t + 12)$$
$$(.25)t = (.20)(t + 12)$$
$$.25t = .2t + 2.4$$
$$.05t = 2.4$$
$$t = \frac{2.4}{.05}$$
$$t = 48$$

Therefore,

$$.25(t) = 12\ seniors$$

4) **Choice A is correct.**
In Algebraic problems of this nature, focus on word translation. "Of" signifies multiplication while "is" signifies an equal sign. This word problem translates into:

$$(\frac{3}{8})p = \$120$$
$$p = 120(\frac{8}{3})$$

$$p = 40(8)$$
$$p = 320$$

5) **Choice C is correct.**
Female change:
From 42 total women, half of all women other than women in the Green Party drop out so:

$$\left(\frac{1}{2}\right)12 + \left(\frac{1}{2}\right)6 + \left(\frac{1}{2}\right)12$$
$$= 15\ females\ dropout$$

Male change:
From 40 male students, 25% quit so:

$$40(.25) = 10\ males\ dropout$$

Therefore, a total of 25 people ($15\ females + 10\ males$) have left the club.

Since p represents the final number of students after both female and male students have left, $p + 25$ tells us how many students there were prior to any drop outs.

6) **Choice B is correct.**
When an item is discounted 20%, 80% of the original price remains. When an item is discounted 40%, 60% remains. Reflect this in an equation:

$$x(.80)(.60) = (.48)x$$

This gives us the total final cost in percentage of the item. The final discount will be the difference from 100%:

$$1 - (0.48) = 0.52$$

7) **Choice D is correct.**
Analyze the pie chart and set up a proportion based on the 1650 students enrolled in the School of Arts & Science.

$$66\%\ of\ total\ t\ student$$
$$= 1650\ arts\ sciences\ students$$

$$(.66)t = 1650$$
$$t = 2500$$

Find the total at the business school:

$$13\%\ of\ total\ students = business\ enrollees$$
$$(0.13)(2500) = 325$$

8) **Choice A is correct.**
Ratio of peanuts to walnuts:
$$P:W = 3:5$$

Ratio of cashews to walnuts
$$C:W = 2:3$$

Since walnuts are in both ratios determine the ratio of all the nuts to one another by determining the lowest common multiple of walnuts:

$$P:W = 3(3):5(3) = 9:15$$
$$C:W = 2(5):3(5) = 10:15$$

Then combine the ratios:

$$P:W:C = 9:15:10$$

If there are 600 cashews, then the actual value of the nuts should correspond in equal multiple of 60, since (10 cashews) (60)=600 cashews.

Multiplying the ratio value of peanuts (9) to 60 yields:

(9 peanuts) (60)=540 peanuts

9) **Choice B is correct.**
Cross multiply then simplify:

$$\frac{5}{5r} = \frac{3+x}{9r}$$

$$\frac{5(9r)}{5r} = (3+x)$$

$$9 = 3 + x$$
$$6 = x$$

10) **Choice A is correct.**
Some exam questions ask for the role of a variable in a formula.

In this instance, one variable represents the rate at which the herd moves (speed) and the other indicates time elapsed. Since t represents time, r must represent speed.

11) **The correct answer is 7.5**
Set up a formula to account for the mixing of both solutions to create a new solution with a concentration of 60%, where x+1.5 represents the total volume of the new solution:

$$.35(1.5) + 0.65x = .6(x + 1.5)$$
$$.525 + .65x = .6x + .9$$
$$.05x = .375$$
$$x = 7.5$$

12) **The correct answer is $\frac{4}{13}$**
Because the problem asks for attendees from just New York, ignore the PA and OH rows to focus on the 26 total attendees from New York. Since 8 have Bachelor's Degrees or PhDs, set up a fraction out of the 26 New Yorkers:

$$\frac{8}{26} = \frac{4}{13}$$

13) **The correct answer is 85**
Convert ice into water then into steam utilizing the correct conversion factors:

$$9\left(\frac{1}{180}\right)(1700) = 85$$

14) **The correct answer is 72 inches**
Pay attention to units! To find the length of the model in inches, since the actual USS Missouri is 864 feet, convert from feet to inches by multiplying by 12. From there, set up an appropriate proportion and solve for the missing variable:

$$scale\ of\ model\ size = \frac{length\ of\ model}{actual\ ship\ length}$$

$$\frac{1}{144\ inches} = \frac{x}{(864\ ft)\ (12\frac{inches}{foot})}$$

$$\frac{864 \times 12 \times 1}{144} = x$$

$$\frac{10368}{144} = x$$

$$72 = x$$

Homework Exercises

1) **Choice D is correct.**
Express the vanilla-preferring 40% of the Chang family and 12 chocolate-preferring family members algebraically:

$$\frac{n}{n+12} = .40$$

Now solve for n:

$$n = .4(n + 12)$$
$$n = .4n + 4.8$$
$$.6n = 4.8$$
$$n = \frac{4.8}{.6}$$
$$n = 8$$

Therefore, the total Chang family members must be $8 + 12 = 20\ members.$

2) **Choice C is correct.**
Since 15 people (8 + 7) prefer vanilla, and there are 40 people total in both families (13 + 12 + 8 + 7), calculate the percentage who prefer vanilla as follows:

$$\frac{15}{40} = \frac{3}{8} = .375(100\%) = 37.5\%$$

3) **Choice B is correct.**
This problem requires proficiency with fraction rules. Choice A multiplies the numerator by 2, but does not do the same to the denominator. Choices C and D incorrectly splits the expression into two terms. Choice B is correct because we maintain a consistent denominator as we break the expression into two terms by splitting up the numerator.

4) **Choice C is correct**
Determine what is needed and only focus on that information.

Probability of finding a business major requires the following steps:

First add the number of all women:

$$235 + 240 + 88 + 237 = 800$$

Now divide the number of female business majors by the total number of women to calculate the correct probability:

$$\frac{240}{800} = \frac{3}{10} = 0.3$$

5) **Choice B is correct.**
Credible + Very Credible for WSJ:

$$37\% + 38\% = 75\%$$

Credible + Very Credible for ABC:

$$24\% + 43\% = 67\%$$

Total students equal 1600, so:

$$1600(.75) = 1200\ WSJ$$
$$1600(.67) = 1072\ ABC$$
$$1200 - 1072 = 128\ Students$$

128 more students find WSJ credible.

6) **Choice D is correct**.
The initial vote has 12 of 16 students voting *for* the measure, which means 75% of voters approve.

$$\frac{12}{16} = 75\%\ approval$$

If all nine additional votes approve the measure the new percentage will be:

$$\frac{21}{25} = 82\%$$

If all nine go against the measure the new percentage will be:

$$\frac{12}{25} = 48\%$$

There is a greater distance between (75% – 48%) than (82% – 75%) so:

$$75\% - 48\% = 28\%$$

7) **Choice D is correct.**
Set up an equation based on the information provided:

Let s equal to the # of shirts sold.

$$Profit = (sale\ price * shirts\ sold) - 40\%\ of\ sale\ price - 50\%\ of\ remaining\ sale\ price$$

$$\$1000 = \$200s - (.4)(\$200)s - (.5)(.6)(\$200)s$$
$$1000 = 60s$$
$$16.667 = s$$

A fraction of a shirt cannot be sold, so the answer must be 17.

8) **Choice A is correct.**

$$Production\ cost\ \% = (\%\ remaining\ after\ investor\ payoff)(50\%\ cost)$$

Since 40% initially goes to the investors, we have 60% remaining. 50% of that yields 30%.

$$= (0.6)(.5)100\%$$
$$= 0.3(100\%)$$
$$= 30\%$$

9) **Choice B is correct.**
Make sure to convert pounds to ounces here. 3.5 ounces of cobalt are required to make 1 ingot, so 87.5 ounces are required to make 25 ingots

$$3.5\ ounces\ per\ ingot\ \times 25\ ingots = 87.5\ ounces$$

Since there are 32 ounces of cobalt in a pack, we divide as follows:

$$\frac{87.5\ ounces}{32\ ounces/pack} \cong 2.73\ packs$$

Since we cannot have 2.73 packs, we round up to get 3 total packs needs.

10) **Choice A is correct.**
Calculate the difference between Kentucky and other states using the information given.

Kentucky: $(.7)(4.2\ million) = 2.94\ million$
Other States: $(.33)(4.2\ million) = 1.4\ million$

Subtract:

$2.94\ million - 1.4\ million = 1.54\ million$

11) **Choice A is correct.**
Follow the information in the word problem and set up a formula that gives us the number of homeowners in Manhattan:

$$30\% \times total\ residents = homeowners$$
$$0.3(8.4\ million) = 2.52\ million$$

Next take 20% of the figure you just calculated to determine how many homeowners spend more than half their income on housing:

$$0.2(2.52\ million) = 504{,}000$$

12) **Choice D is correct.**
We set up the proper conversions like so:

$$Bundles = (162\ kg)(\frac{1\ pound}{0.45kg})(\frac{1\ bundle}{25pounds})$$

$$= 14.4\ bundles$$

Round up to obtain a total of 15 bundles.

13) **Choice C is correct.**

$$= (70\%)(115\%)(37\ rpm)$$
$$= (.7)(1.15)(37\ rpm)$$
$$= 29.7\ rpm$$

Round up to obtain 30 rpm.

14) **Choice A is correct.**
To find out whether Store X or Store Y offers the better price Tar must reduce the initial price at Store X by 20% and then reduce the new price by another 20%:

$$100\% - 20\% = 80\%$$
$$\$499(.8) = \$399.20$$
$$\$399.20(.8) = \$319.36$$

Next Tar needs to calculate the price at Store Y by reducing the initial price by 30%:

$$100\% - 30\% = 70\%$$
$$\$499(.7) = \$349.30$$

Store X offers the better price. Use subtraction to determine how much lower the Store X price is:

$$\$349.30 - \$319.36 = \$29.94$$

15) **Choice D is correct.**

$$\frac{n}{8} = \frac{5}{28}$$
$$\frac{n}{5} = \frac{8}{28}$$

Multiply both sides by 3:

$$\frac{(3)n}{5} = \frac{8(3)}{28}$$

$$= \frac{24}{28}$$

$$= 0.86$$

16) **Choice C is correct.**
Focus on the fact that the ball's velocity has doubled:

$$KE_1 = \frac{mv^2}{2}$$

$$KE_2 = \frac{m(2v)^2}{2}$$

$$KE_2 = \frac{4mv^2}{2}$$

Next, the ratio between KE_1 and KE_2:

$$\frac{KE_1}{KE_2} = \frac{(\frac{mv^2}{2})}{4(\frac{mv^2}{2})}$$

$$\frac{KE_1}{KE_2} = \frac{1}{4}$$

Finally, note that an increase from 1 to 4 is an increase of 300% therefore,

$$\frac{(4-1)}{1} \times 100\% = 300\%$$

17) **The correct answer is 6**
Let t be the total number of members. Set up an equation as follows:

$$\frac{1}{6}t + 9 = \frac{1}{3}(t + 9)$$

$$t = 36$$

To determine the number of sophomores:

$$\frac{1}{6}(36) = 6$$

18) **The correct answer is 5**
Since Marcy drives 65 miles per hour for 8 hours everyday:

$$65 \; miles\; per\; hour \times 8 \; hours = 520 \; miles$$

From 2,427 miles we divide 520 miles to determine the total number of days:

$$\frac{2427 \; miles}{520 \; miles\; per\; day} = 4.66 \; days$$

Round up to obtain 5 *total* days to reach Los Angeles.

19) **The correct answer is 10**
470 students were included in the initial college report since 350 reported acceptance and 120 reported no acceptance.

To determine the minimum number of new students reporting additional acceptances to bring the high school's acceptance rate to 75%, set up the following:

$$\frac{350 + x}{470 + x} = .75$$

$$350 + x = .75(470 + x)$$

$$350 + x = 352.5 + .75x$$

$$.25x = 2.5$$

$$x = 10$$

20) **The correct answer is 3**

$$Garlic: Pepper = 4: 3$$
$$Pepper: Cumin = 5: 2$$

Multiply each ratio by pepper's lowest common multiple:

$$Garlic: Pepper = 4(5): 3(5) = 20: 15$$
$$Pepper: Cumin = 5(3): 2(3) = 15: 6$$

Now determine the ratio of garlic to pepper to cumin as follows:

$$G: P: C = 20: 15: 6$$

Since the recipe calls for 10 oz. of garlic, we can calculate how much cumin is needed:

$$\frac{6}{20} = \frac{x}{10}$$

$$60 = 20x$$

$$\frac{60}{20} = x$$

$$3 = x$$

Mathematics
Lesson 3

Algebra 1

Goals

We will develop our mathematical fluency and gain meaningful understanding by learning to:

1) Use general strategy to isolate and solve for variables
2) Work with various linear equation tasks
3) Understand how inequalities function under different scenarios
4) Create a system of equations from any given scenarios
5) Solve systems of equations for both unique and non-unique values
6) Become familiar with equations with either infinite or no real solutions

Contents

- General Strategy
    - Variable Isolation
    - Data Analysis
    - Polynomial Division
- Systems of Equations
    - Substitution/Combination/Elimination
    - No Solutions & Infinite Solutions
- Inequalities
    - Number Line
    - Note on Inequalities

Lesson 3
Algebra 1

Algebra, Arabic for "reunion of broken parts," is the representation of unknown values with variables. Representing numbers as variables allows us to understand how different operations work under different circumstances.

Variable Isolation

Given a typical algebraic equation like $3x + 5 = 7$, we can determine the value of variable x by isolating it and placing all other terms onto the other side of the equation. To determine the value of x, we'll work backwards by subtracting 5 from both sides, and then dividing 3 from both sides to obtain $x = \frac{2}{3}$.

$$\begin{array}{r} 3x + 5 = 7 \\ -5 \quad -5 \\ \hline 3x = 2 \\ /3 \quad /3 \\ \hline x = \frac{2}{3} \end{array}$$

There may also be cases where we'll be faced with two or more variables. Treat them as any other terms in variable isolation. Oftentimes, words such as "in terms of" will accompany such problems.

eg 1. If $\frac{x+4}{m} = 11$, and $m = 3$, what is the value of x?

eg 2. If given the equation $= \frac{x^2+4}{k}$, where k is a constant, what is x in terms of all other variables?

A) $yk - 2$

B) $\sqrt{yk - 4}$

C) $\sqrt{yk^2 - 2}$

D) $(yk - 4)^2$

Algebra problems may also be given to us as word problems, asking to utilize given data to determine the result. Always make sure to understand the role of each variable and avoid mistakes in computation.

Remember, in general algebra strategy, the words "*in terms of*" asks us to place a variable or term to one side of the equation while expressing the leftovers in the other. When given an equation like $y = 2x + 3$, and the problem asks us to express "x in terms of y," we perform variable isolation for x by subtracting 3 from both sides, then dividing both sides by 2 to obtain $x = \frac{y-3}{2}$.

Another aspect of algebra is analysis of data. Sets of data may be given in the form of charts, graphs or scatterplots where we are asked to construe the given information to ascertain some further deductions. Let's take a look at a typical problem involving use of data:

Species	Offspring
salmon	300
brown rat	24
human	2

eg 3. The mortality rate of a species is roughly estimable by the equation $m = 5\sqrt{s}$ where m represents mortality rate, and s represents the average number of offspring produced by that species. What would be the approximate difference between the mortality rate of brown rats versus humans?

A) 24
B) 23
C) 22
D) 21

Polynomial Division

At times, we may run into problems with difficult problems asking us to simplify problems like $\frac{x^2+6x+8}{x+4}$=?

This is where polynomial division comes in. Polynomial division is essentially the process of long division with whole terms instead of numerical digits. First, we setup the expression like so:

$$x + 4 \overline{\smash{)}x^2 + 6x + 8}$$

Second, we ask ourselves "how many times does x go into x^2?" The answer is x, since x times x is x^2. Now x becomes the first term of our answer, like the way we would find the first digit in long division. Make sure to line up the terms correctly.

$$\begin{array}{r} \downarrow \\ x \\ x + 4 \overline{\smash{)}x^2 + 6x + 8} \end{array}$$

Third, we multiply the divisor $(x + 4)$ to x to obtain $x^2 + 4x$, which we will subtract from $x^2 + 6x + 8$. Make sure to distribute the negative sign to all of the terms properly. This leaves us with the remainder of $2x$.

$$\begin{array}{r} x \\ x + 4 \overline{\smash{)}x^2 + 6x + 8} \\ \underline{-x^2 - 4x} \\ 2x \end{array}$$

We then follow this pattern until we reach the final digit of the dividend. In this case, the next multiplier is a 2. We multiply the divisor $(x + 4)$ to 2, to obtain $2x + 4$. We then subtract as follows:

$$\begin{array}{r|l} & \quad\; x + 2 \\ \hline x + 4 & x^2 + 6x + 8 \\ & --x^2 - 4x \\ \hline & \quad\;\; 2x + 8 \\ & \;\; -2x - 8 \\ \hline & \qquad\quad 0 \end{array}$$

Note that since there is no remainder, we can safely state that $(x + 4)$ is a factor of $(x^2 + 6x + 8)$, and goes into the quadratic evenly.

However, simplifying other expressions may leave us with a remainder. If the given expression was instead $\frac{x^2+6x+9}{x+4}$, we would obtain:

$$\begin{array}{r|l} & \quad\; x + 2 + \frac{1}{x+4} \\ \hline x + 4 & x^2 + 6x + 9 \\ & --x^2 - 4x \\ \hline & \quad\;\; 2x + 9 \\ & \;\; -2x - 8 \\ \hline & \qquad\quad 1 \end{array}$$

Note that the remainder becomes the numerator and the divisor becomes the denominator of the remaining fraction.

It is also worth noting the pattern of our answer. If you see that a question contains polynomials that have a fraction as their final term like our example, it is likely a product of polynomial division.

Using the answer choices can quickly provide a proper methodology to find the correct answer.

Systems of Equations

Systems of equations problems involve two or more equations with two or more variables, where we are usually asked to solve for the values of those variables. With some exception, there are two methods that we can use to solve any given system: substitution or combination (combination is also sometimes known as elimination). First, however, remember this handy dandy rule:

For n number of variables in a system of equations, an n number of *distinct* equations is needed to solve for each variable.

Note that *distinct* means *unique*, and multiples of the same equation are not considered distinct. For example, $2x + 3y = 5$ and $4x + 6y = 8$ are ***not*** distinct because the second equation is merely the first equation multiplied by a factor of two. Essentially, to solve for the value of each and every variable, you will need the same number of equations as there are variables. Try this example problem:

eg 4. Given the system of equations $4x - 6y = -2$ and $y = x - 1$, what is x?

(Think about which method you'd like to employ first, then solve.)

Since the above equation already has one of the variables defined in terms of the other ("y in terms of x") the most prudent method to employ here would be substitution. In this instance, substituting the value of y from the second equation into the first, we would then obtain the following:

$$4x - 6y = -2$$
$$y = x - 1$$

Substitute for y in the first equation with the second:

$$4x - 6(x - 1) = -2$$
$$4x - 6x + 6 = -2$$
$$-2x + 6 = -2$$

Add 2 and 2x to both sides:

$$8 = 2x$$
$$4 = x$$

At other times, despite the system of equations given, the question may ask for an operation of variables, rather than the values of individual variables themselves.

eg 5. For the solution (x, y) to the system of equations below, what is the value of $x + y$?

$$2y - 3x = 16$$
$$8x - 2y = 8$$

A system of equations involving two linear equations will have only one set of values since, graphically speaking, the solution is represented by the point of intersection between two linear equations. As seen below, the equations $y = x + 2$ and $y = -2x + 5$ share a solution at $x = 1$ *and* $y = 3$.

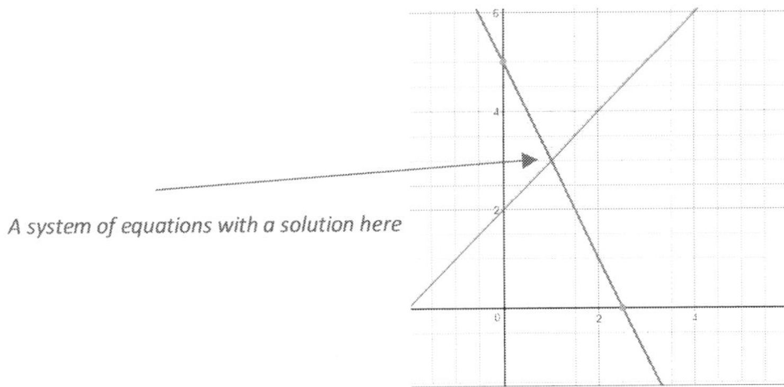

A system of equations with a solution here

No Solution and Infinite Solution Systems

In systems of equations, there are two general instances where we may find no solution or infinite solutions, which, for all practical purposes, yields no solution.

For example, the two linear equations:

$$y = x + 2$$
$$y = x + 5$$

The above two linear equations will never intersect since they are parallel to each other. Another way of ascertaining whether a pair of lines is parallels is to look at their slopes. If they share the same slope but have differing y-intercepts, there is no point of intersection between two linear equations. Therefore, there is no solution.

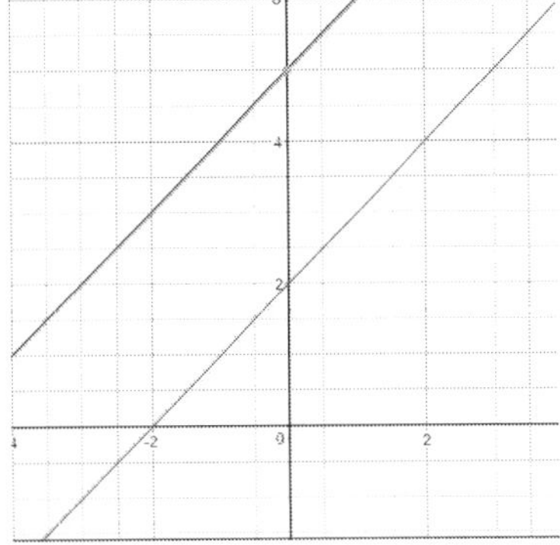

A system of equations with no solution.

The second instance of effectively no solution is when two or more equations presented are actually a multiple of each other, such as $y = x$ and $3y = 3x$. Since they are practically the same equation, there are an infinite number of solutions *which means there is no solution that would satisfy the system.*

Infinite solutions mean that any and every point on the first line is on the second. This means that our two lines overlap and have the same value. To reason it out another way, transposing a line (which is infinite) to another longer line (which is also infinite) will yield the same line, and therefore, will have no real solution.

Inequalities

Inequalities can be solved much like linear equations with one major exception:

Any time we multiply or divide by a negative number, we flip the inequality sign.

For example, given the following inequality:

$$\begin{array}{c} -2x > 18 \\ /-2 \quad /-2 \\ \hline x < -9 \end{array}$$

Note that the inequality sign "flipped" when we isolated the variable *x* by dividing both sides by (- 2). Let's try an example problem:

eg 6. Vaughn works at a coffee shop where the amount of money in his register, c, is to be no more than twenty dollars away from the dollar amount projected by receipts, r. Which of the following inequalities will show Vaughn's register work?

A) $c > 20 - r$

B) $c - r < 20$

C) $|c - r| < 20$

D) $|r - c| \leq 20$

This problem requires us to think about how the inequality is being presented. In choice A, for instance, we could re-write the inequality as $r + c > 20$, which makes no sense. Choice B may seem like a solid option, but if Vaughn's receipts indicate \$100 and his register only has \$20, then we can solve $c - r$ as $-\$80$, which is below \$20 but does not fit our problem's stipulations. In choices C and D, the left sides of the inequality for both options have an absolute value, making $|c - r|$and $|r - c|$ equivalent options. The only variance is in the inequality: can Vaughn's r be twenty dollars away from c? The problem dictates "*no more than twenty dollars away,*" which includes \$20; therefore, Choice D is the best answer.

eg 7. If s is the product of integers from 100 to 200, inclusive, and t is the product of the integers from 100 to 201, inclusive, what is $\frac{1}{s}+\frac{1}{t}$ in terms of t ?

A) $\frac{201^2}{t}$

B) $\frac{(201)(202)}{t}$

C) $\frac{201}{t}$

D) $\frac{202}{t}$

Since this problem is *in terms of t* (defining the answer with the variable t), we should try to eliminate any variable that isn't t. The variable s is given to us in terms of a large operation (100 terms multiplied), but the operation is irrelevant! We should notice how close the terms s and t are, and that the only difference is that t is just s multiplied by one more value, 201. That means $t=(201)s$, or $s=\frac{t}{201}$. Now we can substitute in our new value of s and use algebra to simplify the expression as follows:

Substitute $s=\frac{t}{201}$	$=\frac{1}{(\frac{t}{201})}+\frac{1}{t}$
Simplify the 1st fraction (multiply by reciprocal)	$=\frac{201}{t}+\frac{1}{t}$
Add the fractions	$=\frac{202}{t}$

Therefore, answer choice D is the correct answer.

PITTSBURGH PREP

Algebra 1
Application Exercises

NO CALCULATOR SECTION
Questions 1-5

Time - 20 Minutes

1) If $\frac{3x-6}{4} = 6$, then what is the value of x?

A) $\frac{1}{3}$
B) $\frac{1}{2}$
C) 5
D) 10

2) What is the value of $(b - a)$ if $4b + 3a = 12$, and $2b + a = 6$?

A) 0
B) 1
C) 3
D) 4

3) Which of the following ordered pairs will satisfy both the inequalities shown?

$$y \leq 2x + 3$$
$$10 - y > -5x$$

A) (2,4)
B) (-2,0)
C) (-2, 8)
D) (0,4)

4) Eight years ago, Jason was half as old as Marky Mark. Marky Mark is now 20 years older than Jason. How old will Jason be 15 years from now?

A) 20
B) 28
C) 34
D) 43

5) A compound, made of ingredients m and n, costs \$60. The relation between the cost of the ingredients and the final compound is given by the formula $\frac{1}{2}m - n = 60$, where the cost of ingredient m must be equal to \$160 or less, and the cost of ingredient n must equal at least \$10. Which of the following represents all the values that m could represent?

A) $m \leq 160$
B) $140 \leq m \leq 160$
C) $80 \leq m \leq 160$
D) $20 \leq m \leq 160$

CALCULATOR SECTION
Questions 6-10

6) What is the value of $3x$ if $(2x+3)^2 = 9$, and x is a non-negative integer?

A) 0
B) 3
C) 9
D) 15

7) The sum of three numbers is composed of two unknown values and x, a third value that is 40% larger than the sum of the two other values. If the three numbers add up to 312, what is the value of x?

A) 130
B) 182
C) 208
D) 223

8) The formulas for the tensile strengths of two materials are calculated as $4x^3 - 6x^2 + 5x - 9$ for Material A and $8x^2 + 3x - 3$ for Material B, where x is the width of the material in millimeters. An engineer blends the two materials to make an alloy, which has a tensile strength calculated as the average of the two materials. What is the sum of the coefficients in the formula for the alloy?

A) 13
B) 7
C) 4
D) 1

9) The system of equations $18x - 6y = 29$ and $15x - ay = 15$ has no solution. What is the value of a?

A) 2
B) 3
C) 5
D) The solution cannot be found

10) A power plant worker can store fuel rods in containers of either 4 or 8 rods. The worker must package at least 750 rods today, and must pack exactly 150 containers of fuel rods. What is the minimum number of 8-rod containers the worker must use?

A) 37
B) 38
C) 112
D) 113

GRID-IN SECTION
Questions 11-14

11) The cost of a telephone call using long distance Carrier A is $\$1.00$ for any time up to and including 20 minutes and $\$0.07$ per minute thereafter. The cost using long-distance Carrier B is $\$0.06$ per minute for any amount of time. For a call that lasts t minutes, the cost of using Carrier A is the same as the cost of using carrier B. If t is a positive integer greater than 20, what is the value of t?

12) An orchard maps the supply of bushels of apples with the equation $S = \frac{3}{8}P + 20$ and maps demand of a bushel of apples with the equation $D = 130 - P$, where P is the price of a bushel of apples. When supply equals demand, the optimum price of a bushel can be found. What is the optimum number of bushels for the orchard to supply?

13) A company makes $\$1300$ for standard seminars and $\$1600$ for premium seminars. The company has room for twelve seminars monthly and needs to make at least $\$17{,}200$ per month. What is the minimum number of premium seminars the company can offer per month?

14) Three frenemies are splitting a restaurant tab. The first frenemy ordered the basic meal, costing $\$12$. The second and third frenemy's meals cost 18% and 25% more, respectively. They all also will need to pay for the $8.80 shared order of chicken wings, 10% sales tax, and 20% tip after tax as well. If the three frenemies all split the tab evenly, what will be the approximate amount each frenemy pays, rounded to the nearest dollar?

PITTSBURGH PREP

Lesson 3
Algebra 1
Homework Exercises

NO CALCULATOR SECTION
Questions 1-8

Time - 25 Minutes

1) The quantity x is 8 more than y, and the quantity $xy = 48$. What is one possible value of $x + y$?

A) 16
B) 20
C) 22
D) 23

2) The inequality $8x - 6y \leq 18$ can be translated to which of the following inequalities?

A) $y \leq \frac{4}{3}x + 3$
B) $y \geq \frac{4}{3}x + 3$
C) $y \geq \frac{4}{3}x - 3$
D) $y \leq \frac{4}{3}x - 3$

3) If $4g = 18$, and h is two less than three times the value of g, what is h?

A) $\frac{5}{2}$
B) $\frac{23}{2}$
C) 12
D) 16

4) A certain value x is contained within the inequalities $4x - 5 \geq 15$ and $-3x > -25$. Which of the following choices is equivalent to the inequalities above?

A) $\frac{25}{3} < x \leq 5$
B) $\frac{25}{3} \leq x < 5$
C) $5 \leq x < \frac{25}{3}$
D) $\frac{25}{3} > x \geq 5$

5) The energy of an electron in a hydrogen atom is found with the equation $E = -R(\frac{1}{n^2})$, where E is the energy of the electron, R is a constant, and n is the state the electron is located in. Which of the equations below will find the state of the electron in terms of its energy?

A) $n = -\frac{R}{E}$

B) $n = \sqrt{(-\frac{R}{E})}$

C) $n = \sqrt{-RE}$

D) $n = -\frac{RE}{n^2}$

6) In the system of equations below, what value of q will have no solutions?

$$4x - 3y = 11$$

$$6x - qy = 17$$

A) $\frac{3}{2}$

B) $\frac{9}{2}$

C) 6

D) 9

7) An upcoming banquet has a maximum budget of $6,000 total, which will be spent between VIPs and standard guests. The standard meals will cost $25 per plate, while VIPs will cost $55 per plate. The VIP section will hold 15 people at most, and at least 45 people will be coming to the banquet. If this situation is modeled according to a system of inequalities, which of the following systems best represents a banquet with g standard guests and v VIPs?

A) $55v + 25g \geq 6000$
$g + v \geq 45$
$v \geq 15$

B) $55g + 25v \leq 6000$
$g + v \leq 45$
$v \leq 15$

C) $55v + 25g \leq 6000$
$g + v \geq 45$
$v \geq 15$

D) $55v + 25g \leq 6000$
$g + v \geq 45$
$v \leq 15$

8) A certain number can be found by adding three to four times b. The same number can be found by squaring b and subtracting nine. What is one possible value of b?

A) -6
B) -2
C) 2
D) 12

CALCULATOR SECTION
Questions 9-16

9) The table shows the relative value of $100 worth of goods in several states. If a person in Arizona buys a certain amount of coffee for $85 and then sells it in Alaska, how much money should the person expect to receive?

State	Relative Value of $100
Alabama	$113.90
Alaska	$94.61
Arizona	$103.73
Arkansas	$114.29

A) $77.53
B) $89.84
C) $93.19
D) $113.85

10) Shaun and Indu are working for a company to build a smartphone app. Together, they work a total of 87 hours. Shaun works at a rate of $20 per hour, and Indu earns $18 per hour. If Shaun and Indu earned $1,676 on the project, how much money did Indu earn, rounded to the nearest dollar?

A) 32
B) 576
C) 794
D) 1100

11) A food truck sells $8 burritos and $3 tacos and makes a percentage of those sales as profit, as shown below. If the food truck sells three times as many burritos as it does tacos, what is the minimum number of burritos that needs to be sold to make at least $1,000 in profit?

Item	Profit per Item
Tacos	40%
Burritos	20%
Churros	35%

A) 50
B) 150
C) 500
D) 555

12) In the system of equations below, what is the value of $3x - 2y$?

$$7x + 8y = 119$$

$$2x + 5y = 44$$

A) 8
B) 15
C) 31
D) The answer cannot be determined

PITTSBURGH PREP

$$f(x) = \frac{3x - 5}{2x^3 + 16}$$

13) Which of the following values will NOT produce a value for the function above?

A) -2

B) $\frac{5}{3}$

C) 2

D) 8

14) A judo dojo models its monthly budget and student enrollment based on the two equations below, where x is the cost per class at the school, b is the monthly budget for the school, and s is the student enrollment. At what point will the two equations find equilibrium?

$$b = 18x + 75$$

$$s = 1200 - 85\,x$$

A) 8.95

B) 10.92

C) 13.88

D) 18.19

15) What ordered pair is a solution for the equations $5x + 5y = 75$ and $x - 5 = \frac{y}{9}$?

A) (9,11)

B) (11,9)

C) (6,9)

D) (9,6)

16) A phone store can order either standard or deluxe smartphones if they order a combined 200 phones and make $75,000 in gross profits. If standard phones are sold for $300 and deluxe phones are sold for $500, which of the following is the least number of deluxe phones that must be sold?

A) 50

B) 75

C) 100

D) 125

PITTSBURGH PREP

GRID-IN SECTION
Questions 17-20

17) In the following system of equations, what is the value of $y + z$?

$$x - 3y + 2z = -18$$

$$2x + 2y + 12z = 20$$

18) A tank with 10 gallons of pure peroxide must be diluted with water to reach a 16% concentration. How many gallons of water must be added to reach the desired concentration?

19) An apartment building has room for 350 tenants between students and non-students. The building needs at least 120 students, and charges $600 per month per student and $800 per month per non-student. If the building needs at least $235,000 each month, what is the minimum number of non-students that can occupy it?

20) Jun budgets a certain amount of money each month for college. If Jun starts with an initial investment of n dollars, it will take him two years to reach his goal. If he instead starts with $400, it will take him three years to reach his goal. If he starts with no initial money, it will take him three years and four months. How much money in dollars is Jun's initial investment?

Lesson 3
Algebra 1
Answer Key

Example Exercises	Application Exercises	Homework Exercises
1) 29	1) D	1) A
2) B	2) C	2) C
3) B	3) A	3) B
4) −2	4) D	4) C
5) 20	5) B	5) B
6) C	6) A	6) B
7) D	7) B	7) D
	8) B	8) B
	9) C	9) A
	10) B	10) B
	11) 40	11) C
	12) 50	12) C
	13) 6	13) A
	14) 23.4	14) B
		15) C
		16) B
		17) $\frac{29}{4}$
		18) 52.5
		19) 215
		20) 1600

Application Exercises

1) **Choice D is correct**

$$\frac{3x-6}{4}=6$$
$$3x-6=(6)4$$
$$3x-6=24$$
$$3x=30$$
$$x=10$$

2) **Choice C is correct**
Utilize elimination by first multiplying the second equation:

$$(2b + a = 6)2$$
$$6b + 3a = 18$$

Then eliminate variable b by subtracting from the first equation. Make sure to distribute the negative sign correctly:

$$4b + 3a = 12$$
$$-(6b + 3a = 18)$$

$$-2b = -6$$
$$b = 3$$

Substitute 3 for b into any equation to obtain:

$$2(3)+a=6$$
$$a=0$$

Finally:

$$(b-a)=$$
$$(3-0)=$$
$$3$$

3) **Choice A is correct.**
Plug-in the answer choices to efficiently determine the proper answer choice.

4) **Choice D is correct.**
Assign the following values:

J = Jason's age now
M = Marky Mark's age now

Therefore,

$J - 8$ = Jason's age 8 years ago
$M - 8$ = Mark's age 8 years ago

Translate the word problem properly. This is an important skillset so focus on this aspect of test taking and comprehension.

"Eight years ago, Jason was half as old as Mark" translates to:

$$\frac{M-8}{2} = J - 8$$

"Mark is now 20 years older than Jason" translates to:

$$M = J + 20$$

Utilizing substitution, we then solve:

$$\frac{[(J+20)-8\,]}{2} = J - 8$$

$$J + 12 = 2J - 16$$
$$28 = J$$

Therefore, Jason's age 15 years from now is

$$28 + 15 = 43$$

5) **Choice B is correct.**
From the equation, translate:

$$m \leq 160$$
$$n \geq 10$$
$$\frac{1}{2}m - n = 60$$

When n is at its minimum value, we obtain

$$\frac{1}{2}(m) - 10 = 60$$
$$m = 140$$

Therefore, we obtain:

$$140 \leq m \leq 160$$

6) **Choice A is correct.**
Solve for x:

$$(2x + 3)^2 = 9$$
$$\sqrt{(2x + 3)^2} = \sqrt{9}$$
$$(2x + 3) = 3 \text{ or } (2x + 3) = -3$$
$$x = 0 \text{ or } x = -3$$

7) **Choice B is correct.**
Remember in systems of equations, if we have two distinct equations, we can only solve for two distinct variables. Therefore, assume the two unknown values as one variable, y, since assigning a variable to each would result in three total variables.

Translate, utilizing percentage knowledge properly:

$$x + y = 312$$
$$x = 140\%(y)$$

Substitute $x\ for\ 1.4y$:

$$1.4(y) + y = 312$$
$$2.4y = 312$$
$$y = 130$$

Plug back in:

$$x + 130 = 312$$
$$x = 182$$

8) **Choice B is correct.**
To find the average, add the terms then divide by the number of terms:

$$\frac{(4x^3 - 6x^2 + 5x - 9) + (8x^2 + 3x - 3)}{2}$$

$$2x^3 + 1x^2 + 4x - 6$$

Add the coefficients together to obtain:

$$2 + 1 + 4 = 7$$

Note that "6" is NOT a coefficient. It is merely an integer.

9) **Choice C is correct.**
Solve for the systems that creates equivalency of coefficients between the two equations. This allows for both functions to become parallel lines with *no solution*.

$$18x - 6y = 29$$
$$15x - ay = 15$$

The missing value here can be found by creating a proportion of coefficients:

$$\frac{18}{15} = \frac{6}{a}$$

$$a = 5$$

10) **Choice B is correct.**
Let x be a container of 4 rods and y a container of 8 rods. Eliminate the x variable by multiplying the first equation by 4, then subtract:

$$4(x + y = 150)$$
$$-(4x + 8y = 750)$$

$$-4y = -150$$
$$y = 37.5$$

Since we cannot have half of a container, we round up to obtain 38 containers of 8-rods.

11) **The correct answer is 40**
Translate the word problem correctly, with time t as the total minutes. Make sure to take away the 20 minutes from Carrier A since it has already been factored into the first minute:

$$Cost\ of\ Carrier\ A = Cost\ of\ Carrier\ B$$
$$1 + 0.07(t - 20) = 0.06t$$
$$1 + 0.07t - 1.4 = 0.06t$$
$$-0.4 = -0.01t$$
$$t = 40$$

12) **The correct answer is 50**
Set the supply equal to demand. Then find the value of P, price of a bushel of apples:

$$Supply = Demand$$

$$(\frac{3}{8})P + 20 = 130 - P$$
$$(\frac{11}{8})P = 110$$
$$P = 80$$

Input this value into the supply side:

$$S = (\frac{3}{8})(80) + 20$$
$$S = 50$$

13) **The correct answer is 6**
Define the variables as follows:

$$x = the\ number\ of\ standard\ seminars$$
$$y = the\ number\ of\ premium\ seminars$$

Translate the word problem into appropriate equations:

$$17{,}200 \leq 1300x + 1600y$$
$$12 = x + y$$

Multiply the second equation by 1300 then eliminate the variable x by subtraction. Remember to distribute the negative sign properly:

$$17{,}200 = 1300x + 1600y$$
$$-(15{,}600 = 1300\,x + 1600y)$$

$$1600 = 300\,y$$
$$5.3 = y$$

Since we cannot have 5.3 seminars, we round up to obtain 6 premium seminars.

14) **The correct answer is 22**
Translate the word problem correctly as follows. Note that the tax occurs before the tip:

$$= \frac{[(Total\ cost\ of\ meals)\ sales\ tax]\ tip}{Number\ of\ friends}$$

$$= \frac{(\$12\ +\ 12(1.18) +\ 12(1.25) + 8.80) \times 1.1 \times 1.2}{3}$$

$$= \frac{(\$12 + 14.16 + 15 + 8.8) \times 1.1 \times 1.2}{3}$$

$$= \$21.98$$

$$\cong \$22$$

#frenemiesFTW

Homework Exercises

1) **Choice A is correct.**

$$x = y + 8$$
$$xy = 48$$

Isolate x in Equation 2:

$$x = \frac{48}{y}$$

Substitute into first equation then solve for y:

$$(\frac{48}{y}) = y + 8$$
$$48 = y^2 + 8y$$
$$0 = y^2 + 8y - 48$$
$$0 = (y - 4)(y + 12)$$
$$y = 4\ or\ -12$$

Using y=4, we plug into first equation to determine the x value:

$$x = 4 + 8 = 12$$

Therefore,

$$x + y = 4 + 12$$
$$= 16$$

2) **Choice C is correct.**
Re-express the given inequality in terms of y:

$$8x - 6y \leq 18$$
$$-6y \leq -8x + 18$$
$$y \geq (\frac{4}{3})x - 3$$

Note on inequalities: switch the inequality sign when dividing or multiplying each side by a negative number.

3) **Choice A is correct.**
Translate the words into appropriate equations:

$$4g = 18$$
$$h = 3g - 2$$

Isolate the variable g from the second equation:

$$\frac{h + 2}{3} = g$$

Substitute this value into the first then solve for h:

$$4(\frac{h + 2}{3}) = 18$$
$$(\frac{12h + 24}{3}) = 18$$
$$12h + 24 = 54$$
$$12h = 30$$
$$h = \frac{5}{2}$$

4) **Choice C is correct.**
Isolate x in each inequality as follows:

$$4x - 5 \geq 15$$
$$4x \geq 20$$
$$x \geq 5$$

And in the other, flipping the sign when dividing or multiplying by a negative to both sides:

$$-3x > -25$$
$$x < \frac{25}{3}$$

Then combine to obtain:

$$5 \leq x < \frac{25}{3}$$

5) **Choice B is correct.**
Manipulate the formulae to isolate the variable n:

$$E = -R(\frac{1}{n^2})$$
$$(n^2)E = -R$$
$$n = \sqrt{(-\frac{R}{E})}$$

6) **Choice B is correct.**
Solve for the multiplier that creates equivalency of coefficients between the two equations. This allows for both functions to become parallel lines with *no solution*.

Set up the correct proportion to find the missing value of q:

$$\frac{4}{6} = \frac{3}{q}$$
$$q = \frac{18}{4}$$
$$q = \frac{9}{2}$$

7) **Choice D is correct.**
Translate the word problem correctly as follows, paying attention to translating quantifiers such as "maximum budgets" and "at most".

Assign the following variables:

$$s = number\ of\ standard\ guests$$
$$v = number\ of\ VIP\ guests$$

$$25s + 55v \leq 6000$$
$$g + v \geq 45$$
$$v \leq 15$$

If you've made a mistake here, make sure to pay special attention to the denotations of quantity comparisons in the future.

8) **Choice B is correct.**
Translate this algebraic word problem appropriately as follows:

$$4b + 3 = b^2 - 9$$
$$0 = b^2 - 4b - 12$$
$$0 = (b + 2)(b - 6)$$
$$b = -2\ or\ b = 6$$

Amongst the answer choices, only one of the solutions is viable. In this instance the viable choice is -2.

9) **Choice A is correct.**
One method of solving is to set up a proportion with appropriate values:

$$\frac{\text{Relative Value Arizona}}{\text{Relative Value Alaska}} = \frac{\text{Actual Value Arizona}}{\text{Actual Value Alaska}}$$
$$\left(\frac{103.73}{94.61}\right) = (\frac{85}{x})$$
$$x = \$77.53$$

10) **Choice B is correct.**
Assign the variables properly in these systems of equations:

$$S = \textit{number of hours Shaun worked}$$
$$I = \textit{number of hours Indu worked}$$

Set up the appropriate system of equations:

$$S + I = 87$$
$$20(S) + 18(I) = 1676$$

Solve by either elimination or substitution. As with most problems, the problem will dictate one method or another. Here, use substitution:

$$S = 87 - I$$
$$20\,(87 - I) + 18\,(I) = 1676$$
$$1740I + 18I = 1676$$
$$I = 32 \textit{ hours}$$

Multiply \$18/hr. to the total hours Indu worked to obtain:

$$\$18 \textit{ per hour } (32 \textit{ hours}) = \$576$$

11) **Choice C is correct.**
Assign the proper variables:

$$t = \textit{the number of tacos sold}$$
$$b = \textit{the number of burritos sold}$$

Translate and solve the word problem properly. Pay special attention to the relative setup between the items according to the problem:

$$b = 3t$$
$$\$8(b)(20\%) + \$3(t)(40\%) \geq \$1000$$

$$\$8(b)(0.2) + \$3(t)(0.40) \geq \$1000$$
$$\$1.6(b) + \$1.2(t) \geq \$1000$$

Substitute:

$$t = \frac{b}{3}$$

$$\$1.6b + \$1.2(\frac{b}{3}) \geq \$1000$$

$$\$2b \geq \$1000$$

$$b \geq 500$$

12) **Choice C is correct.**
The most efficient way of solving this particular problem is to find a multiplier that will yield $3x - 2y$ directly.

Multiplying the second equation by (2) then combining both equations will provide this effectively:

$$7x + 8y = 119$$
$$-2(2x + 5y = 44)$$

$$7x + 8y = 119$$
$$-4x - 10y = -88$$

Combine both equations to get:

$$3x - 10y = 31$$

13) **Choice A is correct.**
In this particular problem, plug in answer choices here to find that -2 will yield a denominator value of 0, which will produce no solution.

Note: not every equations need be solved algebraically.

14) **Choice B is correct.**
Set the two equations equal to each other, then solve for x:

$$18x + 75 = 1200 - 85x$$
$$103x = 1125$$

$$x = \frac{1125}{103}$$

$$x \cong 10.92$$

15) **Choice C is correct.**
Simplify the first equation by dividing by 5 to both sides:

$$\frac{5x + 5y}{5} = \frac{75}{5}$$
$$x + y = 15$$

Multiply the second equation by 9 to simplify:

$$9(x - 5) = (\frac{y}{9})9$$
$$9x - 45 = y$$

Substitute for y into the first equation and isolate for x:

$$x + (9x - 45) = 15$$
$$10x = 60$$
$$x = \frac{60}{10}$$
$$x = 6$$

16) **Choice B is correct.**
Assign the proper variables:

$$s = number\ of\ standard\ smartphones$$
$$d = number\ of\ deluxe\ smartphones$$

Translate the word problem into a system of equations:

$$s + d = 200$$
$$300s + 500d = 75{,}000$$

Multiply the first equation by 300 and subtract to eliminate s, *making sure to distribute the negative correctly*:

$$300(s + d) = (200)300$$

$$-(300s + 300d = 60{,}000)$$
$$300s + 500d = 75{,}000$$

$$200d = 15000$$
$$d = \frac{15000}{200}$$
$$d = 75$$

Note: Plug the answer back into the equation to double check, as needed.

17) **The correct answer is 7**
Look for a multiplier that will allow the system of equations to eliminate the unnecessary variable x, directly leading to the sought after equation $y + z$.

Multiplying the first equation by 2 allows this combination effectively:

$$-2(x - 3y + 2z = -18)$$
$$2x + 2y + 12z = 20$$

$$-2x + 6y - 4z = 36$$
$$2x + 2y + 12z = 20$$

Eliminate x by combining both equations, then solve:

$$\frac{8y + 8z = 56}{8}$$
$$(y + z) = \frac{56}{8}$$
$$= 7$$

18) **The correct answer is 52.5**
Assign the variable x as follows:

$$x = gallons\ of\ water$$

Since the definition of percent is:

$$\frac{Part\ Peroxide}{Whole\ Solution} = \%\ of\ Peroxide$$

Translate the word problem accordingly:

$$\frac{10}{10 + x} = 16\%$$
$$10 = (0.16)(10 + x)$$
$$10 = 1.6 + 0.16x$$
$$8.4 = 0.16x$$
$$\frac{8.4}{0.16} = x$$
$$52.5 = x$$

19) **The correct answer is 125**
Assign the proper variables:

$$s = students$$
$$n = nonstudents$$

Translate the word problem appropriately:

$$s + n = 350$$
$$s \geq 120$$
$$600s + 800n \geq 235{,}000$$

Isolate the variable *s* from the first equation:

$$s = 350 - n$$

Substitute:

$$600(350 - n) + 800n \geq 235{,}000$$

$$210{,}000 - 600n + 800n \geq 235{,}000$$

$$200n \geq 25{,}000$$

$$n \geq \frac{25{,}000}{200}$$

$$n \geq 125$$

20) **The correct answer is 1600**
This problem is as intuitive as it is logical to setup algebraically. Assign the variables properly. Convert all years into monthly equivalents:

n = initial investment
x = dollars invested per month

$$n + (24)x = goal$$
$$\$400 + (36)x = goal$$
$$(40)x = goal$$

Setting equations 2 and 3 to each other solves for x:

$$\$400 + 36x = 40x$$
$$\$400 = 4x$$
$$\$100 = x$$

Plug this value back into equation 3 to determine the goal value:

$$40(\$100) = \$4000$$

Utilize equation 1 to determine the value of n:

$$n + (24)x = goal$$
$$n + (24)\$100 = \$4000$$
$$n = \$1600$$

Mathematics
Lesson 4

Algebra 2

Goals

We will develop our mathematical fluency and gain meaningful understanding by learning to:

1) Work with quadratics and all of their applications
2) Understand how functions behave under different operations
3) Perform essential calculations involving complex numbers

Contents

- Quadratics
    - Standard Form and its Components
    - Solving the Quadratic
    - Graphic Representation
- Functions
    - Coordinate Plane
    - Shifts
    - Finding Roots with Polynomial Division
- Complex (Imaginary) Numbers
    - Application
    - Conjugate

Lesson 4
Algebra 2

In Algebra 2, we'll look to explore three more concepts: the quadratic, functions, and imaginary numbers. Much of the heart of algebra requires a deep understanding of the workings of quadratics.

Quadratic Equations

A quadratic, utilizing the Latin term "quad" meaning "squared", involves any variable raised to the power of two. The *standard form* of the quadratic is given as:

$$ax^2 + bx + c = 0$$

The variables a. b and c all represent distinct (different) parts of the parabola. We'll see later on what each symbolizes in our understanding of the parabola. Other quadratic equations may look differently than the standard form, but they can all be manipulated to be expressed as the standard form. Reformulate the following equations into the standard form:

eg 1. $2m(m-4) = 5$

$(g-5)(g+3) = 0$

$x = (4x+4)\frac{1}{x}$

Graphically, every quadratic looks like a smile or a frown on the coordinate plane, otherwise known as a parabola. The highest or lowest point of a parabola is known as the vertex.

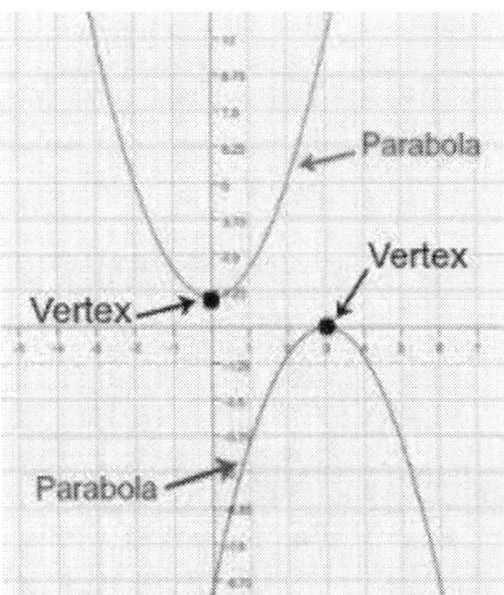

An alternative form, the *vertex form*, is represented as:

$$a(x-h)^2 + k = 0$$

Here, the variables (h, k) represent the vertex. The standard and vertex forms are used commonly so it's a good idea to understand their applications well.

To now actually "solve" for the quadratic, or to find the x-intercepts, we have several options. We can look to *factor*, *complete the square* or utilize the *quadratic formula*. Let's take a deep dive into each method.

Factoring

Factoring involves the reverse of FOIL and can only be utilized when all of the coefficients are workable. More specifically, with standard form, we want to find two numbers that multiply to *ac*, but will add to *b*. For example:

$$x^2 - 7x + 12 = 0$$
$$(x-3)(x-4) = 0$$

Note that in the above example, a = 1, b = - 7, and c = 12. Further, note that the two numbers that multiply to ac will add to b. In this instance, the two numbers are (-3) and (-4) that multiply to (+12) = ac, while they add up to (-7) = b.

Both $(x-3)$ *and* $(x-4)$are considered factors of $x^2 - 7x + 12$. From here, since we know that either of the factors $(x-3)$ or $(x-4)$ must equal to 0, each of these factors therefore can be set to equal to zero. Hence, $x = 3$, or $x = 4$. These are called by variously different names. Known as **solutions**, **zeros**, **roots** or **x-intercepts**. Since they are interchangeable, keep a keen lookout for these terms especially in your word problems.

Factor the following quadratics, and find their respective zeros:

eg 2. $z^2 + 2z - 3 = 0$
$m^2 - 25 = 0$
$\frac{1}{4}x^2 + 2x - 12 = 0$

Completing the Square

Completing the square involves a bit of savvy when conventional factoring just doesn't work. It's a close cousin of the quadratic formula, and they are both to be used when the problem dictates their use.

One method to find the x-intercepts of any quadratic from the standard form $ax^2 + bx + c = 0$ is to subtract c from both sides, then add $(\frac{b}{2})^2$ to both sides. This allows us to find both the *factors* and *vertex* quickly.

For example, given $f(x) = x^2 - 4x - 1$ we quickly realize that since we cannot factor this quadratic, we may complete the square. Setting the equation to 0, we can add +1 to both sides to obtain $x^2 - 4x = 1$. Following the method outlined above, we take -4 (b) and divide by 2, and square that number, which turns out to be +2 then we add that back into both sides of the equation to obtain $x^2 - 4x + 4 = 1 + 4$. This method then allows us to factor the left side of the equation as $(x-2)^2 = 5$. We then take the root of both sides to obtain $(x-2) = \pm\sqrt{5}$, obtaining two possible solutions $x = 2 + \sqrt{5}$ or $x = 2 - \sqrt{5}$. Voila.

Completing the square is generally not altogether useful for finding solutions, *per se,* since either factoring or the quadratic formula is a more efficient method. However, it can be useful when a problem asks to find the values of the coefficients, obtain the standard form, or in coordinate plane problems involving circles.

eg 3. What is the area of a circle, on a coordinate plane, that is represented by $x^2 - 12x + y^2 - 8y = -36$?

A) 4π
B) 12π
C) 16π
D) 24π

Quadratic Formula

$$\frac{-b \pm \sqrt{b^2 - 4ac}}{2a}$$

The quadratic formula above is a handy-dandy formula that is utilized to determine the solution of any quadratic that cannot be factored. The formula itself can be understood as two different parts.

The first part $\frac{-b}{2a}$ is handy for determining the x-coordinate of the vertex.

The second part, also called the discriminant, is under the squared root sign as $(b^2 - 4ac)$. The "determinant" determines how many solutions the quadratic contains. A positive discriminant indicates that the quadratic has two solutions. A zero-value discriminant indicates that the quadratic has one solution. And finally, a negative discriminant means there are no solutions.

Determinant	# of Solutions	Reason
$b^2 - 4ac > 0$	2	A positive discriminant value yields two possible solutions
$b^2 - 4ac = 0$	1	One discriminant value yields one possible solution
$b^2 - 4ac < 0$	No solution	A negative square root is no possible value (ie. imaginary)

In many cases, even after applying the quadratic formula, the answer choices may need to be simplified.

eg 4. What are the roots of the following quadratic $2x^2 - 5x + 2 = 0$?

A) $\frac{4 \pm 3\sqrt{3}}{4}$

B) $\frac{10 \pm 6}{8}$

C) $\frac{2 \pm 1.5}{2}$

D) $1 \pm \frac{6}{4}$

Functions

At their most basic, functions can be thought of in terms of input/output. For every input value of x, we will have one corresponding value of y. Generally, functions are expressed as $f(x)$ or $g(x)$, and equal some expression.

Functions can be expressed algebraically, graphically, and via data sets. They can also shift, shrink or expand when the inputs are modified. And finally, they can be reflected over any defined axis.

Typical graphic representations of some of the more common functions include:

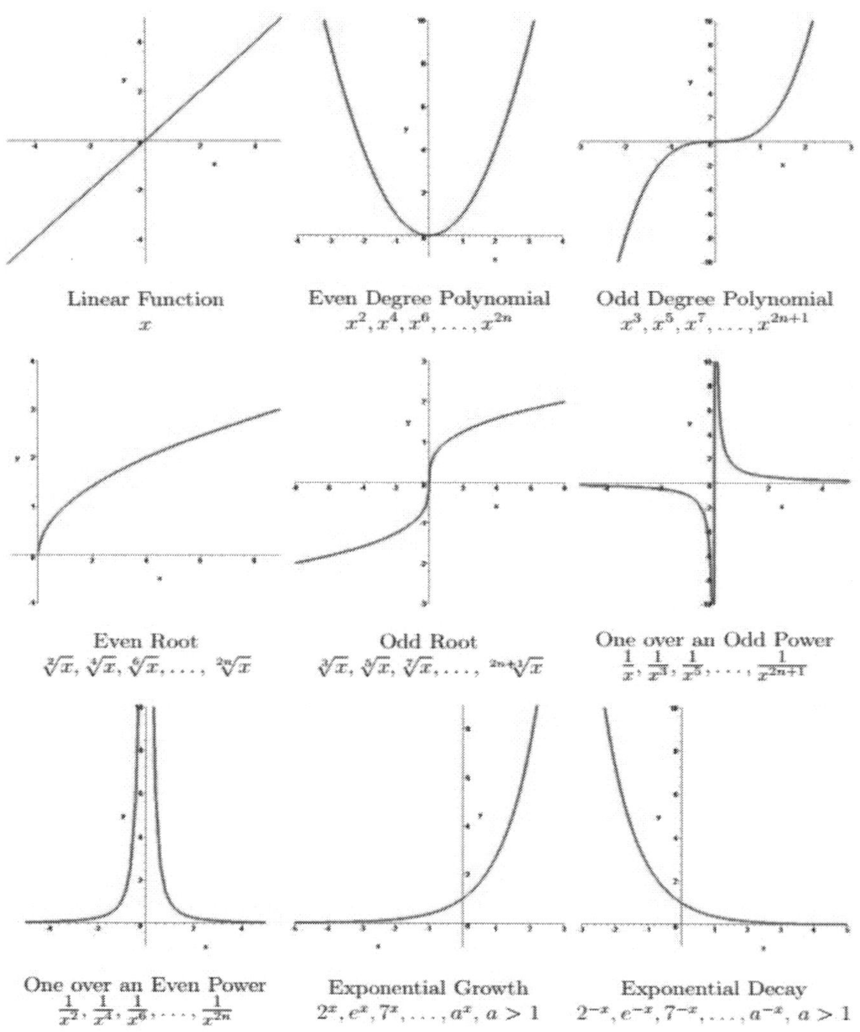

Source: wcsu.edu

Transformations

Functions shift *vertically*, *horizontally*, or *both*. Vertical shifts occur when a value is added to the entire function. For example, when $f(x) + M$, the entire function will shift UPWARDS by M units. When $f(x) - M$, the entire function will shift DOWNWARDS by M units.

On the other hand, horizontal shifts occur when a value is added to the input of the function. For example, $f(x + M)$ will yield a shift to the LEFT by M units. When $f(x - M)$, this will cause a horizontal shift to the RIGHT by M units.

To determine proper transformations, first find the base function, then apply the above shifts accordingly. For example, given $f(x) = (\sqrt{x-3}) + 4$, the base function $f(x) = \sqrt{x}$ will shift UP four units, and RIGHT three units.

Graphically, this $f(x) = \sqrt{x}$ 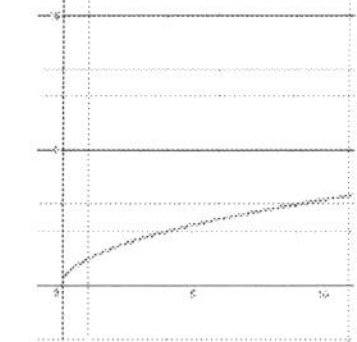 becomes $f(x) = (\sqrt{x-3}) + 4$ 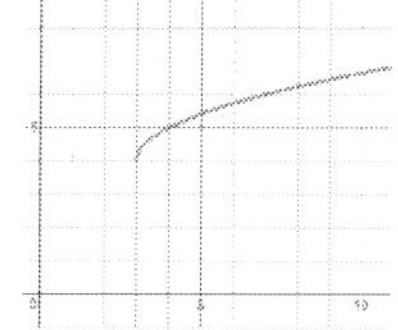

eg 5. If $f(x)$ contains the point $(3, -2)$, and $g(x) = f(x+3) - 3$, what point *must* be in $g(x)$?

Functions within Functions

Sometimes problems will be given where a function will be placed within a function. In these situations, remember to apply the data "inside-out" by solving for the inner function first, then solving for the outer function next. Try the following example:

eg 6. Given $f(x) = 5x + 5$ and $g(x) = x^2 + x$, what is $f(g(5))$?

First, we solve for $g(5)$ by substituting 5 for x, as $g(5) = (5)^2 + 5 = 25 + 5 = 30$. Next, since $g(5) = 30$, we find $f(30) = 5(30) + 5 = 155$.

Functions given as Data

Functions can also be expressed as a set of data points. Remember that the variable, or x-coordinate, is the "input" while the value of the function, or y-coordinate, is the "output". For example, if the data set is given as:

x	f(x)
-2	6
0	5
4	0

We can read the above data in several different ways. When the x value is -2, then the value of f(x) is 6. In other words, f(-2) = 6, according to the data. Also, note that the y-intercept is 5 according to the data.

eg 7.

x	$f(x)$
−2	3
−1	6
0	9
1	12
2	15

x	$g(x)$
3	0
5	−2
9	0
12	3
14	−1

Given the data above, what is the value of $f(g(3))$?

In this example problem, we look for $g(3)$first. Looking at the second data set, we can see from the left-hand column, when $x = 3$, the corresponding value of $g(3) = 0$. Then, we look for $f(0)$ by looking at the first data set. Going down the left-hand column for when $x = 0$, we find that $f(x) = 9$.

Imaginary Numbers

Mathematicians dislike anything that cannot be fathomed. In 50 A.D., Heron of Alexandria tried to ascertain the volume of a peculiar section of a pyramid that led him to a final value represented by $\sqrt{81 - 114}$. At that point, he had to give up and redirect his efforts elsewhere. But mathletes never give up! We've come a long way since then. Complex (or imaginary) numbers are used in all sorts of life applications, from measuring flow of fluids to radio waves.

We can define an imaginary number by the letter $i = \sqrt{-1}$.
Understand that imaginary numbers also act in patterns of 4 as follows, under the rules of exponents:

$i^1 = \sqrt{-1}$
$i^2 = -1$
$i^3 = -\sqrt{-1}$
$i^4 = +1$

$i^5 = \sqrt{-1}$
$i^6 = -1$
$i^7 = -\sqrt{-1}$
$i^8 = +1$

$i^9 = \sqrt{-1}$
$i^{10} = -1$
$i^{11} = -\sqrt{-1}$
... etc.

Let's try out a ferw application problems to solidify our understanding of the concept better:

eg 8. What is the value of $i^{73} - i^{44}$?

A) 0

B) $2i$

C) $1 + i$

D) $i - 1$

The above expression requires us to simplify both of the terms into a reduced form. Note that i^{73} can be reduced down to i^{73} because $\frac{73}{4}$, or $18\frac{1}{4}$, reduces down to i^1. Similarly, i^{44} reduces down to +1. Therefore, the correct answer choice is D.

As an alternate variation, instead of finding the value of a particular expression, at times we'll have to simplify an expression involving imaginary numbers. Try the following problems:

eg 9. Simplify:

$$\frac{6}{3-i}$$

Mathematicians despise irrational or imaginary numbers in the denominator. (They have issues, we know.) in order for us to resolve this, we can multiply the bottom term by what is known as the conjugate. A conjugate retains the terms but are opposing signs. In the problem above, we would manipulate the fraction as follows:

$$(\frac{6}{3-i})(\frac{3+i}{3+i})$$

Distribute the top, while FOIL-ing the bottom as follows:

$$\frac{6(3)+6i}{9-3i+3i-i^2}$$

Cancel out terms:

$$\frac{6(3)+6i}{9-i^2}$$

Substitute for $i^2 = 1$:

$$\frac{18+6i}{9+1} = \frac{18+6i}{10} = \frac{9+3i}{5}$$

Alright, good job! Try our final example problem:

eg 10. Simplify:

$$\frac{5-i}{3-i}$$

Make a note on how conjugates work with complex numbers, and on simplifying large exponential values involving i.

PITTSBURGH PREP

Lesson 4
Algebra 2
Application Exercises

NO CALCULATOR SECTION
Questions 1-5

Time - 20 Minutes

1) If $\frac{x^2+x-12}{x-3} = 5$, then $x =$?

A) 0

B) 1

C) 3

D) 4

2) If $f(x) = x^2 - x - 20$, what is the sum of the solutions of $f(x-2)$?

A) 0
B) 1
C) 5
D) 9

3) What is the value of $\frac{i^{428}}{3-i}$?

A) $\frac{3+i}{10}$

B) $\frac{3+1}{3-i}$

C) 0

D) $\frac{3i-1}{10}$

4) For the parabola $x^2 - 3x + 5$, if m is the number of x-intercepts, and n is the number of y-intercepts, what is mn?

A) 0
B) 1
C) 2
D) The answer cannot be found.

5) If $(a + bi)(1 + i) = 5 + i$ is put into standard form, what is the value of a in the standard form $a + bi$?

A) -1

B) 1.5

C) 3

D) 3.5

PITTSBURGH PREP

CALCULATOR SECTION
Questions 6-10

6) In the functions $f(x)$ and $g(x)$, the value of the $f(3) = 5$, and the value of the $g(-4) = 3$. What is the value of the $f(g(-4))$?

A) -20
B) -12
C) 3
D) 5

7) If $\frac{24x^2+bx+c}{-4x+7} = (-6x+4) + \frac{4x-7}{-4x+7}$, what is the value of $b + c$?

A) -54
B) -51
C) -33
D) 89

8) A quadratic equation has solutions at $\frac{-27}{28} \pm \frac{\sqrt{729-112n}}{28}$. If the equation is put in standard form $ax^2 + bx + c$, what is the value of c?

A) 2
B) n
C) 2n
D) 4n

$$f(x) = x^3 + 3x^2 - 4x - 12$$
$$g(x) = x^2 + 8x + 15$$

9) The above polynomials are divisible by a common binomial. If this binomial is a root of both equations, what is x equal to?

A) -5
B) -3
C) 0
D) 2

10) The function $h(x)$ crosses the x axis at $x = 6$. Which of the following points must be found on the graph of $h(x-3)+2$?

A) 3, -2
B) 3, 2
C) 9, -2
D) 9, 2

GRID-IN SECTION
Questions 11-14

$$\frac{x^2 - 6x + 8}{x - 5} = 0$$

11) If the zeroes of the above equation are added together, and then the impossible solutions for the function are subtracted from that sum, what is the result?

12) A quadratic function f has zeroes at 11 and -3, and a value of 1 for its leading coefficient. If the lowest possible value of $f(x)$ is equal to $-n$, what is the value of n?

$$y = x + 2$$

$$y = x^2 - 6x + 12$$

13) In the system of equations above, what is the y-value of one possible solution to the system?

14) In the quadratic $x^2 - 4x + n$, what value of n will give solutions of $2 + i$ and $2 - i$?

PITTSBURGH PREP

Lesson 4
Algebra 2
Homework Exercises

NO CALCULATOR SECTION
Questions 1-8

Time - 25 Minutes

1) If $g(x) = 3x^2$, what is the value of $g(2x)$?

A) $5x^2$
B) $6x^2$
C) $8x^2$
D) $12x^2$

2) A function $h(x) = x^2 + 12x + n$ has exactly one real root. If so, what is a possible value of n?

A) 0
B) 12
C) 36
D) 40

3) The function $b(x)$ passes through the coordinate $(6,3)$. What must be a coordinate of $b(x-3)+5$?

A) $(9, 8)$
B) $(3, 8)$
C) $(11, 0)$
D) $(11, 6)$

4) The function $f(x) = x^2 - 6x + 8$ is shifted to become $g(x)$, which has one root at (4,0). Which of the following would NOT be an expression of $g(x)$?

A) $(x-4)^2$
B) $x^2 - 8x + 16$
C) $(x^2+1) - 6(x+1)$
D) $(x-1)^2 - 6(x-1) + 9$

5) Which of the following functions will have roots at -2, 3, and 5?

A) $f(x) = (x-2)(x-3)(x-5)$
B) $f(x) = (x-2)(x+3)(x+5)$
C) $f(x) = (x+2)(x-3)(x-5)$
D) $f(x) = (x+2)(x+3)(x+5)$

6) Which of the following choices lists all the zeroes for the function below:

$$f(x) = x^4 - 13x^2 + 36$$

A) -3, -2, 2, 3
B) -2, 2, 3
C) -3, 2, 3
D) 2, 3

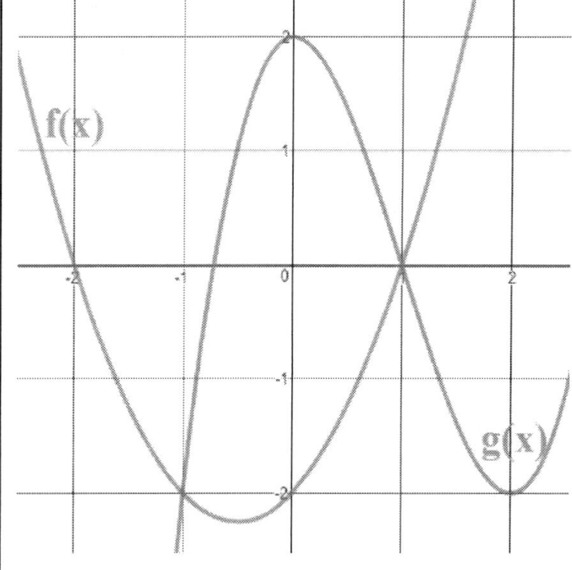

Refer to graph for questions 7 *and* 8*:*

7) The coordinate plane above shows the quadratic function $f(x)$ and the cubic function $g(x)$. What is the $g(f(-2))$?

A) -2
B) 0
C) 1
D) 2

8) For what value of x does $g(x)$ above have a relative minimum?

A) -2
B) -1
C) 0
D) 2

PITTSBURGH PREP

CALCULATOR SECTION
Questions 9-16

9) The expression $x^3 + 3x^2 - 2x - 6$ can be factored into the form $(ax^2 + b)(cx + d)$. Which of the following is equivalent to the expression?

A) $(x - 2)(x^2 + 3)$
B) $(x + 2)(x^2 - 3)$
C) $(x - 3)(x^2 + 2)$
D) $(x + 3)(x^2 - 2)$

$$y = \frac{4x}{x+3} + \frac{2x^2}{2x+4} + \frac{8x}{2x+6}$$

10) What is the maximum number of roots the above function may possess, if graphed on the coordinate plane?

A) 1
B) 2
C) 3
D) 4

11) If the equation $y = hx^2 - 2\pi x - 8$ is graphed on a coordinate plane, the line of symmetry will be at which of the following?

A) $x = \frac{2}{h}$
B) $x = \frac{\pi}{h}$
C) $x = -\frac{2\pi}{h}$
D) $x = \frac{2\pi}{h}$

12) Which of the following is a solution for both the function $f(x) = x - 5$ and the function $g(x) = x^2 - 3x - 2$?

A) $(0, -2)$
B) $(1, -4)$
C) $(1.5, -4.25)$
D) $(3, 0)$

13) A projectile is launched from the top of an 18-foot tower and is modeled by the function $h(t) = -2t^2 + 16t + 18$, where $h(t)$ is the height of the projectile in feet after t seconds. According to the function, after how many seconds will it reach its maximum, and what is the maximum height of the projectile?

A) 4 seconds, 32 feet
B) 4 seconds, 50 feet
C) 9 seconds, 32 feet
D) 9 seconds, 50 feet

14) In the quadratic equation $\frac{1}{2}x^2 - 5 = \frac{3}{2}x$, which of the following are roots of the equation?

A) $-2, 5$
B) -5, 2
C) $\frac{\frac{3}{2}+5}{4}, \frac{\frac{3}{2}-5}{4}$
D) $\frac{\frac{3}{2}\pm\sqrt{-\frac{7}{4}}}{6}$

15) A quadratic function has zeroes at $x = 8$ and $x = -2$. Which of the following is a possible vertex of the function?

A) (3, -25)
B) (3, 0)
C) (4, -24)
D) (5, 21)

$$\frac{3x^2 + 2x + 5}{x + 4}$$

16) The above expression is equivalent to $3x - 10 + m$. Which of the following could be a value of m?

A) 45
B) 35
C) $\frac{35}{x+4}$
D) $\frac{45}{x+4}$

GRID-IN SECTION
Questions 17-20

$$x^2 - 6x + y^2 + 12y = 4$$

17) In the graph of the above circle, what is the maximum distance between any two points on the circle?

18) The function $y = x^2 + kx - 12$ has a root at $x = 2$. What is the value of k?

19) The quadratic equation $y = x^2 - 3x - 88$ has two solutions. What is the sum of the two solutions?

$$\frac{-5}{i^{13} + 2}$$

20) If the above expression is rewritten into the standard form $a + bi$, where a and b are real numbers, what is the value of b?

Lesson 4
Algebra 2
Answer Key

Example Exercises		Application Exercises		Homework Exercises	
1)	$2m^2 - 8m - 5 = 0$	1)	B	1)	D
	$g^2 - 2g - 15 = 0$	2)	C	2)	C
	$x^2 - 4x - 4 = 0$	3)	A	3)	A
2)	$(z+3)(z-1) = 0$	4)	A	4)	C
	$z = 1\ or - 3$	5)	C	5)	C
	$(m+5)(m-5) = 0$	6)	D	6)	A
	$m = \pm 5$	7)	C	7)	D
	$\frac{1}{4}(x+12)(x-4) = 0$	8)	C	8)	D
		9)	B	9)	D
	$x = 4\ or - 12$	10)	D	10)	C
3)	C	11)	1	11)	B
4)	B	12)	49	12)	B
5)	$(0, 5)$	13)	7 or 4	13)	B
6)	155	14)	5	14)	A
7)	9			15)	A
8)	$i - 1$			16)	D
9)	$\frac{9+3i}{5}$			17)	14
10)	$\frac{8+i}{5}$			18)	4
				19)	3
				20)	1

Application Exercises

1. **Choice B is correct.**
Factor the numerator and cancel out like terms:

$$\frac{((x-3)(x+4))}{(x-3)} = 5$$
$$x + 4 = 5$$
$$x = 1$$

2. **Choice C is correct.**
Substitute the term $(x-2)$ for x into the function to obtain:

$$(x-2)^2 - (x-2) - 20 = 0$$
$$(x-2)(x-2) - (x-2) - 20 = 0$$
$$x^2 - 5x - 14 = 0$$

Use the quadratic formula:

$$= \frac{-(-5) \pm \sqrt{-5^2 - 4(1)(-14)}}{2(1)}$$

$$x = -2, 7$$

Therefore,

$$-2 + 7 = 5$$

3. **Choice A is correct.**
Simplify the numerator first, then multiply the fraction by the denominator's conjugate:

$$i^{428} = i^0 = -1$$

Then,

$$= (\frac{1}{3-i})(\frac{3+i}{3+i})$$
$$= (\frac{3+i}{9-i^2})$$
$$= \left(\frac{3+i}{9-(-1)}\right)$$
$$= \frac{3+i}{10}$$

4. **Choice A is correct.**
To determine the number of y-intercepts, n, set the x value of the function to 0:

$$f(0) = x^2 - 3x + 5$$
$$= 0^2 - 3(0) + 5$$
$$= 5$$

Therefore, $n = 1$

To determine the number of x-intercepts, m, utilize the determinant:

$$b^2 - 4(a)(c)$$
$$(-3)^2 - 4(1)(5)$$
$$9 - 20$$
$$-11$$

Since the determinant is less than 0, there is no solution for the function. Therefore, $m = 0$.

Finally,

$$mn = (0)(1) = 0$$

5. **Choice C is correct.**
Isolate the intended quantity $(a + bi)$ by dividing out $(1 + i)$ to both sides, then multiplying the fraction by the conjugate:

$$(a + bi)(1 + i) = 5 + i$$
$$(a + bi) = \frac{(5 + i)}{(1 + i)}$$
$$(a + bi) = \frac{(5 + i)}{(1 + i)}\left(\frac{1-i}{1-i}\right)$$
$$= \frac{5 - 4i - i^2}{1 - i^2}$$
$$= \frac{6 - 4i}{2}$$
$$a + bi = 3 - 2i$$

6. **Choice D is correct.**
Always compute the function inside-out. In this problem, compute $g(-4)$ first, then $f(3)$:

$$f(g(-4)) =$$
$$f(3) =$$
$$5$$

7. **Choice C is correct.**
Multiply the quantity $(-6x + 4)$ by $(\frac{-4x+7}{-4x+7})$ to create a common denominator for all terms, then add all terms to make equivalencies between both sides of the equation:

$$= (-6x + 4)\left(\frac{-4x + 7}{-4x + 7}\right)$$
$$= \frac{24x^2 - 42x - 16x + 28}{-4x + 7}$$
$$= \frac{24x^2 - 58x + 28}{-4x + 7}$$

Add the terms:

$$= \frac{24x^2 - 58x + 28}{-4x + 7} + \frac{4x - 7}{-4x + 7}$$
$$= \frac{24x^2 - 54x + 21}{-4x + 7}$$

Therefore,

$$b = -54$$
$$c = 21$$
$$b + c = -33$$

8. **Choice C is correct.**
Set the given expression equal to the quadratic formula:

$$\frac{-b \pm \sqrt{b^2 - 4ac}}{2a} = \frac{-27 \pm \sqrt{729 - 112n}}{28}$$

Therefore,

$$28 = 2a$$
$$14 = a$$

Based on same deduction, substitute for a:

$$112n = 4ac$$
$$112n = 4(14)c$$
$$2n = c$$

9. **Choice B is correct.**
Find the solutions for $g(x)$ first:

$$0 = x^2 + 8x + 15$$
$$0 = (x+3)(x+5)$$
$$x = -3 \text{ or } x = -5$$

Plug in one of the above solutions of g(x) that will allow for the value of x, for example, (−3):

$$f(x) = x^3 + 3x^2 - 4x - 12$$
$$f(-3) = (-3)^3 + 3(-3)^2 - 4(-3) - 12$$
$$= (-27) + 27 + 12 - 12$$
$$= 0$$

Note: plugging in −5 will NOT yield a zero solution for f(x), therefore, −3 would be the default answer.

10. **Choice D is correct.**
Transformational rules dictate that a coordinate of (6,0) for $h(x-3)+2$ must be moved to the RIGHT three times and moved UP twice. Therefore:

$$(6+3, 0+2) =$$
$$(9,2)$$

11. **The correct answer is 1**
The zeros are the solutions of the function in the numerator, whereas the impossible solution is the zero value of x in the denominator that provides an undefined fraction.

The zeros are found by factoring:

$$(x^2 - 6x + 8)$$
$$x^2 - 6x + 8 = 0$$
$$(x-2)(x-4) = 0$$
$$x = 2 \text{ or } x = 4$$

The x value for a denominator that gives an impossible solution is found by variable isolation:

$$x - 5 = 0$$
$$x = 5$$

Subtract this value from the sum of the solutions:

$$(2+4) - 5 = 1$$

12. **The correct answer is 49**
Work backwards to determine the quadratic:

$$x = 11, or\ x = -3$$

Therefore,

$$(x - 11)(x + 3) = 0$$
$$x^2 + 8x - 33 = 0$$

The x-coordinate of the vertex is found by:

$$x - coor. of\ vertex = -\frac{b}{2a}$$
$$= -\frac{8}{2(1)}$$
$$= -\frac{8}{2}$$
$$= -4$$

Plug this x value back into function to determine y-coordinate of the vertex:

$$f(x) = x^2 + 8x - 33$$
$$= 4^2 + 8(-4) - 33$$
$$= 16 - 32 - 33$$
$$= -49$$
$$-n = -49$$

Therefore,

$$n = 49$$

13. **The correct answer is 7 or 4**
Set the two equations to each other to determine their intersection (solution):

$$x + 2 = x^2 - 6x + 12$$
$$0 = x^2 - 7x + 10$$
$$0 = (x - 2)(x - 5)$$
$$x = 2, or\ x = 5$$

Plug-in the 'x' values to equation 1:

$$(2) + 2 = 4$$
$$(5) + 2 = 7$$

Therefore,

$$y = 4\ or\ y = 7$$

14. **The correct answer is 5**
Solve for the function utilizing the quadratic equation:

$$= \frac{-(-4) \pm \sqrt{(-4)^2 - 4(1)(n)}}{2(1)}$$
$$= \frac{4 \pm \sqrt{16 - 4n}}{2}$$
$$= \frac{4}{2} \pm \frac{\sqrt{4(4-n)}}{2}$$
$$= 2 \pm \frac{2\sqrt{(4-n)}}{2}$$
$$= 2 \pm \sqrt{(4-n)}$$

Since the solutions provided are $2 \pm i$,

$$2 \pm i = 2 \pm \sqrt{(4-n)}$$
$$i = \sqrt{4-n}$$
$$\sqrt{-1} = \sqrt{4-n}$$
$$-1 = 4 - n$$
$$5 = n$$

Homework Exercises

1. **Choice D is correct**
Plug in 2x for x into the function:

$$g(x) = 3x^2$$
$$g(2x) = 3(2x)^2$$
$$= 3(4)x^2$$
$$= 12x^2$$

2. **Choice C is correct**
Utilizing the determinant, the problem can be translated as:

$$0 = b^2 - 4ac$$
$$0 = (12)^2 - 4(1)(n)$$
$$0 = 144 - 4n$$
$$144 = 4n$$
$$36 = n$$

3. **Choice A is correct**
Utilizing transformation theory, starting from (6,3) we move RIGHT three and UP five to obtain:

$$(6 + 3, 3 + 5)$$
$$(9, 8)$$

4. **Choice C is correct**
Simplifying all of the answer choices creates choices A, B, and D equivalent to $(x - 4)^2$ whereas choice C yields:

$$x^2 - 6x$$

To double check, plug in the coordinate value of (4,0) to confirm.

5. **Choice C is correct.**
This conceptual question requires an understanding of how solutions in functions work. When a quantity is multiplied by a quantity, one of them must be equal to zero to solve for the function, like so:

$$(x + 2)(x - 3)(x - 5) = 0$$

Therefore,

$$x + 2 = 0 \; or \; x - 3 = 0 \; or \; x - 5 = 0$$
$$x = -2 \; or \; x = 3 \; or \; x = 5$$

6. **Choice A is correct.**
Factor the expression as follows:

$$0 = x^4 - 13x^2 + 36$$
$$0 = (x^2 - 4)(x^2 - 9)$$
$$0 = (x + 2)(x - 2)(x + 3)(x - 3)$$

Therefore,

$$x = -2, 2, -3, 3$$

7. **Choice D is correct.**
Determine $f(-2)$ first by finding the coordinate on the graph:

$$f(-2) = 0$$

Therefore, $g(f(-2)) = g(0)$:

$$g(0) = 2$$

8. **Choice D is correct.**
A relative minimum is the lowest point shown on the graph for $g(x) = -2$.

Therefore, $g(2) = -2$

9. **Choice D is correct.**
Factor by grouping. Note that (x^2) can be factored out from the first group:

$$= [x^3 + 3x^2] - [2x - 6]$$
$$= (x + 3)[x^2] - [2x - 6]$$

Note that (x+3) can now be factored out from the second group:

$$= (x + 3)[x^2] + (x + 3)[-2]$$

Re-express:

$$= (x + 3)(x^2 - 2)$$

10. **Choice C is correct.**
Simplify the fractions first:

$$0 = \frac{4x}{x + 3} + \frac{x^2}{x + 2} + \frac{x}{x + 3}$$
$$0 = \frac{5x}{x + 3} + \frac{x^2}{x + 2}$$

Multiply both sides of the equation by $(x + 3)(x + 2)$:

$$0 = (5x)(x + 2) + x^2(x + 3)$$
$$0 = 5x^2 + 10x + x^3 + 3x^2$$
$$0 = x^3 + 8x^2 + 10x$$

The equation has a variable raised to the power of 3, therefore, the maximum number of roots it may possess is three.

11. **Choice B is correct.**
The line of symmetry can be determined by the x-coordinate of the vertex:

$$= \frac{-b}{2a}$$
$$= \frac{-(-2\pi)}{2(h)}$$
$$= \frac{\pi}{h}$$

12. **Choice B is correct.**
Set the two equations equal to each other to determine the solutions:

$$x - 5 = x^2 - 3x - 2$$

Solve for x:

$$0 = x^2 - 4x + 3$$
$$0 = (x - 3)(x - 1)$$
$$x = 3 \; or \; x = 1$$

Plug in either answer choice to determine that only one solution $(1, -4)$ will work amongst the answer choices.

13. **Choice B is correct.**
The maximum height of the given quadratic function is the vertex, whose x-coordinate is determined by:

$$x - coordinate = -\frac{b}{2a}$$
$$= -\frac{16}{2(-2)}$$
$$x = 4 \; seconds$$

Plug this value back into the function to obtain:

$$h(t) = -2t^2 + 16t + 18$$
$$h(4) = -2(4)^2 + 16(4) + 18$$
$$y = -32 + 64 + 18$$
$$y = 50 \; feet$$

14. **Choice A is correct.**
Multiply both sides by 2 to obtain:

$$2\left(\frac{1}{2}\right)x^2 - 2(5) = 2\left(\frac{3}{2}\right)x$$
$$x^2 - 10 = 3x$$
$$x^2 - 3x + 10 = 0$$
$$(x - 5)(x + 2) = 0$$
$$x = 5 \; or \; x = -2$$

15. **Choice A is correct.**
Reconstruct the quadratic by FOIL:

$$y = (x - 8)(x + 2)$$
$$y = x^2 - 6x - 16$$

Find the x-coordinate of the vertex:

$$= -\frac{b}{2a}$$
$$= -\frac{(-6)}{2(1)}$$
$$x - coordinate = 3$$

Plug this back into the function to determine the y-value:

$$y = (x - 8)(x + 2)$$
$$y = (3 - 8)(3 + 2)$$
$$y - coordinate = -25$$

16. **Choice D is correct.**
Perform polynomial division:

$$\begin{array}{r} 3x - 10 \\ x+4 \overline{) \; 3x^2 + 2x + 5} \\ 3x^2 + 12x \\ \hline -10x + 5 \\ -10x - 40 \\ \hline 45 \end{array}$$

Therefore, with 45 as the remainder:

$$\frac{3x^2 + 2x + 5}{x + 4} = 3x - 10 + \frac{45}{x + 4}$$

So:

$$m = \frac{45}{x + 4}$$

17. **The correct answer is 14**
The problem asks for the diameter of the given circle. Complete the square:

$$[x^2 - 6x] + [y^2 + 12y] = 4$$

$$[x^2 - 6x + 9] + [y^2 + 12y + 36] = 4 + 9 + 36$$

$$(x - 3)^2 + (y + 6)^2 = 49$$

Therefore,

$$r^2 = 49$$
$$r = 7$$
$$d = 14$$

18. **The correct answer is 4**
Since one of the roots is given, substitute the value into the function then solve for k:

$$y = x^2 + kx - 12$$
$$0 = 2^2 + k(2) - 12$$
$$0 = 2k - 8$$
$$8 = 2k$$
$$4 = k$$

19. **The correct answer is 3**
Utilize the quadratic formula:

$$= \frac{-(-3) \pm \sqrt{(-3)^2 - 4(1)(-88)}}{2(1)}$$
$$= \frac{3 \pm \sqrt{9 + 352}}{2}$$
$$= \frac{3 \pm \sqrt{361}}{2}$$
$$= \frac{3 + 19}{2} \ or \ \frac{3 - 19}{2}$$
$$= \frac{22}{2} or -\frac{16}{2}$$
$$\text{x} = 11 \text{ or } \text{x} = -8$$

Therefore,

$$11 + (-8) = 3$$

20. **The correct answer is 1**
Simplify i^{13} first, then multiply by the conjugate:

$$i^{13} = i^1$$

So,

$$= \frac{-5}{i^1 + 2} (\frac{i - 2}{i - 2})$$
$$= \frac{-5i + 10}{i^2 - 4}$$
$$= \frac{-5i + 10}{(-1) - 4}$$
$$= \frac{-5i + 10}{-5}$$
$$= i - 2$$

In $a + bi$ form:

$$-2 + i = a + bi$$
$$b = 1$$

Mathematics
Lesson 5

Geometry 1

Goals

We will develop our mathematical fluency and gain meaningful understanding by learning to:

1) Identify key concepts of lines and angles on the coordinate plane
2) Create, identify, graph, interpret and solve linear equations and their systems
3) Apply fundamental triangle rules (triangle inequality, etc.) to examples
4) Use special right triangles and Pythagorean triples to quickly and efficiently solve problems
5) Use polygon formulas to quickly find interior and exterior angle measures

Contents

- Lines and Angles
- Linear Equations
- Triangles
- Quadrilaterals & Other Polygons
- Volume

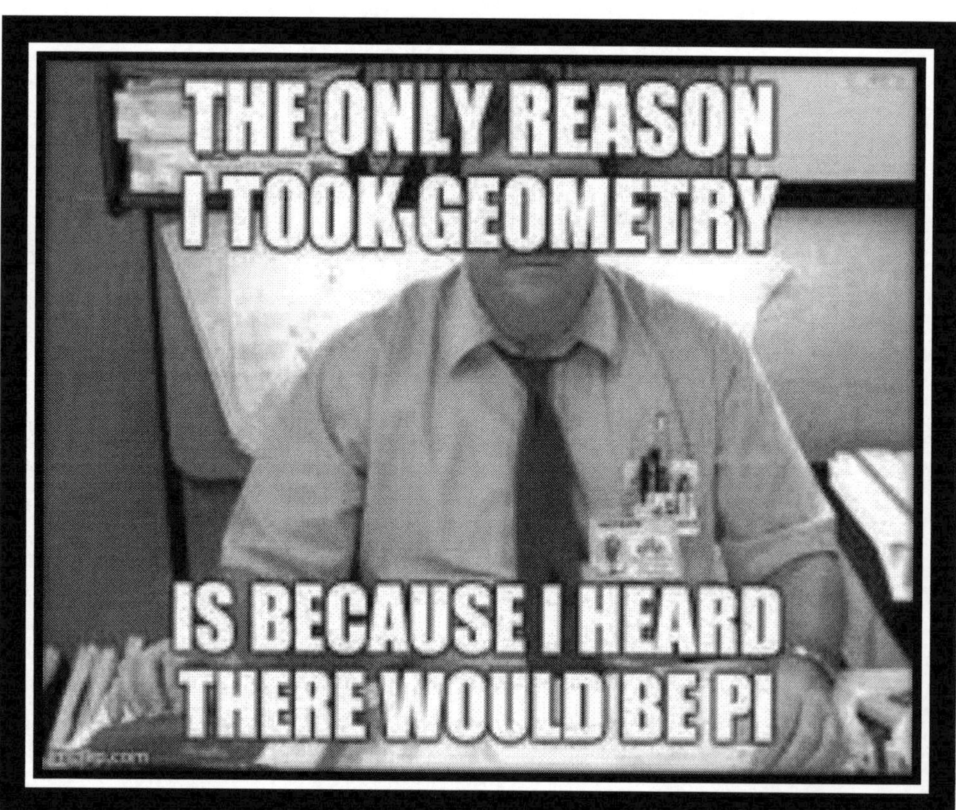

Lesson 5
Geometry 1

Lines & Angles

Lines are imaginary, straight, and infinite. There is a 180 degree measure across a straight line, and can interact with other lines. One of the most common interactions involves two parallel lines cut by a transversal.

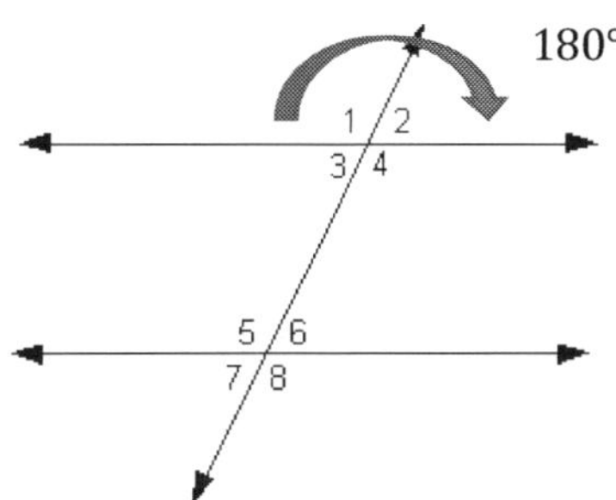

Supplementary angles $\angle 1 + \angle 2 = 180°$, while vertical angles $\angle 1 = \angle 4$. Since both lines are parallel, angles $\angle 1 = \angle 4 \angle = \angle 5 = \angle 8$ and $\angle 2 = \angle 3 = \angle 6 = \angle 7$.

Also, many relationships between lines and angles will center on complementary relationships as well, so it is important to recognize when two angles add up to 90°. Remember, supplementary angles add up to 180°, while complementary angles add up to 90°.

Rudimentary representation of lines and their properties may seem exactly that: rudimentary. However, there are many ways this can be tested, so learn to recognize figures and shapes that contain such lines and angles. Referring to the fundamentals will help you to frame your approach to difficult problems.

Linear equations

Depicting a line on a coordinate plane, linear equations can be expressed in one of two common ways: (1) the slope intercept form and (2) the point-slope form. These forms are derivatives of each other, and our skillset will go well beyond merely recognizing them.

Slope intercept form is represented by the equation $\boldsymbol{y = mx + b}$, where m is the slope and b is the y-intercept. **Slope,** also known as "rise over run," can be found by dividing the difference of y values over the difference of x values using any two coordinates on a line.

The **y-intercept**, or the point where the line touches the y-axis, can be determined by plugging in zero (0) as the x value in the slope intercept equation, leaving us with the value of b.

eg. 1 What is the linear equation of a line that passes through the coordinates $(4, 5)$ and $(0, -3)$? (*Provide your answer in slope intercept form*)

Point-slope form is represented by $y - y_1 = m(x - x_1)$ or $\boldsymbol{y_1 - y_2 = m(x_1 - x_2)}$. We can see that this is really a re-expression of the definition of slope (dividing both sides by $(x_1 - x_2)$ gives us m). This form comes in handy if we are given the slope and just one coordinate, which we can plug into x_1 and y_1.

eg. 2 What is the equation of a line in point-slope form that contains coordinate $(4, -2)$ with a slope of $\frac{2}{3}$?

A typical linear equation is depicted on the coordinate plane to the right. There are several different facets of linear equations we should be familiar with.

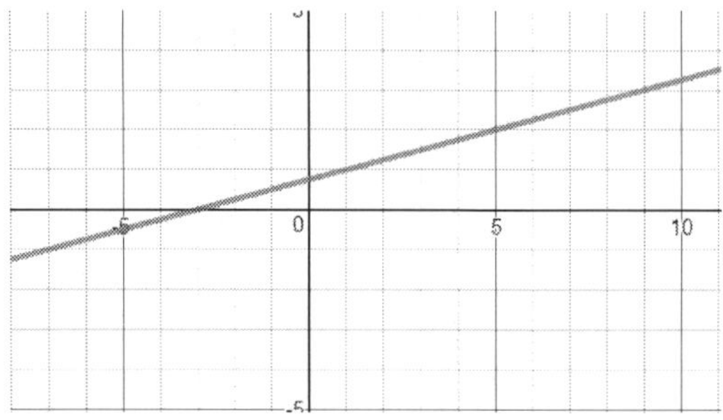

A straight line that is parallel to the x-axis will always have the form $y = n$, where n equals a certain number. This type of line will have a slope of zero (0). On the other hand, a line that is parallel to the y-axis will have the form $x = n$. This type of line will have an undefined slope, since the denominator of m will be a zero value.

An alternate way of determining a slope of a line involves counting the rise vs. run aspect on a coordinate plane – just make sure that the units are "one-to-one".

eg 3. What is the slope of the line shown to the right? (Solve both algebraically and visually)

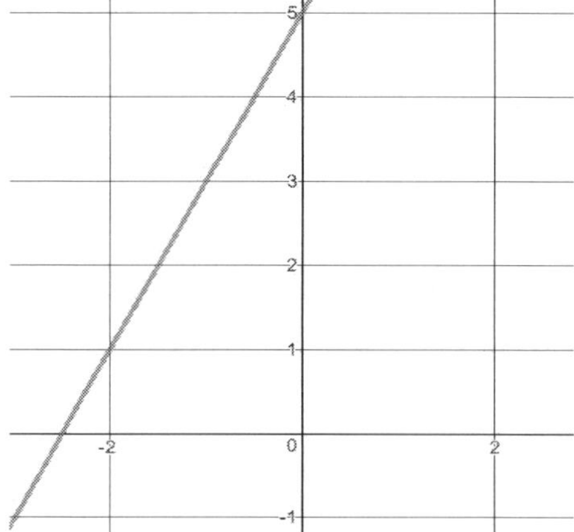

Some other things to note about slopes:

- A positive (+) slope will cross through quadrants I and III, while a negative (-) slope will cross through quadrants II and IV.
- Parallel lines share the same slope.
- Perpendicular lines share slopes that have opposite-reciprocal relationships: if line l has a slope of $\frac{3}{5}$ and is perpendicular to line m, the slope of line m would be $-\frac{5}{3}$.

eg 4. If line m has a slope of $\frac{1}{3}$ and it passes through the point (3,3) what is the y-intercept of perpendicular line n with a coordinate (1,0)?

eg 5. What is the y-intercept of the following equation: $\frac{1}{y}+\frac{3}{2y}=5$?

A) $\frac{1}{2}$

B) $\frac{1}{3}$

C) $\frac{1}{4}$

D) $\frac{1}{8}$

If two linear equations intersect, they share a "solution," or common coordinate. In these circumstances, setting the equations equal will determine the solution. Questions that test this relational aspect will involve systems of equations provided in some form or another.

eg 6. If the two equations below intersect at a certain coordinate, what is the solution to the equation system below?

$$y = 4x + 4$$
$$y = -2x - 2$$

Triangles

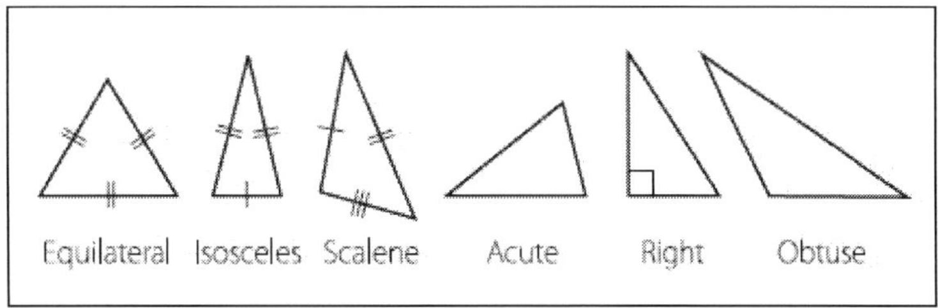

A triangle is a polygon with only three sides. There are many types, as exemplified above. Some essential facts for all triangles are as follows:

- *The Angular Sum*: All three angles of a triangle add up to 180 degrees
- *Area of a Triangle*: The area is equal to half of the base multiplied by the height ($\frac{1}{2}bh$)
- *Perimeter of a Triangle*: The perimeter of a triangle is the sum of the three sides
- *Isosceles Triangles*: In an isosceles triangle, two sides and their opposite angles are equal, but not to the third side and angle
- *Equilateral Triangle*: In an equilateral triangle, all three sides are equal, and their opposing angles are all $60°$
- *Exterior Angle*: An exterior angle of a triangle is equal to the sum of the opposite interior angles, and is also supplemental to the angle with it (adds to $180°$)
- *Triangle Inequality Theorem*: The sum of the lengths of any two sides of a triangle is greater than the length of the third. (Also: The difference of any two sides of a triangle is lesser than the length of the third)

eg. 7 If two sides of a scalene triangle correspond to 12 and 8 respectively, which of the following is a possible value of the third side?

A) 24
B) 22
C) 20
D) 18

Note that in the above example, there can only be one possible answer since the sum of the two given sides is 20, and therefore the third side must be less than 20. Hence, answer choice D.

There are many variations that exists when it comes to triangles: right triangles, angular variations, similar triangles, and inscribed triangles all have different considerations. Learn to work with all of these different types in the Pittsburgh Prep problem sets, and you'll have a greater chance of attaining your best score on exam day.

Right Triangles

Right triangles are special triangles that have been studied for a thousand years. They have one angle with a $90°$ measure, which is opposite the hypotenuse, and two other angles/sides. To determine the length of each side of a triangle, we can look to the Pythagorean Theorem, which states: $a^2 + b^2 = c^2$ where *a, b* are the two sides and *c* is the hypotenuse. Below is a fun explanation from NASA, of all places (note: it uses *h* for hypotenuse instead of *c*):

Pythagorean Theorem

Glenn Research Center

For any right triangle with sides a and b and hypotenuse h, the square of the hypotenuse is equal to the sum of the squares of the other two sides.

$$h^2 = a^2 + b^2$$

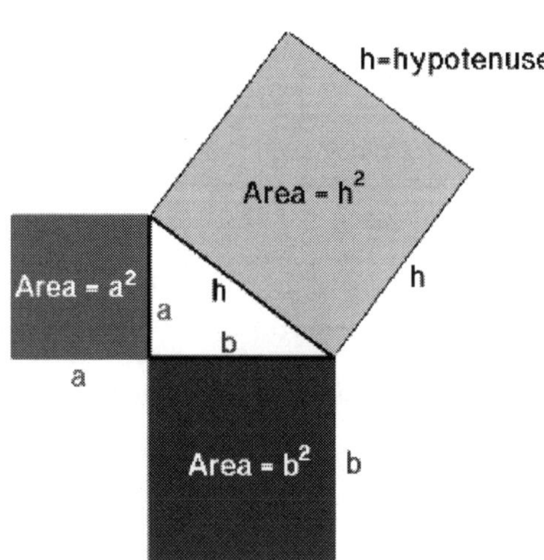

Pythagorean Triplets are right triangles that have all side lengths as integers. Some common triplet right triangles are $3-4-5$, $5-12-13$, and $7-24-25$, as well as any multiples of those sides ($6-8-10$ is a multiple of a $3-4-5$ triplet triangle). The triangles below are all variations of the $3-4-5$ triangle, with multiples of $2x$, $3x$, and $\sqrt{3}x$. Note that respective sides correspond to each other in multiples.

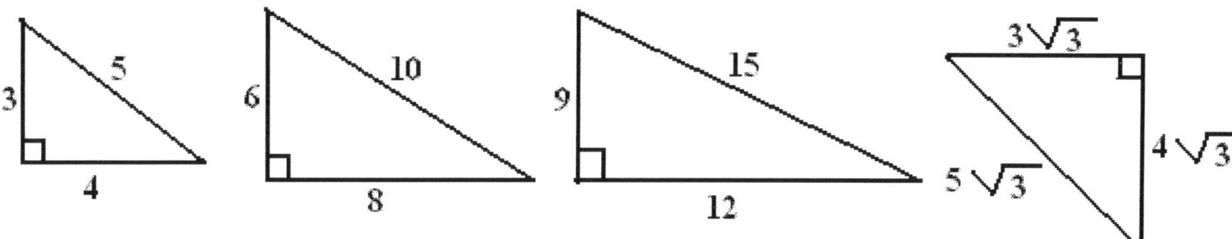

Two incredibly important special right triangles involve *two angular triangles*. They are the $30-60-90$ and $45-45-90$ triangles. The $30-60-90$ is a common triangle that is important not just on its own, but as a pair: two $30-60-90$ triangles, when placed together by the long legs (the $\sqrt{3}$ side), will make an equilateral triangle. With the right isosceles, or the $45-45-90$ triangle, placing two together alongside the hypotenuses, will make a square. The $45-45-90$ and $30-60-90$ all have special side relationships as shown below:

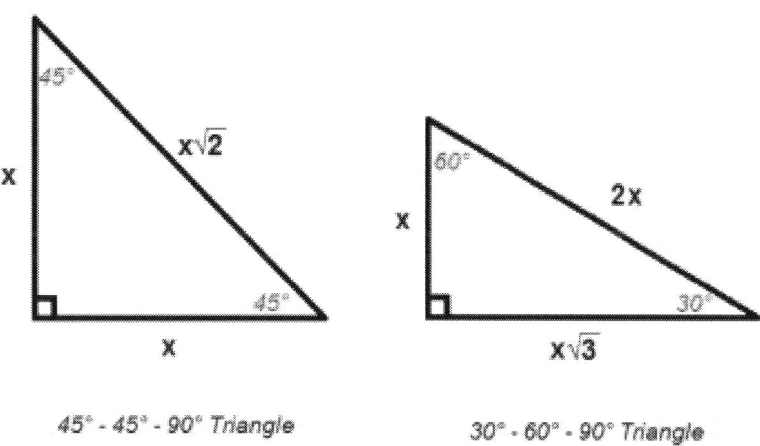

45° - 45° - 90° Triangle

30° - 60° - 90° Triangle

eg. 8 What is the area of an isosceles right triangle whose hypotenuse is 8?

An isosceles right triangle with a hypotenuse of 8 is a 45-45-90 triangle with the long side of 8. Since we know that the hypotenuse is $x\sqrt{2} = 8$, we obtain:

$$x\sqrt{2} = 8$$

$$x = \frac{8}{\sqrt{2}}\left(\frac{\sqrt{2}}{\sqrt{2}}\right) \leftarrow rationalize$$

$$x = \frac{8\sqrt{2}}{2}$$

$$x = 4\sqrt{2}$$

Similar triangles share the same angular measures and different, but proportional, sides. They can be depicted as triangles within triangles, or two separate entities. If we can deduce that at least two angles are the same between two triangles, we can also deduce that the two triangles are similar.

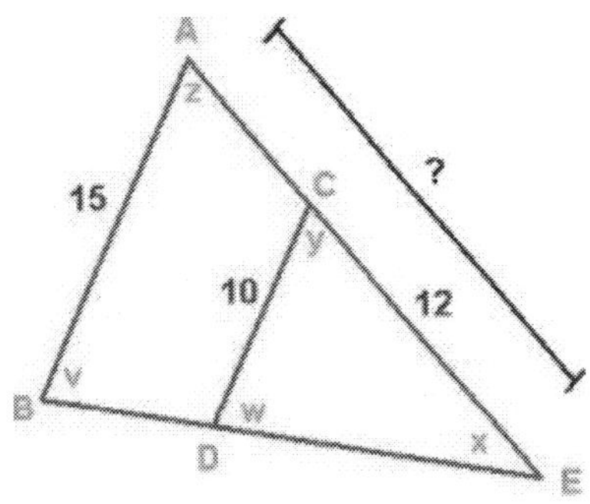

eg. 9 In the figure above, if $\overline{AB} \parallel \overline{CD}$, what is the length of $\overline{AE}$?

A) 12
B) 14
C) 18
D) Cannot be determined

In this problem, we note that the two triangles are in fact similar since parallel lines create corresponding angles when cut by a transversal (plus they both share angle x). Therefore, we can then set up a proportion as follows:

$$\frac{15}{10} = \frac{\overline{AE}}{12}$$

$$\frac{(12)15}{10} = \overline{AE}$$

$$18 = \overline{AE}$$

Inscribed triangles within circles have distinct properties. Within a circle, any inscribed angle whose vertex lies on the circle intercepts an arc that is twice its measure, whereas central angles intercept the arc's actual measure.

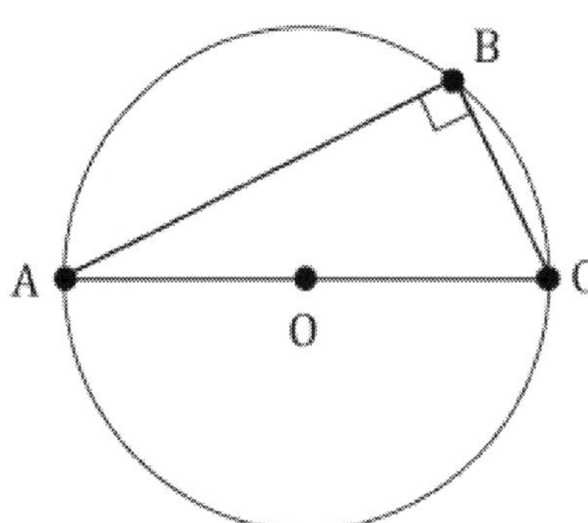

It's important to note that all inscribed triangles have a 90° measure when the hypotenuse is the diameter of the circle. This is because $\angle B$ is a minor angle to the central angle. Minor angles are always $\frac{1}{2}$ the central angle in circles.

Polygons

Of course, there are more shapes than triangles. There are two general aspects of polygons that will be essential to finding both interior and exterior angles of polygons. Let's take a look at both aspects together.

Interior Angles of Polygons

When finding the interior angles of polygons, find a pattern. Look at the four regular polygons below:

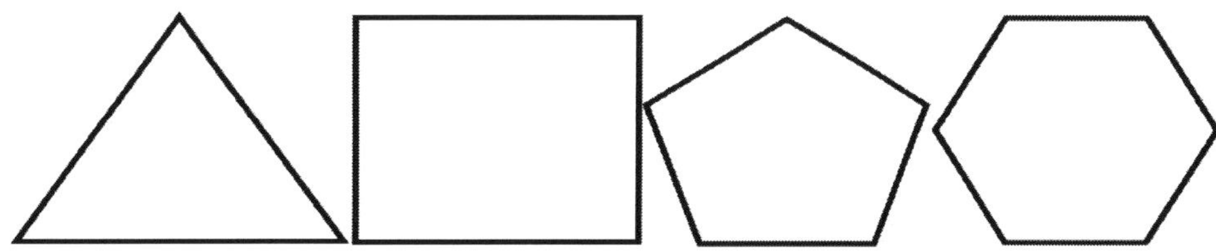

Sides	Three	Four	Five	Six
Interior Angle	60°	90°	108°	120°
Int. Angle Sum	180°	360°	540°	720°

Note that every additional side in a polygon adds 180° to the sum of the interior angles. The formula to express the total angular sum is $(n-2)(180)$, where n is the number of sides in the polygon.

In order to find the individual angular measure of a "regular" polygon, divide the total interior angular measure by the number of sides. A "regular" polygon is a figure with equal sides and angles.

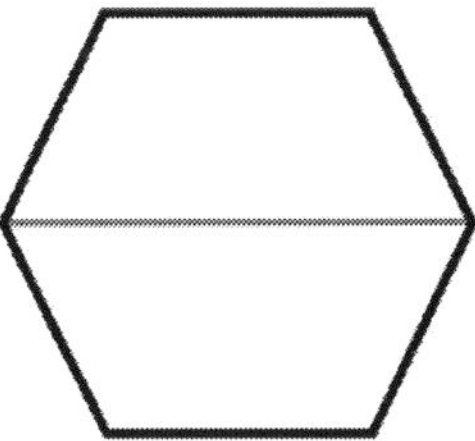

eg. 10 The regular hexagon above is divided along its diameters, as shown. If the individual side lengths is 2, what is the length of the diameter?

A) $2\sqrt{3}$
B) 4
C) $4\sqrt{3}$
D) Cannot be determined

Exterior Angles of Polygons

Exterior angles are created when the side of a polygon is extended. The exterior angle is the *supplement* of the interior angle: adding the two angles gives us $180°$. The more important fact with exterior angles is that the sum of the exterior angles for any polygon is always $360°$.

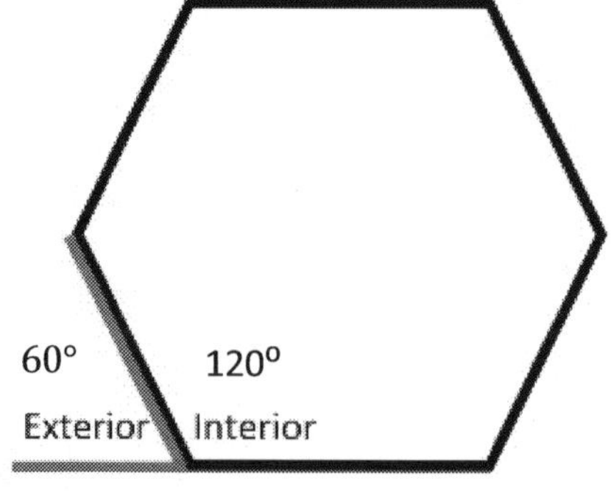

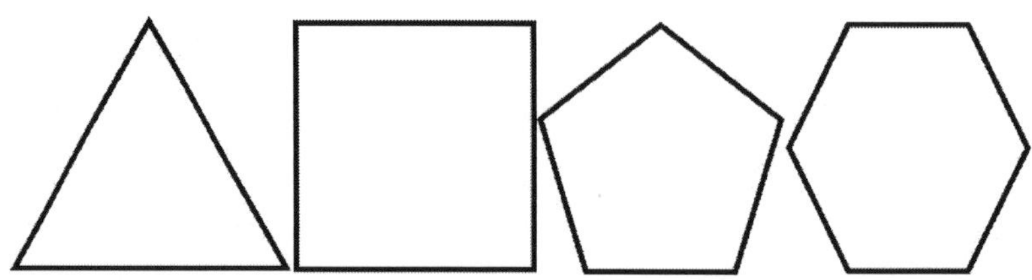

Sides	Three	Four	Five	Six
Exterior Angle	120°	90°	72°	60°
Ext. Angle Sum	360°	360°	360°	360°

eg. 11 How many sides does a polygon have if it's exterior angle measures exactly 40°?

Volume

Volume asks the question: how much space does an object take up? Volume is a three-dimensional object, so it must have three variables to consider. A box, for instance, will have a volume: $v = lwh$, where l = length, w = width, and h = height. A soup can, for instance, is a right circular cylinder whose volume is: $v = (\pi r^2 h)$ where r = the radius of the cylinder and h = the height. Most times, the volume formula of an object will be provided for you on the exam.

eg. 12 What is the difference (rounded to the nearest tenth) in volume between a right cylinder $v = \pi r^2 h$ with a radius of 4 cm and a height of 5 cm, and a rectangular prism ($v = lwh$)with a height of 4 cm, width of 5 cm and a depth of 3 cm?

PITTSBURGH PREP

Lesson 5
Geometry 1
Application Exercises

NO CALCULATOR SECTION
Questions 1-5

Time - 20 Minutes

1) In the figure below, two parallel lines are crossed by a transversal. What is the value of 3x?

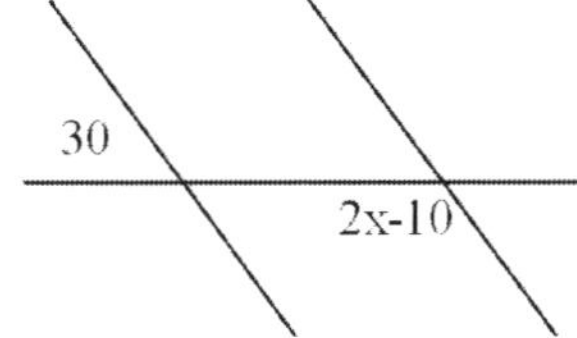

Note: Figure not drawn to scale

A) 80°
B) 180°
C) 360°
D) 240°

2) ΔOSP and ΔQRP are equilateral triangles on $\overline{QO}$, which has a length of 15. What is the total perimeter of the triangles?

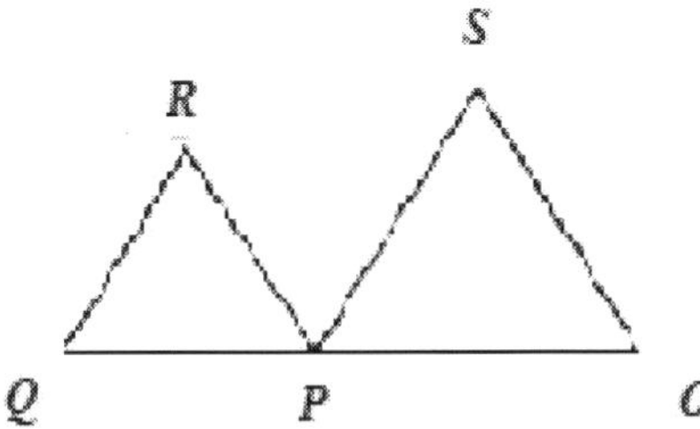

A) 15
B) 30
C) 45
D) 52

3) What is the value of c in terms of b in the figure below, if $a = 4b$?

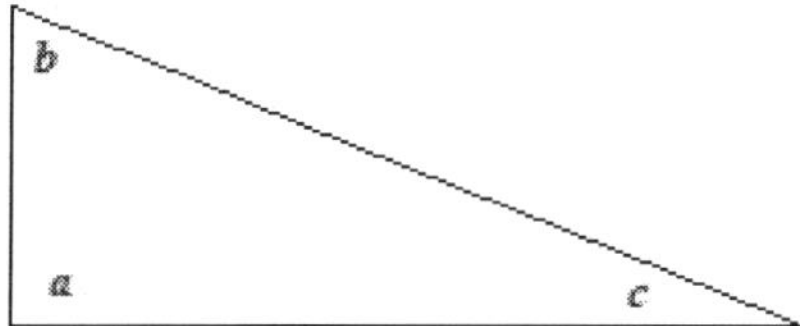

Note: Figure not drawn to scale

A) $180 + 5b$
B) $180 + 4b$
C) $180 - 4b$
D) 180 – 5b

4) A large box with dimensions of $3 \times 4 \times 5$ is filled with large tennis balls with a radius of 1. If the volume of a sphere is found with the formula $V = \frac{4}{3}\pi r^3$, what is the maximum amount of balls that can fit in the box?

A) 4
B) 8
C) 10
D) 12

5) If a certain square has a diagonal that measures exactly 9, then what is the perimeter of the square?

A) 18
B) $18\sqrt{2}$
C) 36
D) $36\sqrt{2}$

CALCULATOR SECTION
Questions 6-10

6) In the figure below, $\overline{ZY} = 13$, $\overline{CZ} = 5$, and $\overline{CX} = 4\sqrt{7}$. What is the length of $\overline{XY}$?

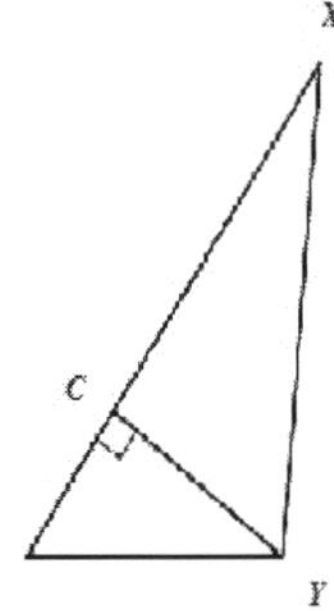

Note: Figure not drawn to scale

A) 12
B) 16
C) 20
D) 35

7) What is the distance between the points $(4, 2)$ and $(8, -3)$ in the coordinate plane?

A) $\sqrt{3}$
B) 3
C) 5
D) $\sqrt{41}$

8) In the figure below, three adjacent squares with sides 3, 5 and x, what is the area of the shaded areas if A, B, and C all lie on line ℓ?

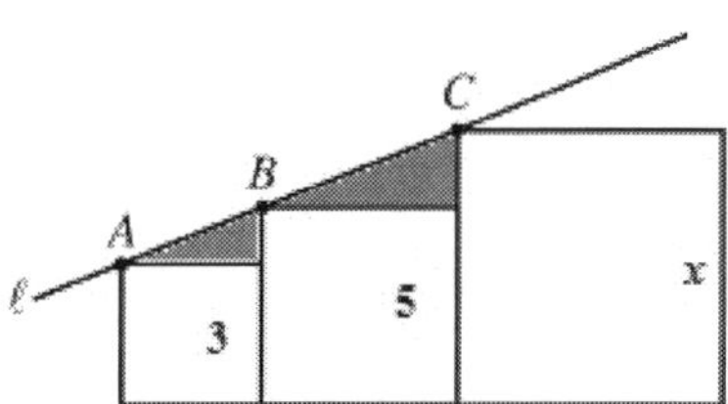

Note: Figure not drawn to scale

A) Cannot be determined from the information given
B) 8
C) $10\frac{1}{3}$
D) $11\frac{1}{3}$

9) In the circle below with center O, $m\angle AOB = 5x + 2y + 6$, $m\angle BOC = 10y - 10$, and $m\angle BCO = 2x + 2y - 5$. What is the value of x?

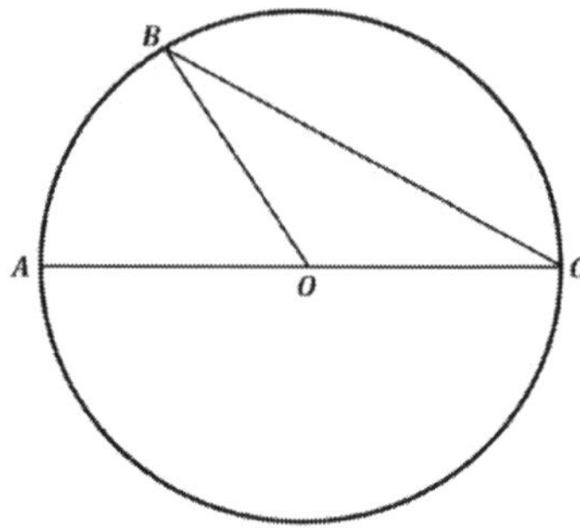

A) 3
B) 8
C) 12
D) Cannot be determined from the information given

10) An equilateral triangle has an area of $\sqrt{48}$. What is the length of one side of the triangle?

A) 4
B) $4\sqrt{3}$
C) 8
D) $8\sqrt{3}$

GRID-IN SECTION
Questions 11-14

11) An isosceles triangle with one internal angle measuring $100°$ has external angles $2n$, $3n + 20$, and $5n - 60$. What is the measure of n?

12) On the coordinate plane, line l can be found with the equation $y = 2x + 5$. Line m is the reflection of line l across the y-axis, and line n is perpendicular to line m. What is the slope of line n?

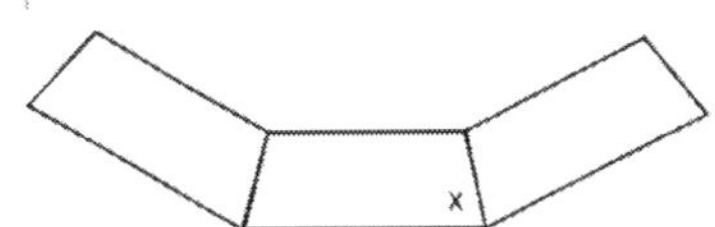

13) A group of trapezoids are placed end to end to make a full regular polygon with n sides, where n is the number of trapezoids making the larger regular polygon. If $m\angle x = 75$, what is the number of trapezoids creating the polygon?

14) If $f(x) = 2x + 2$, $g(x)$ is the reflection of $f(x)$ across the x-axis, and $h(x)$ is the reflection of $f(x)$ across the y-axis, what is the distance between the y-intercept of $f(x)$ and the y-intercept of $h(x)$?

Lesson 5
Geometry 1
Homework Exercises

NO CALCULATOR SECTION
Questions 1-8

Time - 25 Minutes

1) In the figure below, lines l and m are parallel, as are lines n and p. If lines m and n intersect at angle x, what is the measure of angle x?

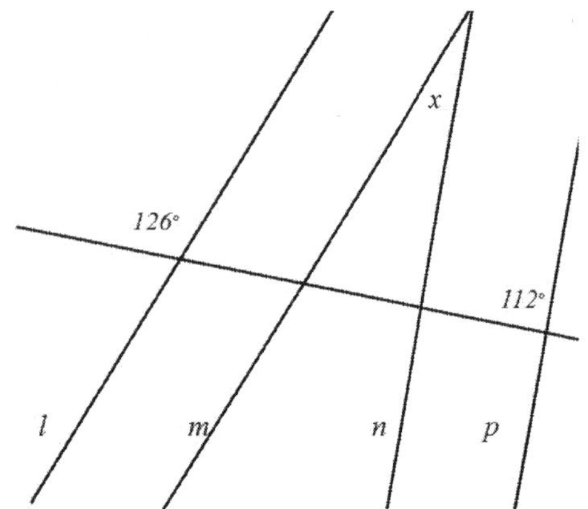

A) 14^0
B) 54^0
C) 58^0
D) 68^0

2) If the line $y = -\frac{2}{3}x - h$ does not pass through the third quadrant, what is a possible value of h?

A) -5
B) 1
C) 3
D) 5

3) An equilateral triangle has a base of 15. What is the height of the triangle?

A) $\frac{15}{2}$

B) $\frac{15\sqrt{3}}{2}$

C) 15
D) $15\sqrt{3}$

4) The line l passes through coordinates $(5, m)$ and $(7, n)$. Which of the following is the slope of l?

A) $\frac{n-m}{2}$

B) $\frac{m-n}{2}$

C) $\frac{n-m}{12}$

D) $\frac{2}{m-n}$

5) In the triangle below, what is a logical value for n?

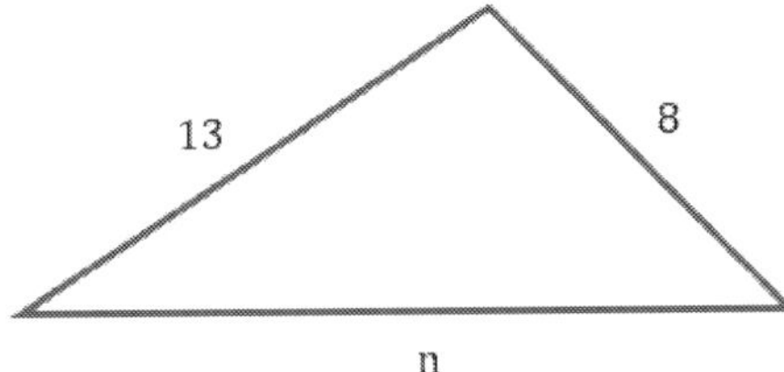

A) 25
B) 21
C) 14
D) 5

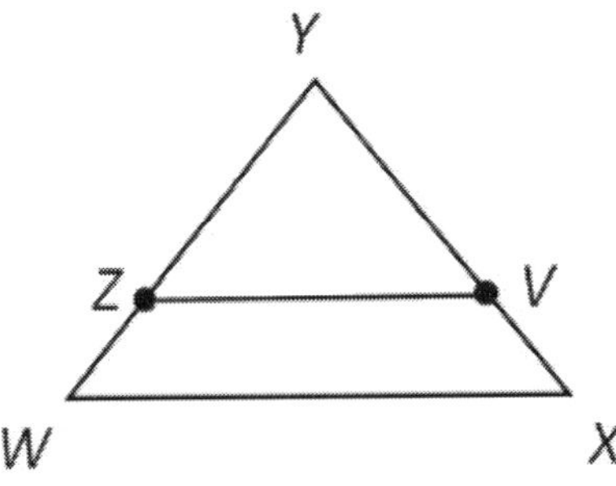

Note: Figure not drawn to scale

6) In the figure above, points Z and V are the midpoint of sides WY and XY respectively. If triangle *WXY* is isosceles and if side WX is m meters long, what is the value of ZV?

A) $2m$
B) m
C) $\frac{m}{2}$
D) $\frac{m}{4}$

7) Which of the following inequalities is shown in the number line below?

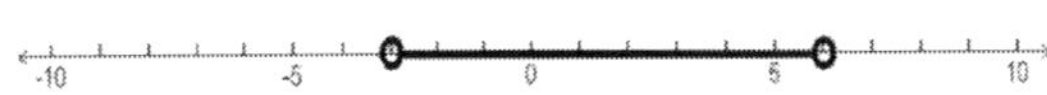

A) $6 < 6 - 2x < 12$
B) $6 > 6 - 2x > 12$
C) $|x - 1.5| > 4.5$
D) $|x - 1.5| < 4.5$

8) In the figure below, what is the value of $x + y$?

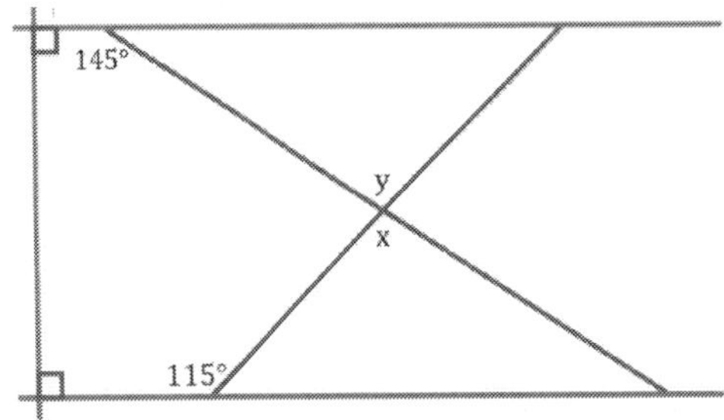

A) 95
B) 105
C) 160
D) 260

PITTSBURGH PREP

CALCULATOR SECTION
Questions 9-16

9) Two points on Line l are at $(3, 2)$ and $(10, 26)$. What is the distance between these two points?

A) 17
B) 23
C) 25
D) 31

10) Which of the following inequalities is true about the side lengths, a and b, of a right triangle whose hypotenuse is equal to 25?

A) $625 < (a+b)^2$
B) $0 < (a+b)^2 < 25$
C) $25 < (a+b)^2 < 50$
D) $25 \leq (a+b)^2 < 625$

11) The volume of Cone A is 16 cubic inches. Cone A's height is tripled, and its diameter is halved to make Cone B. What is the volume of Cone B?

A) $\frac{23}{2}$
B) 12
C) 16
D) 24

12) The roots of the quadratic $x^2 - x - 6$ and the point (3,5) forms a triangle. What is the area of that triangle?

A) $\frac{15}{2}$
B) $\frac{25}{2}$
C) 15
D) 20

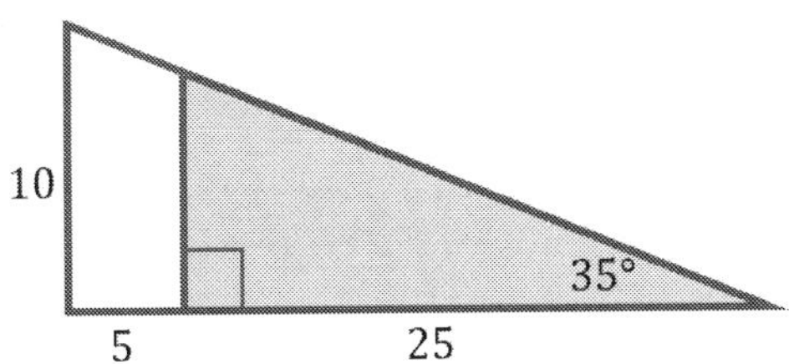

13) A sail is attached to a ten-foot mast, as shown above. The sail is twenty-five feet long at the bottom and is rigged five feet away from the bottom of the mast. If the sail must be perpendicular to the mast. What is the height of the sail?

A) 7
B) $\frac{25}{3}$
C) 9
D) $\frac{29}{3}$

14) A right isosceles triangle has vertices at (3,3) and (7,3). Which of the following are possible areas of the triangle?

i. 4
ii. $8\sqrt{2}$
iii. 8

A) i only
B) iii only
C) i and iii only
D) $i, ii,$ and iii

15) What is the area of the triangle below?

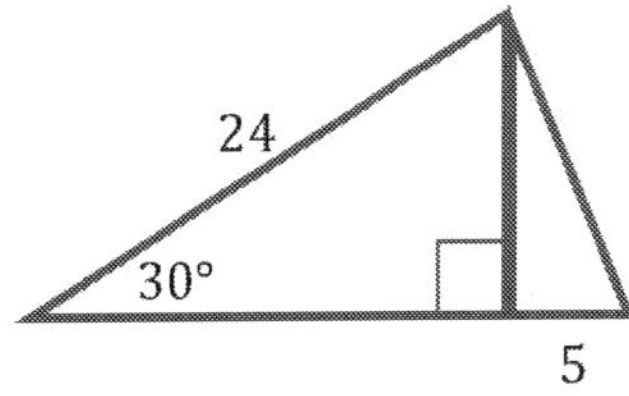

A) 60
B) $72\sqrt{3}$
C) $72\sqrt{3} + 30$
D) $144\sqrt{3}$

16) The lines $y = 0, y = \frac{2}{3}x, and\ y = -\frac{1}{2}x + 7$ form a triangle with a perimeter that rounds to which integer value?

A) 14
B) 18
C) 27
D) 31

GRID-IN SECTION
Questions 17-20

17) If a line has a positive slope and positive y-intercept, and passes through the point (3,5), what is a possible y-intercept of that line?

18) A right isosceles triangle has an area of 180.5 units. What is the perimeter of the triangle, rounded to the nearest integer?

19) A scalene triangle has sides of 9 and 13. What is a possible length of the third side?

20) What is the difference in the measure of the interior angle of a nonagon (nine-sided polygon) and a dodecagon (twelve-sided polygon)?

Lesson 5
Geometry 1
Answer Key

Example Exercises	Application Exercises	Homework Exercises
1) 27	1) D	1) A
2) B	2) C	2) D
3) B	3) D	3) B
4) −2	4) A	4) A
5) A	5) B	5) A
6) (-1,0)	6) B	6) C
7) D	7) B	7) D
8) 16	8) D	8) C
9) C	9) B	9) C
10) 4	10) A	10) A
11) 9	11) 40	11) B
12) 191.3	12) 0.50	12) B
	13) 6	13) B
	14) 23.39	14) C
		15) C
		16) D
		17) $0 < b < 5$
		18) 65
		19) $4 < x < 22$
		20) 10

Example Exercises

1. **The correct answer is y = 2x − 3**
   Find the line's slope (m) by finding the "rise over run":
   $$m = \frac{y_2 - y_1}{x_2 - x_1}.$$
   $$m = \frac{5-(-3)}{4-0}$$
   $$m = \frac{8}{4} = 2.$$
   To find the y-intercept:
   $$y = mx + b$$
   $$b = y - mx$$
   $$b = 5 - (2)(4)$$
   $$b = -3$$
   Substitute into slope intercept equation as $y = 2x - 3$.

2. **The correct answer is $y + 2 = \frac{2}{3}(x - 4)$**
   Substitute the values into the form
   $$y - y_1 = m(x - x_1)$$
   Note that any point that is on the line could be substituted into x_1 and y_1 and fit the equation.

   The same linear equation can be expressed in myriad forms.

3. **The correct answer is 2**
   To solve for slope algebraically, find two points on the line to substitute into the equation with clear coordinates: on this line, $(-2, 1)$ and $(0, 5)$ both have integer values.
   $$m = \frac{y_2 - y_1}{x_2 - x_1}.$$
   $$m = \frac{5-1}{0-(-2)}$$
   $$m = \frac{4}{2} = 2$$

4. **The correct answer is 3**
   We don't necessarily need to solve line m here: to find the slope of the perpendicular line n, we only need to find the negative reciprocal of the slope of $\frac{1}{3}$. With a negative reciprocal of $-\frac{3}{1}$, we can use the given point $(1, 0)$ in point-slope form to find the y-intercept:
   $$y = mx + b$$
   Isolate b:
   $$b = y - mx$$
   Substitute the point and slope:
   $$b = 0 - (-3)(1)$$

5. **Choice A is correct.**
This equation may appear strange because of the two y variables in the denominators of the fractions, but this problem is remedied by finding a common denominator of $2y$ and combining the fractions to find $\frac{5}{2y} = 5$. Solve this equation by multiplying both sides by $2y$ to find $5 = 10y$ and $y = \frac{1}{2}$. Don't be fooled by the lack of an x value: this is a horizontal line.

6. **The correct answer is $(-1, 0)$**
While several methods could be used to solve this system, setting both equations equal (or substituting for y) is the most direct method.

$$4x + 4 = -2x - 2$$
$$6x = -6$$
$$x = -1$$

To find the corresponding y value, substitute -1 for x in one of the equations.

$$y = 4(-1) + 4$$
$$y = 0$$

The coordinate value is $(-1, 0)$.

7. **Choice D is correct.**
Use the Triangle Inequality Theorem to find that the two given sides have a combined value of 20 and a difference of 8 as min/max values. 18 is the only viable option.

8. **The correct answer is 16**
A right isosceles triangle is a $45 - 45 - 90$: the hypotenuse is equal to the leg times $\sqrt{2}$, so the legs will equal $\frac{8}{\sqrt{2}}$. Find the triangle's area:

$$A = \frac{1}{2}bh$$
$$A = \frac{1}{2}\left(\frac{8}{\sqrt{2}}\right)\left(\frac{8}{\sqrt{2}}\right)$$
$$A = \frac{1}{2}\left(\frac{64}{2}\right)$$
$$A = 16$$

9. **Choice C is correct.**
These triangles are similar because they are built on parallel lines with two corresponding angles and share a third angle. Similar triangles are proportional:

$$\frac{x}{15} = \frac{12}{10}$$
$$10x = 180$$
$$x = 18$$

10. **Choice B is correct.**

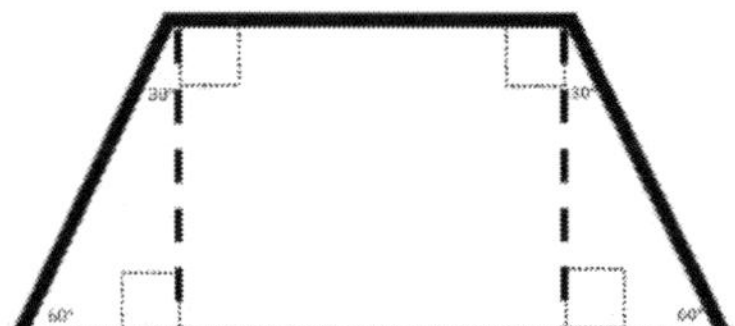

Find the measures of the angles given. All exterior angles add to 360°, so the exterior angles of a regular hexagon are 60° each. The interior angles therefore must be 120°.

Draw altitudes from the diameter to split the 120° angles into 90° and 30°, making a rectangle and two $30 - 60 - 90$ triangles.

Since the hexagon's sides are now the triangles' hypotenuses, the short legs of the triangles that are on the diameter are half that length. The diameter is made of two legs with a length of 1 and a rectangle with a length of 2. Add those dimensions to find the diameter of 4.

11. **The correct answer is 191.3**
Find the volume of the cylinder with given radius and height:

$$V = \pi r^2 h$$
$$V = \pi \times 4^2 \times 5$$
$$V = 251.3$$

Find the box's volume with the given dimensions:

$$V = l \times w \times h$$
$$V = 3 \times 4 \times 5$$
$$V = 60$$

The difference yields $251.3 - 60 = 191.3$

Application Exercises

1) **Choice D is correct.**
Because these are parallel lines, the two angles shown are supplementary angles. Therefore:

$$30 + (2x - 10) = 180°$$
$$2x - 10 = 150°$$
$$2x = 160°$$
$$x = 80°$$

However, since the problem asks for $3x$:

$$3x = 240°$$

2) **Choice C is correct.**
If we give the sides of triangle RQP a length of x and the sides of triangle SPO a length of y, we can describe RQP's perimeter as $3x$ and SPO's perimeter as $3y$. We can then express the total perimeter of the triangles as $3x + 3y$ or $3(x + y)$.

Alternatively, since we are also given the length of line segment $\overline{QO}$ as 15,

$$\overline{QR} + \overline{PS} = 15$$

And

$$\overline{RP} + \overline{SO} = 15$$

Therefore,

$$3(15) = 45$$

3) **Choice D is correct.**
We are asked to find the value of c "in terms of" b. The first step to solving this problem is to express the given information in a clear form: Since a, b, and c are each an angle in the triangle:

$$a + b + c = 180°$$

Substitute $a = 4b$, then isolate for c:

$$4b + b + c = 180°$$
$$5b + c = 180^{o}$$
$$c = 180^{o} - 5b$$

4) **Choice D is correct.**
Here, consider the logic behind the problem: regardless of the volume of the sphere, the ball's diameter limits the amount of balls that fit in the box.

With dimensions given $(3 \times 4 \times 5)$, the box can accommodate one tennis ball in 3 inches of height, two tennis balls in 4 inches of width, and two tennis balls in 5 inches of depth.

That means the total 60 $units^3$ of volume are irrelevant since a dimension of $1\ ball \times 2\ balls \times 2\ balls$ gives us a capacity of 4 actual tennis balls.

Analyze the problem before tackling it. Do not perform rote mechanical computations without an understanding of the problem first.

5) **Choice B is correct.**
A square is composed of two $45 - 45 - 90$ triangles that share a hypotenuse. Since we also know that the hypotenuse of a $45 - 45 - 90$ triangle is $\sqrt{2}$ times larger than a leg, x:

$$9 = x\sqrt{2}$$

Variable isolate, then rationalize:

$$x = \frac{9}{\sqrt{2}}\left(\frac{\sqrt{2}}{\sqrt{2}}\right) = \frac{9\sqrt{2}}{2}$$

Since the perimeter of a square is 4 times each side:

$$4\left(\frac{9\sqrt{2}}{2}\right) = 18\sqrt{2}$$

6) **Choice B is correct.**
This problem gives us two right triangles that share a leg. We should recognize the smaller triangle ΔCZY as a $5 - 12 - 13$ special right triangle, meaning that $\overline{CY} = 12$.

That gives us two legs of the larger triangle ΔXCY as 12 and $4\sqrt{7}$.

Use the Pythagorean Theorem to solve for the hypotenuse $\overline{XY}$:

$$12^2 + (4\sqrt{7})^2 = \overline{XY}^2$$
$$256 = \overline{XY}^2$$
$$16 = \overline{XY}$$

7) **Choice D is correct.**
We can use the Pythagorean Theorem to find the distance between two points if we treat the points like vertices of a right triangle.

We have a distance of 4 on the x-axis and 5 on the y-axis.

$$4^2 + 5^2 = c^2$$
$$41 = c^2$$
$$\sqrt{41} = c$$

8) **Choice D is correct.**
We should start by acknowledging several facts: the squares create three parallel lines extending from points $A, B,$ and C, and because $\overleftrightarrow{AC}$ acts as a transversal to those parallel lines, the angles in the two shaded triangles are congruent, meaning the triangles are similar.

Therefore, the smaller triangle with hypotenuse $\overline{AB}$ has legs of 3 and 2 ($5 - 3 = 2$), and the larger triangle with hypotenuse $\overline{BC}$ has a leg of 5 and a leg of unknown length.

Set up a proportion to find the missing leg:

$$\frac{3}{2} = \frac{5}{c}$$

$$C = \frac{10}{3}$$

Therefore, areas of the triangles are:

$$A_1 = \frac{1}{2}(3)(2) = 3$$

$$A_2 = \frac{1}{2}(5)\left(\frac{10}{3}\right) = \frac{25}{3}$$

$$Total\ area = \frac{34}{3}\ or\ 11\frac{1}{3}$$

9) **Choice B is correct.**
$\angle AOB$ and $\angle BOC$ are supplemental:

$$5x + 2y + 6 + 10y - 10 = 180$$
$$5x + 12y = 184$$

We also know that $\angle AOB$ is twice the measure of $\angle BCO$:

$$5x + 2y + 6 = 2(2x + 2y - 5)$$
$$x - 2y = -16$$

Multiply the second equation by 6 to eliminate the y variable. Use elimination to combine both equations:

$$5x + 12y = 184$$
$$6x - 12y = -96$$

$$11x = 88$$
$$x = 8$$

10) **Choice A is correct.**
Simplify the area

$$\sqrt{48} = 4\sqrt{3}$$

An equilateral triangle always breaks down into two $30 - 60 - 90$ triangles that share a long leg.

Therefore, each of the $30 - 60 - 90$ triangles have an area = $2\sqrt{3}$

We also know the legs have a proportion of x and $x\sqrt{3}$, so

$$2\sqrt{3} = \frac{1}{2}(x)(x\sqrt{3})$$

$$2\sqrt{3} = \frac{1}{2}x^2\sqrt{3}$$

$$x = 2$$

Each leg of equilateral triangle is twice the short leg of the $30 - 60 - 90$ therefore

$$2x = 4$$

11) **The correct answer is 40**
Ignore the angle inside of the triangle: since we know that sum of all exterior angles adds to 360°

$$2n + (3n + 20) + (5n - 60) = 360^{o}$$
$$10n - 40 = 360^{o}$$
$$n = 40^{o}$$

12) **The correct answer is 0.5 or $\frac{1}{2}$**
When we reflect across the y-axis, we keep the y-intercept but change our slope, so line $m = -2x + 5$. Since line n is perpendicular to line m, the slope is the negative reciprocal of -2, so $\frac{1}{2}$ is the slope of line n.

Note that many problems will utilize variables like m that we would normally attribute as the slope of a line, but in this instance is the line itself. Stay focused.

13) **The correct answer is 12**
Since $x = 75°$ and all trapezoids have the same angular measures ("regular polygon"), a full interior angle of the complete polygon is $2 \times 75° = 150°$

Therefore, the exterior angles = 30°

Utilize the exterior angular theorem:

$$30x = 360°$$
$$x = 12^{o}$$

14) **The correct answer is 4**
To find $g(x)$, we need to reflect $f(x)$ across the x-axis, which yields $-f(x)$, aka

$$-f(x) = -(2x + 2)$$
$$= -2x - 2$$

$h(x)$ is the reflection of $f(x)$ across the y-axis, which is $f(-x)$

$$f(-x) = 2(-x) + 2 = -2x + 2$$

The distance between the intercepts:

$$2 - (-2) = 2 + 2 = 4$$

Homework Exercises

1) **Choice A is correct.**
Find the missing angles by taking advantage of the fact that angle x is part of a triangle made from four parallel lines.

One of the missing angles of that triangle is a supplement of $126°$, *or* $54°$. The other angle is a corresponding angle of $112°$.

$$x + 54° + 112° = 180°$$
$$x = 14°$$

2) **Choice A is correct.**
This linear equation must have a negative slope and positive y-intercept. Therefore:

$$h = -5$$

3) **Choice B is correct.**

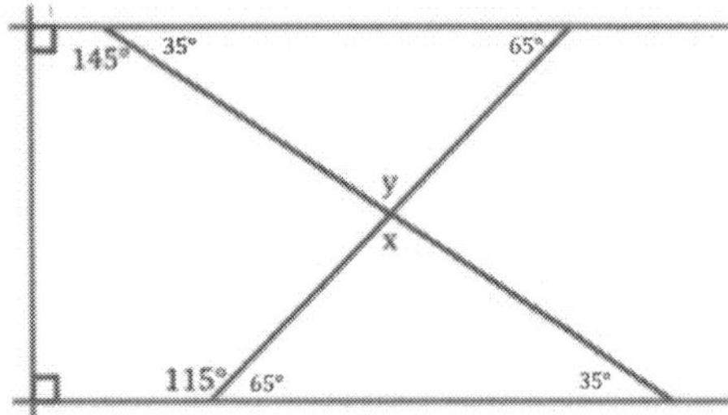

An equilateral triangle can be split into two 30 – 60 – 90 triangles sharing a long base.

Our equilateral triangle's side of 15 is made up of two of the short legs of these 30 – 60 – 90 triangles, giving each short leg, x, a value that is half that of the base.

$$x = \frac{15}{2}$$

The height, h, of the equilateral triangle is $\sqrt{3}$ times longer than its base, therefore:

$$h = \frac{15\sqrt{3}}{2}$$

4) **Choice A is correct.**

$$Slope = \frac{rise}{run} \text{ or } \frac{y_2 - y_1}{x_2 - x_1}$$

Therefore,

$$l = \frac{n - m}{7 - 5} = \frac{n - m}{2}$$

5) **Choice C is correct.**
According to the triangle inequality theorem, we obtain:

$$5 < n < 21$$

Therefore, 14 is the only valid answer.

6) **Choice C is correct.**
Because side ZV is made with the midpoints of sides WY and XY, ΔVYZ is half the area of ΔXYW. That means that each side of the smaller triangle will be half the length of the larger triangle:

$$ZV = \frac{m}{2}$$

7) **Choice D is correct.**
The number line shows the following inequality:

$$-3 < x < 6$$

Choice D will give us an *inclusive* inequality with endpoints that converge.

Incorrect choice C will give us an *exclusive* inequality with endpoints that extend into infinity.

Further, incorrect choices A and B have an endpoint of 0.

8) **Choice C is correct.**
To find x and y, first take advantage of alternate interior angles to fill in the missing angles like so:

From here, since the sum of two triangles is equal to 360:

$$35^{0} + 65^{0} + 35^{0} + 65^{0} + x + y = 360^{0}$$

$$x + y = 160^{0}$$

9) **Choice C is correct.**
Finding the distance between these points can be accomplished with the Pythagorean Theorem, using the distance between the x-values as one leg and the distance between the y-values as the other leg.

$$(26-2)^2 + (10-3)^2 = c^2$$
$$625 = c^2$$
$$25 = c$$

10) **Choice A is correct.**
This problem may seem like the Pythagorean Theorem (based on the squaring of the sum of sides), but $(a+b)^2$ is NOT the same as $a^2 + b^2$.

The only fact that we know about $a + b$ *is that it must be greater than* 25 because of the triangle inequality theorem.

Therefore, $(a+b)^2$, which equals $a^2 + 2ab + b^2$, must be greater than 625, leaving 625 to be less that $(a+b)^2$.

Note: The triangle inequality theorem, like all other theorems listed in our lesson, can and will be tested in many ways.

11) **Choice B is correct.**
Volume of a cone,

$$V_a = \frac{1}{3}\pi r^2 h$$

When the new radius is halved, and height is tripled, the volume of Cone B:

$$V_b = \frac{1}{3}\pi\left(\frac{1}{2}r\right)^2 (3h)$$

$$= (\frac{3}{4})(\frac{1}{3})\pi r^2 h$$

Therefore, volume of Cone B is $\frac{3}{4}$ of Cone A:

$$V_b = 16(\frac{3}{4})$$

$$V_b = 12$$

12) **Choice B is correct.**
The height of the triangle is the y-coordinate given:

$$h = 5$$

The length of the base is the distance between the two roots:

$$= x^2 - x - 6$$
$$= (x-3)(x+2)$$

$$x = 3 \; or \; x = -2$$

Therefore,

$$Base = 3 + 2 = 5$$

$$Area = \frac{1}{2}(5)(5) = \frac{25}{2}$$

13) **Choice B is correct.**
Because both triangles share sides and angles, they are similar.

Build a proportion from the two known legs of the larger triangle (10 *and* 30) and the known & unknown legs of the smaller triangle (x *and* 25).

$$\frac{10}{30} = \frac{x}{25}$$

$$x = \frac{25}{3}$$

Note that the 35^0 angle is not necessarily used in this problem.

14) **Choice C is correct.**
Because this triangle is explicitly labeled as right isosceles, the triangle has two possible side length combinations of four units apart, yielding the following two possible areas:

This could be one of the legs, giving us a hypotenuse of $4\sqrt{2}$, and an area of

$$A_1 = \frac{1}{2} \times 4 \times 4$$
$$A_1 = 8$$

The distance of four could alternatively be the hypotenuse of a $45-45-90$ triangle, which means that our sides are $\frac{4}{\sqrt{2}}$ or $2\sqrt{2}$ and an area of

$$A_2 = \frac{1}{2}(2\sqrt{2})(2\sqrt{2})$$
$$A_2 = 4$$

15) **Choice C is correct.**
The triangle is $30-60-90$. The height, therefore, is 12. As a result, the left side of the base is $12\sqrt{3}$. The total base is $12\sqrt{3}+5$. The area then:

$$Area = \frac{1}{2}(12\sqrt{3}+5)(12)$$
$$Area = 72\sqrt{3}+30$$

16) **The correct answer is D.**
Determine the vertices of the triangle by obtaining the intersections of the three linear functions.

Since $y = 0$ is one of the linear functions, the two coordinates of the base are determined first by the x-intercepts of the other two lines as follows:

$$0 = -\frac{1}{2}x + 7$$
$$14 = x$$
$$0 = \frac{2}{3}x$$
$$0 = x$$

Our two coordinates of the base are:

$$(14,0)\ and\ (0,0)$$

The third point can be found at the intersection of the other two lines:

$$\frac{2}{3}x = -\frac{1}{2}x + 7$$

$$\frac{7}{6}x = 7$$
$$x = 6$$

Plug 6 into $y = \frac{2}{3}x$ to determine the y value:

$$y = \frac{2}{3}(6)$$
$$y = 4$$

Therefore, our third coordinate is (6,4)

This is a right triangle. Utilizing the Pythagorean Theorem, we determine the distances of all sides as:

$$14 + \sqrt{52} + \sqrt{80} \cong$$
$$14 + 7.2 + 8.9 \cong$$
$$\cong 30.15$$

Since the answer approximates to either 30.1 or rounds up to 30.2, either would be acceptable in the grid-in section.

Note that some grid-in questions will have more than one acceptable answer.

17) **The correct answer is $0 < x < 5$**
Since a coordinate on this particular function has a y-value of 5, the y-intercept must be between 0 and 5.

18) **The correct answer is 65**
A right isosceles triangle is a $45 - 45 - 90$ by definition, meaning that the two similar legs will be the base and height in the area formula. Therefore:

$$\frac{1}{2}x^2 = 180.5$$
$$x^2 = 361$$
$$x = 19$$

$$Perimeter = 19 + 19 + 19\sqrt{2}$$
$$Perimeter = 64.87$$

Since the grid-in section only has four spaces for input, the answer is either 64.8 or rounded up to 64.9.

19) **The correct answer is $4 < x < 22$**
A scalene triangle is a triangle with three different sides.

With only two sides of a triangle, calculate a possible value for the third side with triangle inequality theorem.

The third side must be larger than the difference of the two sides (4) but less than the sum (22), therefore, any value between 4 and 22 will suffice.

20) **The correct answer is 10**
The sum of the interior angle of any polygon:

$$180(n - 2)$$

Each interior angle of a dodecagon:

$$\frac{180^{\circ} \times (12 - 2)}{12} = 150^{\circ}$$

Each interior angle of a nonagon:

$$\frac{180^{\circ} \times (9 - 2)}{9} = 140^{\circ}$$

The difference in measure:

$$150^{\circ} - 140^{\circ} = 10^{\circ}$$

Alternatively, determine the exterior angles of any polygon by:

$$\frac{360^{\circ}}{n}$$

The interior angles will then be the supplements of those exterior angles.

Mathematics

Lesson 6

Geometry 2

Goals

We will develop our mathematical fluency and gain meaningful understanding by learning to:

1) Work with circles and all derivatives, including inscribed and central angles
2) Apply concepts utilizing radian measure and able to convert to degree measure
3) Distinguish various formulas to be utilized in coordinate plans

Contents

- Circles
- Coordinate Plane
- Radians
- Distance Formula
- Application Exercises
- Homework Exercises

PITTSBURGH PREP

Lesson 6
Geometry 2

Circles

The area, A, of a circle is determined by $A = \pi r^2$, where r represents the radius of the circle. Pi (π) is an irrational number that is close to $\frac{22}{7}$, and can also be expressed as approximately 3.14

The circumference, C, of a circle is determined by $C = 2\pi r$. Alternatively, $C = \pi d$, where d represents the diameter. Since twice the radius is the length of the diameter, the above two formulas are equivalent.

eg. 1 What is the area of a circle whose radius is 3?

We learned from our lesson in Geometry 1 that a central angle intercepts an arc with the same degree measure, while an inscribed minor angle intercepts an arc that is twice the angular measure of the inscribed angle. We can use this knowledge to determine more information about a circle by understanding that angles and lengths are proportional to each other.

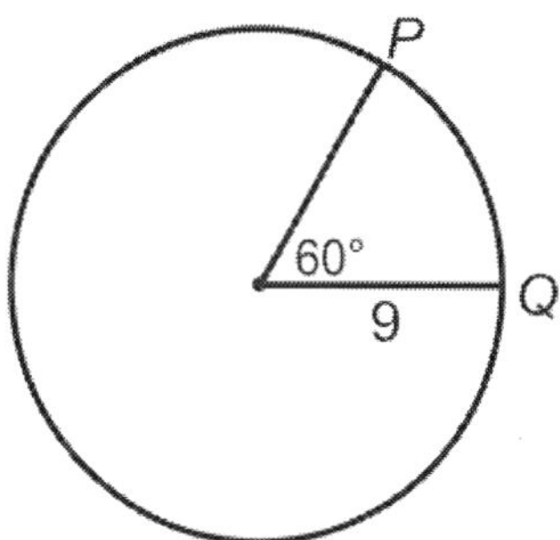

eg. 2 In the figure above, what is the measure of arc $\widehat{PQ}$, given that the radius is 9, and the central angle is 60 degrees?

In this problem, the proper setup would be to create a proportion that shows the reflection of the central to arc PQ as follows:

$$\frac{Central\ Angle}{360°} = \frac{Arc\ PQ}{Circumference\ (2\pi r)}$$

$$\frac{60°}{360°} = \frac{Arc\ PQ}{18\pi}$$

$$(18\pi)\frac{1}{6} = Arc\ PQ$$

$$3\pi = Arc\ PQ$$

Coordinate Plane + Completing the Square

In the coordinate plane, a circle can be measured by the following circle formula:

$$(x - h)^2 + (y - k)^2 = r^2$$

The coordinate (h, k) represents the center of the circle, and r represents the radius of that circle. Note the positive or negative signs that are used in the circle formula to avoid any mistakes. Many times, the concept of a circle formula in a coordinate plane is coupled with the idea of completing the square.

To complete the square from a standard quadratic form of $ax^2 + bx + c = 0$, move the constant c to the right side of the equation to get $ax^2 + bx = -c$, then add $(\frac{b}{2})^2$ to both sides to obtain $ax^2 + bx + (\frac{b}{2})^2 = -c + (\frac{b}{2})^2$. Let's take a look at a few example problems:

eg. 3 Complete the square for the following equation: $x^2 + 6x - 16 = 0$

Since we cannot factor the given quadratic, one option would be to complete the square as follows:

$$x^2 + 6x - 16 = 0$$
$$x^2 + 6x = 16$$
$$x^2 + 6x + 9 = 16 + 9$$
$$(x + 3)(x + 3) = 25$$

eg. 4 If the equation of a circle in the coordinate plane is given as $x^2 - 6x + y^2 + 4y = 131$, what are the coordinates of the center of the circle?

Translation

When a circle is translated (up/down or left/right), we need to apply the correct operation into the equation of a circle. Note that when we ADD a constant to y, the circle shifts DOWNWARDS. The same occurs when we ADD a constant to x, the circle shifts DOWNWARDS. Let's take a look at the following example:

eg. 5 In a circle with the equation $(x - 6)^2 + (y + 3)^2 = 16$, the circle is moved up 4 and to the left 2 spaces, what is the new equation of the circle?

Since we know that the center of the circle lies at coordinate $(6, -3)$ but must then be shifted to $(4, 1)$, we modify the equation as follows: $(x - 6 + 2)^2 + (y + 3 - 4)^2 = 16$. The radius did not change since the circle just moved from one spot to another. Our final circle equation is therefore $(x - 4)^2 + (y - 1)^2 = 16$, which has a center coordinate of $(4, 1)$ correctly as stated in the problem above.

Radians

The measure of a circle in degrees is a representation, not an actual value of the circle. So how do measure the actual length of a circle? Enter: radians. The best way to think about a radian is the measure of circle's radius against the circumference of the circle. So, one radian is equivalent to walking one radius length along the circumference of a circle. In this way, we can measure the actual distance traveled in terms of the radius as a reference.

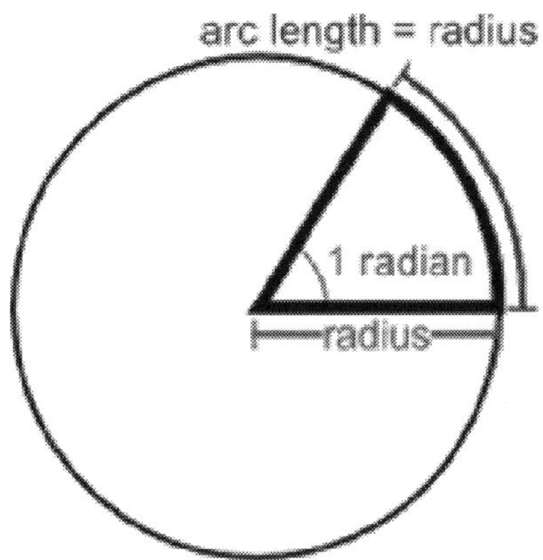

It turns out that when traversing the circumference of a circle, it's total measure is exactly 2π radians. This is why we were always taught that the circumference was exactly $C = 2\pi r$. Which means we can break up the circle as shown in the figure below, by its (degree, radian) equivalencies. For example, 90 degrees is equivalent to $\frac{\pi}{2}$ radians. Note that for conversion purposes, $\pi\ radian = 180\ degrees$. Refer to the diagram below for future reference.

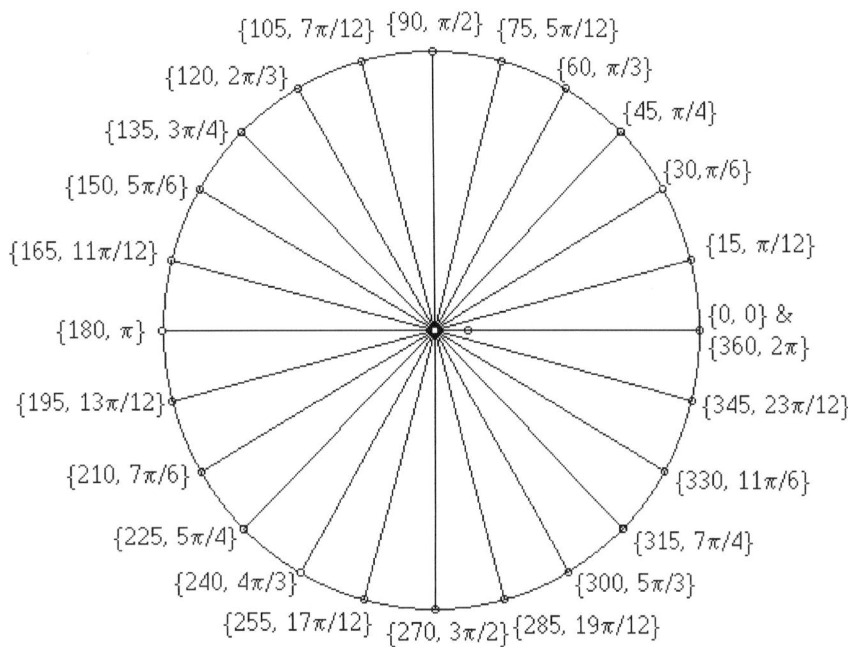

To determine the arc length or sector of a given circle below, we can utilize proportions using either degrees or radians. You'll need to be adept at converting your answers in both forms.

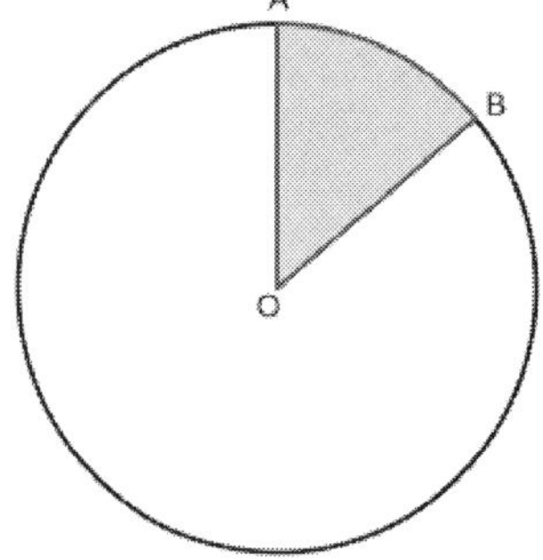

To determine the arc measure of $\widehat{AB}$ we can set a proportion of the arc we are looking for over the total circumference equal to the central angle x over the total angular measure of a circle:

$$\frac{m\widehat{AB}}{2\pi r} = \frac{x}{360}$$

To determine the sector, we note that the ratio of a sector area to the total area of a circle is equal to the ratio of the central angle to the total angular measure of a circle:

$$\frac{area\ of\ sector\ AOB}{\pi r^2} = \frac{x}{360}$$

Pro tip: Radians can come in handy when trying to determine the length of an arc by the formula $s = r\theta$, where s is the arc, r is the radius and θ is the radian measure. This shortcut may come in handy for radian specific problems.

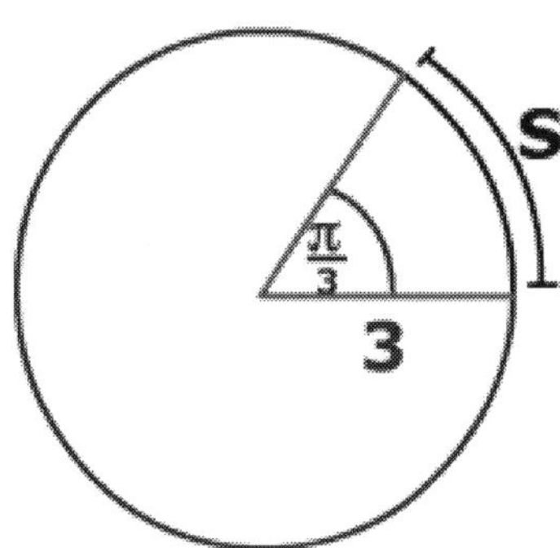

eg. 6 In the figure above, what is the length of arc S and the area of the sector in radian measure?

Distance Formula

In a coordinate plane, the distance formula is a variation of the Pythagorean theorem. The distance formula itself is:

$$d = \sqrt{(x_1 - x_2)^2 + (y_1 - y_2)^2}$$

If we were given two ordered pairs, such as $(6, 1)$ and $(2, -2)$, we can use the above formula to determine the distance as:

$$d = \sqrt{(6 - 2)^2 + (1 - (-2))^2}$$
$$d = \sqrt{(4)^2 + (3)^2}$$
$$d = \sqrt{16 + 9}$$
$$d = \sqrt{25}$$
$$d = 5$$

We can connect the two ordered pairs by drawing a right triangle. Try it out below:

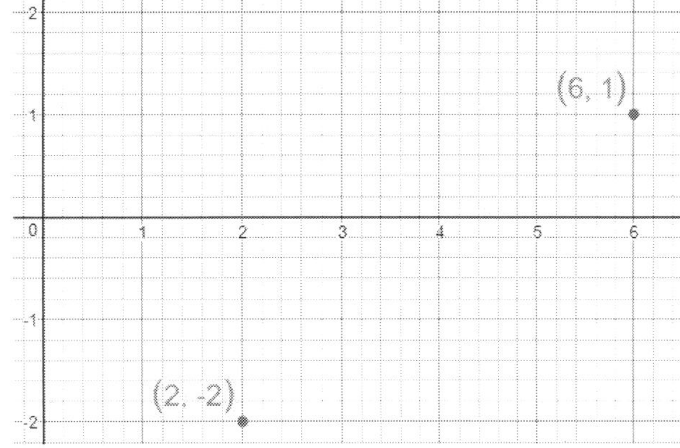

Note that we should now be able to determine the length of the distance between the two points by utilizing the Pythagorean theorem. If we imagine a third point at $(6, -2)$, our right triangle allows us to plug in the values as:

$$c^2 = a^2 + b^2$$
$$c = \sqrt{(6 - 2)^2 + (1 - (-2))^2}$$

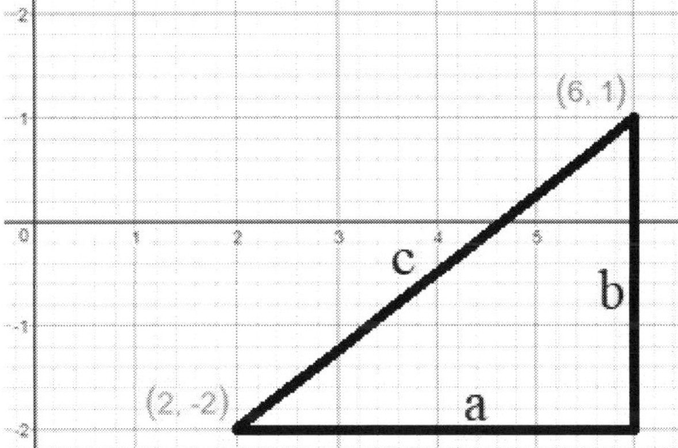

From this point, we get to the same result as above.

PITTSBURGH PREP

Lesson 6
Geometry 2
Application Exercises

NO CALCULATOR SECTION
Questions 1-5

Time - 20 Minutes

1) Line m is a line that is perpendicular to line l, and line m contains the points $(-1, 2)$ and $(1, -2)$. Line ℓ has an x-intercept of 10. What is the y-intercept of line ℓ?

A) -10
B) -5
C) 5
D) 10

2) If a pizza pie with radius r can serve exactly 8 people, how many more people can a pizza pie with $2r$ serve?

A) 8
B) 16
C) 24
D) 32

3) What is the area of a circle with a circumference that is exactly twice as large?

A) 16π
B) 2π
C) π
D) 1

4) If a certain square has a diagonal that measures exactly 9, then what is the area of the square?

A) $\frac{9}{\sqrt{2}}$
B) $18\sqrt{2}$
C) $\frac{81}{2}$
D) $81\sqrt{2}$

5) In the figure below, where $f(x) = y$ for some constant x, for how many values of x does $f(x) = 3$ if $-9 \leq x \leq 5$?

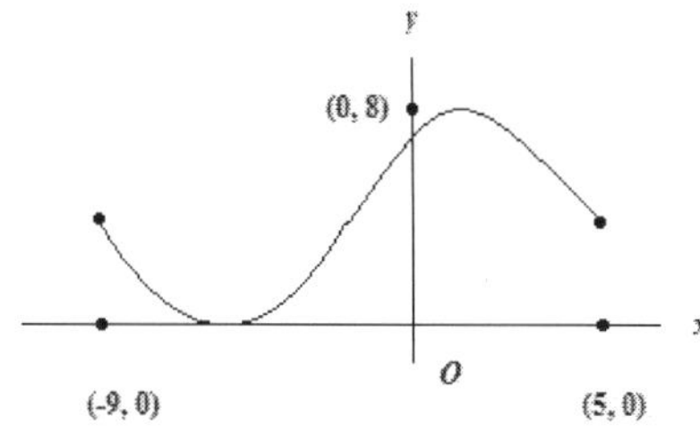

Note: Figure not drawn to scale

A) 3
B) 2
C) 1
D) It cannot be determined from the information given

CALCULATOR SECTION
Questions 6-10

6) A circle is cut into congruent five segments by radii, creating five angles. What, in radians, is the measure of each of the angles created by the radii?

A) $\frac{\pi}{5}$
B) $\frac{2\pi}{5}$
C) $\frac{3\pi}{5}$
D) 72

7) A circle C has a radius of 7, and contains equilateral triangle ABC, where two of the triangle's sides act as radii for circle C. If points A and B are on the circumference and form an arc, what is the length of arc AB?

A) $\frac{7\pi}{3}$
B) $\frac{7\pi}{2}$
C) $\frac{49\pi}{6}$
D) $\frac{49\pi}{3}$

8) A paper cone with a height of four inches and a circumference of 18π is completely filled with water, and is then emptied into a can with a diameter of four inches. How much of the can's depth in inches will be filled with water?

(Note: A cone's volume is found with $\frac{1}{3}\pi r^2 h$)

A) 4
B) 18
C) 27
D) 36

9) The linear function $f(x)$ contains the point (0,4) and bisects the circle $(x-3)^2 + (y+2)^2 = 25$. Which of the following is a possible point on $f(x)$?

A) (2, 1)
B) (-2, 0)
C) (6, -8)
D) (6, -6)

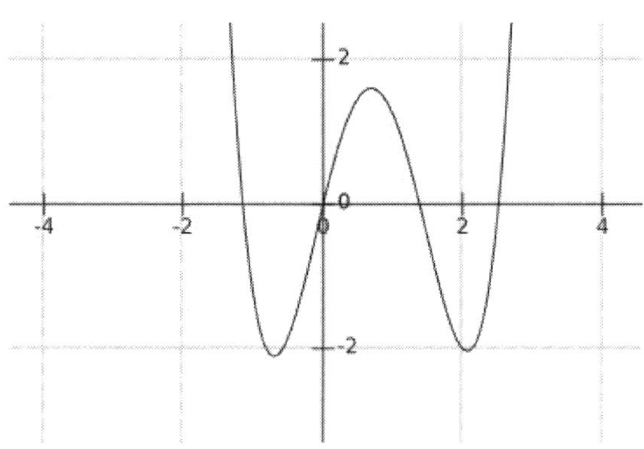

10) In the graph above, the function $f(x)$ has a first term of x^n, where n is a positive integer. Which of the following is a possible value of n?

A) 3
B) 4
C) 5
D) The answer cannot be determined with the given data.

GRID-IN SECTION
Questions 11-14

11) A tire has a diameter of 36 inches and is rolled down a road. How many radians, rounded to the nearest radian, will the wheel have rotated once it has rolled 1,760 yards? (There are 36 inches in a yard)

12) A line l extends from $(-1, 4)$ to a point 25 units away at $(6, n)$. If n is a positive integer, what is the value of n?

13) If $f(x) = 2x + 2$, $g(x)$ is the reflection of $f(x)$ across the x-axis, and $h(x)$ is the reflection of $g(x)$ across the y-axis, what is the positive difference between the y-intercept of $f(x)$ and the y-intercept of $h(x)$?

14) What is the radius of the circle $y = \frac{11-x^2}{y-10}$?

PITTSBURGH PREP

Lesson 6
Geometry 2
Homework Exercises

NO CALCULATOR SECTION
Questions 1-8

Time - 25 minutes

1) If a circle with a radius r is expanded to double its circumference, what is the percent increase in area?

A) 100%
B) 200%
C) 300%
D) 400%

2) A circle has a sector measure of 72π and an area of 180π. What is the measure in degrees of the angle θ that defines the sector?

A) 20
B) 40
C) 50
D) 144

3) What is the circumference of the circle $x^2 + y^2 - 6y = 7$?

A) 7π
B) 8π
C) 16π
D) 36π

4) A pizza parlor sells small and medium pizzas, with respective diameters of 10 and 16 inches. Which of the following represents the increase, rounded to the nearest percentage, of pizza purchased when upgrading from a small to a medium?

A) 25%
B) 39%
C) 56%
D) 156%

5) What is the maximum number of solutions possible for the functions $f(x) = ax^2 + b$ and $g(x) = (x - c)^2 + (x - d)^2 = e$, where $a, b, c, d,$ and e are all distinct integers?

A) Two
B) Four
C) Infinitely Many
D) The answer cannot be determined from the given information

6) What is the distance between the origin and the solution of the functions $f(x) = 3x + 15 = y$ and $g(x) = -4x - 13$?

A) -5
B) 5
C) 3
D) 7

7) What is the radius of the circle with the equation $x^2 + y^2 - 12 = 9$

A) $\sqrt{3}$
B) 3
C) $\sqrt{21}$
D) 21

8) What is the area of the triangle formed by the lines $x = 2$, $3x + 6y = 12$, and the reflection of $3x + 6y = 12$ across the x axis?

A) 2
B) 4
C) $\frac{17}{2}$
D) 8

PITTSBURGH PREP

CALCULATOR SECTION
Questions 9-16

9) A circle C is shifted 3 units to the right and 2 units down, then has its radius change from 4 to 8 to become circle D. If circle D has a center of $(4, -3)$, what is the equation of circle C?

A) $(x-1)^2 + (x+1)^2 = 8$
B) $(x-1)^2 + (x+1)^2 = 16$
C) $(x+1)^2 + (x-1)^2 = 16$
D) $(x+1)^2 + (x-1)^2 = 64$

10) A company is looking to double the volume of a cylindrical container, but not alter the height 9 cm height. If the new container must hold 750 cm^3, what is the nearest width of the old can?

A) 3.64
B) 6.63
C) 7.72
D) 13.27

11) If an angle in a right triangle has a radian measure of $\frac{\pi}{9}$, what is a possible measure of one of the other angles?

A) $\frac{7\pi}{9}$
B) $\frac{8\pi}{9}$
C) $\frac{7\pi}{18}$
D) $\frac{8\pi}{9}$

12) A circle with a square inscribed inside of it will have an area that is what percentage greater than the square?

A) 57
B) 144
C) 157
D) 314

13) The circle shown below has a circumference of 12π, and $\theta = 50°$, what is the area of the shaded sector shown below?

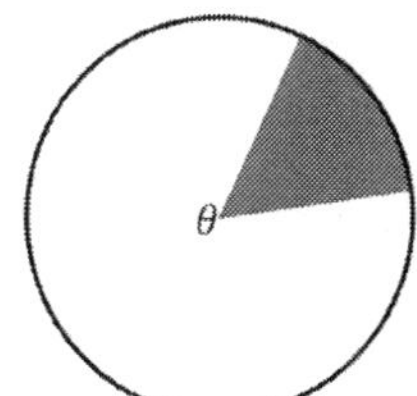

A) $\frac{12\pi}{5}$
B) 5π
C) 6π
D) 12π

14) Given two end points of a diameter are $(-1, -4)$ and $(9{,}20)$ what is the circumference of the circle?

A) $144\ \pi$
B) $169\ \pi$
C) $196\ \pi$
D) $225\ \pi$

15) A circle has an equation $(x - n)^2 + (y + k)^2 = 25$, where $n^2 + 5 = 14$ and k is an integer. Which of the following points will the circle pass through?

I. $4, 2$
II. $8, 0$
III. $-3, 5$

A) I only
B) II only
C) I and II only
D) I, II, and III

16) A square is inscribed into a circle with an area of 128π. The area of the square is what percentage of the circle, rounded to the nearest percentage?

A) 33%
B) 50%
C) 64%
D) 67%

GRID-IN SECTION
Questions 17-20

17) An arc on a circle with an area of 64π has an angle measure θ, where $0° < \theta < 90°$. If the angle n is a measure of θ in radians, and n is an integer, what is a possible measure of n?

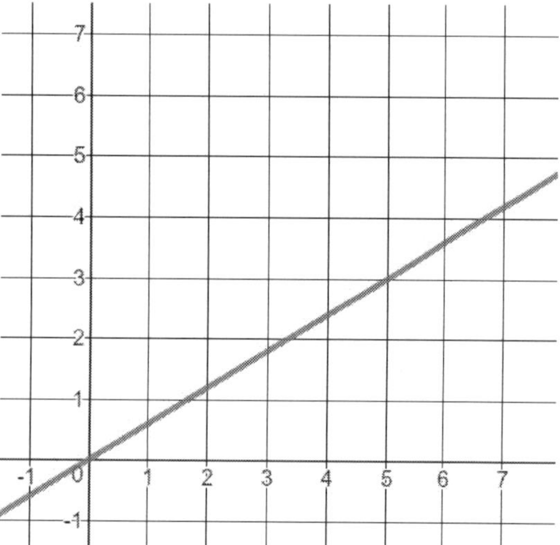

18) In the figure above, line A is not shown, but it is parallel to the line drawn above, and passes through the points (0,5) and (3,y). What is the value of y?

19) A circle with a radius of 8 has an arc of 12π. What is the area of the sector made by that arc, rounded to the nearest integer?

20) A right isosceles triangle is inscribed in a circle, where the triangle's hypotenuse acts as a diameter of the circle. If the area of the circle is 4π, what is the area of the triangle, rounded to the nearest tenth?

PITTSBURGH PREP

Lesson 6
Geometry 2
Answer Key

Example Exercises		Application Exercises		Homework Exercises	
1)	9π	1)	B	1)	C
2)	3π	2)	C	2)	D
3)	$(x+3)^2-25=0$	3)	C	3)	B
4)	$(3,-2)$	4)	C	4)	C
5)	Given	5)	D	5)	B
6)	$S=\pi$, Area $=\frac{3\pi}{2}$	6)	B	6)	B
		7)	A	7)	D
		8)	C	8)	A
		9)	C	9)	B
		10)	B	10)	A
		11)	3520	11)	C
		12)	28	12)	A
		13)	4	13)	B
		14)	6	14)	B
				15)	B
				16)	C
				17)	1
				18)	0
				19)	151
				20)	4

Example Exercises

1. **The correct answer is 9π or 28.3**
Plug in the given values:

$$A = \pi r^2$$

$$A = \pi(3)^2$$

$$A = 9\pi \text{ or } 28.3$$

2. **The correct answer is 3π or 9.42**
An arc is a fraction of the circumference of a circle defined by a central angle. The fraction of that central angle out of the 360° in a circle is the same as the fraction of the arc.

$$\frac{60°}{360°} = \frac{1}{6} \text{ of the circle}$$

$$C = 2\pi r$$

$$C = 2 \times \pi \times 9$$

$$C = 18\pi$$

$$\frac{1}{6} \text{ of } 18\pi = 3\pi.$$

3. **The correct answer is $(x + 3)^2 = 25$**
Complete the square to find a value to factor with $x^2 + 6x$.

$$c = \left(\frac{1}{2}b\right)^2$$

$$c = \left(\frac{1}{2} \times 6\right)^2$$

$$c = 9$$

Add 9 to both sides of the given equation:

$$x^2 + 6x + 9 - 16 = 9$$

We can factor the first three terms:

$$(x^2 + 6x + 9) - 16 = 9$$

$$(x + 3)(x + 3) - 16 = 9$$

Finally, combine constants:

$$(x + 3)^2 = 25$$

4. **The correct answer is (3, −2)**
To find the center's coordinate, complete the square twice in this equation: once for x and once for y. With x-values of $x^2 - 6x$, complete the square:

$$c = \left(\frac{1}{2}b\right)^2$$

$$c = \left(\frac{1}{2} \times 6\right)^2$$

$$c = 9$$

Add 9 to both sides of the equation

$$(x-3)^2 + y^2 + 4y = 140$$

Do the same procedure to $y^2 + 4y$

$$c = \left(\frac{1}{2}b\right)^2$$

$$c = \left(\frac{1}{2} \times 4\right)^2$$

$$c = 2$$

add the 9 and 4 to both sides of the equation, and factor

$$(x-3)^2 + (y+2)^2 = 144$$

Compare to $(x-h)^2 + (y-k)^2 = r^2$: notice $h = 3$ and $k = -2$, so the center is $(3, -2)$.

5. **The correct answer is π**
Since the arc's angle is measured in radians, plug the angle and the radius into the arc formula:

$$s = r\theta$$

$$s = 3 \times \frac{\pi}{3}$$

$$s = \pi$$

Application Exercises

1. **Choice B is correct.**
Finding perpendicular lines and reflections requires the original line's equation. Find the slope of line m:

$$m = \frac{(-2) - 2}{1 - (-1)}$$

$$m = \frac{-4}{2}$$

$$m = -2$$

Then plug that slope and one of the points into the slope intercept form:

$$y = mx + b$$

$$2 = -2(-1) + b$$

$$b = 0$$

Line m is $y = 2x$.

Since lines l and m are perpendicular, the negative/inverse reciprocal of the slope of 2 is $\frac{1}{2}$. With line l's slope and a given (10,0), find the y-intercept by again plugging the slope and point into slope intercept form:

$$y = mx + b$$

$$0 = \frac{1}{2}(10) + b$$

$$b = -5$$

2. **Choice C is correct.**
People eat the area of pizza, and since the pizza's area pizza serves 8 people with a radius r, $8 = \pi r^2$. The second pizza has a radius of $2r$. Use $2r$ in the area equation:

$$A = \pi(2r)^2$$
$$A = 4\pi r^2$$

Since $4\pi r^2$ is four times the original πr^2, the second pizza feeds four times as many people ($4 \times 8 = 32$).
The problems ask for how many *more* people. That means $32 - 8 = 24$.

3. **Choice C is correct.**
Start by translating the given info into an equation:

$$2\pi r = 2(\pi r^2)$$
$$2\pi = 2\pi r$$
$$r = 1$$

Substitute 1 into πr^2 for an area of π.

4. **Choice C is correct.**
A square is made with a pair of $45 - 45 - 90$ triangles that use their hypotenuses as diagonals of the square. Since the hypotenuse is $\sqrt{2}$ times larger than the legs (and sides of the square), translate that to:

$$\sqrt{2} \times l = 9$$
$$l = \frac{9}{\sqrt{2}}$$

With the leg length, find the area of the square:

$$A = \left(\frac{9}{\sqrt{2}}\right)^2$$
$$A = \frac{81}{2}$$

5. **Choice D is correct.**
This problem gives us a function f but no way to know exactly how many times it crosses $f(x) = 3$ since the figure is not drawn to scale. It may cross twice or three times. Therefore, the answer cannot be determined.

6. **Choice B is correct.**
A full circle has 2π radians, and this circle is split into five segments, so divide $\frac{2\pi}{5}$ to find the radian value of each individual segment.

7. **Choice A is correct.**
Points A and B of triangle B are on the circumference of circle C, which means that $\overline{BC}$ and $\overline{AC}$ are radii, and that arc AB has a 60° angle from the equilateral triangle. Find the arc length

$$C = 2\pi r$$
$$C = 14\pi$$

Then set that circumference in a proportion:

$$\frac{x}{14\pi} = \frac{60}{360}$$
$$360x = 840\pi$$
$$x = \frac{7\pi}{3}$$

Alternatively, convert 60° into radians

$$60° \times \frac{2\pi\ radians}{360°} = \frac{\pi}{3}$$

And then find the arc length

$$S = r\theta$$
$$S = 7(\frac{\pi}{3})$$

8. **Choice C is correct.**
First find the radius of the cone

$$2\pi r = C$$
$$r = \frac{C}{2\pi}$$
$$r = \frac{18\pi}{2\pi}$$
$$r = 9$$

Then use that radius with the given height to find the volume of water

$$V = \frac{1}{3}\pi r^2 h$$
$$V = \frac{1}{3}\pi(9)^2(4)$$
$$V = 108\pi$$

The water's volume of 108π is then poured into the can with a radius of 2:

$$\pi r^2 h = V$$
$$\pi(2)^2 h = 108\pi$$
$$4\pi h = 108\pi$$
$$h = \frac{108\pi}{4\pi}$$
$$h = 27$$

9. **Choice C is correct.**
Find the given line by using the point (0,4) and the center of the circle $(3, -2)$. First, find the slope of $f(x)$

$$m = \frac{y_2 - y_1}{x_2 - x_1}$$
$$m = \frac{(-2) - 4}{3 - 0}$$
$$m = -2$$

Then substitute the y-intercept (0,4) to find $y = -2x + 4$. Finally, use the answer choices to determine that (6, –8) fits the line.

10. **Choice B is correct.**
Estimate the function's greatest exponent by examining the endpoints and number of turns the function makes. Both ends of the function extend in the same direction, so the function must have an even exponent. The power of a function is usually one greater than the amount of turns (relative minimums and maximums). With three turns in this function, the equation starts with x^4.

11. **The correct answer is 3520 radians**
This problem involves the conversion of units as much as the geometry of a circle. The tire has a circumference of 36π inches (from $C = \pi d$), or $\frac{1\ rotation}{\pi\ yards}$, so measure the amount of rotations by taking $\frac{1760\ yards}{1} \times \frac{1\ rotation}{\pi\ yards} \times \frac{2\pi\ radians}{1\ rotation} = 3520\ radians.$

12. **The correct answer is 28**
Distance on a coordinate plane can be drawn as a right triangle, so the 25 unit distance is a hypotenuse. One of the legs is the distance between x-values and the other is the distance between 4 and whatever y is. Input these values into the Pythagorean Theorem:

$$a^2 + b^2 = c^2$$
$$\left(6 - (-1)\right)^2 + (n - 4)^2 = 25^2$$
$$49 + n^2 - 8n + 16 = 625$$
$$n^2 - 8n - 560 = 0$$

Factor this quadratic to find n:

$$(n + 20)(n - 28) = 0$$
$$n = -20 \text{ or } n = 28$$

Since n must be positive, $n = 28$

13. **The correct answer is 4**
Reflections across x can be described as $-f(x)$, so distribute the negative across $f(x)$ to $g(x) = -2x - 2$. Reflections across y can be described as $g(-x)$, so $h(x) = 2(-x) - 2$. Since $f(x)$ has a y-intercept of 2 and both $g(x)$ and $h(x)$ have y-intercepts of -2, find a difference of $2 - (-2) = 4$

14. **The correct answer is 6**
This equation's form is unusual, but we can put it in standard circle form:

$$y = \frac{11 - x^2}{y - 10}$$

$$y^2 - 10y = 11 - x^2$$

$$x^2 + y^2 - 10y = 11$$

Complete the square for y to find:

$$x^2 + (y - 5)^2 = 11 + 25$$

Since a circle is $x^2 + y^2 = r^2, r = 6$

Homework Exercises

1. **Choice C is correct.**
Start with the standard area equation

$$A = \pi r^2$$

Doubling the circumference of a circle doubles the area, so

$$A = \pi(2r)^2$$

$$A = 4\pi r^2$$

This shows a quadrupled area, which is an increase of 300% (increase doesn't include the original 100%).

2. **Choice D is correct.**
Find the angle of a sector by finding the proportion of the sector to the total circle:

$$\frac{72\pi}{180\pi} = \frac{2}{5}$$

$$\frac{2}{5} \times 360° = 144°$$

3. **Choice B is correct.**
Finding the circumference will require the radius: in this problem, finding the radius means completing the square.

$$x^2 + y^2 - 6y = 7$$

$$x^2 + y^2 - 6y + 9 = 7 + 9$$

$$x^2 + (y - 3)^2 = 16$$

Since $r^2 = 16, r = 4$.Then find the circumference:

$$C = 2\pi r$$

$$C = 2\pi(4)$$

$$C = 8\pi$$

4. **Choice C is correct.**
Diameters of 10 and 16 inches mean radii of 5 and 8 inches, and since $A = \pi r^2$, they each have areas of 25π and 64π respectively. Then find the percentage increase:

$$P = \frac{New - Old}{Old} \times 100\%$$

$$P = \frac{64\pi - 25\pi}{25\pi} \times 100\%$$

$$P = 156\%$$

Since the new pizza is 156% of the old pizza, we have an *increase* of 56%.

5. **Choice B is correct.**
A quadratic equation like $f(x)$ can overlap a circle like $g(x)$ up to four times, as shown:

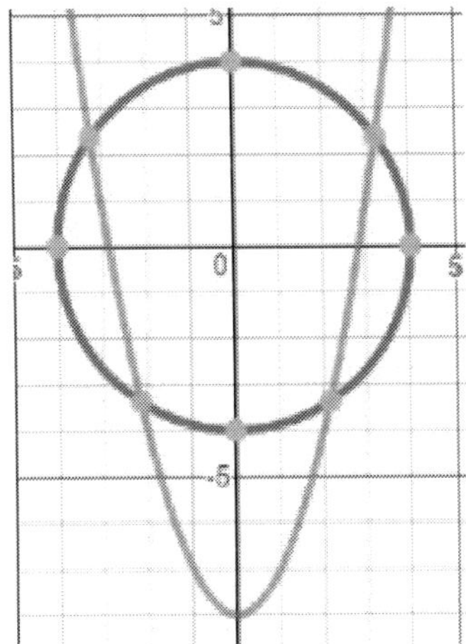

6. **Choice B is correct.**
Finding distance requires two points, and our second point is the solution of $f(x)$ and $g(x)$

$$f(x) = g(x)$$

$$3x + 15 = -4x - 13$$

$$x = -4$$

Plug 4 into one of the functions to find y:

$$y = 3x + 15$$

$$y = 3(4) + 15$$

$$y = 3$$

The distance between (0,0) and (−4,3) is found with the Pythagorean Theorem:

$$a^2 + b^2 = c^2$$

$$\left(0 - (-4)\right)^2 + (0 - 3)^2 = c^2$$

$$16 + 9 = c^2$$

$$5 = c$$

7. **Choice C is correct.**
Since there are no x or y terms here (only x^2 and y^2), move the constants to one side:

$$x^2 + y^2 - 12 = 9$$

$$x^2 + y^2 = 21$$

Since $r^2 = 21$, $r = \sqrt{21}$

8. **Choice A is correct.**
Area requires base and perpendicular height. The "height" is the distance between $x = 2$ and the intersection of the other two functions, and the "base" is the distance between the points of the two functions when $x = 2$

$$Area = \frac{1}{2} \times base \times height$$

$$Area = \frac{1}{2}(2)(2)$$

$$Area = 2$$

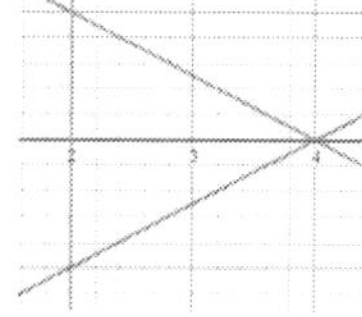

9. **Choice B is correct.**
Start with the coordinate of $(4, -3)$ and reverse the function shift 2 units up and 3 units left to find $(1, -1)$ as the center of circle C. Since circle C has a radius of 4, the area will be 16, yielding $(x - 1)^2 + (x + 1)^2 = 16$

10. **Choice A is correct.**
Start by halving the new volume to find $\frac{750\ cm^3}{2} = 375\ cm^3$. Since $Vol = \pi r^2 h$, substitute to find $375 = \pi r^2 \times 9$, simplify to find $13.27 = r^2$ and $3.64 = r$.

11. **Choice C is correct.**
Since the triangle is a right triangle, two of the angles are known ($\frac{\pi}{9}$ and $\frac{\pi}{2} = 90°$). The sum of the angles must be 180°, aka π radians. Thus $x + \frac{\pi}{9} + \frac{\pi}{2} = \pi$, $x = \pi - \frac{11\pi}{18}$, and $x = \frac{7\pi}{18}$

12. **Choice A is correct.**
If the circle has a radius of x, then

$$Area = \pi x^2$$

The diagonal of an inscribed square is the diameter of the circle, so the square has a diagonal of $2x$, a side of $\frac{2x}{\sqrt{2}}$, and an area of $\frac{4x^2}{2}$ or $2x^2$. Divide the circle's area by the square's:

$$\frac{\pi x^2}{2x^2} = \frac{\pi}{2} = 1.57$$

The circle is 57% larger than the square.

13. **Choice B is correct.**
The sector is a fraction of the area, so $\frac{50}{360}$ of the circle's area. The circumference of 12π means the radius is 6.

$$Area = \pi r^2$$
$$Area = \pi 6^2$$

36π, and $\frac{5}{36}$ of 36π is 5π

14. **Choice B is correct.**
Aside from utilizing the Pythagorean theorem, the triangle that can be formed here is a multiple of a 5-12-13 special right triangle as follows:

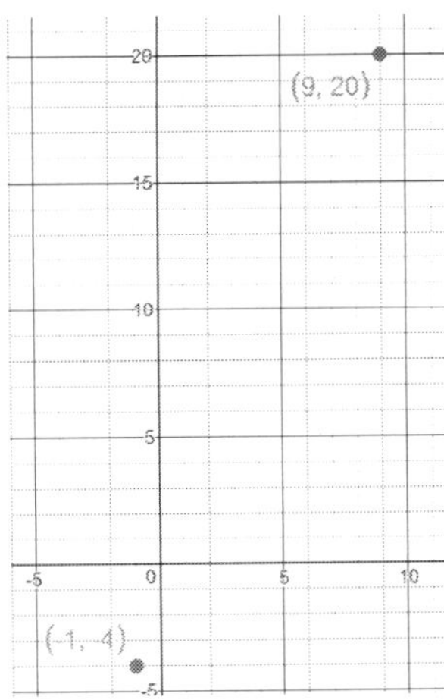

Given thus, we recognize that the radius is 13. Circumference therefore is:

$$C = \pi r^2$$
$$C = \pi(13^2)$$
$$C = 169\pi$$

15. **Choice D is correct.**
First, solve $n^2 + 5 = 14$ and find that $n = \pm 3$. If $n = \pm 3$ and $r = 5$ (since $r^2 = 25$), we have infinite possible circles aligned along x=3 and x=-3. One method to solve this problem would be to plug in the x and y values of the given points and solve each equation for k. Another would be to understand that any point within 5 units of $x = 3$ or $x = -3$ with integer units should work.

16. **Choice C is correct.**
First, find the circle's radius:

$$\pi r^2 = Area$$
$$\pi r^2 = 128\pi$$
$$r = 8\sqrt{2}$$

Since $radius = \frac{1}{2} diameter$,
$d = 16\sqrt{2}$, and the sides are 16. $Area = s^2$

$$Area = 256$$

Then find the square's percentage:

$$\frac{Square}{Circle} \times 100\%$$
$$\frac{256}{128\pi} \times 100\%$$
$$64\%$$

17. **The correct answer is 1**

$$360° = 2\pi \text{ radians}$$

Therefore, $90° = \frac{\pi}{2} = 1.57$ radians. Since n must be an integer, 1 is the only logical answer.

18. **The correct answer is 0**
The equation of the line drawn is:

$$y = \frac{3}{5}x$$

Line A is perpendicular, therefore, it has a negative reciprocal slope, with a given y-intercept of 5.
Line A =>

$$y = -\frac{5}{3}x + 5$$

Plug in the given x-coordinate of (3,y) to obtain the following:

$$y = -\frac{5}{3}x + 5$$
$$y = -\frac{5}{3}(3) + 5$$
$$y = 0$$

19. **The correct answer is 151**

Find the circumference:

$$C = 2\pi r$$
$$C = 2\pi(8)$$
$$C = 16\pi$$

The portion is $\frac{12\pi}{16\pi} = \frac{3}{4}$ of the full area (πr^2):

$$\frac{3}{4} \times \pi(8)^2$$
$$48\pi$$
$$150.8$$

The nearest integer is 151.

20. **The correct answer is 4**

An inscribed right triangle resembles the figure shown with the hypotenuse as diameter. Find the radius:

$$\pi r^2 = Area$$
$$\pi r^2 = 4\pi$$
$$r = 2$$

The diameter of 4. Since the hypotenuse of a right triangle is $\sqrt{2}$ times longer than the legs, the legs must be $\frac{4}{\sqrt{2}}$ (or $\frac{4\sqrt{2}}{2}$).

Now, find the area:

$$Area = \frac{1}{2}(base)(height)$$
$$Area = \frac{1}{2} \times \frac{4}{\sqrt{2}} \times \frac{4}{\sqrt{2}}$$
$$Area = \frac{16}{4} = 4$$

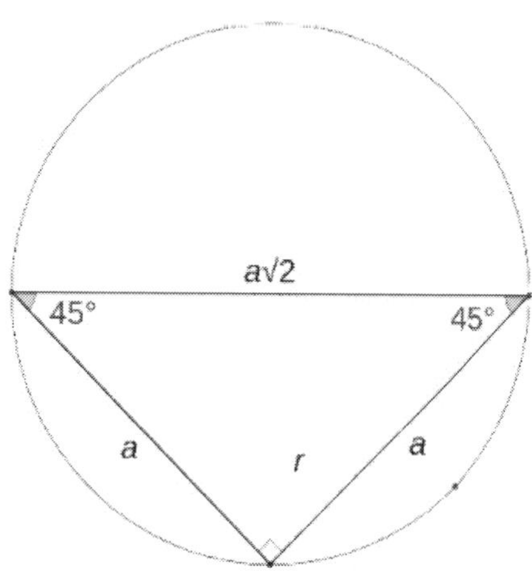

Mathematics
Lesson 7

Trigonometry

Goals

We will develop our mathematical fluency and gain meaningful understanding by learning to:

1) Identify the role of trigonometry and basic trigonometric functions
2) Apply trigonometric identities to common scenarios
3) Use trig ratios in combination with other concepts (geometry, algebra, etc.) to solve problems
4) Use advanced trigonometric functions in preparation for challenging problems

Contents

- Trig Fundamentals
- Trig Functions
- Trig Identities
- Secant, Cosecant, Tangent
- Inverse Functions

Lesson 7
Trigonometry

Trigonometry Fundamentals

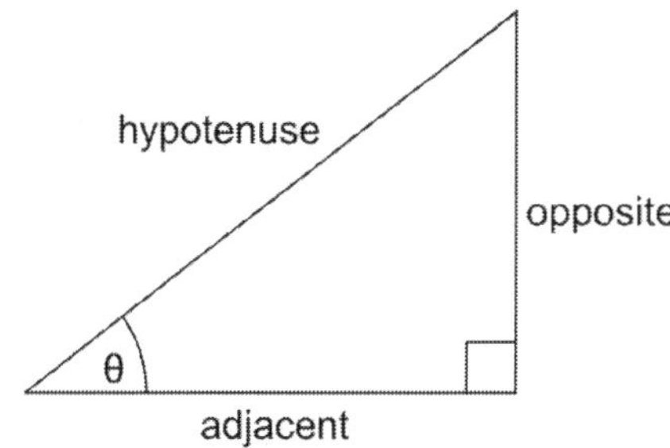

Trigonometry, or "trig", is the study of the relationship between sides and angles in right triangles. The core of trig is realizing that **all triangles have fixed ratios based on their sides**. The ratio of sides in any right triangle with the same angle measures will remain the same if that triangle has a hypotenuse of 9 or 9,000. Because of this, all similar right triangles will have the same trig values.

Most people think of trigonometry in terms of functions. All trig functions will give a value that measures the ratio of sides. For example, if we know $\sin 30° = \frac{1}{2}$, the hypotenuse of *any* right triangle with a $30°$ angle will be twice the length of the opposite side of that angle. This is true of all such triangles, despite the differences in their actual sizes. *Note that most trig problems will be measured in radians.*

Trigonometry Functions

Fundamental trig functions are sine, cosine, and tangent. They are tied to the acrostic mnemonic device:

SOH-CAH-TOA

SOH: Sine θ is equal to Opposite over Hypotenuse ➡ $\sin\theta = \frac{Opp}{Hyp}$

CAH: Cosine θ is equal to Adjacent over Hypotenuse ➡ $\cos\theta = \frac{Adj}{Hyp}$

TOA: Tangent θ is equal to Opposite over Hypotenuse ➡ $\tan\theta = \frac{Opp}{Adj}$

Sine measures the ratio of an angle's opposite side to the hypotenuse ($\sin\theta = \frac{Opposite}{Hypotenuse}$).

Cosine measures the ratio of the adjacent side to the hypotenuse ($\cos\theta = \frac{Adjacent}{Hypotenuse}$). Since every angle is made up of two lines, it may seem like we have two adjacent sides, but the hypotenuse never counts as the adjacent side for trig measures.

Tangent measures the ratio of the opposite and adjacent sides ($\tan\theta = \frac{Opposite}{Adjacent}$) and is the only one of the three basic functions that is without the hypotenuse.

	$\sin\theta = \frac{Opposite}{Hypotenuse}$	$\cos\theta = \frac{Adjacent}{Hypotenuse}$	$\tan\theta = \frac{Opposite}{Adjacent}$
30°	$\frac{1}{2}$	$\frac{\sqrt{3}}{2}$	$\frac{1}{\sqrt{3}}$ or $\frac{\sqrt{3}}{3}$ rationalized
60°	$\frac{\sqrt{3}}{2}$	$\frac{1}{2}$	$\frac{\sqrt{3}}{1}$
90°	1	0	Undefined

eg 1. The Burj Khalifa, pictured on the right, is the world's tallest existing structure at approximately 825 meters of height. If the base of the tower is 175 meters from the coast of the lake surrounding it, and a line is drawn from the coast to the top of the tower, what is the ratio of the tower's height to the distance to the beach?

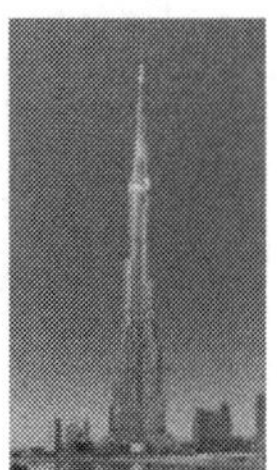

Trigonometry Identities

Trig functions can also be understood by treating the related sides as variables. Let's take some time to understand where the rules come from and how to use algebra to solve complicated trig issues.

- $\frac{\sin x}{\cos x} = \tan x$ is a rule that can be proven with nothing more than some critical reasoning and our knowledge of fractions. Since we know the definition for sine and cosine as fractions, we can substitute them in as $\frac{(\frac{Opposite}{Hypotenuse})}{(\frac{Adjacent}{Hypotenuse})} = \tan x$ (remember, this only works if all the trig functions use the same angle).

  When we divide by a fraction, we can instead multiply by the reciprocal, giving us $\frac{Opp}{Hyp} \times \frac{Hyp}{Adj} = \tan x$, and we can eliminate the two Hyp to give us $\frac{Opp \times \cancel{Hyp}}{Adj \times \cancel{Hyp}}$, the very definition of tangent.

eg 2. If the sine of an angle measures $6x$ and the cosine of the same angle measures $11x$, what is the tangent of the angle?

- $\boldsymbol{sin^{\,2}x + cos^2x = 1}$. The best way to understand this rule is to think about the terms not as just trig functions but as side relations. Note that $sin^2x = (\sin x)^2$. Then, rewrite the equation as $(\frac{O}{H})^2 + (\frac{A}{H})^2 = 1$, and simplify to $\frac{O^2}{H^2} + \frac{A^2}{H^2} = 1$ and $\frac{O^2+A^2}{H^2} = 1$. Think about the Pythagorean Theorem now and see that $O^2 + A^2$ is equal to H^2 ($leg^2 + leg^2 = hypotenuse^2$). That leaves $\frac{h^2}{h^2} = 1$, which proves our identity. This work took centuries to develop in Persia and Greece, but we just proved it in a few lines. Nice job!

eg 3. If $\sin\theta = x^2 - 2x - 8$ and $\cos\theta = x - 4$, what is of $\tan\theta$ in terms of x?

- $\boldsymbol{\sin\theta = \cos(90 - \theta)}$. To better understand this relationship, we refer to the triangle figure to the right. The sine of α is the $\frac{Opposite}{Adjacent}$, so in this case $\sin\alpha = \frac{a}{c}$. We also note that $\cos\beta = \frac{a}{c}$, therefore $\sin\alpha = \cos\beta$. Furthermore, since we know $\alpha + \beta + 90 = 180$, we simplify the equation to $\beta = 90 - a$. We then substitute to obtain $\cos(90 - \alpha) = \frac{a}{c}$. Therefore, we can conclude $\sin\alpha = \cos(90 - \alpha)$.

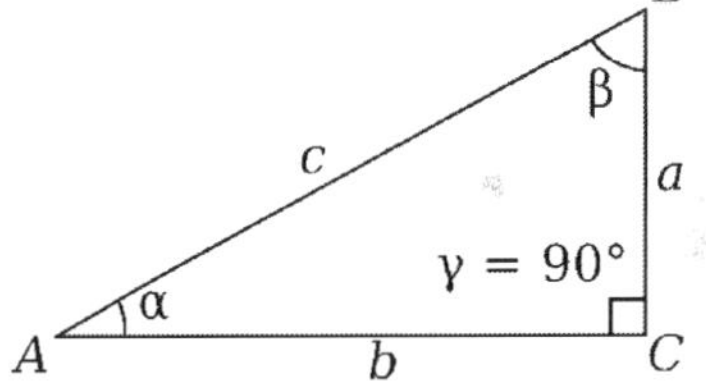

eg 4. If $\sin\theta = \sqrt{4n - n^2 - 3}$, what is $\cos\theta$ in terms of n?

Secant, Cosecant, and Cotangent

Let's take a look at three new trig functions cosecant (cosec), secant (sec) and cotangent (cot). We define these functions as follows:

$$cosec\ \theta = \frac{1}{sin\ \theta}$$

$$sec\ \theta = \frac{1}{cos\ \theta}$$

$$cot\ \theta = \frac{1}{\tan\theta}$$

Cosecant measures the ratio of the hypotenuse to the opposite side.

Secant measures the ratio of the hypotenuse to the adjacent side.

Cotangent measures the ratio of the adjacent and opposite sides.

$\sin\theta = \frac{Opposite}{Hypotenuse}$	$\cos\theta = \frac{Adjacent}{Hypotenuse}$	$\tan\theta = \frac{Opposite}{Adjacent}$
$\csc\theta = \frac{Hypotenuse}{Opposite}$	$\sec\theta = \frac{Hypotenuse}{Adjacent}$	$\cot\theta = \frac{Adjacent}{Opposite}$

Inverse Functions

For every trigonometric functions, there is an inverse function that works in reverse. These functions are also called by the same name but with an "arc-" in front of them. All inverse trig functions have an angle (in degrees or radians) as its output. If $y = \arcsin x$ then $\sin y = x$. For example:

$$sin\ \theta = \frac{\pi}{2}$$

$$arcsin\ \frac{\pi}{2} = \theta$$

$$cos\ \theta = \pi$$

$$arcos\ \pi = \theta$$

$$tan\ \theta = \frac{\pi}{3}$$

$$arctan\ \frac{\pi}{3} = \theta$$

Inverse functions are also sometimes denoted as:

$$sin^{-1}\ \frac{\pi}{2} = \theta$$

For all intents and purposes, $arcsin = sin^{-1}$ and they are used interchangeably, but most use the arc-format.

eg 5. Given $\sin\theta = \frac{3}{4}$, what is the value of $\sec\theta$?

eg 6. What are all the sides of the right triangle if $\arcsin x = \theta$?

Lesson 7
Trigonometry
Application Exercises

NO CALCULATOR SECTION
Questions 1-5

Time - 20 Minutes

1) Which of the following is equivalent to the tangent of angle G?

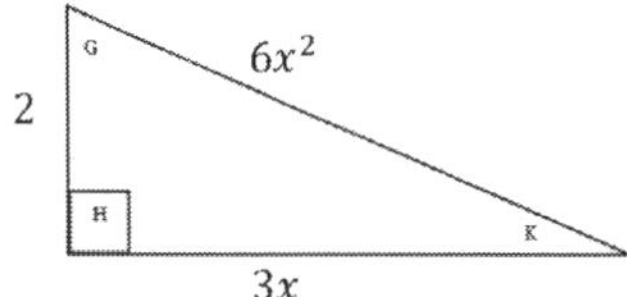

A) $\frac{3x}{2}$

B) $\frac{6x^2}{2}$

C) $\frac{2}{3x}$

D) $\frac{6x^2}{3x}$

2) What is $\sin 30°$ equivalent to?

A) $\sin -30°$
B) $\cos 60°$
C) $\sin 210°$
D) $\tan 150°$

3) Which of the following equals the cosine of θ?

A) $\frac{\tan\theta}{\sin\theta}$

B) $\tan(90-\theta)$

C) $\frac{\cos\theta}{\sin\theta}$

D) $\frac{\sin\theta}{\tan\theta}$

4) In the right triangles below, $\overline{AE}$ and $\overline{BD}$ are parallel. The length of $\overline{BD}$ is equivalent to which of the following?

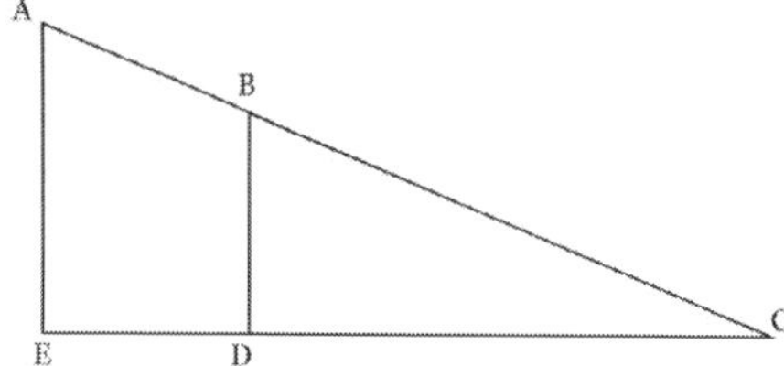

A) $\tan(CAE) \times \overline{CD}$

B) $\cos(CAE) \times \overline{CD}$

C) $\frac{1}{\tan(CAE)} \times \overline{CD}$

D) $\sin(CAE) \times \overline{CD}$

5) Two right isosceles triangles are placed together so that a hypotenuse is formed from the leg of each triangle, as shown below. If the altitude of the greater triangle is 5, what is the length of the greater hypotenuse?

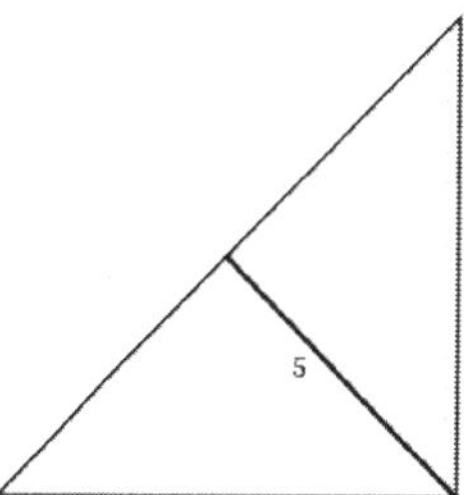

A) 5
B) $5\sqrt{2}$
C) $\frac{10}{\sqrt{2}}$
D) 10

CALCULATOR SECTION
Questions 6-10

6) A professional football field is 300 feet long and 160 feet wide. Two players, A and B, are located on a football field as shown below. Player A started at the midpoint of the bottom boundary and walked 60 feet towards the midpoint of the field, and Player B walks 36 feet from the right edge of the field on the bottom boundary. What is the shortest distance, *in yards*, between the two players? (1 yard = 3 feet)

A) 23.3
B) 42.9
C) 70
D) 128.8

7) If $\sin a = \frac{3}{5}$, what is the value of $\cos a$?

A) 0.8
B) 0.6
C) 0.5
D) 0.4

8) If $\cos\theta = 10x + 5$, and $\sin\theta = 2x + 1$, which of the following must be equivalent to $\tan\theta$?

A) 5

B) 2.8 or $\frac{14}{5}$

C) $\frac{1}{5}$ or .2

D) $\frac{2}{5}$ *or* .4

9) If $\sin x = 1$, $\cos x = 0$, and $x \geq 0$, what is the value of x?

A) 0
B) 1
C) 90
D) θ

10) If $sin(a°) = cos(b°)$, and $2a = b$, what is the measure of a?

A) 30
B) 45
C) 60
D) The answer cannot be determined from the information given

GRID-IN SECTION
Questions 11-14

11) In the diagram below, $\angle IOP$ is measured in radians. If $\angle IOP$ has a measure of $\frac{\pi}{n}$, what is the value of n?

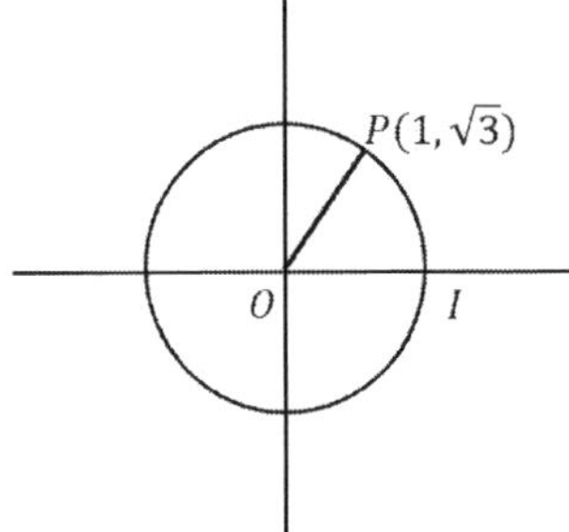

12) A support wire goes from the top of a fifty-foot building to a point on the ground so that the wire contacts the ground to make an angle θ (measured in degrees). If the support wire is anywhere from 70 to 100 feet long, what is a possible integer value of θ?

13) In the rectangle below, $\overline{AD} = 8$ and $\angle ABD = 32$. If $sin\ 32 = 0.53$, $cos\ 32 = 0.848$, and $tan\ 32 = 0.624$, what is the length of $\overline{CD}$ to the nearest integer?

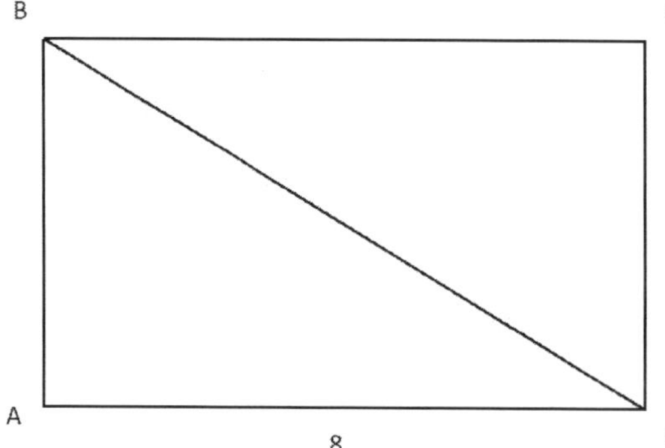

14) In right triangle JFK, $\sin \angle JKF = \frac{x-2}{x+6}$ and $\cos \angle JKF = \frac{x+5}{x+6}$. What is the value of x?

Lesson 7
Trigonometry
Homework Exercises

NO CALCULATOR SECTION
Questions 1-8

Time - 25 Minutes

1) In the triangle below, the $\sin x = .85$. What is the value of side A if the hypotenuse has a length of 20?

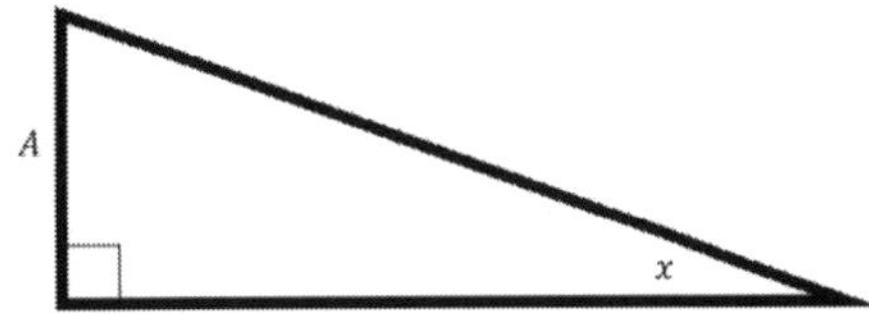

A) 8
B) 10
C) 17
D) 23.5

2) In a right triangle with a 40-degree angle, which of the following will have the greatest measure?

A) $\sin 40$
B) $\cos 40$
C) $\sin 50$
D) $\tan 50$

3) If $\sin(90 - x) = \frac{1}{2}$, what is the value of $\cos x$?

A) $\frac{1}{2}$
B) $\frac{1}{\sqrt{3}}$
C) $\frac{\sqrt{3}}{2}$
D) 2

4) Which of the following cannot be a measure of $\cos \theta$, if $0° < \theta < 90°$?

A) $\frac{5}{3}$

B) $\frac{3}{5}$

C) $\frac{1}{2}$

D) $\frac{3}{8}$

5) The sine of $x^2 + 9$ is equal to the cosine of $8x + 33$. Which of the following could be equal to x?

A) -11
B) -8
C) 1
D) 4

6) A triangle with an angle θ has a sine of 0.2. Which of the following is the best approximation of the tangent of θ?

A) $\frac{1}{4}$
B) $\frac{\sqrt{6}}{12}$
C) $\sqrt{3}$
D) 4

7) A triangle with an angle θ has a cosine of 0.25. Each side of the triangle is increased by a constant x, and this changes the cosine to 0.4. What is the value of x?

A) 0
B) 1
C) 5
D) The answer cannot be determined from the information given.

8) Which of the following is equal to the function $f(\theta)$, if the function f is equal to $f(x) = ((\sin x) + 1)((\sin x) - 1)$?

A) $\tan x$
B) $-\cos^2 x$
C) $\sin^2 x$
D) $-\tan x$

PITTSBURGH PREP

CALCULATOR SECTION
Questions 9-16

9) A triangle has a hypotenuse of 25 and an angle θ with a sine of 0.573. What is the measure of the side opposite θ, rounded to the nearest tenth?

A) 14.3
B) 20.5
C) 43.6
D) The answer cannot be determined from the information given.

10) A right triangle contains an angle β, which has a sine of $\frac{3}{7}$. If the hypotenuse of the triangle is 42, then what is the length of side β?

A) 18
B) 21
C) 24
D) 49

11) In a triangle with angle α, the cosine of angle α is approximately 0.91 and the sin of angle α is approximately 0.42. If the hypotenuse of the triangle has a length of 10, what is the perimeter of the triangle?

A) The answer cannot be determined from the information given.
B) 23.3
C) 67
D) 58

12) A line $f(x) = \frac{2}{5}x$ is mapped on the coordinate plane. At what angle does the line intercept the origin, rounded to the nearest degree?

A) 22
B) 24
C) 66
D) 68

13) In Circle P, $\overline{RQ}$ is a diameter of circle P with a length of 18. If the measure of angle $\angle SPQ$ is $42°$, and $\overline{PS}$ is 9, what is $\cos \angle SRP$, rounded to the nearest hundredth?

A) .21
B) .74
C) .93
D) 88.6

14) If a twenty-five-foot-tall building casts a shadow of sixty feet, what is the measure of the angle the shadow strikes the ground at (to the nearest degree)?

A) 23
B) 25
C) 65
D) 67

15) A right triangle has angles of $x^2 + 2x$, $-x + 70$, and 90. If $x > 0$, what is a possible value for x?

A) 4
B) 5
C) 10
D) 11

16) If $\sin \theta = x^{4n}$, $\cos \theta = x^{5n+1}$, and $\tan \theta = x^{3n+6}$, what is the value of n?

A) -2
B) $\frac{-7}{4}$
C) 3
D) 5

GRID-IN SECTION
Questions 17-20

17) If the sine of angle θ is 0.6, what is the sine of $(90 - \theta)$?

18) A roof's pitch, or steepness, can be measured in slope and degrees from the bottom of the roof. If a roof has a 25 foot diagonal length and has a pitch of 30 degrees, how high will the roof rise, in meters to the nearest tenth?

19) A wheelchair ramp must descend a 5-foot drop. According to the Americans with Disabilities Act, the maximum angle for the ramp is 4.8°. What is a possible length of the ramp, rounded to the nearest meter?

20) In the diagram below, β is four times the size of α. What is the measure of $\sin\alpha$?

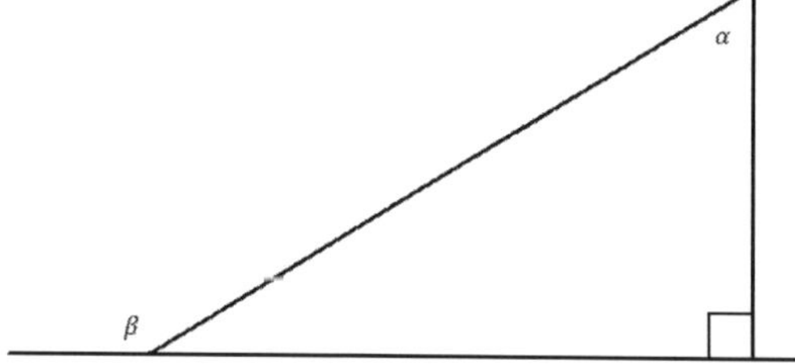

Lesson 7
Trigonometry
Answer Key

Example Exercises	Application Exercises	Homework Exercises
1) $\frac{33}{7}$	1) A	1) C
2) $0.\overline{54}$	2) B	2) D
3) $x+2$	3) D	3) A
4) $n-2$	4) C	4) A
5) $\frac{4}{\sqrt{7}}$	5) D	5) D
6) $1, x, \sqrt{1-x^2}$	6) B	6) B
	7) A	7) B
	8) C	8) B
	9) C	9) A
	10) A	10) A
	11) 3	11) B
	12) $30 \leq x \leq 45$	12) A
	13) 13	13) C
	14) 7	14) A
		15) A
		16) B
		17) 0.8
		18) 12.5
		19) $x \geq 20$
		20) 0.5

Example Exercises

1) **The correct answer is** $\frac{33}{7}$
Imagine making a right triangle with the tower and beach as legs of a right triangle, since we can assume the tower isn't leaning. We can set up a fraction to express this ratio: $\frac{Tower}{Beach} = \frac{825\ m}{175\ m} = \frac{33}{7}$

2) **The correct answer is** $0.\overline{54}$
Since $\frac{sin}{cos} = tan$, we only need to fill in the functions that we have. $\frac{6x}{11x} = 0.545454\ ...$

3) **The correct answer is** $x+2$
This problem may seem like mixing geometry and trig, but we can solve it with fundamentals. The only rule we need is $\frac{\sin x}{\cos x} = \tan x$. From here, treat the problem like algebra: sub $\frac{\sin\theta}{\cos\theta}$ for $\tan\theta$, then plug in given values to get $\frac{x^2-2x-8}{x-4}$, a problem type we've seen. With quadratics in fractions, see if they factor and reduce before resorting to polynomial division. Since the numerator factors to $(x-4)(x+2)$, reduce to $\frac{\cancel{(x-4)}(x+2)}{\cancel{(x-4)}} = \tan\theta$.

4) **The correct answer is** $n-2$
This problem is notable because it lacks a fraction. Since $\sin\theta = \frac{\sqrt{4n-n^2-3}}{1}$, we can set up a triangle with a side of $\sqrt{4n-n^2-3}$ and hypotenuse of 1. Use the Pythagorean Theorem to find the other leg: $leg^2 + \sqrt{4n-n^2-3}^2 = 1^2$. Isolate to get $leg^2 = n^2-4n+4$ and factor to $leg = n-2$.

5) **The correct answer is 78**
This problem uses the ratios from the first example. Since the tower is opposite the observer and the beach is adjacent to the observer, we should use arctangent to find the angle. $\arctan\frac{825}{175} = 78°$.

Application Exercises

1) **Choice A is correct.**
Fill in the definition of tangent:

$$Tangent\ (G) = \frac{Opposite}{Adjacent}$$

$$Tangent\ (G) = \frac{3x}{2}$$

2) **Choice B is correct.**

$$\sin\theta = \cos(90-\theta)$$
$$\sin 30 = \cos(90-30)$$
$$\sin 30 = \cos(60)$$

3) **Choice D is correct.**

$$\tan\theta = \frac{\sin\theta}{\cos\theta}$$
$$\tan\theta \times \cos\theta = \sin\theta$$
$$\cos\theta = \frac{\sin\theta}{\tan\theta}$$

4) **Choice C is correct.**
Because $\Delta ACE \cong \Delta BCD$, $\angle CBD \cong \angle CAE$. $\overline{BD}$ is adjacent to $\angle CAE$, and each choice is multiplied by the opposite side:

$$n \times Opposite = Adjacent$$
$$n = \frac{Opposite}{Adjacent}$$
$$n = \frac{1}{\tan\theta}$$

5) **Choice D is correct.**
The greater hypotenuse is made from two legs of the lesser triangles, so $5 + 5 = 10$.

6) **Choice B is correct.**
Find the distance between the players by making a right triangle: Player A walks 60 feet upward, and Player B walks 112 feet ($\frac{300}{2} - 36 = 112$). Then use the Pythagorean Theorem:

$$a^2 + b^2 = c^2$$
$$60^2 + 114^2 = c^2$$
$$3600 + 12996 = c^2$$
$$12996 = c^2$$
$$128.8 = c$$

Since this answer is in feet, and the problem asks for the distance in yards, $128.8\, feet \times \frac{1\, yard}{3\, feet} = 42.9\, yards$

7) **Choice A is correct.**

$$\sin\theta = \frac{Opposite}{Hypotenuse}$$
$$\sin a = \frac{3}{5}$$

Therefore, Opposite=3 and Hypotenuse= 5. Then recognize the Pythagorean Triple 3 – 4 – 5 and apply:

$$\cos\theta = \frac{Adjacent}{Hypotenuse}$$
$$\cos a = \frac{4}{5}$$

8) **Choice C is correct.**

$$\tan\theta = \frac{\sin\theta}{\cos\theta}$$
$$\tan\theta = \frac{2x+1}{10x+5}$$
$$\tan\theta = \frac{2x+1}{5(2x+1)}$$
$$\tan\theta = \frac{1}{5}$$

9) **Choice C is correct.**
Remember that 1 is the maximum value for a standard trig function. Since $\sin x$ is the maximum value, x must be the maximum angle: 90.

10) **Choice A correct.**
Start with a trig identity:

$$\sin\theta = \cos(90-\theta)$$

Since $\sin a = \cos b$, $b = 90 - a$. Use the given $2a = b$ to substitute:

$$(2a) = 90 - a$$
$$3a = 90$$
$$a = 30$$

11) **The correct answer is 3**
Create a triangle out of the coordinates as shown and use the Pythagorean Theorem to find the radius:

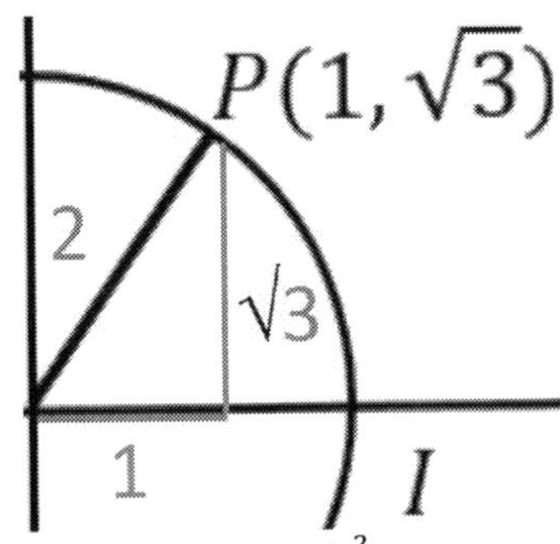

$$1^2 + (\sqrt{3})^2 = 2^2$$

Recognize the $30 - 60 - 90$ triangle that makes $\angle IOP = 60°$. Finally, convert to radians:

$$60° \times \frac{2\pi\ radians}{180°} = \frac{\pi}{3}$$

12) **The correct answer is $30 \le x \le 45$**
If the wire is the hypotenuse of the right triangle and 50 foot building is the side opposite theta.

$$\sin\theta = \frac{50}{hypotenuse}$$

A maximum length of 100 would give us

$$\sin\theta = \frac{50}{100} = \frac{1}{2}$$

We can recognize $\frac{1}{2}$ as the sine of 30° or use $\sin^{-1}\frac{50}{x} = \theta$.

The minimum length of 70 yields $\sin^{-1}\frac{50}{70} =$ 45.58°, but since the answer must be an integer, 45° is acceptable.

13) **The correct answer is 13**
Since this is a rectangle, $\overline{CD} \cong \overline{AB}$, set up a trig function:

$$\tan\angle ABD = \frac{8}{x}$$

$$0.624 = \frac{8}{x}$$

$$x(0.624) = 8$$

$$x = 12.9$$

Round the answer to 13.

14) **The correct answer is 7**
Given sine and cosine with the same denominator, infer a triangle with legs of $x - 2$ and $x + 5$, and use the Pythagorean Theorem to build an equation:

$$(x-2)^2 + (x+5)^2 = (x+6)^2$$

$$x^2 - 4x + 4 + x^2 + 10x + 25 = x^2 + 12x + 36$$

$$2x^2 + 6x + 29 = x^2 + 12x + 36$$

$$x^2 - 6x - 7 = 0$$

$$(x-7)(x+1) = 0$$

$$x = 7, x = -1$$

Since x must be a positive integer, $x = 7$.

Homework Exercises

1) **Choice C is correct.**
Solve by adding $\sin x = \frac{85}{100}$ to a proportion with the given side:

$$\frac{85}{100} = \frac{x}{20}$$

$$1700 = 100x$$

$$17 = x$$

2) **Choice D is correct.**
A 40° angle indicates a triangle as shown: substitute values or use deduction to see that the tangent of 50° gives the middle value divided by the smallest value.

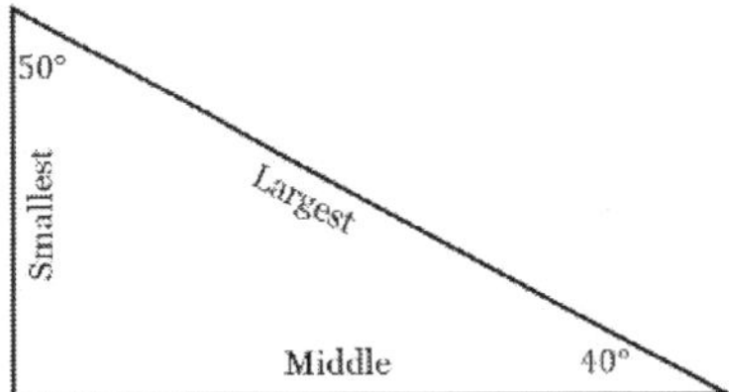

3) **Choice A is correct.**
Apply trigonometric identities to the given information:

$$\sin(x) = \cos(90 - x)$$

Therefore,

$$\sin(90 - x) = \cos(x)$$

$$\frac{1}{2} = \cos(x)$$

4) **Choice A is correct.**
Cosine and sine have maximum values of 1. Therefore, any value greater than 1 cannot be a measure of $\cos\theta$.

5) **Choice D is correct.**
If $\sin a = \cos b$, then $a = 90 - b$. Because of this,

$$x^2 + 9 = 90 - (8x + 33)$$
$$x^2 + 9 = 57 - 8x$$
$$x^2 + 8x - 48 = 0$$
$$(x + 12)(x - 4) = 0$$
$$x = -12, x = 4$$

6) **Choice B is correct.**
Since $0.2 = \frac{2}{10}$, $\sin\theta = \frac{Opposite}{Hypotenuse} = \frac{2}{10}$. With the opposite side and hypotenuse, we can use the Pythagorean Theorem to find the adjacent:

$$a^2 + 2^2 = 10^2$$
$$a^2 = 96$$
$$a = \sqrt{96} = 4\sqrt{6}$$

Find $\tan\theta = \frac{Opposite}{Adjacent}$:

$$\tan\theta = \frac{2}{4\sqrt{6}}$$

Rationalize the fraction

$$\frac{2}{4\sqrt{6}} \times \frac{\sqrt{6}}{\sqrt{6}} = \frac{2\sqrt{6}}{24} = \frac{\sqrt{6}}{12}$$

7) **Choice B is correct.**
Convert 0.25 to $\frac{1}{4}$ and translate the given information:

$$\frac{1 + x}{4 + x} = \frac{40}{100}$$
$$160 + 40x = 100 + 100x$$
$$60 = 60x$$
$$1 = x$$

8) **Choice B is correct.**
Recognize the difference of squares and distribute:

$$((\sin x) + 1)((\sin x) - 1)$$
$$\sin^2 x + \sin x - \sin x - 1$$
$$\sin^2 x - 1$$

Use the trig identity $\sin^2 x + \cos^2 x = 1$

$$\sin^2 x + \cos^2 x - 1 = 0$$
$$\sin^2 x - 1 = -\cos^2 x$$

9) **Choice A is correct.**
Put the given values into the definition of sine:

$$\sin\theta = \frac{Opposite}{Hypotenuse}$$
$$0.573 = \frac{x}{25}$$
$$25 \times 0.573 = x$$
$$14.3 = x$$

10) **Choice A is correct.**
Since $\sin\beta = \frac{3}{7}$, set a proportion with the actual value of the hypotenuse:

$$\frac{3}{7} = \frac{x}{42}$$
$$7x = 126$$
$$x = 18$$

11) **Choice B is correct.**
Since $\cos\alpha = \frac{91}{100}$ and $\sin\alpha = \frac{42}{100}$, use given hypotenuse of 10 to find the opposite side:

$$\frac{91}{100} = \frac{Opp}{10}$$
$$910 = 100 \times Opp$$
$$9.1 = Opp$$

Perform the same procedure to find the adjacent:

$$\frac{42}{100} = \frac{Adj}{10}$$
$$420 = 100 \times Adj$$
$$4.2 = Adj$$

Find the three sides' sum to yield the perimeter:

$$4.2 + 9.1 + 10 = 23.3$$

12) **Choice A is correct.**
Use the slope of the line to build a right triangle with legs of 5 as opposite the angle and 2 as adjacent to the angle:

$$\tan^{-1}\frac{2}{5} = \theta$$
$$21.8 = \theta$$

13) **Choice C is correct.**
Start by drawing the circle.

$$\angle SPQ = 42°$$

S
R
P
Q

$$\angle SRP = \frac{1}{2}\angle SPQ$$
$$\angle SRP = \frac{1}{2}(42°)$$
$$\cos\angle SRP = \cos 21°$$
$$\cos 21° = .93$$

14) **Choice A is correct.**
Find the angle by using the definition of tangent:

$$\tan x = \frac{Opposite}{Adjacent}$$
$$\tan x = \frac{25}{60} = 5/12$$
$$\tan^{-1}\frac{5}{12} = 22.6°$$

15) **Choice A is correct.**
Use the sum of angles to solve for x:

$$(x^2 + 2x) + (-x + 70) + 90 = 180$$
$$x^2 + x - 20 = 0$$
$$(x + 5)(x - 4) = 0$$
$$x = -5, x = 4$$

Since $x > 0$, $x = 4$.

16) **Choice B is correct.**
Use the definition of tangent to solve:

$$\frac{\sin x}{\cos x} = \tan x$$
$$\frac{x^{4n}}{x^{5n+1}} = x^{3n+6}$$

Combine terms using exponent rules:

$$x^{4n} = x^{3n+6} \times x^{5n+1}$$
$$x^{4n} = x^{8n+7}$$
$$4n = 8n + 7$$
$$-4n = 7$$
$$n = -\frac{7}{4}$$

17) **The correct answer is 0.8**
Use the definition of sine to find sides that will work with the given angle:

$$\sin\theta = \frac{Opposite}{Hypotenuse}$$
$$\frac{6}{10} = \frac{Opposite}{Hypotenuse}$$

Use the Pythagorean Theorem to find the third side:

$$a^2 + 6^2 = 10^2$$
$$a^2 = 64$$
$$a = 8$$

Since $\sin(90 - \theta) = \cos\theta$, find $\cos\theta$:

$$\cos\theta = \frac{Adjacent}{Hypotenuse}$$
$$\cos\theta = \frac{8}{10}$$

18) **The correct answer is 12.5**
Find the rise of the roof by using sine:

$$\sin\theta = \frac{Opposite}{Hypotenuse}$$
$$\sin 30° = \frac{Height}{25}$$
$$25 \times \sin 30° = Height$$
$$12.5 = Height$$

19) **The correct answer is $x \geq 20$**
To find ramp length (hypotenuse), use the given information in sine:

$$\sin\theta = \frac{Opposite}{Hypotenuse}$$
$$\sin 4.8° = \frac{5}{Ramp}$$
$$.084 = \frac{5}{Ramp}$$
$$Ramp = \frac{5}{.084}$$
$$Ramp = 59.75$$

Since 4.8° is the maximum angle, a length of 60 feet or greater is sufficient, but the answer must be recorded in meters, meaning $x \geq 20$ (3 feet= 1 meter)

20) **The correct answer is 0.5**
Solve for the angle by setting equations with the triangle's right angle, α, β, and the triangle's third unknown angle x:

$$\alpha + x + 90 = 180$$
$$\beta + x = 180$$

Combine the equations:

$$\alpha + x + 90 = \beta + x$$
$$\alpha + 90 = \beta$$

Substitute 4α for β:

$$\alpha + 90 = 4\alpha$$
$$90 = 3\alpha$$
$$30 = \alpha$$

Finally, $\sin 30 = \frac{1}{2}$

Reading Comprehension Lesson 1

Reading Fundamentals

Goals

We will develop our grammatical fluency and gain meaningful understanding by learning to:

1) Read properly and powerfully
2) Differentiate between the four various passage types common on all exam types
3) Put into practice applicable skills of reading
4) Understand the nuances of reading methodology

Contents

- Reading Methods
- Analytical vs. Problem-Based Methods of Reading
- Reading Fundamentals + Example Problems
- Short Passage Exercises

Lesson 1
Reading Fundamentals

Reading Fundamentals

For many, the reading section is an either/or proposition. Either you'll like it, or you won't care for it. However, since building competency in reading comprehension is a necessity for all academics, we at Pittsburgh Prep have developed **the fundamentals of reading.** These fundamentals include introductions on how to read (yes, literally learning to read all over again) and how to process what we've read. We can rebuild and reinforce these fundamentals to expect better results not just on exams, but in just about any activity where reading is required.

There are **five fundamental processes** of reading that we all must master from the onset. Resolve to master the following processes individually. It will take some time for you to become competent readers by unlearning past poor habits and learning the methodologies outlined here. These are, in order of importance:

I. Identify the **Passage Type**
II. Outline the **Structure**
III. Create **Blueprints**
IV. Be **Metacognitive**
V. Increase **Speed**

I. Identify the **Passage Type**

In our readings, there will be four major **passage types**:

1) Narrative
2) Historical
3) Rhetorical
4) Expository

A <u>narrative</u> passage can be either fiction or nonfiction, and will ask the reader to be **empathetic,** and to shed the reader's prior beliefs, and share in the very **struggle** of the author or subject at issue. This is the main task of any narrative prose reader: find the struggle. Then determine its surrounding parts, such as resolution, tone, perspective, and method of argument. Narrative prose, by definition, is storytelling.

A <u>historical</u> passage will focus on the experiences of the author at their time and their engagement of the issues that continue to influence our civic life. It is important to grasp the **position** the author takes, as it relates to the **central issue** at discussion, with the sole purpose of **attempting to influence** the reader. Themes of justice, freedom, human dignity, and morality all come to the forefront. Though not necessary, it is highly recommended that we have read many variously different readings that tackle historical issues. We must not let ourselves get overwhelmed with the older style or tone of historical passages; instead, focus on the author's position and issues.

An <u>expository</u> passage will seek to present a **general inquiry** with objective **factual findings** that are more meaningful or **insightful**, often paired with some **data**. Your task is to determine, from the general question, the insight or deeper meaning, incorporating the data as need be here.

A <u>rhetorical</u> passage will have a central theme or **thesis** that the author will formulate a personal **point of view** for or against. Unlike historical passages, rhetorical passages will not overtly try to shape your perspective. It is to **inform** the reader of a different perspective altogether.

For every passage you will read, the very first paragraph will indicate the passage type. Try your hand on the following exercises:

Identify the following passages as either narrative, historical, rhetorical or expository.

Example 1: _______________

Tendinitis is a condition that affects nearly 70,000 people each year, causing them to miss their work and suffer needlessly. The only good news here is that, although it is painful, tendinitis is a curable disease. It does, however, take time, rehabilitation, proper rest, and lots of ice cubes. Still, tendinitis can turn into a more dangerous form called tendinosis if not cared for appropriately.

Example 2: _______________

"People object to the demands of those whom they choose to call the strong-minded, because they say 'the right of suffrage will make the women masculine.' That is just the difficulty in which we are involved today. Though disfranchised, we have few women in the best sense; we have simply so many reflections, varieties, and dilutions of the masculine gender. The strong, natural characteristics of womanhood are repressed and ignored in dependence, for so long as man feeds woman she will try to please the giver and adapt herself to his condition."

\- Elizabeth Cady Stanton

Example 3: _______________

He took the sandwich into the next room. His dad was watching TV, sitting in that periscope stoop of his, crookback, like he might tumble into the rug. His dad had infirmities still waiting for a name. Things you had to play one against another. If one thing required a certain medication, it made another thing worse. There were setbacks and side effects, there was a schedule of medications that Richard and his mother tried to keep track of through the daily twists of half doses and warning labels and depending on this and don't forget that.

\- Don DeLillo

Example 4: _______________

The first thing that strikes me about education is knowledge gain. Education gives us a knowledge of the world around us and changes it into something better. It develops in us a perspective of looking at life. It helps us build opinions and have points of view on things in life. People debate over the subject of whether education is the only thing that gives knowledge. Some say education is the process of gaining information about the surrounding world while knowledge is something very different. They are right.

\- Kafoumba Doumbia

II. Outline the **Structure**

As we read a passage, learn to identify and reconstruct its **structure** – at first, do so explicitly on paper, then become so good at this skill that you can do so mentally come test day. Note that structures of passages will differ greatly. Some may have a central thesis, some may not. Others will end with a conclusion, while others will begin with one. Some passages may be full of evidence ripe for deduction, while others will ask the readers to make strong inferences. This is our very first skillset we will develop.

Practice outlining the structure (and other aspects of reading) for the following short passages.

Example 5:

Young Ha-Kim, a Korean author known for his debut novel "I have the right to destroy myself," is also a social commentator of bleak urban relationships. His peers often lament his terse prose, while giving credence to its powerful reflection of living inside a large metropolis like Seoul, Korea. In 1998, two years after publication, Ha-Kim spoke at the annual Housing and Urban Development conference, providing a much-needed voice to the policy wonks making top-level decisions for the residents.

(i) What is the passage type? ____________

(ii) How is the passage structured?

(iii) The author suggests which of the following about Ha-Kim?

A) He does not care much about the opinions of his peers
B) He had written prolifically throughout his career
C) He feels strongly for the people living in urban poverty
D) He prefers to make policy decisions when he is not writing

Example 6:

Many cultures have their own individual accounts of Bigfoot, or the portrayal of a very large humanoid creature, with minor variances. Hunters, scientists, Youtubers and even philosophers have all quipped one way or another about Bigfoot's existence. The pseudoscientific field of Cryptozoology aims to address this, and other folklore questions, with definitive answers. However, the question that I carry with me as I read through these texts is: why doesn't any museum house any sort of fossil record for these creatures?

(i) What is the passage type? ____________

(ii) How is the passage structured?

(iii) The author implies that Cryptozoologists are

A) facades
B) charlatans
C) pragmatists
D) pugilists

III. Create **Blueprints**

When we **blueprint**, we are paraphrasing what the **author wants us to take away**, **NOT what we want to take away from it**. We must disengage with our usual way of reading by disassociating our own personal biases when reading any written material from here onwards. Remember, always read from the author's point of view, without personal bias.

Limit your paraphrase to 10 words or less, and create a blueprint for every paragraph in the passage, since we can safely assume that each paragraph contains a separate and distinct idea.

Create blueprints for the following passages

Example 7:

The truth of these words is beyond doubt, but the mission to which they call us is a most difficult one. Even when pressed by the demands of inner truth, men do not easily assume the task of opposing their government's policy, especially in time of war. Nor does the human spirit move without great difficulty against all the apathy of conformist thought within one's own bosom and in the surrounding world. Moreover, when the issues at hand seem as perplexing as they often do in the case of this dreadful conflict, we are always on the verge of being mesmerized by uncertainty; but we must move on.

(i) What is the passage type? ___________

(ii) How is the above passage structured?

(iii) What is the blueprint? (or, what does the AUTHOR want you to take away?)

(iv) The statement ("Nor does the human spirit... surrounding world") serves to

(A) support the author's main thesis
(B) express the author's disapproval
(C) analyze a hidden agenda of the government
(D) provide a counterargument against the main point

Example 8:

Passage 1

Reformers in the scientific community have long since argued that there will come a time when the carbon footprint will cross a threshold the world cannot turn back from. That time is now. An International Energy Agency analysis shows that global CO2 emissions in 2040 will actually be slightly higher than it is today. This is far short of the Paris Climate Accord target set by the US and other industrial nations.

Passage 2

The Earth has a way of resolving its own issues, with or without human intervention. The much-talked about Ozone Layer depletion in 1987, scientists argued, came about as a result of releasing CFCs (chlorofluorocarbons) into the air. Now, three decades later, the great Ozone hole above "the Antarctic is gradually filling up," Jo Haigh at the Grantham Institute of Imperial College London said. Whence told the proposition that all environmental atrocities be held seriously, need not be taken *primae facia* when calls for the same arise.

(i) What is the passage type? ____________

(ii) How is passage 1 structured?

(iii) What is the blueprint for passage 1?

(iv) How is passage 2 structured?

(v) What is the blueprint for passage 2?

(vi) What best describes the relationship between the two passages?

A) Passage 1 defines a scientific phenomena, while Passage 2 examines the impact on the world's populace
B) Passage 1 describes the International Energy Agency's crusade for the preservation of natural resources, while Passage 2 argues against it
C) Passage 1 suggests causes for environmental degradations, while Passage 2 explores the reasons for them
D) Passage 1 suggests a call to action, while Passage 2 challenges any action at all

IV. Be **Metacognitive**

Metacognition will come naturally. By definition, metacognition means "to be aware of what you are reading." The basic question you will ask after pertinent moments of reading passages will be: **why**? Or, more specifically, *why did the author state what she/he did?* We don't need to ask this question at every moment of our reading, and we will need to understand exactly when we should do so, but this is a fundamental area of reading we will develop fully.

The following types of statements should prompt us to think metacognitively – why do you think this is the case? In your readings, pay special attention to these types of sentences that ask us to think deeper.

Example 9: Write down your metacognitive thoughts after reading each sentence.

(i) Some of the pastors at congregation decided collecting dues was a bad idea.

(ii) Despite the policy ban, bikers performed their errands marvelously throughout the city.

(iii) Isn't it always better to catch adequate sleep than not?

(iv) The rodents are in a hurry now.

(v) Craters landed in this place, affecting this many miles, and ultimately this many people.

(vi) "It was a defining moment," the lawyer argued.

V. Increase **Speed**

To increase **speed**, we look to focus less on technical aspects, but the mental capacity to read with intensity. If you are of the type that loses concentration after a few minutes or sentences, practice high-intense reading at all times. Practice reading in 5 minute, then 10 minute, then 15 minute increments of high-intensity and high-focus. Turn off all cellphones and step away from all distractions while doing so. Take frequent breaks from high intensity reading, usually about a minute (max. two) after each high-intensity reading session (HIRS). Over time, you'll notice a dramatic difference in your ability to read quickly and comprehend better.

Homework Exercises

Short Passage Practice 1
Directions: Attempt the first 10 questions first. Then the more formal questions after class review.

Why is it that those who are experts in a specialty field are the ones with the least amount of care for basic knowledge? Take Professor EJ Monahan, a virtual superstar in the field of electromagnetism. Although he has won the prestigious Nobel Prize, has authored 17 authoritative textbooks, and is oft-recited in dissertations throughout US & European research institutions, he is just as famous for leaving his home and forgetting his shoes, or getting lost on his way to work every single day. Or take Dr. Prajathan Rippamann, an India-born physicist who was well known for forgetting how to use email so often that his Ph.D students had to virtually manage his entire email account for him for years. “We have a reserved sort of reverence for him,” a student once chirped.

1) How is this passage structured by the author?

2) What is your blueprint? Or, to put it another way, what is the author want you to take away from this passage?

3) What is the function of the first sentence?

4) Why is the 1st sentence posed as a question?

5) What should you expect to read after the first sentence? Why?

6) What are the two qualities that every example must embody, according to the author’s thesis?

7) How many examples are given by the author? Where are they?

8) Do the examples embody the two qualities of the thesis?

9) What are the functions of “17 *written textbooks*” & the student quote?

10) We can infer from the passage (lines 3 – 11) that Prof. Monahan's priorities

A) are juxtaposed with mundane daily functions
B) seems to lie solely in academic pursuits
C) seems to not befit a man of his genius level
D) are really harmless to anyone

11) According to the passage (lines 11-17) the author would most likely agree that Dr. Rippamann

A) has contributed greatly to the field of physics
B) would lose his shoes just as many times as Prof. Monahan
C) may win the Nobel Peace Prize
D) holds great respect from his students and peers

12) The student's tone in lines 16-17 can best be summed up as

A) gentle and sarcastic
B) jocular and staid
C) respectful and mocking
D) scolding and carefree

13) The main purpose of this passage is

A) to rebuke a general principle by giving contradictory statements
B) to discuss an odd phenomenon and present a hypothesis against it
C) to argue for an opinion by providing exemplary persons
D) to censure the general idea that savants are perfect beings

Short Passage Practice 2
Directions: Attempt the first 10 questions first. Then the more formal questions thereafter.

The generally accepted statement that Abe Lincoln fought for, created, and signed into law the freedom of slaves has been challenged recently. While it is true that Lincoln is attached to the historically significant Proclamation of 1862, his Vice President, Hannibal Hamlin, was the real force behind the idea the Union needed slaves as soldiers to win the civil war. Further, the Republican leader of the House, Thaddeus Stevens was the first to declare war against the rebellion, especially those who held slaves in their territories. Yes, it is true that Lincoln set the momentum for the freedom of all slaves; however, the law that he signed only pertained to slaves in the Confederacy, which meant that, ironically, slaves in the north were not free even after the proclamation went into effect. It would take three years, when the 13th amendment was created, to achieve this result.

Questions:

1) What is your <u>blueprint</u>?

2) How is this passage structured and organized?

3) How is this passage different from the last passage, in terms of structure?

4) What is the tone of the author?

5) Where is the thesis of this passage located?

6) What should you expect to read after the thesis?

7) Is this a well written passage, in your opinion?

8) Why does the author use the word "Yes"? What function does it have?

9) In the sentence "Further, the Republican... territories" (lines 8 – 12) the author attempts to distinguish between the

A) true versus fake author
B) early versus late motivator
C) executive branch versus the legislative one
D) forceful versus timid

10) The author describes the Proclamation (lines 12-19) in a tone that is

A) massaging the idea that it was not what it seemed to be
B) clearly defying all other interpretations
C) defensively backing the accepted ideals of it
D) challenging the fallacious notions surrounding the topic

11) The author would agree with which of the following statements?

A) The Emancipation Proclamation was a sham, and was not clear in its ideals
B) Abe Lincoln had very little, if any, influence on the abolition of slaves, instead, others should be given more credit for it
C) Americans are unequivocally wrong in their understanding of how the Emancipation Proclamation came into place
D) Slaves in the Union north were not as enthusiastic about the Emancipation Proclamation as the slaves in the Confederacy states

Lesson 1
Reading Fundamentals
Answer Key

Example Exercises

1) Expository

2) Historical

3) Narrative

4) Rhetorical

5) (i) Expository
(ii) Thesis -> Reason -> Example
(iii) Choice (C) is the correct answer

6) (i) Rhetorical
(ii) Claim -> Example -> Conclusion
(iii) Choice (B) is the correct answer. ***Note the subject shift from third person voice to first person voice to indicate the author's opinion is being introduced. Important*! **

7) (i) Historical (by MLK Jr. "Beyond Vietnam, 1967")
(ii) Thesis -> Counterargument #1 (Man's nature) -> Counter #2 (inertia) -> Counter #3 (complex issue) -> Conclusion
(iii) Author provides three specific counter-reasons but still concludes otherwise.
(iv) Choice (D) is the correct answer

8) (i) Rhetorical
(ii) Fact -> Conclusion -> Evidence -> Opinion
(iii) Author urgently calls for action, citing expert analysis
(iv) Fact -> Expert opinion -> Fact -> Conclusion
(v) The Earth heals itself so no need to take any action
(vi) Choice (D) is the correct answer

9) (i) "Some" should lead us to ask about "most"
(ii) Contrasting words like "despite" should prompt us to think further. Other such words like however, moreover, therefore, since, until are all indicatives of emphasis
(iii) Rhetorical questions should always give us pause for further thought
(iv) The usage of the word "now" indicates an emphasis on time
(v) Repetition of words, in this instance "this" is a clear indication of emphasis that the author wants us to realize
(vi) Using quotes should always make us think further about the quote itself and why the author had placed it

Short Passage Practice 1

1) The passage structure has a thesis then two examples that follow

2) The blueprint should correspond with: Experts don't care about basic knowledge.

3) The first sentence functions as a rhetorical question that serves as the passage's thesis as well

4) As stated above, it's rhetorical

5) The reader should expect to read supporting statements about experts who do not care about basic knowledge

6) The two qualities are (1) whether they are experts and (2) whether they don't care about basic knowledge

7) The author provides two examples, and they follow each other

8) Both examples factually embody both qualities, but the second example does not specifically state that he is an expert. We must, therefore, infer that he is.

9) The "17 written textbook" functions to support the author's contention that the example given is an expert, while the student quote provides support for the second example that he is both an expert (since the students respect him) and that he does not care for basic knowledge (since the students do not respect him fully – they have a reservation about it)

10) **Choice B is correct.**
Because experts do not think of basic things, instead, they must be thinking of their academic pursuits. This is a classic inference type.

11) **Choice A is correct.**
Because we know that the author defines an expert as someone who is accomplished according to the resume provided by the author for example #1 (EJ Monahan). Therefore, it follows that any other example will also be an expert who has accomplished much.

12) **Choice B is correct.**
Tone can be determined by diction + context. Jocular implies a friendly, joking manner, which can be inferred from the "reserved reverence." At the same time, the student's comment maintains a level of respect that fits the definition of "staid." If unsure about vocabulary, use elimination

13) **Choice C is correct.**
The opinion is the author's thesis, and two examples follow to support this thesis.

Short Passage Practice 2

1) Your blueprint should be similar to: "a generally accepted statement has been challenged recently." Note that this passage is about a particular statement that has been challenged – it is NOT about Lincoln or any other character.

2) The passage gives us a thesis, then three examples.

3) The last short passage had two examples, and it furthered developed the two examples into two parts.

4) The tone here is more academic in nature. The author uses words like "while it is true" and "further" to convey wording that you'd find in a typical history textbook or mag.

5) The thesis is the first sentence.

6) We should expect to read about the three ways the generally accepted statement has been challenged.

7) The correct answer here is: who cares. Rarely will an exam ask for your opinion on the passage. Most times exams test you on your ability to critically analyze the passage, not your personal opinions.

8) One of the reasons for why an explicit agreement or disagreement is used to begin a sentence is to signify that there will be a counterpoint later.

9) **Choice B is correct.**
The challenge that is developed here the question "who created the law that freed slaves?" According to the author, this is a question that's best answered by looking at the earlier motivator, Thaddeus Stevens, who prompted the eventual creation of the law by declaring war.

10) **Choice D is correct**.
The author is indeed challenging the notions surrounding the proclamation. Choice A doesn't fit the definition of massage, as the author does not manipulate the information for a favorable result.

11) **Choice D is correct.**
As an inference question, this may have been difficult, but we can reasonably infer that the Slaves in the North were not as happy as the Slaves in the South since only the Southern Slaves were freed. All other choices are not supported by the passage.

Reading Comprehension Lesson 2

Narrative Passages

Goals

We will develop our grammatical fluency and gain meaningful understanding by learning to:

1) Dissect narrative type passages
2) Implement specific strategies for narrative passages
3) Answer different question types based on narrative passages

Contents

- Narrative Passage Types
- Note on Personal Bias
- Short Passage Exercises
- Long Passage Exercises

Lesson 2
Narrative Passages

Narrative Passages

Remember that narrative passages ask the reader to be **empathetic**, to avoid personal **biases**, and identify the author's **struggle** or subject at issue. Start by identifying the struggle from the onset, and develop all other points surrounding that struggle accordingly.

A general outline of a narrative mindmap tends to look like this:

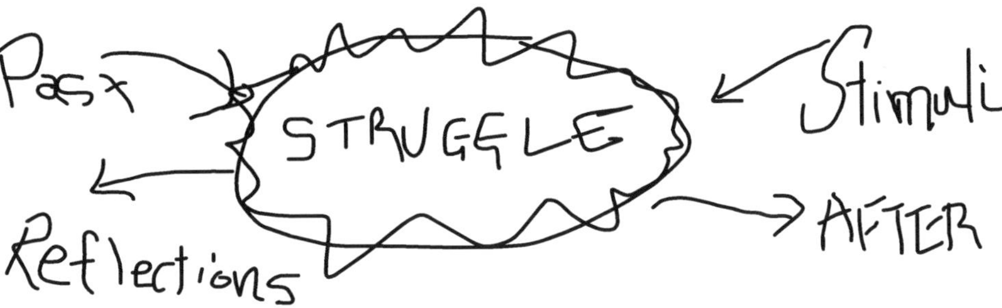

Understand that each of the components above will be a significant part of the passage, and they help us to analyze the passage deeply and meaningfully. If this understanding comes naturally to you as a reader, then great, soldier on. If you do not consider yourself an avid reader (or just plainly hate to read) then treat this lesson more like a puzzle that needs to be solved.

Questions to be asked when reading a narrative passage are:

- What is the central struggle of the author?
- What are the past events that led up to the struggle?
- What are the reflections of the author on the struggle?
- What are the consequences of having gone through the struggle?
- What are the stimuli that feeds into the struggle currently?

This is the very first step. Let us talk a bit further about the individual components.

Central Struggle:	In Narrative passages, the central **struggle** can be something a character may have gone through, presently going through, or will be going through. Identify this conflict first, since it is pertinent as a basis for analyzing the entire passage.
Past Events:	Past events that led up this moment in time present us with **facts** and history. This important info will be introduced at some point in the passage. Provides us with cause.
Reflections:	The author's **personal opinion**. A subjective shift from third-person to first-person ("he, she or it" → "I, me, my") marks a very important moment for both the author and the reader. Recognize when this occurs!

After Events: This is where the author discusses possible **resolutions** to the issue at hand, changes of emotions or outlook moving forward. Many times, this particular paragraph or two is dark or filled with despair, but not always, since the author is usually gripped by some meaningful problem.

Stimuli: The idea of a stimuli revolves around current pressures, or things left unsaid that the reader must skillfully **infer** or **deduce**. Pairing our metacognitive skills will allow us to become stronger in this area.

Remember, all of the above occurs while you read, and much of how you process the information will be incorporated into the structure of the passage that you will outline. A paragraph may contain only one or more of the above topics, so be sure to stay attentive as they occur.

Note on Personal Bias

Do not incorporate any prior knowledge into your readings. Since many of the passages are adapted from actual, written works of literature from well known authors, you may find that you are familiar with some passages you encounter. Even so, make sure to not let any of your prior knowledge come into play as you both read and answer questions based on that passage.

Application Exercises

Narrative Short Passage 1: Emmanuella

While visiting inside the catacombs, Emmanuella decided then and there to become an archeologist. Her adoptive parents, both medical doctors, were simply elated upon hearing the news. As long as anyone can remember, everyone in their family were physicians, dating back to the Civil War for seven generations, filling the pages and ledgers of crisp, white medical journals from ghostly past. Her parents were overjoyed, even, for they knew: in diversity there is beauty and strength.

Narrative Passage Analysis:

1) What is the central struggle of the author?

2) What are the past events that led up to the struggle?

3) What are the reflections of the author on the struggle?

4) What are the consequences of having gone through the struggle?

5) What are the stimuli that feed into the struggle currently?

"Outside of a dog,
a book is a man's best friend.
Inside of a dog, it's too dark to read."
-Groucho Marx

Narrative Short Passage 2: The Beach

The beach was the place where I found my discomfort, thank goodness. Watching the people commiserating under the hot, dull sun, drenched in sweat and full of coerced conversation muted by endless waves, perhaps it reminded me a wee bit much of home. Either way, no one was able to sway my dim disposition one way or another once I sat down on my Grandpaw's rickety beach chair, with nary a moment to be missed on the grand stage of sand.

Narrative Passage Analysis:

1) What is the central struggle of the author?

2) What are the past events that led up to the struggle?

3) What are the reflections of the author on the struggle?

4) What are the consequences of having gone through the struggle?

5) What are the stimuli that feeds into the struggle currently?

Final Note on Narrative Passage Analysis

Narrative passages are usually structured chronologically. Events leading up to and events that follow the author's struggle can be identified in this way.

Analysis should occur as your read the passage. Your analysis should be incorporated into your identification of structure and blueprints. Remember that the analysis occurs in your head, not explicitly, for every passage. Otherwise it will take too long to complete a reading comprehension passage and time will be a concern.

The next step is to follow through with Pittsburgh Prep's methodology of proper reading. These include outlining of structure, creating blueprints, being metacognitive, and increasing speed.

Homework Exercises

Narrative Long Passage 1: Call of the Wild, Jack London (1903)

When Buck earned sixteen hundred dollars in five minutes for John Thornton, he made it possible for his master to pay off certain debts and to journey with his partners into the East after a fabled lost mine, the history of which was as old as the history of the country. Many men had sought it; few had found it; and more than a few there were who had never returned from the quest. This lost mine was steeped in tragedy and shrouded in mystery. No one knew of the first man. The oldest tradition stopped before it got back to him. From the beginning there had been an ancient and ramshackle cabin. Dying men had sworn to it, and to the mine the site of which it marked, clinching their testimony with nuggets that were unlike any known grade of gold in the Northland.

But no living man had looted this treasure house, and the dead were dead; wherefore John Thornton and Pete and Hans, with Buck and half a dozen other dogs, faced into the East on an unknown trail to achieve where men and dogs as good as themselves had failed. They sledded seventy miles up the Yukon, swung to the left into the Stewart River, passed the Mayo and the McQuestion, and held on until the Stewart itself became a streamlet, threading the upstanding peaks which marked the backbone of the continent.

John Thornton asked little of man or nature. He was unafraid of the wild. With a handful of salt and a rifle he could plunge into the wilderness and fare wherever he pleased and as long as he pleased. Being in no haste, Indian fashion, he hunted his dinner in the course of the day's travel; and if he failed to find it, like the Indian, he kept on travelling, secure in the knowledge that sooner or later he would come to it. So, on this great journey into the East, straight meat was the bill of fare, ammunition and tools principally made up the load on the sled, and the time-card was drawn upon the limitless future.

To Buck it was boundless delight, this hunting, fishing, and indefinite wandering through strange places. For weeks at a time they would hold on steadily, day after day; and for weeks upon end they would camp, here and there, the dogs loafing and the men burning holes through frozen muck and gravel and washing countless pans of dirt by the heat of the fire. Sometimes they went hungry, sometimes they feasted riotously, all according to the abundance of game and the fortune of hunting. Summer arrived, and dogs and men packed on their backs, rafted across blue mountain lakes, and descended or ascended unknown rivers in slender boats whipsawed from the standing forest.

The months came and went, and back and forth they twisted through the uncharted vastness, where no men were and yet where men had been if the Lost Cabin were true. They went across divides in summer blizzards, shivered under the midnight sun on naked mountains between the timber line and the eternal snows, dropped into summer valleys amid swarming gnats and flies, and in the shadows of glaciers picked strawberries and flowers as ripe and fair as any the Southland could boast. In the fall of the year they penetrated a weird lake country, sad and silent, where wildfowl had been, but where then there was no life nor sign of life—only the blowing of chill winds, the forming of ice in sheltered places, and the melancholy rippling of waves on lonely beaches.

And through another winter they wandered on the obliterated trails of men who had gone before. Once, they came upon a path blazed through the forest, an ancient path, and the Lost Cabin seemed very near. But the path began nowhere and ended nowhere, and it remained mystery, as the man who made it and the reason he made it remained mystery. Another time they chanced upon the time-graven wreckage of a hunting lodge, and amid the shreds of rotted blankets John Thornton found a long-barrelled flint-lock. He knew it for a Hudson Bay Company gun of the young days in the Northwest, when such a gun was worth its height in beaver skins packed flat, and that was all—no hint as to the man who in an early day had reared the lodge and left the gun among the blankets.

1) What is the passage type?

A) Narrative
B) Rhetorical
C) Historical
D) Expository

2) What is the structure of the passage? (*Think of your narrative analysis*)

3) Write down blueprints for each paragraph:

4) Which choice best summarizes the passage?

A) A character and his companion travel down a river to seek freedom
B) An adventurer seeks fortune after a small windfall despite mysterious lore
C) A crew of pioneers experience unmitigated optimism after earning some money
D) A band of travelers find nothing but despair at the end of their journey

5) What is the purpose of the sentence "With a handful of salt...he pleased" in lines 31-34?

A) To show that John was an experienced traveler in the wild
B) To indicate that John was a competent cook in the wild
C) To express John's gratitude for being able to spend time in the wild
D) To establish John's inner conflict with the wild

6) The fifth paragraph ("The months...beaches") is primarily concerned with establishing a contrast between

A) illusions of grandeur and false promises
B) sultry winters and bountiful summers
C) harsh landscapes and tidings of hope
D) happiness of desire and sadness of rejection

7) The passage indicates that after Buck had earned sixteen hundred dollars, John had found

A) nothing but depression
B) true happiness in life
C) proper perspective
D) freedom to pursue his dreams

8) The reference to John Thornton finding a long-barrelled flint-lock serves to

A) prove his vast knowledge base on things related to firearms
B) emphasize the thematic significance of the length of John Thornton's trek
C) show the marketability of the rifle that he found on the trails
D) draw an analogy on the solitude felt by John and his companions

9) The phrase used in lines 41-43, "the time-card was drawn upon the limitless future" most nearly means

A) that the travelers had no concept of time as they started their quest
B) that John and Buck were not hindered by obligations
C) that the adventurers did not possess a watch
D) that John and his companions needed to balance their work and their desire for gold

10) The narrator shows us that the travelling company of John, Pete and Hans were

A) skilled woodsman
B) meandering adventurers
C) desperate seekers
D) greedy merchants

11) Which choice provides the best evidence for the answer to the previous question?

A) Lines 13-17 (“Dying men ... Northland.”)
B) Lines 43-45 (“To Buck ... places.”)
C) Lines 53-58 (“Summer arrived ... forest.”)
D) Lines 86-91 (“He knew ... blankets.”)

Narrative Long Passage 2: Gulliver's Travels, Jonathan Swift (1892)

My father had a small estate in Nottinghamshire: I was the third of five sons. He sent me to Emanuel College in Cambridge at fourteen years old, where I resided three years, and applied myself close to my studies; but the charge of maintaining me, although I had a very scanty allowance, being too great for a narrow fortune, I was bound apprentice to Mr. James Bates, an eminent surgeon in London, with whom I continued four years. My father now and then sending me small sums of money, I laid them out in learning navigation, and other parts of the mathematics, useful to those who intend to travel, as I always believed it would be, some time or other, my fortune to do. When I left Mr. Bates, I went down to my father: where, by the assistance of him and my uncle John, and some other relations, I got forty pounds, and a promise of thirty pounds a year to maintain me at Leyden: there I studied physic two years and seven months, knowing it would be useful in long voyages.

Soon after my return from Leyden, I was recommended by my good master, Mr. Bates, to be surgeon to the Swallow, Captain Abraham Pannel, commander; with whom I continued three years and a half, making a voyage or two into the Levant, and some other parts. When I came back I resolved to settle in London; to which Mr. Bates, my master, encouraged me, and by him I was recommended to several patients. I took part of a small house in the Old Jewry; and being advised to alter my condition, I married Mrs. Mary Burton, second daughter to Mr. Edmund Burton, hosier, in Newgate-street, with whom I received four hundred pounds for a portion.

But my good master Bates dying in two years after, and I having few friends, my business began to fail; for my conscience would not suffer me to imitate the bad practice of too many among my brethren. Having therefore consulted with my wife, and some of my acquaintance, I determined to go again to sea. I was surgeon successively in two ships, and made several voyages, for six years, to the East and West Indies, by which I got some addition to my fortune. My hours of leisure I spent in reading the best authors, ancient and modern, being always provided with a good number of books; and when I was ashore, in observing the manners and dispositions of the people, as well as learning their language; wherein I had a great facility, by the strength of my memory.

The last of these voyages not proving very fortunate, I grew weary of the sea, and intended to stay at home with my wife and family. I removed from the Old Jewry to Fetter Lane, and from thence to Wapping, hoping to get business among the sailors; but it would not turn to account. After three years expectation that things would mend, I accepted an advantageous offer from Captain William Prichard, master of the Antelope, who was making a voyage to the South Sea. We set sail from Bristol, May 4, 1699, and our voyage was at first very prosperous.

It would not be proper, for some reasons, to trouble the reader with the particulars of our adventures in those seas; let it suffice to inform him, that in our passage from thence to the East Indies, we were driven by a violent storm to the north-west of Van Diemen's Land. By an observation, we found ourselves in the latitude of 30 degrees 2 minutes south. Twelve of our crew were dead by immoderate labour and ill food; the rest were in a very weak condition. On the 5th of November, which was the beginning of summer in those parts, the weather being very hazy, the seamen spied a rock within half a cable's length of the ship; but the wind was so strong, that we were driven directly upon it, and immediately split. Six of the crew, of whom I was one, having let down the boat into the sea, made a shift to get clear of the ship and the rock. We rowed, by my computation, about three leagues, till we were able to work no longer, being already spent with labour while we were in the ship.

1) What is the passage type?

A) Rhetorical
B) Expository
C) Narrative
D) Historical

2) What is the developmental pattern of the passage above? (*Think of your narrative analysis*)

3) Write blueprints for the five paragraphs of the passage. (*Note that a blueprint must be less than 10 words or so*)

4) What choice best describes what occurs in the entire passage?

A) Narrator recounts his past while tackling his financial troubles
B) Narrator questions the value of his medical profession considering his family life
C) Narrator analyzes the circumstances laid before him by his Master and father
D) Narrator critiques the old-fashioned method of apprenticeship and rebels by travelling on ships

5) As used in line 33, the word "condition" most nearly means

A) bachelorhood
B) medical illness
C) mental faculties
D) sobriety

6) Why does the author state that he "not suffer *{me}* to imitate the bad practice of too many among my brethren" (line 42-43)?

A) He was full of spite
B) He was unaccustomed to failure
C) He refused to deviate from his standards
D) He suffered many trepidations

7) What is the best definition of "fortune" (line 47) as it is used in the passage?

A) luck
B) happiness
C) wealth
D) divinity

8) The "good master" (line 38) would most likely have thought of the author's continuation of his medical practice in London as

A) ambivalent
B) repugnant
C) recommended
D) ill-advised

9) Which choice provides the best evidence for the answer to the previous question?

A) Lines 23-26 ("Soon after ... commander.")
B) Lines 29-31 ("to which...patients.")
C) Lines 38-40 ("But my ... fail.")
D) Lines 40-42 ("for my ... brethren.")

10) We can infer from the passage that the narrator

A) comes from a well-to-do, but not egregiously wealthy, family
B) is greedy
C) neglects his wife and family
D) attempts, in vain, to seek great wealth

Narrative Long Passage 3: Heart of Darkness, Joseph Conrad (1899)

"'What a loss to me—to us!'—she corrected herself with beautiful generosity; then added in a murmur, 'To the world.' By the last gleams of twilight I could see the glitter of her eyes, full of tears—of tears that would not fall.

"'I have been very happy—very fortunate—very proud,' she went on. 'Too fortunate. Too happy for a little while. And now I am unhappy for—for life.'

"She stood up; her fair hair seemed to catch all the remaining light in a glimmer of gold. I rose, too.

"'And of all this,' she went on mournfully, 'of all his promise, and of all his greatness, of his generous mind, of his noble heart, nothing remains—nothing but a memory. You and I—'

"'We shall always remember him,' I said hastily.

"'No!' she cried. 'It is impossible that all this should be lost—that such a life should be sacrificed to leave nothing—but sorrow. You know what vast plans he had. I knew of them, too—I could not perhaps understand—but others knew of them. Something must remain. His words, at least, have not died.'

"'His words will remain,' I said.

"'And his example,' she whispered to herself. 'Men looked up to him—his goodness shone in every act. His example—'

"'True,' I said; 'his example, too. Yes, his example. I forgot that.'

"'But I do not. I cannot—I cannot believe—not yet. I cannot believe that I shall never see him again, that nobody will see him again, never, never, never.'

"She put out her arms as if after a retreating figure, stretching them back and with clasped pale hands across the fading and narrow sheen of the window. Never see him! I saw him clearly enough then. I shall see this eloquent phantom as long as I live, and I shall see her, too, a tragic and familiar Shade, resembling in this gesture another one, tragic also, and bedecked with powerless charms, stretching bare brown arms over the glitter of the infernal stream, the stream of darkness. She said suddenly very low, 'He died as he lived.'

"'His end,' said I, with dull anger stirring in me, 'was in every way worthy of his life.'

"'And I was not with him,' she murmured. My anger subsided before a feeling of infinite pity.

"'Everything that could be done—' I mumbled.

"'Ah, but I believed in him more than any one on earth—more than his own mother, more than—himself. He needed me! Me! I would have treasured every sigh, every word, every sign, every glance.'

"I felt like a chill grip on my chest. 'Don't,' I said, in a muffled voice.

"'Forgive me. I—I have mourned so long in silence—in silence.... You were with him—to the last? I think of his loneliness. Nobody near to understand him as I would have understood. Perhaps no one to hear....'

"'To the very end,' I said, shakily. 'I heard his very last words....' I stopped in a fright.

"'Repeat them,' she murmured in a heart-broken tone. 'I want—I want—something—something—to—to live with.'

"I was on the point of crying at her, 'Don't you hear them?' The dusk was repeating them in a persistent whisper all around us, in a whisper that seemed to swell menacingly like the first whisper of a rising wind. 'The horror! The horror!'

"'His last word—to live with,' she insisted. 'Don't you understand I loved him—I loved him—I loved him!'

"I pulled myself together and spoke slowly.

"'The last word he pronounced was—your name.'

"I heard a light sigh and then my heart stood still, stopped dead short by an exulting and terrible cry, by the cry of inconceivable triumph and of unspeakable pain. 'I knew it—I was sure!'... She knew. She was sure. I heard her weeping; she had hidden her face in her hands. It seemed to me that the house would collapse before I could escape, that the heavens would fall upon my head. But nothing happened. The heavens do not fall for such a trifle. Would they have fallen, I wonder, if I had rendered Kurtz that justice which was his due? Hadn't he said he wanted only justice? But I couldn't. I could not tell her. It would have been too dark—too dark altogether...."

1) What type of passage is this?

A) Rhetorical
B) Narrative
C) Expository
D) Historical

2) What is the structural integrity of the passage? (*aka. Narrative analysis*)

3) Create a blueprint of the main ideas of the passage. (*Note: since this narrative contains many paragraphs/quotes, you may want to separate the passage into 2-3 chunks of ideas.*)

4) The woman's correction in the first sentence indicates that she is afflicted with

A) tragedy
B) self-centeredness
C) magnanimity
D) spite

5) The declaration of how the narrator's "anger subsided before a feeling of infinite pity" (line 45) serves to

A) illustrate the dark hatred he felt towards her
B) explain the reason for the tragedy
C) provide cause for his reluctant agreeableness
D) foreshadow the lady's desire for lost love

6) As presented in the passage, the narrator's desire to speak Kurtz's last words was

A) instead stifled by the narrator's conscience
B) ultimately fulfilled despite author's hesitations
C) mainly replaced by immense sadness
D) terribly overcome with an irrational sense of doom

7) We can point to the following lines for evidence to the question answered above:

A) Lines 58-59 ("To the ... fright")
B) Line 72 ("The last ... name")
C) Line 76 ("I knew ... knew.")
D) Lines 86-87 ("It would ... altogether")

8) Which choice best summarizes the passage?

A) A man struggles but ultimately acquiesces to a woman's wishes
B) A man creates havoc for a recent widow who is simply seeking remorse
C) A man exhibits his deep anger at a woman who seeks compassion
D) A man takes a strange interest in dark fantasies while conversing with a woman

9) In line 2, the word "generosity" most nearly means

A) kindness
B) lavishness
C) latitude
D) altruism

10) What, in fact, were the last words spoken by Kurtz?

A) Line 67 ("The horror... horror.")
B) Line 68 ("to live ... with")
C) Line 72 ("The last ... name.")
D) Lines 76 ("I knew ... sure!")

Narrative Long Passage 4: "A Wrester's Life," Miranda Bellefonte (2007)

The passage below is an excerpt from an author who defied social stereotypes and pressure as the first female wrestler in her high school. She writes about her experience ten years afterwards in an interview.

People always ask me, "was it strange to be on an all-boys wrestling team as a female?" and of course I answer deftly, "not really, it was always fun to kick boys' butts." After the laughter subsides, the strange reality sets in my audience. They wonder if I'm serious or not, but I leave before they can ask me any more questions. When I was a sophomore, my original reason for trying out for the wrestling team was innocuous, really. Little did I know that my life would be changed forever.

I was always walking to school since the only family car that was available was driven by my older brother. Of course, he refused to give me a ride, being the bratty jock that he was. He said something like if I beat him in arm wrestling, I could have the car. On the spot, I upped the ante with him; I said if I tried out for his wrestling team, and made varsity, then he should give me his car. We shook hands, and I tried out for the team that day.

Yes, I had the usual jeers, and lascivious remarks directed at me. And yes, faculty, deans, and friends and family all said I couldn't do it. Isn't this always the case though? Every time a girl decides to do something that society doesn't believe she shouldn't do, someone somewhere makes a big hoopla about it. But I really don't want to talk about that. This is old news by now.

Amazingly, the wrestling coach, Mr. Chapman, allowed me try out as a 112 pounder, and even decided that I had enough of a natural potential to stay on the team. This did several things for me: one, I was sure right then and there that I had a fair shot at making the varsity team, and two, embarrassed my older brother so much that he in turn was getting harassed by his teammates. That in itself was enough for me to stay on the team.

All joking aside, however, it took me two full years of hard work and dedication to make it to varsity. I was tall for a girl, and I was naturally athletic, but don't let anyone fool you, I worked my butt off to get to where I was going. I trained harder, ran longer, woke up earlier, and practiced better than anyone else on my team. I actually lost weight because my body changed from a typical girly body to a more robust muscular and toned one. By my senior year, I made it into varsity as a 108 pounder.

Winning 20 matches in wrestling is like a professional baseball player winning 20 games. I personally amassed a year-end record of 19-6 as a senior. It was a very difficult feat, and I was happy with it. When the newspapers came, and I made national headlines after placing 3rd in the State championships, I had no idea that it was all that big of a deal. No one gave the record to me. I faced the same competition as all the other boys in my division, and in my State. I practiced with the same coach, same teammates, and same facilities. Furthermore, I never felt out of place within the team. I was eventually treated equitably like everyone else.

Best thing of all? I drove to school every day in what used to be my brother's car. That was nice.

1) The word "innocuous" (line 10) most likely means

A) little
B) innocent
C) humble
D) profound

2) It can be inferred from the passage that the author

A) entirely dismisses her hardships as a female wrestler
B) is proud of her accomplishments
C) demands others to acknowledge her as a great female athlete
D) wrestled and beat her older brother fairly

3) The primary purpose of the passage is to show that the author

A) never gave up in the face of hardship and difficulty as a pioneering athlete
B) had a tough time as a first female wrestler
C) faced barriers, but not the barriers that society would normally attribute
D) surprisingly lost weight as a result of her making the varsity team

4) In line 23, the word "lascivious" most closely means

A) confusing
B) lonely
C) lewd
D) unkempt

5) The author declares that her troubles as a female wrestler is "old news by now" (line 30) in order to

A) dismiss the notion that she had a tough time
B) show there were bigger factors to overcome
C) dismantle social stereotypes
D) ignore disdainful remarks made against her

6) The author would characterize her statement "...embarrassed my older brother..." (line 37) as

A) mendacious
B) serious
C) facetious
D) pusillanimous

7) In lines 42-52 the author mentions her losing weight primarily in order to

A) show that girls can diet in other ways and lose weight just as effectively
B) appeal to the public that a girl can train as hard as any boy in high school
C) emphasize the grueling nature of her training regimen
D) examine medically spurious statements that contradict healthy body types in females

8) The passage indicates the author's mood as

A) smug
B) content
C) elitist
D) humble

9) The word "equitably" (line 65) most closely means

A) mainly
B) faintly
C) regularly
D) impartially

Lesson 2
Narrative Passages
Answer Key

Narrative Short Passage 1:
Emmanuella

1) The central struggle of the author revolves around Emmanuella who decides to go against family tradition.

2) Past events indicated by the passage involve a long lineage of medical doctors.

3) The author, in the third person, reflects upon Emmanuella's decision positively.

4) The consequences are that the parents and heroine both found diversity to be a good thing within the family.

5) Stimuli in this instance was a simple family visit to the catacombs that became the impetus for the decision.

Narrative Short Passage 2:
The Beach

1) The central struggle here involves the main protagonist finding comfort in her own discomfort and her belief and observation of the people around her feeling the same.

2) Past events of her home life allows the protagonist, perhaps, to share in the misery of being on the hot beach.

3) Interestingly, the author reflects on her current condition with a some nostalgia.

4) The consequences of the author's struggle seems to be a certain level of contentment at her miserable state.

5) The stimuli are many: unbearable climate, dreary disposition, sweaty people around her.

Narrative Long Passage 1:
Call of the Wild

1) **Choice A is correct.**
This is a narrative passage.

2) The structure of the passage is:

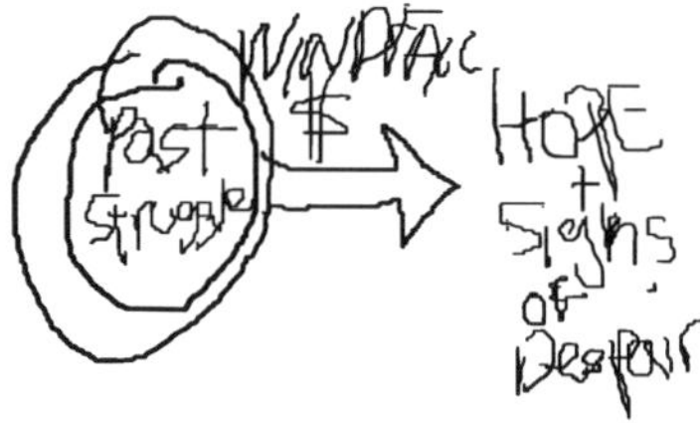

3) Blueprints are as follows:

(1) Small windfall allows adventurers to seek fortune despite historical forebodings

(2) Past has nothing to do with current – let's begin journey!

(3) John + co. were able, experienced men in the wild + ex.

(4) Dogs POV and description of outdoor living

(5) Juxtaposition of actual barrenness vs. hope as seasons pass

(6) Examples of dwindling hope as time and distance increases

4) **Choice B is correct.**
John the adventurer, along with his companions, seek fortune despite lore that warns of risks.

5) **Choice A is correct.**
The prior sentence states that John was "unafraid of the wild", indicating his experienced nature.

6) **Choice C is correct.**
The barren landscape of "uncharted vastness" is contrasted with hopes of "if Lost cabin were true".

7) **Choice D is correct.**
John paid off his "debts" freeing him to pursue his quest.

8) **Choice B is correct.**
John notes that the gun *once* was "worth its height in beaver skins packed flat" but since it is no longer, the change emphasizes the prolonged period of time John and co. spent in the wild.

9) **Choice B is correct.**
As adventurers without debt, the metaphor of a "time-card" drawn upon a "limitless future" indicates that John and his companions were not held back by debts or other obligations – they can take their time searching for fortune as long as they liked.

10) **Choice A is correct.**
Line 56-57 shows us that they "whipsawed boats from the standing forests" – essentially making canoes from trees that they cut down themselves.

11) **Choice C is correct.**

Narrative Long Passage 2:
Gulliver's Travels

1) **Choice C is correct.**
Narrative.

2) The outline of the passage is:

3) Blueprints should correlate to the following:

   (1) Author discusses family upbringing and desire for travel
   (2) Found job a surgeon on ship, returns to London, marries

   (3) Loses money, finds job at sea, learns of other cultures

   (4) Returns wanting to stay with family, but leaves to sea again

   (5) Shipwreck! Meets severe trouble at sea

4) **Choice A is correct.**
There's a consistent theme of the author's past and his financial troubles despite his best attempts to be stable.

5) **Choice A is correct.**
The condition can be argued to be two-fold: (i) his bachelor status or (ii) his desire to be financially stable. His marriage plus the 400 pounds addressed both in the story.

6) **Choice C is correct.**
Author states that his "conscience" would not let him suffer the "bad practice" of his fellow surgeons. We do not know what the bad practice actually may be, but we can infer that it would deviate from the author's standards.

7) **Choice C is correct.**
For the narrator, sailing to sea results in an increase in his monetary earnings.

8) **Choice C is correct.**
The narrator states that his master had encouraged him to settle down and keep his practice on land (line 30-33).

9) **Choice B is correct.**

10) **Choice A is correct.**
Line 1 and line 8 indicates that his family had a small estate but was of a "narrow fortune" – all indications that they were not of immense wealth, but certainly well-to-do.

Narrative Long Passage 3: Heart of Darkness

1) **Choice B is correct.**
   Narrative.
2)

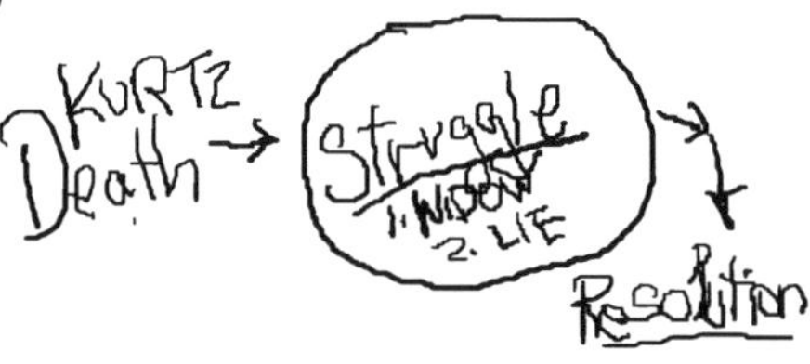

3) Idea #1 (lines 1-30): Author sympathizes a widow's loss of her lover, despite self-centeredness
   Idea #2 (lines 32-70): Author angers, then pities widow, lying to assuage her
   Idea #3 (lines 71-85): Author reconciles his internal struggle, acquiesces to woman's wishes

4) **Choice B is correct.**
   The lady saying that SHE is the one who is suffering, then correcting to the third person ("us") implies a self-centeredness.

5) **Choice C is correct.**
   The narrator's change of heart follows her murmur that indicated real loss, not just a need for attention.

6) **Choice A is correct.**
   The narrator cannot tell the true words spoken because he feels that it would have broken the lady's heart to do so.

7) **Choice D is correct.**

8) **Choice A is correct.**
   The narrator finds himself distraught due to his conscience and the woman's sadness but ultimately gives in to her desire to hear what she wants.

9) **Choice C is correct.**
   In correcting herself, she is giving herself a lot of latitude for understanding her own self-centered mistake when she first proclaimed that the death of her betrothed was a loss to *her* only.

10) **Choice A is correct.**
    Although somewhat unclear, it becomes evident that when the narrator asks: "Don't you hear them?" (lines 63 – 64) he is referring to Kurtz's actual last words spoken, which turns out to be "The horror! The horror!" (line 67).

Narrative Long Passage 4:
A Wrestler's Life

1) **Choice B is correct.**
Innocuous in this instance means innocent, since this is how the author conveys her original reasons for trying out for the team.

2) **Choice B is correct.**
We can infer this form the words that the author uses, such as "I was happy with it" (lines 56 – 57)

3) **Choice C is correct.**
Choice (A) may seem correct but the author does not wish to talk about herself as a pioneering athlete, therefore choice (C) is best. The barriers that society would normally attribute would have something to do with Miranda's gender.

4) **Choice C is correct.**
The sexist comments are lewd or lascivious.

5) **Choice B is correct.**
The expression "old news by now" is an indication that the author acknowledges the old event, but want to move on and talk about something else. In this particular context, Miranda wants to talk of bigger factors that she had overcome., as indicated by paragraphs 5.

6) **Choice C is correct.**
As clearly indicated by line 42, the author was joking about this statement.

7) **Choice C is correct.**
The entire paragraph focuses on the difficulty that the author faced as an athlete, and losing weight was a significant part of said hardship.

8) **Choice B is correct.**
The author is not arrogant, nor elitist, nor humble. There are no words that we can point to that would justify these wrong answer choices, therefore the author can best be described as content.

9) **Choice D is correct.**
The author was treated impartially – or without bias or discrimination. Since bias and discrimination can exist in regular treatments of people, the best word here is impartial. Remember, the author was treated the same as everyone else.

Reading Comprehension
Lesson 3

Historical Passages

Goals

We will develop our grammatical fluency and gain meaningful understanding by learning to:

1) Analyze historical or global type passages
2) Implement specific strategies for historical passages
3) Answer different question types based on historical passages

Contents

- Historical Passage Types Lecture
- Note on Paired Passages
- Historical Passage Analysis
- Note on Logic
- Short Passage Exercises
- Long Passage Exercises

Lesson 3
Historical Passages

Historical Passages

Herodotus, the grandfather of modern historians, in 425 BC, published his magnus opus "The Histories" - a literary account of the Greco-Persian Wars "to show what caused them to fight one another." Setting the stage for all future historical prose, his work provided the general structure of modern-day historical accounts of events that incorporate the **position** of the author, the **central issue** at stake, with the goal of **attempting to influence** the reader.

Many of us are quite familiar with historical passages since we've encountered them in our readings in school. Quite often, however, we've only read for general understanding of events occurred, rather than deep comprehension of the written material.

Finally, since historical passages deal in strong opinions, it lends itself nicely to paired-passage phenomena where one opinion is argued, then another follows.

<u>Mindmap</u>

A general outline of a historical paired -passage mindmap should look something like this:

POSITION #1 ← ISSUE → POSITION #2

INFLUENCE

Understand that each of the components above will be a significant part of the passage, and they help us to analyze the passage deeply and meaningfully. If this comes naturally to you as a reader, then great, soldier on. If you do not consider yourself an avid reader (or just plainly hate to read) then treat this lesson more like a puzzle that needs to be solved and get your gameface on, dawg.

Note on Paired Passages

Our general strategy for reading and comprehending paired passages will be as follows:

1) Read & analyze the first passage
2) Answer questions based on the first passage
3) Read & analyze the second passage
4) Answer questions based on the second passage
5) Answer questions that compare both passages

The reason we break up each passage into two distinct (different) passages is to avoid any confusion that may arise by mixing up two different points of view after reading two passages at once. Therefore, read the first passage first then answer the corresponding questions that follow. Then do the same with passage two thereafter.

Historical Passage Analysis

Questions to be asked when reading historical passages are:

- What is the **main issue** at large?
- What is the **position** of the author?
- What method does the author engage in to **influence** the author?

Let's look at the questions in detail:

Main Issue:	In historical passages, the **main issue** will form the basis for one or two arguments the author(s) will pose. Vital issues such as freedom, justice, human dignity, and fundamental rights all have shaped a global conversation from the British American colonies to current US climate.
Position:	The author will have a very specific **position** on the main issue – our job is to recognize this viewpoint with proper justification and reasoning. Requiring more than a simple acknowledgement here, the actual process of identifying the point of view involves a checklist of (1) finding the author's actual words and (2) the logical reasons for that point of view.
Engagement Method:	Exactly what are the methods the author(s) use to **influence** the reader? Popular methodologies include but are not limited to: pathos (emotional appeal), ethos (standards agreement), logos (logic), analogy, counterarguments, exemplification, cause/effect, appeal to tradition, discrediting the source, morality, biology, and many others. It is imperative that we understand which method(s) the author engages in.

Note on Logic

In our volatile political climate, it is easy to get lost in fallacies of argument. These include: *ad hominem attack, mysterious "they", causation vs. correlation, strawman arguments* to name a few. It's not important to know these, per se, but since we may bring in improper logic while reading a passage with strongly opinionated stances like women's rights or gun control legislation, make sure to distance yourselves from these and other common fallacies.

Application Exercises

Historical Short Paired Passage 1:

Passage 1 is adapted from an article published from the NYTimes in 1913, "Come to Counsel Japanese Here" by Kametaro Iijima. Passage 2 is adapted from *An Overland Journey*, letter 26, by Horace Greeley, 1859.

Passage 1

The Japanese people in California have helped the economic growth of that State. When the anti-Japanese agitators say that the Japanese settlers in that State are detrimental to the Californians, they know that they are not sincere. Some of them say that if a Japanese farmer buys a farm, the value of the surrounding farms is depreciated. That is untrue. I studied the status of the Japanese farmers in that State, and my investigations showed me that after they had done so, the price of land went up instead of down. The landowners know this, and they have never complained against the Japanese famers, but have welcomed them.

Passage 2

They are hardly used here. He is popularly held to spend nothing, but carry all his gains out of the country and home to his nativeland – a charge disproved by the fact that he is an inveterate gambler, an opium smoker, a habitual drinker, and a devotee of every sensual vice. But he is weak in body, and not allowed to vote, so it is safe to trample on him; he does not write English, and so cannot tell the story of his wrongs; he has no family here, so enjoys no social standing.

Historical Passage Analysis:

1) What is the main issue here?

2) What are the positions of the authors? (*Remember: Use justification & reasoning here for each author*)

3) How do the authors try to influence the reader?

THE YELLOW TERROR IN ALL HIS GLORY

Racist propaganda circulated in CA (1899)

Historical Short Paired Passage 2:

Passage 1 is an excerpt from President Truman's address to Joint Session of Congress (1947); Passage 2 is adapted from Chris Nichols essay on "Consequence of the Truman Doctrine"

Passage 1

The gravity of the situation which confronts the world today necessitates my appearance before a joint session of the Congress. The foreign policy and the national security of this country are involved. One aspect of the present situation, which I present to you at this time for your consideration and decision, concerns Greece and Turkey. The United States has received from the Greek Government an urgent appeal for financial and economic assistance. Preliminary reports from the American Economic Mission now in Greece and reports from the American Ambassador in Greece corroborate the statement of the Greek Government that assistance is imperative if Greece is to survive as a free nation.

Passage 2

The major ideological shift represented by the Truman Doctrine and the aid to Greece and Turkey is its simultaneous rejection of the long-standing injunction to "steer clear of foreign entanglements" and an embrace of a heightened expansion of a sphere of influence logic. For the first time in US history, the nation's peacetime vital interests are extended far outside of the Western Hemisphere to include Europe and, indeed, much of the world. According to Truman, it is "the policy of the United States to support free peoples who are resisting attempted subjugation by armed minorities or by outside pressures." This new logic of pro-active aid and intervention to support "vital interests" worldwide undergirds the ways in which the United States continues to debate the nation's internationalist as well as unilateralist options abroad in faraway countries.

Narrative Analysis:

1) What is the main issue at large?

2) What are the positions of the authors?

3) What are the methods the authors use to influence the reader?

President Truman

Final note on historical passage analysis

Like all analysis, historical passage analysis should occur as your read the passage. Your analysis should be incorporated into your identification of structure and blueprints. Remember that this analysis occurs in your head (not explicitly) for every passage. Otherwise it will take too long to complete a reading comprehension passage and time will be a concern. Finally, do not get bogged down by details of events and opinions. Identify a central issue, determine the proper positions, and ascertain how the author influences the reader.

The next step is to follow through with Pittsburgh Prep's methodology of proper reading. These include outlining of structure, creating blueprints, being metacognitive, and increasing speed.

Homework Exercises

Historical Long Paired Passage 1:

Passage 1 is from Common Sense *by Thomas Paine (1776); Passage 2 is written by King Frederick II, from "Political Statement of 1752" where he outlines his political philosophy as the King of Prussia.*

Passage 1

MANKIND being originally equals in the order of creation, the equality could only be destroyed by some subsequent circumstance; the distinctions of rich, and poor, may in a great measure be accounted for, and that without having recourse to the harsh ill sounding names of oppression and avarice. Oppression is often the consequence, but seldom or never the means of riches; and though avarice will preserve a man from being necessitously poor, it generally makes him too timorous to be wealthy.

But there is another and greater distinction for which no truly natural or religious reason can be assigned, and that is, the distinction of men into KINGS and SUBJECTS. Male and female are the distinctions of nature, good and bad the distinctions of heaven; but how a race of men came into the world so exalted above the rest, and distinguished like some new species, is worth enquiring into, and whether they are the means of happiness or of misery to mankind.

To the evil of monarchy we have added that of hereditary succession; and as the first is a degradation and lessening of ourselves, so the second, claimed as a matter of right, is an insult and an imposition on posterity. For all men being originally equals, no one by birth could have a right to set up his own family in perpetual preference to all others for ever ... One of the strongest natural proofs of the folly of hereditary right in kings, is, that nature disapproves it, otherwise she would not so frequently turn it into ridicule by giving mankind an ass* for a lion.

Secondly, as no man at first could possess any other public honors than were bestowed upon him, so the givers of those honors could have no power to give away the right of posterity, and though they might say "We choose you for our head," they could not, without manifest injustice to their children, say "that your children and your children's children shall reign over ours for ever." Because such an unwise, unjust, unnatural compact might (perhaps) in the next succession put them under the government of a rogue or a fool. Most wise men, in their private sentiments, have ever treated hereditary right with contempt; yet it is one of those evils, which when once established is not easily removed; many submit from fear, others from superstition, and the more powerful part shares with the king the plunder of the rest.

This is supposing the present race of kings in the world to have had an honorable origin; whereas it is more than probable, that could we take off the dark covering of antiquity, and trace them to their first rise, that we should find the first of them nothing better than the principal ruffian of some restless gang, whose savage manners or pre-eminence in subtility obtained him the title of chief among plunderers; and who by increasing in power, and extending his depredations, over-awed the quiet and defenseless to purchase their safety by frequent contributions.

**A donkey, or, plausibly, current ruler*

Passage 2

A well conducted government must have an underlying concept so well integrated that it could be likened to a system of philosophy. All actions must be well reasoned, and all financial, political and military matters must flow towards one goal: which is the strengthening of the state and the furthering of its power. However, such a system can flow but from a single brain, and this must be that of the sovereign. Laziness, hedonism and imbecility, these are the causes which restrain princes in working at the noble task of bringing happiness to their subjects ... a sovereign is not elevated to his high position, supreme power has not been confined to him in order that he may live in lazy luxury, enriching himself by the labor of the people, being happy while everyone else suffers. The sovereign is the first servant of

the state. He is well paid in order that he may sustain the dignity of his office, but one demands that he work efficiently for the good of the state, and that he, at the very least, pay personal attention to the most important problems....

You can see, without doubt, how important it is that the King of Prussia govern personally. Just as it would have been impossible for Newton to arrive at his system of attractions if he had worked in harness with Leibnitz and Descartes, so a system of politics cannot be arrived at and continued if it has not sprung from a single brain ... All parts of the government are inexorably linked with each other. Finance, politics and military affairs are inseparable it does not suffice that one be well administered; they must all be ... a Prince who governs personally, who has formed his own political system, will not be handicapped when occasions arise where he has to act swiftly: for he can guide all matters towards the end which he has set for himself ...

Catholics, Lutherans, Reformed, Jews and other Christian sects live in this state, and live together in peace: if the sovereign, actuated by a mistaken zeal, declares himself for one religion or another, parties will spring up, heated disputes ensue, little by little persecutions will commence and, in the end, the religion persecuted will leave the fatherland and millions of subjects will enrich our neighbors by their skill and industry.

Is it of no concern in politics whether the ruler has a religion or whether he has none. All religions, if one examines them, are founded on superstitious systems, more or less absurd. It is impossible for a man of good sense, who dissects their contents, not to see their error; but these prejudices, these errors and mysteries made for men, and one must know enough to respect the public and not to outrage its faith, whatever religion be involved.

1) What is the passage type?

A) Narrative
B) Rhetorical
C) Historical
D) Expository

2) What is the structure of Passage 1? (Incorporate your historical analysis here)

3) What is the structure of Passage 2? (Incorporate your historical analysis here as well)

4) Write down your blueprints for Passage 1:

5) Write your blueprints for Passage 2 here:

6) As used in line 10, the term "avarice" most closely means

A) healthy
B) eccentric
C) greedy
D) disruptive

7) In Paragraph 1, Thomas Paine makes what point about the wealth inequality of mankind?

A) That it stems from bad accounting
B) That it needs to be destroyed to attain equality for all
C) That it need not necessarily be from oppressive rule
D) That it is necessary to keep the status quo for the wealthy

8) Which choice provides the most proper evidence for the previous question?

A) Lines 1-4 ("Mankind being... circumstance")
B) Lines 4-8 ("The distinctions ... avarice")
C) Lines 10-12 ("Oppression is ... riches")
D) Lines 12-15 ("and though ... wealthy")

9) What is the central claim of the author of Passage 2?

A) Government cannot be run by lazy imbeciles
B) Factors such as speed, servant, and respect all necessitate a single ruler
C) Inseparable aspects of rule like finance, politics and military must be considered
D) Any one particular religious sect cannot be favored by the sovereign ruler of the land

10) Frederick makes what point about the *role* a ruler must take?

A) A sovereign must always defer to the needs of the country
B) A ruler must be benevolent
C) A dictator cannot have a religion of his own to practice in private
D) A leader of such stature must be paid nominally due to his expansive responsibilities

11) Which choice gives the best support for the question prior?

A) Lines 83-89 ("However, such ... sovereign")
B) Lines 94-95 ("The sovereign ... state")
C) Lines 95-100 ("He is ... problems")
D) Lines 113-117 ("a Prince ... himself")

12) Based on the passages, both authors would agree on which of the following claims?

A) Religion has no place in monarchical rule
B) Kings and subjects are distinguished by oppressive rule
C) Hereditary succession is necessary for the good of the state
D) Sovereign rulers should not be lazy nor hedonistic

13) Frederick II, the author of Passage 2, would most likely have reacted to lines 13-17 ("But there ... SUBJECTS") of Passage 2 with

A) disdain, because he believes rulers should not enrich himself at the expense of his subjects
B) regret, because he believes many dictators before him took advantage of their subjects without sympathy
C) understanding, because he believes hereditary succession is a folly
D) disagreement, because he believes that all aspects involving the state must stem from a single dictator

Historical Long Paired Passage 2:

Passage 1 is adapted from Wealth *by Andrew Carnegie (1889); Passage 2 is from "New Nationalism Speech" by Theodore Roosevelt (1910)*

Passage 1

The price which society pays for the law of competition, like the price it pays for cheap comforts and luxuries, is also great; but the advantages of this law are also greater still, for it is to this law that we owe our wonderful material development, which brings improved conditions in its train. But, whether the law be benign or not, we must say of it, as we say of the change in the conditions of men to which we have referred: It is here; we cannot evade it; no substitutes for it have been found; and while the law may be sometimes hard for the individual, it is best for the race, because it insures the survival of the fittest in every department. We accept and welcome therefore, as conditions to which we must accommodate ourselves, great inequality of environment, the concentration of business, industrial and commercial, in the hands of a few, and the law of competition between these, as being not only beneficial, but essential for the future progress of the race.

Having accepted these, it follows that there must be great scope for the exercise of special ability in the merchant and in the manufacturer who has to conduct affairs upon a great scale. That this talent for organization and management is rare among men is proved by the fact that it invariably secures for its possessor enormous rewards, no matter where or under what laws or conditions. The experienced in affairs always rate the MAN whose services can be obtained as a partner as not only the first consideration, but such as to render the question of his capital scarcely worth considering, for such men soon create capital; while, without the special talent required, capital soon takes wings. Such men become interested in firms or corporations using millions; it is inevitable that that they must accumulate wealth. Nor is there any middle ground which such men can occupy, because the great manufacturing or commercial concern which does not earn at least interest upon its capital soon becomes bankrupt. It must either go forward or fall behind: to stand still is impossible. It is a law, as certain as any of the others named, that men possessed of this peculiar talent for affair, under the free play of economic forces, must, of necessity, soon be in receipt of more revenue than can be judiciously expended upon themselves; and this law is as beneficial for the race as the others.

We start, then, with a condition of affairs under which the best interests of the race are promoted, but which inevitably gives wealth to the few. Thus far, accepting conditions as they exist, the situation can be surveyed and pronounced good. The question then arises, What is the proper mode of administering wealth after the laws upon which civilization is founded have thrown it into the hands of the few? And it is of this great question that I believe I offer the true solution. This is not *wealth,* but only *competence* which it should be the aim of all to acquire.

Thus is the problem of Rich and Poor to be solved. The laws of accumulation will be left free; the laws of distribution free. Individualism will continue, but the millionaire will be but a trustee for the poor; entrusted for a season with a great part of the increased wealth of the community, but administering it for the community far better than it could or would have done for itself. This day already dawns.

Passage 2

But I think we may go still further. The right to regulate the use of wealth in the public interest is universally admitted. Let us admit also the right to regulate the terms and conditions of labor, which is the chief element of wealth, directly in the interest of the common good. The fundamental thing to do for every man is to give him a chance to reach a place in which he will make the greatest possible contribution to the public welfare. Understand what I say there. Give him a chance, not push him up if he will not be pushed. Help any man who stumbles; if he lies down, it is a poor job to try to carry him; but if he is a worthy man, try your best to see that he gets a chance to show the worth that is in him. No man can be a good citizen unless he has a wage more than sufficient to cover the bare cost of living, and hours of labor short enough so after his day's work is done he will have time and energy to bear his share in the management of the community, to help in carrying the general load. We keep countless men from being good citizens by the conditions of life by which we

surround them. We need comprehensive workman's compensation acts, both State and national laws to regulate child labor and work for women, and, especially, we need in our common schools not merely education in book-learning, but also practical training for daily life and work. We need to enforce better sanitary conditions for our workers and to extend the use of safety appliances for workers in industry and commerce, both within and between the States.

Also, remember what I said about excess in reformer and reactionary alike. If the reactionary man, who thinks of nothing but the rights of property, could have his way, he would bring about a revolution; and one of my chief fears in connection with progress comes because I do not want to see our people, for lack of proper leadership, compelled to follow men whose intentions are excellent, but whose eyes are a little too wild to make it really safe to trust them.

National efficiency has many factors. It is a necessary result of the principle of conservation widely applied. In the end, it will determine our failure or success as a nation. National efficiency has to do, not only with natural resources and with men, but it is equally concerned with institutions. The State must be made efficient for the work which concerns only the people of the State; and the nation for that which concerns all the people. There must remain no neutral ground to serve as a refuge for lawbreakers, and especially for lawbreakers of great wealth, who can hire the vulpine legal cunning which will teach them how to avoid both jurisdictions. It is a misfortune when the national legislature fails to do its duty in providing a national remedy, so that the only national activity is the purely negative activity of the judiciary forbidding the State to exercise power in the premises.

I do not ask for...over-centralization; but I do ask that we work in a spirit of broad and far-reaching nationalism where we work for what concerns our people as a whole. We are all Americans. Our common interests are as broad as the continent.

1) What is the passage type of both passages?

A) Narrative
B) Historical
C) Rhetorical
D) Expository

2) What is the structure of passage 1?

3) Write the blueprint for passage 1:

4) What is the structure of passage 2?

5) Create blueprints for passage 2 here:

6) In Passage 1, Carnegie contends that we as people as it regards to the law of competition

A) should capitulate to its conditions
B) move forward or stay behind
C) should seek wealth
D) decry its utilitarian values

7) What choice below provides most accurate evidence to the question prior?

A) Lines 15-22 ("We accept ... race")
B) Lines 27-31 ("That this ... conditions")
C) Lines 46-47 ("It must ... impossible")
D) Lines 66-64 ("This is ... acquire")

8) In line 24, the word "exercise" can be understood to mean

A) talent
B) application
C) tenacity
D) perseverance

9) The sentence in lines 66-68 ("This is ... acquire") primarily serves which function in Passage 1?

A) It brings up a possible counterpoint and refutation to Carnegie's main thesis
B) It offers a conclusive statement from Carnegie's central argument regarding the law of competition
C) It distinguishes a weakening point in the main argument brought up by Carnegie
D) It creates a separate, but equally relevant exemplification of Carnegie's line of reasoning

10) In Passage 2, Roosevelt indicates that national lawmakers should

A) distribute wealth to every citizen in America
B) follow leaders who have excellent intentions
C) do more than just regulate States' abuse of its powers
D) not have the right to regulate wealth as a the public interest

11) Which choice best provides evidence to the previous question?

A) Lines 129-135 ("National efficiency ... institutions")
B) Lines 135-138 ("The State ... people")
C) Lines 143-148 ("It is ... premises")
D) Lines 150-152 ("but I ... whole")

12) Based on the passages, both Carnegie and Roosevelt hold similar views in that they believe laws should help every man

A) administer wealth prudently
B) not be wealthy, per se, but be able to subsist properly
C) to become as wealthy as possible
D) create more capital for firms and corporations alike

13) The primary purpose of both passages is to

A) build rapport with the reader through usage of first person pronouns inclusively
B) Appraise potential negative consequences associated with accumulation of great wealth
C) rebut any argument that individuals should be placed at a higher value than the State
D) highlight the pitfalls of socialism and the advancement of free market capitalism

14) In line 136, the word "efficient" can best be understood as

A) streamlined
B) organized
C) accomplished
D) well-ordered

Lesson 3
Historical Passages
Answer Key

Historical Short Paired Passage 1

1) The **central argument** here revolves around whether Japanese farmers are really good for the State of California

2) **Position #1**: Japanese landowners actually help, not harm, the surrounding towns.
Position #2: In fact, they have many vices and no standing as citizens.

3) **Method of Influence 1**: Author incorporates an economic argument that Japanese landowners actually increase land value around their farms. (Logos)

   Method of Influence 2: Horace Greeley attempts an attack on the person, establishing facts that are not widely held. (Pathos)

Historical Short Paired Passage 2

1) The **main issue** here involves the Truman Doctrine, an argument for helping war torn nations after debilitating wars (in this instance World War II)

2) **Position #1:** President Truman "urgently" appeals for economic help from Congress to help Greece after war citing "policy and national security" as reasons.
Position #2: Author notes the first time US becoming involved in "foreign entanglements" and expanding "influence" with internationalist and unilateralist policies.

3) **Method of Influence 1:** Emotional appeals are made here, as well as logical arguments that it is in the best interest of the US to intervene.

   Method of Influence 2: A logical argument is made to show how the US is changing its stance for the first time in history.

Historical Long Paired Passage 1

1) **Choice C is correct.**
This is set of historical passages.

2) Structure of Passage 1:

3) Blueprints for Passage 1:

   i. Inequality can be explained for some aspects of life

   ii. Cannot be explained for Monarchy rule

   iii. Monarchy lessens our value, while successive rule is bad for future generations (posterity) – (1) Not natural

   iv. (2) Our children have no say so successive monarchy is unfair

   v. (3) Origin of monarchy comes from plundering gangsters

4) Structure of Passage 2:

5) Blueprints for Passage 2:

   i. Well governed State must stem from one ruler, some are lazy, but is the first servant of State.

   ii. Like scientists, and for efficiency sake, one ruler needed for Prussian rule

   iii. In diverse religious land, ruler is wrong if he favors one over another

   iv. Ruler must respect his people, in religion and otherwise

6) **Choice C is correct.**
Even if we didn't know the meaning of avarice, we could have made a strong deduction that it has something to do with money since the author mentions "poor" and "wealthy" in its description. No other answer choice associates with money in this way.

7) **Choice C is correct.**
Paine's assertion in the first paragraph, as evidenced in lines 8 – 9 is that oppression is often a consequence of the wealth gap.

8) **Choice C is correct.**
Paine states that the wealth gap can be explained without oppressive rule behind the cause – oppression, in fact, is a "consequence" of the wealth gap, not a cause.

9) **Choice B is correct.**
This is the main point.

10) **Choice A is correct.**
The author contends that the ruler's role is that of a servant of the State.

11) **Choice B is correct.**
Lines 94 – 95 supports the claim that "The sovereign is the first servant of the state."

12) **Choice A is correct.**
Both Passage 1 (lines 13-17) and passage 2 (lines 132-136) state that religion has no place for a ruler.

13) **Choice D is correct.**
Line 79-83 states that all actions of the state must stem from a single dictator.

Historical Long Paired Passage 2

1) **Choice B is correct.**

2)

Position → ISSUE → INFLUENCE

Don't dictate how wealthy ppl. spend their money | $ + wealthy | -LAW -Talent -Acceptance

3) The following blueprints should mirror your paraphrases for passage 1:

   i. Inequalities are necessary consequences of competition

   ii. By natural law, individuals deserve wealth

   iii. Policy should support competence, not wealth

   iv. We should not dictate what people do with their money

4)

POSITION → ISSUE → INFLUENCE

We should regulate wealth | Proper legislation of wealth | -UNIVERSAL ACCEPTANCE -Role of legislature -reformers

5) The following blueprints should mirror your paraphrases for passage 2:

   i. Regulating wealth = regulating labor

   ii. Following the lead of "reactionaries" yields no benefit to the general public

   iii. Wealth should be legislated in same way as the poor

   iv. Goal: Nationalism but not over-centralization

6) **Choice A is correct.**
   If you answered this question incorrectly, perhaps you should look to brush up on your vocab. To "capitulate" is to give in: this is a vocab word that you absolutely need to know.

7) **Choice A is correct.**
   Carnegie clearly stipulates that "we" "accept," "welcome," the law of competition. His use of the third person is also used to draw agreement from the reader.

8) **Choice B is correct.**
   The word "exercise" here is closely related to the application of the special ability of the merchant, who, Carnegie argues, will do so on a grand scale. Talent is incorrect because the special ability is the talent, not the exercise of it.

9) **Choice B is correct.**
   Paragraph three is a rhetorical argument where Carnegie draws logical conclusions based on previous statements. He starts this argument by arguing that some people will be wealthy, because it's somehow good for the entire human race. Then he ends this argument by stating that wealth is not for the masses, but *competence* (or living wages) is.

10) **Choice C is correct.**
   According to Roosevelt, to fail legislatively is to fail to provide a national remedy, and solely act to provide a "negative activity."

11) **Choice C is correct.**
   Roosevelt's contention here is that national legislature should do more than the "negative activity" of "forbidding" State impinging on national concerns, which would amount to an abuse of power by the States.

12) **Choice B is correct.**
   Lines 66-68 and lines 98-104 shows the authors' similar views as it relates to their living wages or "competency".

13) **Choice B is correct.**
   Both authors discuss the issue of accumulated wealth with different points of view: Carnegie believes that wealth accumulation will lead to able administration by the rich, while Roosevelt believes that government needs to intervene. Choice A is correct, but not the sole purpose of either author.

14) **Choice A is correct.**
   The author notes that the work must be that which "concerns only the people of the State," implying that no extraneous work should be performed.

Reading Comprehension Lesson 4

Expository Passages

Goals

We will develop our grammatical fluency and gain meaningful understanding by learning to:

1) Analyze expository type passages
2) Implement specific strategies for expository passages
3) Answer different question types based on the passages

Contents

- Expository Passage Types Lecture
- Note on Expository Passages
- Expository Passage Analysis
- Note on Blueprinting
- Short Passage Exercises
- Note on Conclusions
- Long Passage Exercises

Lesson 4
Expository Passages

Expository Passages

Expository passages contain **factual findings** that answer a **general inquiry** often coupled with **insightful** or meaningful commentary with data or stats to ultimately **inform** the reader. Words such as "next" or "first, second, third" will be used to denote a progression of logical ideas to categorically present them in an orderly fashion.

Science passages are considered expository types, since many contain objective findings designed to inform the reader of a particular topic. These, too, are often accompanied with charts or graphs that require interpretation.

<u>Mindmap</u>

A general outline of an expository mindmap should look something like this:

INQUIRY → Objective facts / INSIGHT + DATA → INFORM

Much of expository writing will utilize the third person voice when objectively describing an event or a person who is associated with it. However, we must take care to recognize when subjects shifts occur in the passage. A shift into the first person usually will indicate the author's own personal commentary, or conclusive statement.

Note on Expository Passages

Our general strategy for reading and comprehending expository passages will be as follows:

1) Identify the **general inquiry** at large
2) Find the objective **facts**
3) Determine, if any, the author's personal **commentary**
4) Correspond the data to the **information** given in the passage

Expository Passage Analysis

Questions to be asked when reading historical passages are:

- What is the **general inquiry** of the passage?
- What are the **objective facts** of the passage?
- Are there any **insights or inferences** to be made?
- In what ways does the author use **data** to support the inquiry?

Let's look at the questions in detail:

Inquiry:	In expository passages, there exists a **general inquiry** that the passage will seek to answer. Social or natural science-based passages tend to have questions such as: • Where do the particulates comes from? • How does social media articulate the way we communicate in real life? • Can agriculutural methods of different cultures give us further insight into the way mammals migrated throughout Earth?
Objective Facts:	The **objective facts** tell the background history relevant and necessary to the discussion of the inquiry. It is not important to memorize all of the details, but rather, to understand the function of these facts and where they are placed in the passage for understanding the passage's structure.
Insights/inferences:	Look for the author's own commentary – this is usually indicated by a change in the pronoun shift from third person to first person. This change also tends to occur in a new paragraph.
Data:	Exactly what are the methods the author uses to **inform** the reader?

Note on Blueprinting

Blueprinting is our terminology for paraphrasing what the author wants us to take away. Expository passages present the biggest challenge for readers due to the sheer volume of information that is involved when discussing a general inquiry.

We will put this into practice together in the following short & long passages as you have done in our prior reading lessons. Also, pay special attention to the author's words and avoid personal bias!

Application Exercises

Expository Short Passage 1:

For several decades digital communications meant sending soundwaves over long telegraph wires from one place to another. Quick bursts of sounds, or "dots", combined with long ones referred to as "dashes" represented either a letter or a single digit of a number. Developed by Sam Morse, Morse code, as it was known, could tolerate noise in the communication channel that other subsequent radio waves could not. Still, it wasn't long until two-way radios and voice communications took over as the primary form of digital communication, making way for efficiency and preference for the users. The US Coast Guard was the last maritime communications service that ended the use of Morse Code in 1995.

Expository Passage Analysis:

1) What is the general inquiry here?

2) What are some objective facts?

3) Are there any insights we can take away or inferences?

4) Does the author provide data that helps the general inquiry?

Expository Short Passage 2:

The passage below is adapted from "A Dancer Dies Twice" by Maroosha Muzaffar

Fulltime ballet dancers in dance companies are often asked to take classes at affiliate universities. Troupes from Alvin Ailey are offered classes at Fordham University but dual pursuits are rare for dancers because of the extraordinarily high level of passion and time commitment needed for their career pursuits. The "first death" for a ballet dancer happens when a younger member takes over the lead role previously held by the older dancer; the "second death" occurs when the inevitable happens: facing an unprepared transition into the real world.

Expository Passage Analysis:

1) What is the general inquiry here?

2) What are some objective facts?

3) Are there any insights we can take away or inferences?

4) Does the author provide data that helps the general inquiry?

Expository Short Passage 3:

Mosquitoes actually are not as bad as they seem, the latest study finds. First, over 50% of mosquitoes are not harmful to humans – this is because males do not bite. Second, female mosquitoes are just "doing their job" as any decent mother should. They propagate over 2000 babies in one summer, and the need for warm, blood protein requires all the incessant biting. Third, mosquitoes have actually helped save the rainforest. The study argues that the perceived (and very real) danger of dengue, yellow fever, and malaria has prevented humans from entering natural rainforests, thereby saving the world's ecology. Certainly, there is some merit to the study – but I doubt it will prevent us from unremittingly swatting away these buzzing insects.

Expository Passage Analysis:

1) What is the general inquiry here?

2) What are some objective facts?

3) Are there any insights we can take away or inferences?

4) Does the author provide any data that helps the general inquiry?

5) The author states that female mosquitoes are just "doing their job" in line 4 to

   A) argue that mosquitoes are not much different from mothers who care for their young
   B) censure the notion that insects can have feelings
   C) underlie the fact that mosquitoes have a job that has significant meaning in ecology
   D) contend that we humans should not kill the mosquitoes without understanding them first

6) The author's tone is best described as

   A) daunted, but not excited
   B) serious, but not congenial
   C) candid, but not suspicious
   D) amused, but not convinced

Note on Conclusions

What's in a conclusion?

A conclusion can be thought of as either **summation** of the author's main idea or providing some sort of **closure** to the author's main argument. There are many ways to establish a conclusion, but it's generally accepted that a conclusive statement can be placed almost anywhere in the paragraph or a passage. It need not be at the very end of a long discussion, and it need not necessarily be in the passage at all but if it does occur, it's important to identify it as such.

A *general inquiry* is what the author wants to explore. A *conclusion* is a statement that the author uses to provide closure or summation to the inquiry.

So, how do you identify a conclusion?

In logic, a conclusion can be determined by looking for the following three factors:

- Opinionated statements
- Conclusive indications
- Author's main point

Opinions are the strongest clues that a statement is a conclusive one. Facts are normally used to provide data or evidence. **Conclusive indications** are specific words like "in sum" or "conclusively" or "therefore" that serve to indicate closure. Finally, the **author's main point** is a logical catch-all. If you can argue that the statement does not serve its purpose as a conclusion then it most likely won't be.

Let's try the following identification exercises so that we can put this new skillset into practice. For the following statements, identify the conclusive statement and write down your reasons why.

Ex. 1 Science has continually debunked myths about the shape of the Earth and its rotation. Furthermore, scientists spend years attempting to debunk myths through controlled trials. Ergo, scientific methods are a much more credible source of evidence than other sources of info.

What is the conclusive statement? Why?

Ex. 2 I deserve a goddamn raise. I've worked here for 3 months. Also, I'm the only one qualified to do all the tasks here.

What is the conclusive statement? Why?

Ex. 3 My grandad told me when the stock market is down, that's the best time to invest in companies. Interest rates are low, and most other things are just cheaper then.

What is the conclusive statement? Why?

Expository Short Passage 4:

The idea that obesity is caused by fatty foods is prevalent in our society. One legislator has proposed that his State heavily tax any foods that contain large percentage of fat. This is clearly the wrong approach. Fatty food consumption is merely one component of a healthy, balanced lifestyle. We should not needlessly punish companies that sell fatty foods while people continue to make poor choices for their health. After all, no one is holding a gun coercing people to buy fat-laden ring-dings and eat them.

Expository Passage Analysis:

1) What is the general inquiry here?

2) What are some objective facts?

3) Are there any insights we can take away or inferences?

4) Does the author provide any data that helps the general inquiry?

5) According to the passage, state legislature should not heavily tax fatty foods because

A) people are forced to make ill-advised decisions
B) high-fat food makers are at fault
C) people do not make correct choices about their health
D) a balanced lifestyle is a difficult thing for most people

6) The primary purpose of the passage is to

A) disguise the truth about fatty foods
B) illustrate the dangers of an unbalanced lifestyle
C) argue against a fallacious proposal
D) validate the veracity of legislative action

Homework Exercises

Expository Long Passage 1:

Microeconomic theory nicely proposes that when a resource is scarce, there are certain rules that affect human behavior. Macroeconomics, a related field, looks at the behavior of an entire economy as a whole; yet both theories ominously miss a point. Microeconomics studies the smaller supply & demand cycles of certain items, and macroeconomics studies overall trends to set policies for nations or large-scale economies. But, it's very odd that two theories are used as foundations instead of just one super-theory. Economists rarely attempt to cross paths with each other in these respective fields. Ever since the late 19th century, economists developed intricate rules and methods to explain various esoteric behaviors in both of these theories. The issue, however, is that economics should be regarded as a whole, and trying to explain just a large event with one set of rules is *ignoring the fact* that small events affect large events too, and vice versa.

Economics as a science began in earnest even before the popular definition was coined by Robbins, who said that "economics strives to study human behavior when resources are scarce." In other words, economics tries to understand how human beings make choices when given a limited amount of resources.

A market is defined as a product or a service in microeconomic theory. So circuit board production for computers or available private tutors for college students can both be considered a market. Within this theory, the demand for the product and the supply for the product will determine the market. If there is a great demand, then there will be short supply, and therefore the product will cost more. On the other hand, if there is low demand, then there will be a surplus, and the prices will adjust accordingly. Microeconomic theory assumes that the market will naturally and always reach a state of equilibrium.

Indicators give a whole economy how a particular country is doing in macroeconomic theory. So measurement tools such as inflation, unemployment, and Gross National Product (GDP) indicates if the economic system is growing or receding. Furthermore, whole economies are not assumed to reach a state of equilibrium by itself. That is, a country falling deep into a recession with high unemployment rates will not naturally reach a state of equilibrium. In fact, macroeconomics exists to prevent such imbalances, so that politicians and financial advisors of states can make proper policies to alleviate these potential issues.

By and large, microeconomic and macroeconomic theories are incompatible with each other. In reality, however, both macro and micro approaches are intertwined. Policies made by large nations will always have consequences that affect raw materials to increase in price. This in turn will affect people who all make decisions on what to buy, when to buy etc. But no theory exists at this point that cohesively tackles both the small and the large. Why is that? Has the field of economics become so specialized, so compartmentalized, that we just blissfully ignore this issue? Natural sciences have approached this with an all-encompassing theory: biology has "theory of evolution", physics has "superstring theory", so where is this theory for economics? No one master equation exists, and I believe it's high time someone came up with one.

1) What is the passage type?

A) Narrative
B) Historical
C) Rhetorical
D) Expository

2) What is the primary purpose of this passage?

A) Monitor the progress of contrasting theories
B) Propose a resolution of an issue in social science
C) Discuss the relevancy of macroeconomic theory
D) Question an odd phenomenon

3) The word "ominously" in line 5 is most likely synonymous with

A) portentously
B) shakily
C) gloomily
D) sheepishly

4) The passage uses italics in lines 19 – 20, to

A) underscore a beneficial relationship
B) resolve a major defection
C) bolster a hypothesis
D) highlight an emphatic point

5) Which of the following could potentially be defined as a "market" as given in lines 29 – 30?

A) America needing natural oil, gas, and coal, versus Russia needing the same
B) Bananas in a supermarket stand, and those same bananas being sold in the same day
C) The fervor with which people want to contract cobblers, and the actual amount of shoe repairmen in a given area
D) The amount of coal in a small mining town, and the lack of diamonds in the same town

6) Which of the following would best fit the scenario of a perfect microeconomy?

A) Price of lemons fall when there is an increase in demand of vegetables
B) Price of lemons fall when people require more lemonades during a hot summer
C) Price of lemons rise when lemonade stands double in a city
D) Price of lemons rise due to a shortage of fruits nationwide

7) The author's main contention would be BEST resolved by

A) discarding all current economic theories
B) promulgating microeconomic theory over macroeconomic theory
C) creating a market for economic theory to resolve supply and demand
D) emulating the scope of natural science theorists

8) The economists of both microeconomics and macroeconomics would most likely agree that

A) something needs to be done about their incompatibility
B) large events necessarily require a set of rules that also applies to small events
C) natural sciences have no place in economics
D) it would be best to ignore each other's theories for the moment

9) The economists of both microeconomics and macroeconomics from the previous question would most likely disagree about

A) how prices can affect an entire country's economy
B) the fact when given its natural course, all markets will reach a state of equilibrium
C) *laissez faire* as a viable option for governmental policy
D) the fact that both theorists rarely cross paths with each other

Expository Long Passage 2:

For 30 years, annually, a significant number of villagers in the southwestern Chinese villages in the Yunnan province suddenly died of cardiac arrest. Consequently, the deaths were referred to as Yunnan Sudden Death Syndrome. "We heard amazing stories about how people would drop dead in the middle of a conversation," stated Zhang Shu, a cardiologist who took part in a study organized by the Chinese Centre for Disease Control and Prevention (CCDCP) to determine the cause of these mysterious deaths.

The study showed that year after year Yunnan Sudden Death Syndrome almost always occurred during the summer rainy season from June to August and at an altitude of 5900 – 7900 feet. The Yunnan province is well-known for its wild mushrooms and the deaths coincided with the harvesting season, so researchers had a clear starting point for their investigation.

Some circumstantial challenges surfaced immediately after research was underway. Primarily, villages were distanced from one another, scattered around the province. As the prime period for this occurrence was during the rainy season, torrential downpours and mudslides further encumbered lengthy travel. Also, as a result of their remote locations, many of the villages in the Yunnan province had their own dialect, complicating communications between villagers and researchers. Finally, the quick completion of burials – significant to the culture of the area – made conducting autopsies difficult.

In 2008, approximately four years into the study, patterns began to emerge. Most victims had consumed surface water, had eaten mushrooms, and had experienced notable emotional stress. Furthermore, a particular mushroom called the "Little White" was often found in the victims' homes. The Little White is not usually sold at the markets because of its small size and tendency to turn brown shortly after picking. It therefore has very low market value and is seemingly ideal as a snack for those families making their living off of the harvesting and selling of mushrooms. Investigators, suspicious of this small snack, issued a warning against the consumption of these mushrooms and have since seen a dramatic decrease in Yunnan Sudden Death Syndrome.

While this correlation was helpful in narrowing down the cause of the deaths, further testing needed to be conducted. The mushrooms themselves contain several toxins; however, these toxins were determined to be non-lethal. Another possible explanation is that the combination of the toxins from the mushrooms and another factor contributed to the fatalities. The victims also had high levels of barium, a heavy metal found in the water supply that seeps into the soil and, therefore, is easily absorbed by the mushrooms and any other plant-life that may have been consumed by the victims. It is possible that the combination of barium and the Little White's toxins could have led to cardiac arrest in the victims. More research will have to be performed in order to make a more definitive determination.

It is difficult to believe that a small, delicate mushroom could be responsible for the sudden deaths of over 400 southwestern Chinese residents. Even the name, "Little White," seems anodyne. Yet the medical mystery Yunnan Sudden Death Syndrome for which it is responsible is anything but delicate.

1) What is the passage type?

A) Narrative
B) Rhetorical
C) Historical
D) Expository

2) What is the structure of Passage 1?

3) Write the blueprint for Passage 1:

4) The quote from Dr. Zhang Shu in the first paragraph (lines 6-7) acts as

A) the thesis of the argument
B) an exploration into a broader statement
C) an initial refutation of the argument
D) a qualifying support to begin the discussion

5) The list of basic facts in the second paragraph serves to

A) expound on all of the evidence in a condensed manner
B) provide readers with an initial basis for further research
C) outline the remainder of the passage
D) examine a small subset of related facts

6) In the context of line 20, the word "circumstantial" most nearly means

A) coincidental
B) environmental
C) unintentional
D) conditional

7) The author suggests that "Little White" (line 38) is an unlikely lone killer because

A) it may be lethal when combined with barium
B) it is too small in dosage
C) its toxins are not fatal
D) snacks are not a normal cause of death

8) In the fifth paragraph, the author suggests that this medical mystery is

A) mystical
B) resolved
C) insubstantial
D) unsolved

9) The word "anodyne" in line 72 most nearly means

A) harmless
B) culpable
C) horrific
D) abashed

10) The organization of the passage serves to

A) illustrate the process of scientific inquiry
B) examine complex scientific details
C) prove a specific point
D) employ narrative format

11) This passage was likely published in a(n)

A) work manual
B) elementary school textbook
C) scientific journal
D) public news magazine

Lesson 4
Expository Passages
Answer Key

Short Passage 1

1) The general inquiry delves into the changing landscape of digital communications as it pertains to Morse code and its demise.

2) Facts provided include bursts of sound, other communication devices, and the US Coast Guard signaling the end of Morse code usage.

3) One insight may be that despite Morse code's high tolerance for "noise", people generally preferred efficiency when the telephone was invented.

4) Data here is limited to a specific date when More Code ended in 1995.

Short Passage 2

1) The passage asks how fulltime ballet dancers transition from their career in the arts to the real world.

2) Dancers are fully committed to their craft and have little time to seek education outside of their craft.

3) "Death" is a metaphoric term that can be ascribed to dancers as they age, and when they transition into the real world.

4) No particular data is provided.

Short Passage 3

1) The general inquiry revolves around a study that found Mosquitos to be less harmful that originally thought.

2) Three facts are given from the study.

3) The author utilizes intended humor, which is more important to recognize for readers than the actual humor itself. This is evidenced by the author's reference of the mosquito as a "buzzing insect".

4) The author provides data in terms of percentages (50% of mosquitos are not harmful!) and numbers (2000 babies!)

5) **Choice A is correct.**
Because the author justifies female mosquitoes in the second part of the study, where the insects are doing their jobs as mothers.

6) **Choice D is correct.**
Note that the author is amused because of the subject shift that occurs (usage of the first person pronoun "I" towards the end of the passage) and also not convinced since the author "doubts" anyone will listen to the study to any great effect.

Note on Conclusions

Ex.1: The conclusive statement here is "ergo, scientific methods are much more credible than other sources of info" because it's an opinion, contains a conclusive indicator, and is the logical main point of the paragraph. All other statements are facts that acts to support the conclusive statement.

Ex.2: The conclusive statement here is "I deserve a goddamn raise" because it's an opinion, and it she logical main point of the paragraph. Note that it does not contain a indicative word like "therefore" or "ergo". The facts that the author worked for 3 months and is the only one who is qualified to do the job serve to support the conclusive statement.

Ex.3: The conclusive statement here is "My grandad told me when the stock market is down, that's the best time to invest in companies" because it's someone's opinion and is the main assertion of the author. Interest rates being low, and other things being cheaper are both factual evidences that serve to support the conclusive statement.

Short Passage 4

1) The author is concerned with fatty foods and taxation.

2) Facts given are: idea of obesity caused by fatty foods, tax proposal, fatty foods as a part of a balanced diet.

3) The most prominent insight is to recognize the main point of the passage by utilizing the tools in finding the conclusive statement. Many readers initially tackle the passage too nonchalantly – pay attention! The main point (and conclusive statement) is that the taxing of fatty foods is "clearly the wrong approach." It is an opinion, contains a conclusive indicator, and remains the main point of the short passage.

4) The author provides some ambiguous data, such as "large percentage of fat" but nothing concrete.

5) **Choice C is correct**.
Because as indicated in the passage, "people continue to make poor choices".

6) **Choice C is correct**.
The passage is an argument against a faulty, or fallacious, proposal to tax fatty foods.

Long Passage 1

1) **Choice D is correct.**
It is an expository passage.

2) **Choice D is correct**
Our blueprint should give us a big clue – this is a passage written by an author who is questioning the reasons why economics does not have a big all-encompassing theory. Hence, choice B is the best one. All others lack this understanding.

3) **Choice A is correct.**
A high-level vocab word, "portentous" means "ominous" or, in this case, something that is dangerous to ignore.

4) **Choice D is correct.**
This is a structure question. In this instance, the italics serve to highlight the importance of the statement.

5) **Choice B is correct.**
A market is either a product or a service. Bananas are clearly a product.

6) **Choice D is correct.**
As given by the definition in microeconomic theory within the passage, lemons will rise if there is shortage. Or, if there is a surplus, then prices will fall. Only D succinctly describes this relationship.

7) **Choice D is correct.**
Imitating the scope of scientists in the natural sciences would mean that economists would have to inevitably pose the question of how to resolve the discrepancies of micro vs. macro economics.

8) **Choice D is correct.**
The only inference to be made here is that both sides of economics theories cannot be resolved at this time, therefore, the best course of action is to simply ignore it.

9) **Choice B is correct.**
Only microeconomics assumes that there is a natural state of equilibrium. Macroeconomics, however, does not assume this to be the case. Remember to always verify your answer choices as you complete them.

Long Passage 2

1) **Choice D is correct.**
If you answered this wrong, you have problems.

2) The structure:

What was cause → FINDINGS
Facts → of deaths in Yunnan
INQUIRY

3) Blueprint:

P1: Intro to a problem, and quest to determine cause

P2: Facts about the initial stages of research into the public health issue

P3: Initial challenges listed – four specific instances.

P4: Breakthrough! Mushrooms (along with other consumption factors) determined as initial causes.

P5: Different theories on the actual cause proposed – more research needed

P6: Conclusive paragraph: author's opinion given.

4) **Choice D is correct.**
This discussion seems fantastical, therefore a quote from a real doctor to begin the discussion acts as “qualifying support.”

5) **Choice B is correct.**
This list of facts are statements that provide the readers with the factors the researchers had started with.

6) **Choice D is correct.**
From context clues we can assume that “circumstantial” is closest in meaning to “conditional.” Note that there are four conditions, and even though some are purely environmental, not all of them are, therefore choice (D) fits best.

7) **Choice C is correct.**
The passage states that scientists looked for additional causes because the toxins in “Little White” were not harmful as stated in line 54

8) **Choice D is correct.**
The author suggests that scientists are still looking for a definitive cause, therefore the medical mystery remains unsolved.

9) **Choice A is correct.**
In context, the emphatic word “Even” gives the reader indication that anodyne means harmless.

10) **Choice A is correct.**
The passage leads readers through the discovery of the problem, investigation of facts, and discovery of a possible solution, thereby illustrating the process of scientific inquiry. Furthermore, none of the other answer choices satisfy the question.

11) **Choice D is correct.**
This passage is told simply, without complex details; it is likely in a public news magazine meant to inform people of the issues but not at the level of a scientific journal. It qualifies as an expository passage.

Reading Comprehension Lesson 5

Rhetorical Passages

Goals

We will develop our grammatical fluency and gain meaningful understanding by learning to:

1) Analyze rhetorical type passages
2) Implement specific strategies for rhetorical passages
3) Answer different question types based on rhetorical passages

Contents

- Rhetorical Passage Types Lecture
- Short Passages Exercise
- Long Passages Exercise

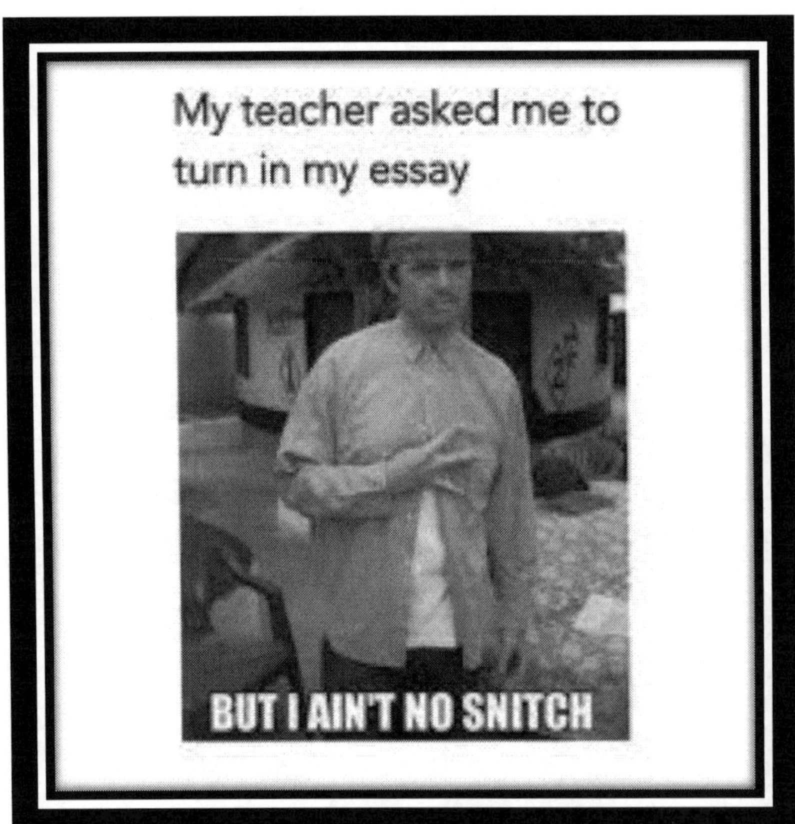

Lesson 5
Reading Comprehension

Rhetorical Passages

The good news about rhetorical passages is that these sorts of passages are the ones you are very much used to writing at your school. Otherwise known as persuasive writing, rhetorical passages focus on an author making a point of view (usually with a thesis) and then building on that POV with facts, reasons, and emotional persuasion.

Mindmap

A general outline of a rhetorical mindmap should look something like this:

THESIS / POV ⇒ INFORM

Rhetorical Passage Analysis

Our general strategy for reading and comprehending rhetorical passages will be to identify answers to the following questions:

- What is the thesis? Rhetorical passages universally contain a **thesis.** It is important to be as correct and specific as possible here.

- What is the author's point of view? The function of the **POV** is to attempt to prove the thesis. To identify the POV, we as readers can look to the actual words used by the author. Clear indicators such as "even though" and "first" provide us with strong clues on both the author's POV and any counterarguments presented in the passage.

- How does the author try to inform the reader? Unlike a fictional narrative or historical documents, rhetorical passages will not try to overtly shape your perspective. Each statement will be clear and succinct, relying on data and logic to **inform** the reader.

In concept, rhetorical passages are quite similar to historical passages. The key difference, however, is that the author is clearly trying to establish by logic and reason that his position is a credible one. Keep this in mind as you tackle this final type of passages on your exams.

Note on Terrible Test Taking for Reading Comprehension

Here is a list of terrible test-taking for the reading comprehension section:

- Reading the questions first: it's a waste of time, read the passage first and develop a deep understanding of the material
- Skipping over vocabulary words: stop and understand its meaning via context
- Not paraphrasing after every paragraph: Laziness will get you nowhere
- Dismissing strategy: Go into every passage type with a specific strategy

Application Exercises

Short Rhetorical Passage 1

In the philosophical question "*what is consciousness?*" David Chalmers posits that we may never know exactly what it is, even though we can determine everything about it. The "easy" problem is explaining how the mind integrates information, where in the brain such activity occurs, and when our mind is attentive. The "hard" problem, on the other hand, is explaining why the brain functions the way it does. An apt analogy in physics would be knowing all the equations in predicting how mass and gravity interact but not knowing why they do so in the way they do.

Rhetorical Passage Analysis:

1) What is the thesis here?

2) What is the author's POV?

3) What points does the author make to inform the reader?

Short Rhetorical Passage 2

Many professionals in the food industry are formally educated with advanced degrees in management, theory and accounting; however, when it comes to chefs, we have quite a different set of circumstances. In the paradigm of cooks, we are looking at apprenticeship, informal structures, emotional intelligence and experience. After learning techniques in food safety and knife handling, the chef has the long journey of finding her own style of leadership. All the while developing her preference – and her trademark - for the cuisine the world has to offer.

Rhetorical Passage Analysis:

1) What is the thesis here?

2) What is the author's POV?

3) What points does the author make to inform the reader?

Rhetorical Long Passage 1

The following passage is adapted from a NYTimes Magazine article on workplace efficiency © 2016

Companies know a great deal on how to maximize effectiveness in the workplace, implementing tried and true methods like clear goal-setting, arranging frequent staff meetings, and placing like-minded people together. Yet tech giants these days have found that the most effective groups within their faculty utilize much more than these traditional methods.

At the end of a three-year research cycle, Anita Woolley from Project Aristotle at Google tells us that when employees in groups have equal communication time ("distribution of conversation") and are sensitive to each other's emotions ("social sensitivity"), the group will perform at a much higher effectiveness than their counterparts with all other factors being equal.

Woolley isn't necessarily the first one to correctly postulate this finding. Jasper Sorensen's *Note on Organizational Culture* (Harvard Business Review, 2009) notes how "group norms" often dictate performance. Incredibly hard to measure, norms or traditions exhibited by any particular group often influence how the individuals function. Individuals may work independently or may dislike working under an authoritative leader. "I've been on some teams that left me feeling totally exhausted and others where I got so much energy," states one Google employee.

Group intelligence, on the other hand, has been measured for well over half a century by major institutions and psychologists from M.I.T., Carnegie Mellon University and Union College. Unsurprisingly, statistics show that the right set of norms raises the collective group's intelligence, while wrong norms hinder it, even if the individuals in the group are all highly educated, bright and motivated to succeed.

"What we are talking about is psychological safety in the workplace," Dr. Mariposa Cohen-Wilkes explains. "There is tremendous benefit to the entire group when you can share how you feel without the fear of judgment or negativity." Effective groups are different. Some have strong leaders who are outspoken yet individual members are still able to communicate in roughly equal measure either at the end of meetings or in other forms, while other groups had average members who focused on their individual strengths and talked to each other in small factions that was eventually shared with the group. One experiment that demonstrates social sensitivity is the Reading the Mind in the Eyes test where participants are asked to determine the accurate emotion of a person by looking at only the eyes of a person. The test was developed by a psychologist in the 70's and is used by large corporations ubiquitously.

Woolley realizes that measuring psychological safety is inherently different from creating one in the workplace. Sometimes, forcing the issue for ineffective working groups creates more dissonance – a seemingly paradoxical result. But she believes that the first step is to acknowledge these factors in a safe environment and to share the data which allows for further (and presumably healthy) discussion.

All of this is to say that none of this is particularly groundbreaking work. Like any other insightful principle, however, the value of Woolley's research is really inside of the individual to understand and to act appropriately. Culture is nigh-impossible to dictate, but when each individual team member of that team can take the results of research and is able to use it plainly, we may have broken at least one barrier to understanding how group can work more effectively. "I had research telling me that it was OK to follow my gut," one employee admitted, "and that was something I wouldn't have known three years ago."

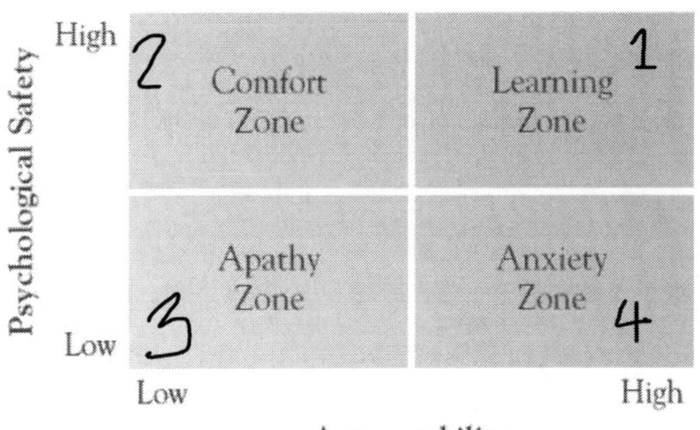

Figure 4.1. Psychological Safety and Accountability

Source: Edmondson, A. C. "The Competitive Imperative of Learning," *HBS Centennial*

1) What type of passage is this?

   A) Narrative
   B) Expository
   C) Historical
   D) Rhetorical

2) One central idea of the passage is that

   A) group intelligence is far more important than individual intelligence
   B) effective working groups exhibit two common traits
   C) creating a strong culture in the workplace is necessary for profitability
   D) employees should engage in social activities to encourage interaction

3) Which choice best describes the overall structure of the passage?

   A) A hypothesis about organization structure, detailed understanding of the risks, and a final refutation by research
   B) A question regarding research methods, explanation of the past findings, and recommendation into future research
   C) A statement about workplace effectiveness, historical underpinnings, and proper usage of research findings
   D) An overview of two distinct viewpoints on workplace safety, an insightful realization into increasing productivity, and final resolution by professional opinion

4) As used in line 18, "postulate" most nearly means

   A) dictate
   B) assume
   C) help
   D) relinquish

5) Which of the following constitutes "psychological safety" according to the passage?

A) The ability to communicate equally and to have emotional sensitivity to other group members
B) Abstaining from violent behaviors in the workplace
C) High level of group and individual intelligences
D) Adhering to group norms strictly, without dissonance

6) What "other forms" would the author deem as acceptable in lines 48 – 49?

A) An email to all group members individually
B) Distribution of pamphlets to every group member after meetings
C) Talking to a few members around the water cooler after every meeting
D) Discussions at the start of meetings by all group members

7) We can infer that the "data" in line 67 would be effective

A) because researchers from Harvard had procured the methods to obtain them
B) since all companies will use them, increasing their productivity within their workgroups
C) for lower level employees
D) only if the organization had enough resources to conduct its own research

8) In a workplace where there is strong leadership where individuals do not like authority, in what quadrant would this group fall under according to figure 4.1?

A) Quadrant 1
B) Quadrant 2
C) Quadrant 3
D) Quadrant 4

9) As used in line 59, "ubiquitously" most nearly means

A) spaciously
B) essentially
C) universally
D) thoroughly

10) Which choice provides the best evidence for the claim that measuring psychological safety is easier than actually implementing it?

A) Lines 26 – 29 ("I've been ... employee")
B) Lines 34 – 38 ("Unsurprisingly ... succeed")
C) Lines 62 – 65 ("Sometimes ... result")
D) Lines 74 – 79 ("Culture is ... effectively")

Reading Comprehension
Lesson 5
Answer Key

Short Rhetorical Passage 1

1) The thesis: We may never know what consciousness is, even though we may be able to determine quite a lot about the subject.

2) The author's POV aligns closely with the thesis here – she believes that consciousness has both easy and hard components.

3) The author attempts to inform the reader by providing two different scenarios as well as a analogous relationship in another field of study.

Short Rhetorical Passage 2

1) The thesis: Unlike other food professionals, chefs adhere to a different paradigm.

2) The author's POV is one that shows her firm belief that chefs are educated informally.

3) The author shows the steps chefs need to take to accumulate knowledge in cuisine, food safety, knife handling, and her leadership style – all to support the POV.

Rhetorical Long Passage 1:

1) **Choice D is correct.**
This is a rhetorical passage.

2) **Choice B is correct.**
As stated in paragraph 2, the two factors are equal communication time and sensitivity to each other's emotions.

3) **Choice C is correct.**
The first paragraph gives a statement on workplace effectiveness, then the next two paragraphs present prior research on the topic, while the final paragraphs discuss the difficulty and proper usage of the findings.

4) **Choice B is correct.**
Although Woolley clearly determined the two factors for workplace effectiveness at Google, others like Prof. Sorenson at Harvard correctly *assumed* the same in an earlier publication.

5) **Choice A is correct.**
This is a factual question – we can find the answer in the second paragraph.

6) **Choice D is correct.**
Any other form that would qualify would mean that every individual in the group must get equal time communicating. Choices (A) and (C) do not work, because communication is conveyed to some members, so it does not qualify. Choice (B) is a one-way method of communication so it also does not qualify.

7) **Choice D is correct.**
Because if organizations didn't conduct its own research, no such data would exist *in the first place* to help the organization in the first place. Choice (B) may seem correct, but there is no guarantee that all companies will use them, nor is there a guarantee that the data presented *without psychological safety* will be effective in improving workplace productivity.

8) **Choice D is correct.**
In a workgroup that has strong authority (*ie.* high accountability) but comprised of individuals who do not like authority (low psychological safety), according to figure 4.1 that workgroup would most likely fall under quadrant 4.

9) **Choice C is correct.**
The author wants to convey that the Mind in the Eye test is used by corporations everywhere. Choice (D) is incorrect because thoroughness indicates completeness, an odd word choice.

10) **Choice C is correct.**
The difficulty of implementing psychological safety is exemplified when organizations attempt to force the issue.

PITTSBURGH
PREP

SAT Practice Test #1
Pittsburgh Prep

Editor's note:

Our practice test, like all other third party practice tests, is to be used solely as a learning tool. Your best source to accurately measure your score and ability is to utilize the College Board's official exams found on their website www.collegeboard.com , coupled with the lessons presented in this study guide.

READING TEST 1: Section 1

65 MINUTES, 52 QUESTIONS

Turn to section 1 of your answer sheet to answer the questions in this section.

Directions

Each passage or pair of passages is followed by a set of questions. After reading each passage or pair, choose the best choice based on the what is stated or implied in the passage(s) and in any other graphics.

Questions 1-9 are based on the following passage.

This passage is an excerpt from the Brothers Karamazov by Fyodor Dostoyevsky published in 1880

A visitor looking on the scene of his conversation with the peasants and his blessing them shed silent tears and wiped them away with her handkerchief. She was a sentimental society lady of genuinely good disposition in many respects. When the elder went up to her at last she met him enthusiastically.

"Ah, what I have been feeling, looking on at this touching scene!" She could not go on for emotion. "Oh, I understand the people's love for you. I love the people myself. I want to love them. And who could help loving them, our splendid Russian people, so simple in their greatness!"

"How is your daughter's health? You wanted to talk to me again?"

"Oh, I have been urgently begging for it, I have prayed for it! I was ready to fall on my knees and kneel for three days at your windows until you let me in. We have come, great healer, to express our ardent gratitude. You have healed my Lise, healed her completely, merely by praying over her last Thursday and laying your hands upon her. We have hastened here to kiss those hands, to pour out our feelings and our homage."

"What do you mean by healed? But she is still lying down in her chair."

"But her night fevers have entirely ceased ever since Thursday," said the lady with nervous haste. "And that's not all. Her legs are stronger. This morning she got up well; she had slept all night. Look at her rosy cheeks, her bright eyes! She used to be always crying, but now she laughs and is gay and happy. This morning she insisted on my letting her stand up, and she stood up for a whole minute without any support. She wagers that in a fortnight she'll be dancing a quadrille. I've called in Doctor Herzenstube. He shrugged his shoulders and said, 'I am amazed; I can make nothing of it.' And would you have us not come here to disturb you, not fly here to thank you? Lise, thank him- thank him!"

Lise's pretty little laughing face became suddenly serious. She rose in her chair as far as she could and, looking at the elder, clasped her hands before him, but could not restrain herself and broke into laughter.

"It's at him," she said, pointing to Alyosha*, with childish vexation at herself for not being able to repress her mirth.

If anyone had looked at Alyosha standing a step behind the elder, he would have caught a quick flush crimsoning his cheeks in an instant. His eyes shone and he looked down.

"She has a message for you, Alexey Fyodorovitch. How are you?" the mother went on, holding out her exquisitely gloved hand to Alyosha.

The elder turned round and all at once looked attentively at Alyosha. The latter went nearer to Lise and, smiling in a strangely awkward way, held out his hand to her too. Lise assumed an important air.

"Katerina Ivanovna has sent you this through me." She handed him a little note. "She particularly begs you to go and see her as soon as possible; that you will not fail her, but will be sure to come."

"She asks me to go and see her? Me? What for?" Alyosha muttered in great astonishment. His face at once looked anxious.

"Oh, it's all to do with Dmitri Fyodorovitch and- what has happened lately," the mother explained hurriedly. "Katerina Ivanovna has made up her mind, but she must see you about it... Why, of course, I can't say. But she wants to see you at once. And you will go to her, of course. It is a Christian duty."

"I have only seen her once," Alyosha protested with the same perplexity.

"Oh, she is such a lofty, incomparable creature If only for her suffering... Think what she has gone through, what she is enduring now. Think what awaits her! It's all terrible, terrible!

"Very well, I will come," Alyosha decided, after rapidly scanning the brief, enigmatic note, which consisted of an urgent entreaty that he would come, without any sort of explanation.

"Oh, how sweet and generous that would be of you" cried Lise with sudden animation. "I told mamma you'd be sure not to go. I said you were saving your soul. How splendid you are I've always thought you were splendid. How glad I am to tell you so!"

"Lise!" said her mother impressively, though she smiled after she had said it.

"You have quite forgotten us, Alexey Fyodorovitch," she said; "you never come to see us. Yet Lise has told me twice that she is never happy except with you."

**Note: Alexei's nickname is Aloysha*

1) Which below best describes the main summary of the passage?

A) An invalid in recovery beseeches an elder man of faith to visit her home along with a request for his young apprentice.
B) An elder priest is given high praise from the mother of a sickly daughter, who is delighted.
C) An elder provides blessings to the Russian people, and is given specific directions by one visiting family.
D) A young girl miraculously recovers, and delivers an urgent message to a young apostle, who is surprised through it all.

2) The purpose of the first sentence is to accomplish which of the following?

A) To create a false sense of acknowledgement for the elder's actions.
B) To help understand the visitor's background and emotional state.
C) To provide a contrast between the visitor and the elder as it pertains to their beliefs.
D) To establish how Lise's recovery was bolstered by the visitor's genuine beliefs on the power of priests.

3) When Lise is instructed to thank the elder, her face becomes solemn yet changes because

A) she cannot contain her joy from seeing Alexey.
B) she is ecstatic about her recovery from her illness.
C) she demands that Alexey also be happy with her recovery.
D) she does not really care about her illness.

4) Which choice gives the best evidence for the answer chosen above?

A) Lines 42 – 45 ("She rose… laughter")
B) Lines 46 – 48 "It's at him… mirth."
C) Lines 49 – 52 "If anyone … down."
D) Lines 56 – 60 "The elder … Alyosha."

5) The passage indicates that Katerina deserves Alexey's visit due to

A) a moral obligation that compels Alexey as a person of faith.
B) his desire to do so.
C) a complicated, but clear reason that only Lise knows.
D) the grave danger Katerina faces presently.

6) We can infer that Katerina is suffering as a direct result of

A) Alyosha not visiting her as frequently as he should.
B) Alexey's family member that Katerina is somehow involved with.
C) Lise's sickness and her surprising recovery.
D) the mystery surrounding the circumstances that Katerina is facing that only Alyosha can solve.

7) The passage indicates that Lise considers

A) her mother to be overbearing.
B) Alexey to be a likable character to whom she would like to marry.
C) Katerina's request to be approached with merriment and joy rather than caution.
D) her recovery from her sickness to be a secondary concern over her fondness for Alyosha.

8) Which choice best provides evidence for the question above?

A) Lines 25 – 28 ("What do you… haste.")
B) Lines 41 – 45 ("Lise's pretty … laughter.")
C) Lines 81 – 84 ("Very well… explanation.")
D) Lines 93 – 96 ("You have quite … you.")

9) On line 82, the word "enigmatic" can best be defined as

A) hasty
B) short
C) mysterious
D) questionable

Questions 10-21 are based on the following passage

The following is an excerpt from the New Yorker magazine, published April 25, 2016, titled "*Why Banks Don't Play It Safe, Even When It Costs Them.*"

Better late than never. That's one way of looking at the proposed new restrictions on banker compensation that U.S. regulators released last week. The rules will require top earners at big financial institutions to wait four years to receive a substantial portion of their incentive-based pay, and will force companies to claw back bonuses from employees whose decisions turn out to be responsible for big losses. The new regulations, which were mandated by the 2010 Dodd-Frank financial-reform bill, were supposed to have been put in place soon after that legislation was passed, but it took five years for the six responsible agencies to put together a reasonable proposal. (And it will be months yet before the individual agencies approve the rules and put them into effect.)

The delay means that, to some extent, the impact of the new rules will be less significant than it would once have been, since, in the wake of the financial crisis, banks already made changes in the ways that they pay top executives. Almost all of them now defer some portion of bonuses for three years, and some defer them for longer than that. Many have clawback provisions as well. Still, the regulations should make a difference: they apply to a wider group of employees, make pay susceptible to clawbacks for seven years, and extend the bonus-deferral period.

If the rules are approved, then, they will, at least on the margin, discourage reckless behavior by bank employees—it will hold them more accountable for their actions and make it harder for them to reap short-term gains from decisions that have negative long-term effects (such as making risky trades or loans, both of which happened regularly during the run-up to the financial crisis). This should, in turn, benefit the banks, by aligning employee incentives with firms' long-term health. Which raises an interesting question: Why didn't the banks put stronger rules in place long ago?

Some might reflexively answer that bankers are greedy bastards who don't care what happens to their companies in the long run. But, even if that were true of individual employees, bank shareholders and boards of directors (which set compensation rules) presumably care quite a bit about the health of their companies. The financial crisis demolished bank stocks—shares of Citigroup and Bank of America, for example, are still trading well below where they were a decade ago. Preventing cavalier risk-taking is clearly something that boards of directors should want to do. And, in fact, they did take some steps to reform pay practices, but only after it became obvious that tougher regulations were eventually coming down the pike.

To understand both why the banks didn't go further on their own and why the threat of regulation helped things along, even before the rules were agreed upon, it's worth consulting a famous essay from 1973 by the social scientist Thomas Schelling, written on the subject of hockey helmets. At the time Schelling was writing, the N.H.L.* had yet to require players to wear helmets, which had been around for decades. Players were allowed to wear them, but the vast majority did not, even though this increased their chances of serious injury, and despite the fact that informal polls suggested that many players would have preferred to use them. The problem was that, while not doing so had obvious costs, it also had perceived benefits: a player's peripheral vision was slightly better, for one, and it conveyed a sense of toughness. As a result, players tended to believe that anyone who wore a helmet was, in effect, hurting his performance relative to everyone else on the ice.

Schelling's point was that in situations where the consequences of a choice depend on the choices that everyone else makes, "people can get trapped at an inefficient equilibrium, everyone waiting for the others to switch." And individually rational choices, such as the choice not to hurt your performance by wearing a helmet, can add up to a collectively irrational outcome. As Schelling notes, there are a variety of potential ways to get out of an inefficient equilibrium, but one obvious (and effective) way is to have an external authority change the rules. The N.H.L. did so, in 1979, requiring helmets for everyone but those players who had already entered the league; now everyone wears them.

**NHL = National Hockey League*

10) The primary purpose of the passage is to

A) deconstruct the psychology of bankers and NHL players
B) consider the pros and cons of equilibrium in business
C) describe the historical underpinnings for certain inactions in banking
D) propose a solution for a longstanding issue in the financial sector

11) Which choice best outlines the author's claim?

A) He begins with a legislative action that has less power than originally intended, then asks and provides the reasons for why such legislation was not enacted earlier.
B) He creates an issue around an ineffective legislation that seems to be rooted in the same issue a sports league once had in the past.
C) He starts off with the 2010 Dodd-Frank law, then proposes we amend this law similarly to the way the NHL had enacted its law.
D) He describes a law that should have been enacted long ago in the banking industry, then provides justifications for why it should not be enacted.

12) According to the passage, the narrator expects which of the following criticisms against laws to protecting banks and their long-term interests?

A) There is no law that can be enacted to prevent losses within banks.
B) With the threat of regulation is almost as powerful as the regulation itself, no laws are needed.
C) Laws such as 2010 Dodd Frank should be enacted as slowly as possible.
D) Individual bankers are overwhelmingly self-interested without regard to their employers.

13) What evidence can be found within the passage to justify your answer above?

A) Lines 18 – 22 ("The delay… executives.")
B) Lines 31 – 34 ("If the rules… employees")
C) Lines 44 – 46 ("Some might… long run.")
D) Lines 75 – 76 ("The problem… benefits.")

14) The main purpose of the second paragraph (lines 18 – 29) is to

A) provide deeper context for the creation of the 2010 Dodd Frank law
B) present a balanced view on the effects of the 2010 Dodd Frank law
C) describe a novel method of regulating banks
D) highlight the ineffective approach of regulatory bodies

15) As used in line 54, the word "cavalier" can best be described as

A) careful.
B) careless.
C) carefree.
D) caring.

16) Which paragraph does the author present an analogy to grasp why banks had not regulated their own employees more strictly in the past?

A) Paragraph 2 (lines 18 – 29)
B) Paragraph 3 (lines 31 – 42)
C) Paragraph 4 (lines 44 – 59)
D) Paragraph 5 (lines 61 – 80)

17) It can be reasonably inferred from the passage that the author's assertion "it will be months yet" (lines 14 – 15) is used to

A) convey a strict timeline that will be followed by the regulatory bodies
B) criticize the methods employed by the six regulatory bodies
C) show confidence in the banking industry post 2010 Dodd Frank law
D) assert that a much longer delay is expected

18) The author contends that "inefficient equilibrium" (line 85) regarding banking implies:

A) individual banks not regulating their own employees, leading to collectively irrational outcomes
B) when two sides, in this case banks and regulatory agencies, do not see eye to eye
C) situations where the threat of a law becomes more powerful than the law itself
D) the inevitable delay in enacting banking law

19) Which of the following statements gives the best indication that the 2010 Dodd-Frank law will create meaningful changes in banking?

A) Line 31-34 ("If the rules… employees.")
B) Line 51-52 ("Financial crisis… stocks.")
C) Line 89-90 ("Can add… outcome.")
D) Line 97 ("Now everyone…them.")

Questions 20-30 are based on the following passage

Hemophilia Patient or Drug Seller?
Originally published on Jan. 14, 2016 by the NYTimes

LaQuenta Caldwell-Moody considered it improper when a pharmacy sales representative tried to take her teenage son, when he was still a minor, to dinner without her.

The salesman was the father of someone with hemophilia, the same disease her son has. But this invitation seemed mercenary, taking advantage of their friendship and shared illness to try to woo the business of her son, Austin Caldwell, whose drug treatments cost more than $1 million a year.

"He's a cash cow," said Ms. Caldwell-Moody, who lives in Concord, N.C. "He's wanted by a lot of people."

Drugs for hemophilia are so expensive and therefore so lucrative for the pharmaceutical industry that they have created an unusual conflict of interest, blurring the lines between being a patient and drug seller. More and more, manufacturers of hemophilia drugs and the specialty pharmacies that dispense the medicines are hiring patients and their relatives to gain an inside track and access in selling their products.

"There are a lot more patients that work in industry now than ever before," said Michelle Rice, vice president for public policy and stakeholder relations at the National Hemophilia Foundation.

The companies, and some patients, say the practice can improve service, because no one understands the special needs of hemophiliacs more than someone with the disease.

But some patient advocates say that having people with dual, and sometimes dueling roles, can result in patients being misled by someone they think of as their friend but who puts profits over their health. The owners of a specialty pharmacy in Alabama were convicted of inflating bills to Medicaid by paying huge commissions to some members of the hemophilia community to recruit patients.

"I think it's a shame that with so much money comes a lot of ugliness," said Charlene Cowell, executive director of Hemophilia of North Carolina, an advocacy group. "A few people have let the revenues and the benefits of the money just outweigh their love for this community."

Ms. Caldwell-Moody, whose son is now 18, said she had stopped attending meetings of Hemophilia of North Carolina to avoid the sales pitches. Some local support groups are establishing rules to identify attendees of events as patients or sales representatives.

The phenomenon of patients working for the industry is not unique to hemophilia, but is much more common for that disease, according to various patient advocates. This could be because of fierce competition among specialty pharmacies and the lingering distrust of drug companies among some people with hemophilia because many of them were infected decades ago with H.I.V. or hepatitis from drugs made from contaminated blood plasma.

In the Alabama case, the owners of the specialty pharmacy MedfusionRx were convicted after prosecutors charged that they hired a man with hemophilia to get him and his relatives with the disease as customers.

Also convicted was the mother of a young man with hemophilia, who was paid 45 percent of the profit MedfusionRx made from each customer she recruited. Prosecutors said she encouraged patients to order more of the drugs than they needed. They also said her son switched to a more expensive drug so she could earn $20,000, which allowed her husband to buy a pickup truck.

About 20,000 Americans, overwhelmingly males, have hemophilia, an inherited disease marked by a deficiency of a protein needed for blood to clot. To prevent or stanch bleeding, which could otherwise be life-threatening, hemophiliacs infuse themselves with the missing protein, known as a clotting factor.

The drugs cost from $30,000 to a few hundred thousand dollars a year per patient. Costs can be much higher, even over $1 million, for patients whose bodies produce "inhibitors" — antibodies that render the clotting factor less effective, or those with other diseases that can cause bleeding.

The global market for hemophilia drugs is now worth about $10 billion a year, according to Ronny Gal, an analyst at Sanford C. Bernstein & Company. The biggest supplier is Baxalta, which was recently spun off from Baxter and agreed this week to be bought by Shire. Other big companies include Bayer, CSL, Pfizer and Novo Nordisk.

The attractiveness of the market is spurring new drug development. Biogen, a newcomer, entered the market with clotting factors that require less frequent infusions. Roche is developing a drug to help overcome inhibitors. Several companies are making progress on gene therapy, which could conceivably cure the disease.

20) The major issue that the author describes within the passage is that patients with hemophilia have been

A) improperly taken to dinners with salesmen.
B) misinformed about the way Medicaid applies to them.
C) unethically targeted by pharmacies looking to increase revenue.
D) unfairly treated by pharmacists looking to gain a competitive advantage.

21) The word "mercenary" (line 7) as used in this context is best defined as

A) unprincipled.
B) pathetic.
C) degrading.
D) aggressive.

22) Ms. Caldwell-Moody describes her son, Austin, as "a cash cow" (line 11) to emphasize the

A) completely unethical way drug sellers view her son.
B) cavalier attitude of the pharmacological industry.
C) exponentially growing market for hemophilia drug makers.
D) hatred parents have for all drug sellers.

23) The passage claims that patients with hemophilia look to other patients as advocates for support because

A) drug sellers are inherently regarded as untrustworthy members in the community.
B) of the harmful effects of drugs in the past and growing competition among pharmacies.
C) other parents with hemophiliac children have proven to be the most trustworthy.
D) the criminal justice system unfairly targets advocates who are trying to make a decent living.

24) Which of the below provides the best answer evidence of the answer to the above question?

A) Line 14 – 18 ("Drugs for hemophilia .... seller.")
B) Line 27 – 30 ("The companies… disease.")
C) Line 35 – 39 ("The owners… patients.")
D) Line 55 – 60 ("This could… plasma.")

25) The function of the fifth paragraph (lines 27 – 30) is to

A) juxtapose the author's position with that of the patients.
B) provide a grounding for the counter argument that follows.
C) level the criticism sure to come against patient advocates.
D) sway the opinions of the masses to the unpopular side.

26) It can be deduced logically that Austin is a patient who

A) undergoes frequent, sometimes frustrating therapy for his medical condition.
B) has to seek compromises in order to seek effective treatment.
C) suffers from a specific medical condition that produces "inhibitors".
D) relies solely on his mother to make proper medical decision, rather than patient advocates.

27) Which pairs of lines best provides evidence for the question above?

A) Lines 6 – 10 ("But this… a year.") and lines 81 – 86 ("Costs can … bleeding.")
B) Lines 14 – 18 ("Drugs for… seller") and lines 49 – 51 ("Some local… representatives.")
C) Lines 1 – 4 ("LaQuenta Caldwell-Moody…her.") and lines 46 – 49 ("Ms. Caldwell-Moody … pitches.")
D) Lines 61 – 65 ("In the Alabama… customers.") and lines 98 – 100 ("Several companies… disease.")

28) The author contends that drug companies are spinning off their hemophiliac divisions because

A) the market is pressuring them to do so.
B) the divisions are so profitable.
C) demand and supply ratios have flipped recently.
D) gene therapy threatens to replace all drug makers in the near future.

29) The best place to find evidence for the question above lies on

A) line 61-65 ("In the Alabama … customers.")
B) line 74 – 76 ("About 20,000 …clot.")
C) line 80 – 81 ("The drugs … patient.")
D) line 87 – 90 ("The global… company.")

30) The author would agree with which of the following assertions?

A) Drug sellers and patients will soon adopt policy guidelines that no longer blur the lines between salesman and patient advocate.
B) Patients will continue to distrust patient advocates in the face of continued industry growth.
C) Many drug makers will no longer be viable as they sell of their most profitable divisions.
D) Patients such as Austin face more difficult decisions than other hemophiliac patients.

Questions 30-42 are based on the following passages

Reprinted with full permission: Weisberg M, Paul DB (2016) Morton, Gould, and Bias: A Comment on "The Mismeasure of Science". PLoS Biol 14(4): e1002444. doi:10.1371/journal.pbio.1002444

Passage I

Stephen Jay Gould famously used the work of Samuel George Morton (1799–1851) to illustrate how unconscious racial bias could affect scientific measurement. Morton had published measurements of the average cranial capacities of different races, measurements that Gould reanalyzed in an article in ***Science*** and then later in his widely read book ***The Mismeasure of Man***. During the course of this reanalysis, Gould discovered prima facie evidence of unconscious racial bias in Morton's measurements. More than 30 years later, Lewis et al. published a critique of this analysis, denying that Morton's measurements were biased by his racism. Instead, they claim that their "results falsify Gould's hypothesis that Morton manipulated his data to conform with his a priori views."

Morton was a Philadelphia physician and highly respected scientist who avidly collected and measured human skulls. Between 1830, when he began his collection, and his death in 1849, Morton had amassed over a thousand specimens, making his the largest collection of human skulls in the world. To measure cranial capacity (a proxy for brain size), Morton filled the cranial cavities with spherical materials: "white pepper seed" for his 1839 measurements and BB shot for his 1844 measurements. He then computed racial averages using the 5-fold classification—Caucasian, Mongolian, Malayan, Ethiopian, and American—invented by Johann Friedrich Blumenbach (1752–1840). He also computed averages for families and subfamilies within these racial groups. His measurements indicated that the "Teutonic Family" (consisting primarily of Germans, Anglo-Saxons, Anglo-Americans, and Anglo-Irish) within the modern Caucasian group had by far the largest brains.

Gould's argument for Morton's unconscious racial bias is based on a comparison between two sets of measurements using two different materials. In his 1839 ***Crania Americana***, Morton used "pepper seeds," but he switched technique to using lead BB shot for the measurements presented in his later works, especially the 1844 ***Crania Aegyptiaca***. Morton made this switch because the pepper seeds were light, variable in size, and easily compressed, and as a result his measurements were highly variable. It is important to note that Gould agrees with Morton about the superiority of the shot measurements. Gould calls these measurements "objective, accurate, and repeatable".

After tabulating and reanalyzing Morton's data, Gould was struck by a systematic difference between the two sets of measurements. The mean cranial capacity for Africans, Americans, and Caucasians had all increased between 1839 and 1844, as is shown in Fig 1. However, they did not change by the same amounts. The African skulls have a much larger increase in mean cranial capacity than the Americans and Caucasians. If this difference were the result either of lack of precision or of a systematic measurement error, the change should be approximately the same for the different races, but it was not. Gould thought that the best explanation for the more dramatic change in the African mean was unconscious manipulation on Morton's part in 1839, when technique made that manipulation possible.

Why, then, do Lewis et al. think Morton has been vindicated? Their 2011 paper reports on the remeasurement of about half the skulls in Morton's original set. They found that Morton's shot measurements were mostly accurate, and that such errors as existed did not support a charge of bias. They also considered Gould's other criticism of Morton's methods and analysis, which they also judged to be mostly without merit (we are here only concerned with the measurement issue). They concluded that "Morton did not manipulate data to support his preconceptions, contra Gould".

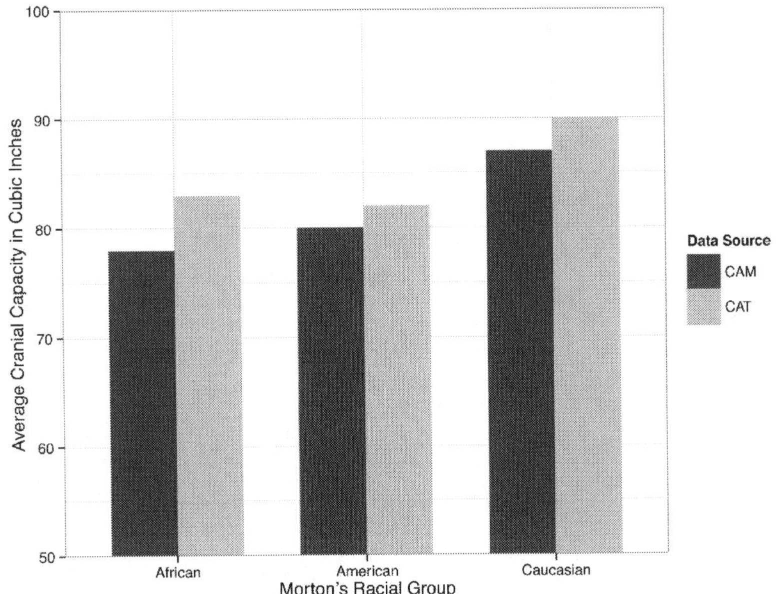

Average Cranial Capacity in Cubic Inches
100
90
80
70
60
50
African
American
Caucasian
Morton's Racial Group
Data Source
CAM
CAT

Passage II

We take no issue with Lewis et al.'s remeasurements, but argue that these measurements are not and cannot be evidence for their conclusion. Although Lewis et al. found Morton's shot-based measurements to be accurate, Gould already accepted this. Indeed, Gould had to assume that Morton's shot measurements were accurate, as he relied on them in his own analysis. Gould never made, nor did he ever claim to make, nor did he have any reason to make any measurements himself. Gould's argument depends on the difference between the two sets of measurements. Thus, as a matter of logic, there is no way that the results of Lewis et al.'s remeasurement program could be used to adjudicate the issue of who was biased. The many commentators who cite as a major failing of Gould's that he "never bothered to measure the skulls himself" have also, though perhaps more understandably, missed the point.

It is perfectly reasonable for a reader to have further questions about Morton's measurements and samples before drawing a final verdict. Perhaps there are other explanations for the anomalously small African mean cranial capacity reported in ***Crania Americana***. However, Lewis et al.'s remeasurements shed no light on this anomaly and only serve to highlight it further by demonstrating that Morton's measurements with shot were indeed accurate. Gould's claim that this is prima facia evidence of unconscious bias in ***Crania Americana*** remains intact.

Lewis et al. also allege that, according to Gould, studies of human variation are inevitably biased. Or, as is their view, "are objective accounts attainable, as Morton attempted?" But here, too, the critique misses its mark.

Gould argued that unconscious bias is ubiquitous in science. He actually praised Morton for the "rare and precious gift" of having published all his primary data, thus enabling others to check his work. Gould did not believe that biased results are inevitable. In his view, the tendency to fudge could and should be countered by "vigilance and scrutiny;" that is, by greater self-reflection and by cultivating, "as Morton did, the habit of presenting all our information and procedures, so that others can assess what we, in our blindness, cannot". In his view, only if we "understand and acknowledge inevitable preferences" can we countermand their influence. Lewis et al. conclude that, contra Gould, "biased scientists are inevitable, biased results are not." But this was precisely Gould's own view!

Lewis et al. have charged that Gould's "own analysis of Morton is likely the stronger example of bias influencing results". We maintain that this accusation, which continues to reverberate, is undeserved, and we hope that this will prompt at least some readers to reevaluate the evidence and arguments.

31) In Passage 1, Lewis et al.'s contention is that

A) they agree wholeheartedly with the original findings of Morton.
B) Gould's famous declaration of Morton's racial bias was in fact incorrect.
C) the text *The Mismeasure of Man* is an antiquated book.
D) Morton and Gould were both incorrect in their measures, regardless of racial bias.

32) Which choice provides the best justification for the question above?

A) Line 1 – 4 ("Stephen Jay Gould … measurement.")
B) Line 4 – 8 ("Morton had … *Man.*")
C) Line 8 – 10 ("During the course… measurements.")
D) Line 11 – 16 ("More than … views.")

33) The author of Passage 1 argues that the newer method of measuring cranial capacity utilized by Morton is

A) not flawed, and repeatable.
B) not flawed, but unrepeatable.
C) flawed, but repeatable.
D) flawed, and unrepeatable.

34) Gould believes Morton exhibited "unconscious racial bias" (line 10) because

A) the differences in measurements should have been the same across all races.
B) Lewis et al. were inherently right in their assertions.
C) BB shots are more "objective, accurate, and repeatable".
D) he had personally re-measured all of the skulls and found Morton to be inaccurate.

35) Data in the chart most strongly supports which of the following statements?

A) The difference in measurement within the Caucasian group was greater than the median.
B) The difference in measurement within the American group was the smallest difference overall.
C) The difference in measurement within the African group was smaller than the difference within the American group.
D) The difference in measurement within the African group was smaller than the difference within the Caucasian, but larger than the difference within the American, groups.

36) Data in the graph identifies which of the following correctly?

A) The CAM measures were conducted after the CAT measures.
B) The CAM measures are more accurate than the CAT measures.
C) The CAT measures were conducted after the CAM measures.
D) The CAT measures are more error prone than the CAT measures.

37) The data in the chart most strongly supports which aspect discussed within Passage 1?

A) The greater CAM measures within the African group shows a plausible greater intellect than the American group, but lesser than the Caucasian group.
B) The CAT measures are less likely to be repeated with consistency than the CAM measures.
C) The fact that the CAM versus CAT measures in American and Caucasian groups increased in similar amounts, coupled with a much greater difference indicated in the African group, shows a possible racial bias in the original CAT measures.
D) The largest cranial capacity measured in both CAT and CAM in Caucasian groups shows a superior intellect versus all other measured ethnic groups.

38) The author of Passage 2 states "it is perfectly reasonable for a reader to have further questions about Morton's measurements and samples before drawing a final verdict" in order to

A) present a viewpoint that not all factors have been considered in analyzing Morton's data.
B) show inherent flaws within Gould's analysis that Lewis at al. point out.
C) emphasize that all scientific measures contain bias, thus making it impossible to draw a final verdict.
D) recommend that readers partake in their own research by measuring Morton's skulls themselves.

39) What is the function of the question that Lewis et al. pose on line 121 – 122: "Are objective accounts attainable, as Morton attempted?"

A) It serves as a rhetorical question, essentially stating that, in fact, objective accounts are not attainable.
B) It serves as a question that has befuddled scientists and researchers alike for some time.
C) It serves as a question that provides an opposing view to Gould's belief that "studies of human variation are inevitably biased."
D) It serves no purpose in determining the validity to Gould's conclusion that Morton held "unconscious racial bias" (line 10).

40) As used in line 116, "prima facia" most closely means

A) obvious.
B) heavy.
C) perplexing.
D) clean.

41) Which choice best describes the relationship between the two passages?

A) Passage 2 refutes much of the original claims made in Passage 1
B) Passage 1 allows for some discrepancies within Passage 2 to be examined, but not refuted, to complete the original analysis
C) Passage 2 specifies in greater detail Passage 1's criticisms to conclude Gould's methods do not justify Lewis et al.'s contention.
D) Passage 2 wholeheartedly agrees with Morton's original thesis presented by Gould and Lewis et al. first encountered within Passage 1

42) The authors of both passages would most likely agree with which of the choices below?

A) Renewed calls for measuring the skulls with shots should be heeded to resolve any issues in racial bias from Morton's original experiments.
B) Based on the evidence at hand, it is difficult to refute the conclusions Morton presents, despite Gould's contentions.
C) Lewis et al. likely do not provide sufficient evidence to refute Gould's claim.
D) Morton shows unconscious racial bias as described by Lewis at al. but refuted by Gould in his analysis.

Questions 43-52 are based on the following passage

Abraham Lincoln, Alton, Ill. October 15, 1858

Fellow-citizens, I have not only made the declaration that I do not mean to produce a conflict between the states, but I have tried to show by fair reasoning that I propose nothing but what has a most peaceful tendency. The quotation that "a house divided against itself cannot stand," and which has proved so offensive to Judge Douglas, was part of the same thing. He tries to show that variety in the domestic institutions of the different states is necessary and indispensable. I do not dispute it. I very readily agree with him that it would be foolish for us to insist upon having a cranberry law here in Illinois where we have no cranberries, because they have a cranberry law in Indiana where they have cranberries. If we here raise a barrel of flour more than we want and the Louisianians raise a barrel of sugar more than they want, it is of mutual advantage to exchange. That produces commerce, brings us together and makes us better friends.

But is it true that all the difficulty and agitation we have in regard to this institution of slavery springs from office seeking, from the mere ambition of politicians? Is that the truth? How many times have we had danger from this question? There never was a party in the history of this country, and there probably never will be, of sufficient strength to disturb the general peace of the country. Parties themselves may be divided and quarrel on minor questions. Yet it extends not beyond the parties themselves.

The Judge alludes very often in the course of his remarks to the exclusive right which the states have to decide for themselves. I agree with him very readily that the different states have the right. Our controversy with him is in regard to the new territories. We agree that when the states come in as states they have the right and the power to do as they please. We have no power as citizens of the free states or in our federal capacity as members of the federal Union through the general government to disturb slavery in the states where it exists. What I insist upon is that the new territories shall be kept free from it while in the territorial condition. Judge Douglas assumes that we have no interest in them, that we have no right whatever to interfere. I think we have some interest. I think that as white men we have. Do we not wish for an outlet for our surplus population, if I may so express myself? Do we not feel an interest in getting to that outlet with such institutions as we would like to have prevail there? If you go to the territory opposed to slavery and another man comes to the same ground with his slave, upon the assumption that the things are equal, it turns out that he has the equal right all his way and you have no part of it your way.

The real issue in this controversy is the sentiment on the part of one class that looks upon the institution of slavery as a wrong, and of another class that does not look upon it as wrong. It is the sentiment around which all their actions, all their arguments circle, from which all their propositions radiate. They look upon it as being a moral, social, and political wrong. Has anything ever threatened the existence of this Union save this very institution of slavery? How do you propose to improve the condition of things by enlarging it? You may have a cancer upon your person and not be able to cut it out lest you bleed to death, but surely it is no way to cure it to graft it and spread it over your body. That is no proper way of treating what you regard as wrong.

That is the real issue. That is the issue that will continue in this country when these poor tongues of Judge Douglas and myself are silent. It is the eternal struggle between these two principles, right and wrong, throughout the world. They are the two principles that have stood face to face from the beginning of time, and will ever continue to struggle. The one is the common right of humanity and the other is the divine right of kings. It is the same principle in whatever shape it develops itself. It is the same spirit that says, "You work and toil and earn bread and I'll eat it." No matter in what shape it comes, whether from the mouth of a king who seeks to bestride the people of his own nation and live by the fruit of their labor, or from one race of men as an apology for enslaving another race, it is the same tyrannical principle.

43) According to the passage, Douglas takes issue with the statement "a house divided against itself cannot stand" (lines 5 – 6) because

A) Douglas believes every State should necessarily make legislative decisions for itself.
B) Lincoln is incorrect to declare war on Slavery.
C) cranberry laws in Illinois should also apply to neighboring States, such as Indiana.
D) he does not believe commerce is more important than Slavery.

44) What sentence or combination of sentences best provide evidence for the answer above?

A) Lines 1 – 5 ("Fellow-citizens…tendency.") and Lines 5 – 8 ("The quotation…thing.")
B) Lines 5 – 8 (The quotation…thing.") and Lines 8 – 10 ("He tries … indispensable.")
C) Line 10 ("I do… it.") and Line 17 – 18 ("That produces… friends.")
D) Line 15 – 17 ("If we… exchange.") and Line 17 – 19 ("That produces… friends.")

45) The word "tendency" (line 5) most closely means

A) growth.
B) consequence
C) intent.
D) outline.

46) The sentence below (line 52 – 57) can be reasonably inferred to mean that

"If you go to the territory opposed to slavery and another man comes to the same ground with his slave, upon the assumption that the things are equal, it turns out that he has the equal right all his way and you have no part of it your way."

A) Douglas should find a compromise when it comes to the issue of slavery in the territories.
B) slaves who are free would find themselves no longer free in the territories of the United States.
C) slave owners should be afforded the same rights they enjoy regardless of their location.
D) slaves and slave owners alike should be afforded the same rights within the United States.

47) As utilized in line 69, what is the closest meaning to the word "cancer"?

A) The issue of slavery.
B) Disparate income gaps.
C) Gender inequality.
D) Rights of free and indentured slaves.

48) The central problem that Lincoln addresses in the passage is that white men

A) do not have the right to interfere in the issue of slavery unless it is an issue within their state of residence.
B) are too weak to act even though they see slavery as morally, socially, and politically wrong.
C) need to veer away from office seeking matters, and stride towards allowing States to make independent decisions.
D) should have a strong concern that slavery should not exist in the territories of the US as a matter of common right of humanity.

49) Which of the choices below would Lincoln and Judge Douglas agree wholeheartedly?

A) Slavery should be allowed within the states that already have laws allowing slavery.
B) Slaves should never be free in the territories of the United States.
C) Slavery should be a decision made by the legislative branch rather than the executive.
D) Slavery is an issue that will divide the Union.

50) What sentences below provides the best evidence for the answer above?

A) Lines 5 – 10 ("The quotation… dispute it.")
B) Lines 21 – 25 ("But is …question.")
C) Lines 25 – 31 ("There never … themselves.")
D) Lines 33 – 38 ("The Judge… territories.")

51) The final paragraph is most concerned with establishing a principle that

A) regardless of its origin, its effect is plainly wrong.
B) applies only to the royal families and not to the common man.
C) will end its timeless struggle after Lincoln takes office.
D) will always be won over by tyrannical men.

52) In context, the word "bestride" (line 88) most closely means

A) harbor
B) aid
C) dominate
D) relegate

WRITING AND LANGUAGE TEST 1: Section 2

35 MINUTES 44 QUESTIONS

Turn to section 2 of your answer sheet to answer the questions in this section.

Directions:

Each passage that follows require you to utilize your skillset in recognizing errors in proper sentence structure, rhetorical usage, and/or punctuation. Some may contain charts or graphs for you to decipher or revise.

Answer each carefully, as best as you can. If there are no errors, choose NO CHANGE.

Questions 1-11

Astronomers find a new way of observing a new phenomenon of black holes

For the first time in history, Japanese astronomer Mariko Kimura from Kyoto University, led significant [1] founds of bursts of visible lights "escaping" a black hole as it devoured a nearby star in the Cygnus constellation. Furthermore, located approximately 7,800 light-years away from Earth, these visible lights came about as a result of relativistic jets consisting of streams of plasma heated to 10 million degrees Celsius (18 million degrees Fahrenheit) from what is known as an accretion disk – an incredibly intensely heated formation near the event horizon just as a whole star is about to be consumed into the gaping maw of a black hole. Such research is significant not only for the event itself but also for scientific research in general.

1)

A) NO CHANGE
B) findings
C) determinants
D) resolutions

2)

A) NO CHANGE
B) However, located
C) Subsequently, located
D) Located

Kimura [3] led a team of 26 astronomers, who unilaterally pointed their optical telescopes throughout the world to observe this two-week phenomenon. In the article published in *Nature*, the team, working night and day, [4] has noted that a mere 20-cm telescope was sufficient to observe what they believe were x-rays from the center of the accretion disk irradiating outer regions. This allows astronomers to observe "without the use of x-ray or gamma ray telescopes," said Kimura; by 2015, he estimates that amateur telescopes will be sufficient [5] to observe black hole phenomena such as the one he discovered.

3)

The author is considering adding the following phrase:

, seeking validation from peers,

Should the author do so?

A) Yes, because it provides the reason for why Kimura led a team of 26 peers
B) Yes, because it creates a deeper understanding into the event horizon phenomenon
C) No, because it adds unnecessary interruption to the logical flow of the sentence
D) No, because it focuses on another subject matter away from astronomers

4)

A) NO CHANGE
B) noted
C) had noted
D) noting

5)

A) NO CHANGE
B) for observing
C) with observations
D) as observations

Reminding us that absolutely nothing, including light itself, can escape a black hole once matter has been completely sucked in, Kimura notes the importance of finding not only the phenomenon itself, but of the new method that has been identified, controlled, and [6] validated by his team of scientists. Being a part of history, as well as a group of like-minded astronomers, should bring forth further funding and interest in the field. [7] In reality, science is always threatened with budget cuts. This news should bolster the argument that more research is needed to understand our galaxy and their functions.

6)

A) NO CHANGE
B) validating
C) full of validation
D) to validate

7)

Which of the choices below combine the two sentences correctly?

A) In reality, because science is always threatened, this news should bolster the argument that more research is needed to understand our galaxy and their functions.
B) In reality, since science is always threatened with budget cuts, this news should bolster the argument that more research is needed to understand our galaxy and its functions.
C) The news that science is always threatened with budget cuts should bolster the argument that more research is needed to understand our galaxy and its functions.
D) Bolstering the argument that more research is needed to understand our galaxy and their functions, reality is that science is always threatened with budget cuts.

To wit, this major finding creates a ripple effect for all of science as it relates to funding further research, garnering public interest, and [8] making stronger the way we realize things about the cosmos. Even though such studies accomplish much in the way of gaining public interest, [9] yet there are thousands of other research projects that do not capture the public imagination. [10] Furthermore, each and every one are relevant and meaningful. [11] To sum up, the event horizon is important and Kimura's research puts a spotlight on black holes, over teamwork among scientists to gain insight and validity, and on scientific research itself.

8)

A) NO CHANGE
B) increasing our understanding of the cosmos.
C) our realizing things about the cosmos.
D) strengthening our relationship with the cosmos.

9)

A) NO CHANGE
B) And
C) But
D) DELETE this underlined word altogether

10)

A) NO CHANGE
B) Still
C) In addition
D) However

11)

Which of the choices below summarizes the passage's main claim in the most concise way possible?

A) NO CHANGE
B) The event horizon, along with Kimura's research, provides a nice summary on the power of black holes, teamwork among scientists, and on scientific research itself.
C) To sum up, Kimura's research puts a spotlight on black holes, on teamwork among scientists to gain insight and validity, and on scientific research itself.
D) On the other hand, black holes and scientists have teamed up to put a spotlight on Kimura's research to provide insight and validity on scientific research itself.

Questions 12-22

Calypso's long history

I never understood the true meaning of Calypso music. [12] That is, until I visited my homeland of Trinidad. Rich in history, and steeped in political impressions, Calypso was always around my house in Jersey City, Jersey. Growing up, I can hear the [13] singer's, Lord Invader's, high notes and the vocal melodies that my father would listen to every weekend as he prepared his traditional roti, doubles and curries for our Sunday family gatherings. Without worry, cared for by my parents, surrounded by four walls and a roof as a child in a loving home, I was beyond words when I finally discovered what [14] it meant to all Caribbean islanders, including myself.

12)

A) NO CHANGE
B) Because
C) For example,
D) However,

13)

A) NO CHANGE
B) singer, Lord Invader's
C) singer Lord Invader's,
D) singer Lord Invader's

14)

A) NO CHANGE
B) they meant
C) the meaning meant
D) Calypso meant

Rhythms of Calypso can be traced back to the very first African slaves who were brought to the island to work in the various plantations throughout Trinidad. [15] Many toiled for long hours, often without voice or interaction, since slaves were forbidden from talking to each other for fear of insurrection. So African slaves then began to sing songs, rooted in West African kaiso sounds, to "talk" with other slaves, to act out against their slave [16] <u>masters, their</u> brutalities. In many instances, slaves had no family and no friends, separated completely from their past, yanked away from their ancestral home, and felt isolated.

:: 3::

Since I now have visited Trinidad, I have learned that it was first colonized by the Spanish, then faced a rash of French immigrants, and later British rule took over. Calypso took shape in the language of patois – an informal dialect that consists of many roots but designated by specific locations. In Jamaica, for example, their dialect is called the "patwa," and [17] <u>this is a language that is a mixture of Islanders and European rule.</u> These songs led the way of communication and freedom when the British abolished slavery in the 1830's, starting an annual tradition that we now know as Carnival. Celebrated throughout the Caribbean and South America, Calypso music was a vehicle for political expression and emancipation of slaves.

15)

At this juncture the author is contemplating about inserting an addition in the form of the following:

> Historians note that the slave trade in the Caribbean were much more prevalent, but more likely to be forgotten about, than the trade that occurred in the North and South American mainlands.

(A) Yes, because it adds a valuable note about how slave trade was perceived in Trinidad.
(B) Yes, because it explains further the origins of Calpyso via the slave trade as it relates to other locations, such as North and South America.
(C) No, because it interrupts the discussion focused on the African slaves themselves, as they relate to Calypso music.
(D) No, because it insinuates that the slave trade in the North and South Americas were more important than the slave trade in the islands.

16)

A) NO CHANGE
B) masters, and their
C) masters and their
D) masters,

17)

Which answer choice gives another exemplification that is similar to the one already provided by the author?

A) NO CHANGE
B) in French Guinea their dialect is called "creole."
C) there are other languages just like "patwa" in many other Islands in the Caribbean.
D) it shares many of the same roots with Calypso music, including influences from the French, Spanish and British.

Harry Belafonte, perhaps the most famous Calypso musician, created and sang [18] <u>*Jean and Dinah*. It marked</u> a new age of political and social movements for Trinidadians. It sold over a million copies for the first time in history, and the song's deeply heartfelt lyrics celebrated the departure of US troops from Trinidad in the 1950's. In fact, much of Calypso has always provided social and humanitarian commentary against the backdrop of the current political landscape, satire and parody against the brutal realities, and [19] <u>a beat that brings rhythm and joy to the listeners despite their destitute living conditions.</u> No longer a mystery, I now find Calypso to be much more than just mere Sunday music.

18)

Which of the following best combines the two sentences at this juncture?

A) *Jean and Dinah*, by marking
B) *Jean and Dinah*, with it marking
C) *Jean and Dinah*, in marking
D) *Jean and Dinah*, marking

19)

Which choice, stylistically, matches the written prose established earlier in the sentence?

A) NO CHANGE
B) a beat that brings rhythm and joy to the listeners within their destitute living conditions.
C) destitute living conditions with a beat that brings rhythm and joy to the listeners.
D) destitute living conditions, that despite it, brings a beat with rhythm and joy to the listeners.

Walking through a country that I know houses such history has given [20] myself a newfound appreciation of the why. Why my father listened to Calypso with such acceptance, why it was an integral part of our lives, and why I will always carry with me these fond memories for the rest of my life. [21] Created with more than just entertainment in mind, my father and my people understood the true meaning of Calypso. But what was the origin of Calypso? How did it come about? These were mysteries that still swirled in my mind.

20)

A) NO CHANGE
B) me a newfound appreciation
C) for myself a newfound appreciation
D) I a newfound appreciation

21)

A) NO CHANGE
B) Created with an intent more than just for entertainment value, my father and my people understood the true meaning of Calypso
C) My father and my people understood the true meaning of Calypso, created with more than just entertainment in mind
D) My father and my people understood, created with more than just entertainment in mind, the true meaning of Calypso.

Think about the passage as a whole for the following question:

22) To make the passage more logical, paragraph 5 should be placed

A) Where it is now.
B) After paragraph 1.
C) After paragraph 2.
D) After paragraph 3.

Questions 23-33

Body detox, mind transformation

For the past two decades, many a guru and health evangelists have proposed a simple, seemingly easy to digest concept of [23] detox: otherwise, to drink healthy juices will yield a cleaner body, and rid itself of toxins that are harmful to your health. Nothing can be further from the truth. When given surveys to list the exact levels of toxins by type and quantity, almost everyone remains baffled by what it is they think they are trying to get rid of. [24] However, with the help of gastroenterologists, we can come to terms with how detox actually occurs, if it does at all, and begin to understand the actual science behind the commonly accepted fad.

23)

A) NO CHANGE
B) detox; otherwise
C) detox: namely,
D) detox. Furthermore,

24)

A) NO CHANGE
B) Moreover,
C) Nevertheless,
D) In sum,

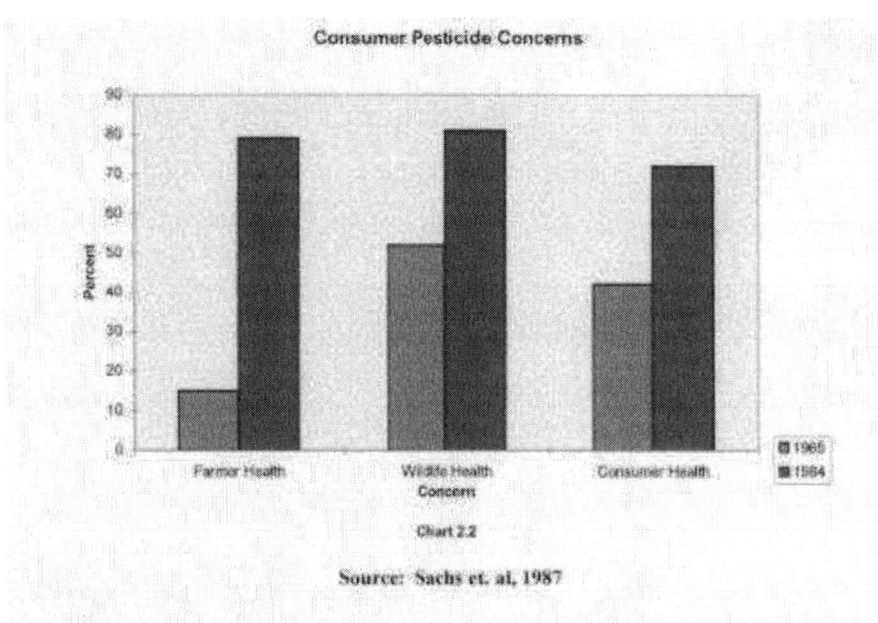

Chart 2.2

Source: Sachs et. al, 1987

Part of the reason for why we attribute the idea of detox so strongly stems from the [25] <u>greatest change in perception within consumers in how pesticides have come to be regarded over time</u> (see chart above). [26] Surely, people argued, less pesticides means less harmful chemicals consumed into our bodies. And any pesticides we consumed, we should be able to "detox" by flushing it out with other, more helpful nutrients, such as organic fruits and vegetables. Simple enough, right? Wrong.

25)

Which choice offers the most accurate interpretation of the chart presented above?

A) NO CHANGE
B) greatest change in perception within farmers in how pesticides have come to be regarded over time
C) greatest change in perception within wildlife activists in how pesticides have come to be regarded over time
D) greatest change in perception occurs amongst all three groups of farmers, wildlife activists, and consumers equally in how pesticides have come to be regarded over time

26)

The author is considering adding the following sentence:

> To put it more clearly, farmers were most directly able to promote healthier living by either denouncing the use of pesticides altogether (which they couldn't do unless they wanted to face severe economic consequences) or promoting alternatives to continued use of pesticides (which is, in fact, what happened over a thirty-year period.)

Should the author do so?

A) Yes, because it establishes the key point about detox that many people could not debunk, including the general population's belief that detox occurs from ingesting certain foods.
B) Yes, because it establishes the logical explanation between the information given in the chart to the reason why the biggest change in farmers' perceptions led to our current beliefs on detox.
C) No, because it is irrelevant to the development of detox and people's beliefs.
D) No, because it does not promote detox in the way the data from the chart allows.

Dr. Woodson Merrell, in "The Detox Prescription", writes with authority. Yet he has received mixed reviews from his peers. He [27] writes, that juicing "allows the body to have more of the resources it needs to support the phases of detoxification." But when couched in such vague terms, his statement is actually [28] vacuous. "What does it even mean?" says a frustrated Dr. Antoinette Sadler, a gastroenterologist at the George Washington University School of Medicine & Health Sciences.

27)

A) NO CHANGE
B) writes – that
C) writes with that
D) writes that

28)

A) NO CHANGE
B) innocent
C) mellifluous
D) rapacious

The main workhorses within [29] their organs are the kidney and the liver. These two function almost exclusively to filter out all of the negative toxins that may accrue within our bodies. Actual toxins, recognized by the medical field, include harmful chemicals such as pesticides and lead. Toxins also include common household items such as acetaminophen found in Tylenol, [30] or too much vitamin A if ingested too much. Dr. Merrell readily agrees that nutrients found in organic foods converted to colorful juices may not actually directly detox anything in the body; however, [31] saying things he might not really be happy to admit that these foods may act to help the important organs – kidney and liver – by way of increasing general overall health.

29)

A) NO CHANGE
B) they're
C) our
D) its

30)

A) NO CHANGE
B) or vitamins like A, especially when people ingest them too much.
C) or vitamin A in large doses.
D) or vitamin A, when ingested in large amounts.

31)

A) NO CHANGE
B) he disagrees
C) he reluctantly but happily says
D) he does assert

The health and self-help industry is a 2 billion-dollar economy, bolstered even more by fitness regimens that promise to change everything within our bodies that are harmful to something altogether positive and beneficial. There are countless books and websites that feature beautifully chiseled yogis, highly accomplished medical doctors, and [32] testimonials from those who are proud to show their before and after pictures to the world. Yet, despite all the fanfare, the very notion that we can detox our bodies simply from what we consume is a fallacy, [33] a grave mistake; that had never before been challenged and continues to this day.

32)

A) NO CHANGE
B) testimonials from proud athletes.
C) testimony from proud athletes.
D) proud athletes and their testimonials.

33)

A) NO CHANGE
B) a grave mistake –
C) a grave, mistake,
D) a grave mistake,

Questions 34-44

Government policies and entrepreneurship

Entrepreneurship has led the way in top business school curricula for the past generation. This is not simply [34] happenstance. Our country has gone through at least three major changes when it comes to governmental policy designed to promote business. From the earliest periods in the 18th to early 19th [35] century - American policy focused on local agriculture, focusing on tight, parochial communities that foster sustainability, rather than nation-wide prosperity. [36] The advent of crop rotation, livestock utilization and [37] stationary farming on arid lands paved the way for greater diversity and successful production of grains and livestock, allowing famers and regional populations to benefit greatly. Federal subsidies and other policies were aimed not only at the local farms in existence, but also in the expansion of American settlement, granting free land – up to 160 acres to pioneering families - to those who would venture out West to risk, insure, and sustain development of farmlands.

34)

A) NO CHANGE
B) chance
C) improbable
D) happening

35)

A) NO CHANGE
B) century;
C) century:
D) century,

36)

The author is pondering whether to add the following sentence here:

Germans immigrants, who had the most background in farming and agriculture from their homeland, at the time were the most willing constituents who sought to take advantage of these governmental policies.

Should the author do so?

A) Yes, because it adds value to how government policies actually worked to help new American immigrants during that time period.
B) Yes, because it expands reader understanding of the "tight, parochial communities" the policies affected most.
C) No, because it distracts the reader from the general description of the particulars of the policies the author is developing in the paragraph.
D) No, because it has zero relevance to how policies shaped America and its existing non-immigrant population.

37)

A) NO CHANGE
B) farm to be done on dry lands
C) farming on stationary, but dry, lands
D) farming that is stationary and dry on land

With the advent of the Industrial Revolution [38] , and with many of the population coming back from war, farms started to decline. Automation in processes and a public perception that shifted jobs from familial rural life to employment within urban cities eventually paved the way for governmental intervention that focused on checks and balances from the vigorous *laissez-faire* expansion of big business.

By the end of World War I, American policy took a decided shift from fostering production of mass-scale processed goods [39] into a focus on laws that fostered reliance on regional or State expertise. During this time period, governmental acts such as the Federal Reserve Act of 1913 created not one central bank, but 13 regional ones to create healthy competition and a system of distribution of wealth between States. Other concurrent acts during the Progressive area had one shortcoming, however: the overt reliance on local and State expertise to regulate the [40] diverse and intricately woven growth in almost all areas of business, including communication, technology, travel and education.

38)

A) NO CHANGE
B) and with many of the population coming back from war
C) , many of the population coming back from war,
D) and with many of the population coming back from war,

39)

A) NO CHANGE
B) into focusing
C) to focusing
D) to a focus

40)

A) NO CHANGE
B) diversion
C) diversity
D) diversely

This policy created an unintended consequence of poaching talent from one location to another. Since this quickly became a zero-sum game of sorts, by the middle of the 20th century, government policies reflected the new mood of the times. That is, instead of big businesses vying for the talents of the few, [41] creating unhealthy competition that prevented overall net-positive growth, States realized that developing their own local community-oriented entrepreneurs was the only option to achieve national goals of prosperity and leadership in global business industry. [42] Hence, government policies that fostered entrepreneurism [43] was shaped and still exists today.

41)

A) NO CHANGE
B) that created unhealthy competition
C) which created unhealthy competition
D) having created an unhealthy competition

42)

A) NO CHANGE
B) Theretofore,
C) Moreover,
D) However,

43)

A) NO CHANGE
B) were
C) has been
D) had thus been

The final question corresponds to the passage as a whole:

44)

Where should the final paragraph be placed for the entire passage to remain logical?

A) Where it is now.
B) After the first paragraph.
C) After the second paragraph.
D) It may be deleted since it does not correspond with the logical progression overall.

MATHEMATICS TEST 1, NO CALCULATOR: Section 3

25 MINUTES, 20 QUESTIONS

Turn to section 3 of your answer sheet to answer the questions in this section.

Directions

For questions 1-15, solve each problem, choose the best answer from the choices provided, and fill in the corresponding circle on your answer sheet. For questions 16-20, solve the problem and enter your answer in the grid on the answer sheet. You may use any available space in your test booklet for scratch work.

Notes

1. The use of a calculator is permitted.
2. All variables and expressions represent real numbers unless otherwise indicated.
3. Figures provided are drawn to scale unless indicated.
4. All figures lie in a plane unless indicated.
5. Unless indicated, the domain for each function is all real numbers.

Reference Formulas and Shapes

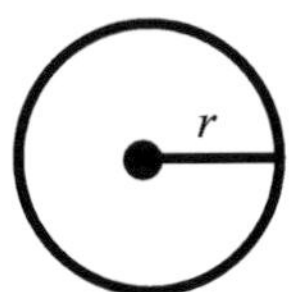

$A = \pi r^2$

$C = \pi d \text{ or } 2\pi r$

$A = l \times w$

$P = 2(l + w)$

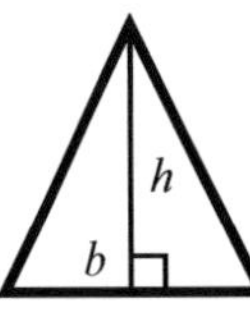

$A = \frac{1}{2}(b \times h)$

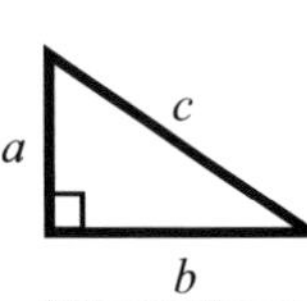

Pythagorean Theorem

$a^2 + b^2 = c^2$

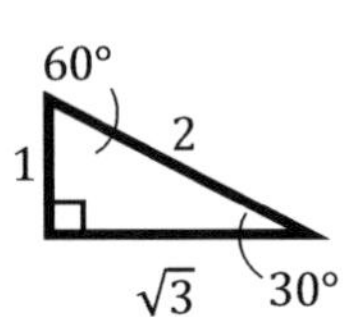

Common Right Triangles

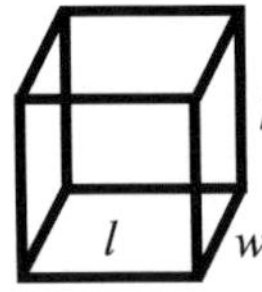

$V = l \times w \times h$

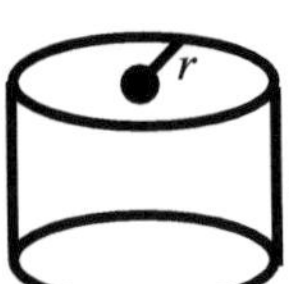

$V = \pi r^2 h$

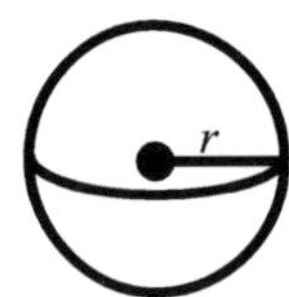

$V = \frac{4}{3}\pi r^3$

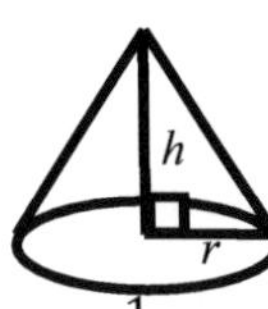

$V = \frac{1}{3}\pi r^2 h$

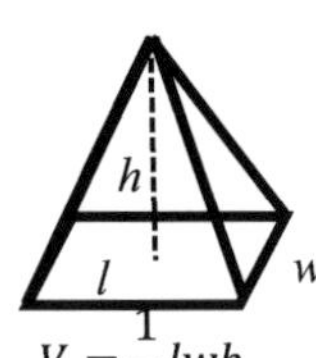

$V = \frac{1}{3}lwh$

A circle contains 360 degrees and 2π radians.
The sum of the angles of a triangle is 360.

---

1) If function f is defined by $f(x) = |x - 5| + 3$, what is the minimum value for f?

A) -3
B) -2
C) 0
D) 3

2) If $x + y = 9$ and $x - y = 15$, what is the value of y?

A) -6
B) -3
C) 3
D) 6

3) Diego works at a sales firm, where he is paid \$64 daily and an additional \$5 commission for each sale he makes after his seventh sale each day. What formula could Diego use to model his income if he makes at least eight sales?

A) 64+5s-7
B) 64+7s
C) 64+5(s-7)
D) 7s+64

4) A building that is 15 feet long, 20 feet wide, and 20 feet tall is being powerwashed. If the four outside walls (excluding the roof) are being washed by a company that washes 200 square feet an hour, how long will it take for the building's cleaning to be completed?

A) 4 hours
B) 5 hours
C) 6 hours
D) 7 hours

5) If a particular circle doubles its radius, what is the ratio of the new area to the old?

A) 1:1
B) 1:2
C) 2:1
D) 4:1

6) The chart shows the estimated amount of E.Coli bacteria after some number of days in an incubator. If the pattern of growth was estimated to continue, what is the pattern of growth and how many bacteria will be estimated to be in the incubator on Day 6?

Size of incubated *E.Coli* Population (in thousands)	
Days	Est. Amount
1	11
2	13
3	16
4	20

A) Linear, with 28,000 bacteria on Day 6
B) Linear, with 32,000 bacteria on Day 6
C) Exponential, with 25,000 bacteria on Day 6
D) Exponential, with 31,000 bacteria on Day 6

7) What is the value of the expression $3i(5+i) - 2i(4-i)$ in $a+bi$ form?

A) $7+5i$
B) $5-23i$
C) $-5+7i$
D) $-1-23i$

8) Mirepoix, a common recipe in cooking, has a usual ratio of two parts onions, one part carrots, and one part celery. If preparing 38 grams of mirepoix for a recipe, how much of the mixture should be onions?

A) 10 grams
B) 19 grams
C) 25 grams
D) 27 grams

9) A certain line $g(x)$ has a y-intercept of 8 and a point at $(3,13)$. Which of the following lines is perpendicular to $g(x)$?

A) $h(x) = -\frac{3}{5}x - 8$
B) $h(x) = \frac{5}{3}x + 8$
C) $h(x) = \frac{3}{5}x - 8$
D) $h(x) = -\frac{5}{3}x + 8$

10) What quadrant contains part of the function $h(x) = (x-5)(x+2)$?

A) Quadrant II
B) Quadrant III
C) Quadrant IV
D) Each quadrant contains a part.

11) Given the system of equations below, what is the value of $x + y$?

$$4x - 3y = -36$$
$$2y - x = 19$$

A) 3
B) 5
C) 7
D) 12

12) If $y = x - 5$, and $\frac{8^y}{2^{x+3}} = 16$, what is the value of x?

A) -11
B) 5
C) 3
D) 11

13) In the function $f(x) = \frac{x+5}{x-3} + x + 5$, where does $f(x)$ cross the x-axis?

A) $(5,0)$
B) $(3,0)$
C) $(-5,0)$ and $(3,0)$
D) $(-5,0)$ and $(2,0)$

14) The kinetic energy of a solid can be found with the formula $K = \frac{1}{2}mv^2$, where m is the mass and v is the velocity of the object. If the object triples its velocity and halves its mass, what is the ratio of the second object's kinetic energy to the original object?

A) $\frac{2}{9}$
B) $\frac{2}{3}$
C) $\frac{3}{2}$
D) $\frac{9}{2}$

15) If a quadratic function has x-intercepts at 4 and 10, which of the following is an expression of the function?

A) $f(x) = (x - 4)^2 - 9$
B) $f(x) = (x - 7)^2 - 9$
C) $f(x) = (x + 7)^2 - 9$
D) $f(x) = (x - 4)^2 + 9$

GRID-IN

16) If one third of the square of a positive number is 48, what is the number?

17) In the map below, Samir drives from point A to B, which is 4 miles, and then drives from point B to C, which is 3 miles. If the distance from point A to point D is 20 miles, and roads BC and DE run parallel, what is the distance from point D to point E?

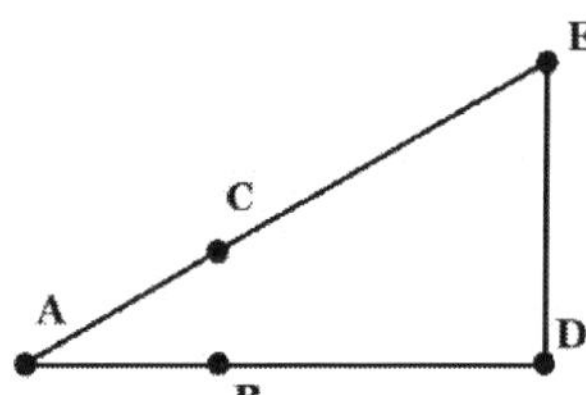

18) The data below tracks profits in three companies that would come from a hypothetical investment of $1,000 in a company in 1996. What year showed the largest percent increase for any company?

Profit from a Hypothetical Investment			
	Apple	Microsoft	IBM
2001	4000	2955	2784
2006	8023	4432	2796
2011	39486	5342	6369
2016	117413	10374	7917

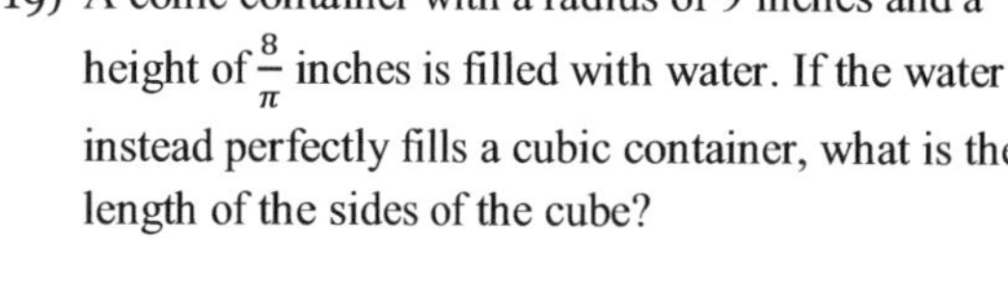

19) A conic container with a radius of 9 inches and a height of $\frac{8}{\pi}$ inches is filled with water. If the water instead perfectly fills a cubic container, what is the length of the sides of the cube?

20) The cosine of an angle is $\frac{\sqrt{3}}{2}$. What is the sine of the same angle?

MATHEMATICS TEST 1, CALCULATOR: Section 4

55 MINUTES, 38 QUESTIONS

Turn to section 4 of your answer sheet to answer the questions in this section.

Directions

For questions 1-29, solve each problem, choose the best answer from the choices provided, and fill in the corresponding circle on your answer sheet. For questions 30-38, solve the problem and enter your answer in the grid on the answer sheet. You may use any available space in your test booklet for scratch work.

Notes

1. The use of a calculator is permitted.
2. All variables and expressions represent real numbers unless otherwise indicated.
3. Figures provided are drawn to scale unless indicated.
4. All figures lie in a plane unless indicated.
5. Unless indicated, the domain for each function is all real numbers.

Reference Formulas and Shapes

$A = \pi r^2$

$C = \pi d \text{ or } 2\pi r$

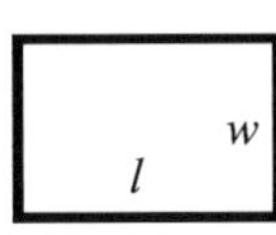

$A = l \times w$

$P = 2(l + w)$

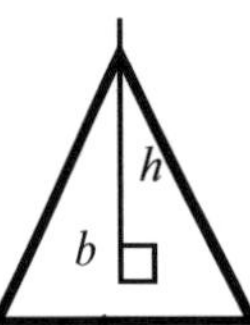

$A = \frac{1}{2}(b \times h)$

a, b, c

Pythagorean Theorem

$a^2 + b^2 = c^2$

60°, 2, 1, $\sqrt{3}$, 30°

1, 45°, $\sqrt{2}$, 45°, 1

Common Right Triangles

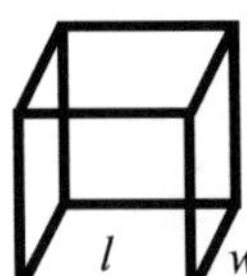

$V = l \times w \times h$

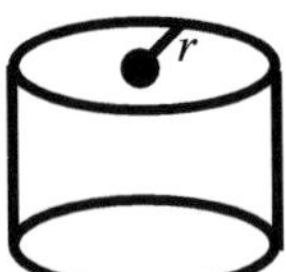

$V = \pi r^2 h$

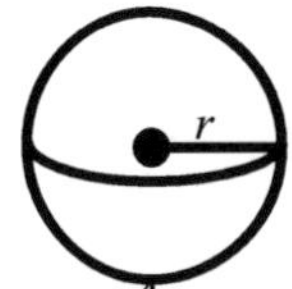

$V = \frac{4}{3}\pi r^3$

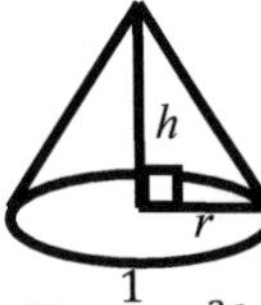

$V = \frac{1}{3}\pi r^2 h$

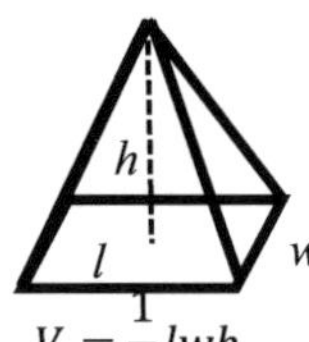

$V = \frac{1}{3}lwh$

A circle contains 360 degrees and 2π radians.
The sum of the angles of a triangle is 360.

---

1) If nine more than three times x is fifteen, what is the value of x?

   A) 2
   B) 3
   C) 12
   D) 27

2) A triangle has a height that is four times its base. If the area of the triangle is 50, what is the base of the triangle?

   A) 4
   B) 5
   C) 7
   D) $5\sqrt{2}$

3) Carlos is buying a computer that $899, but is on clearance for 30% off, and he has a coupon for an additional 10% off. What is the final cost of the computer, rounded to the nearest dollar?

A) \$297
B) \$360
C) \$539
D) \$566

4) In the visual, two parallel lines are transected by a third line. The measure of angle A is equal to $5x + 9$ and angle B is equal to $3x + 3$. What is the value of x?

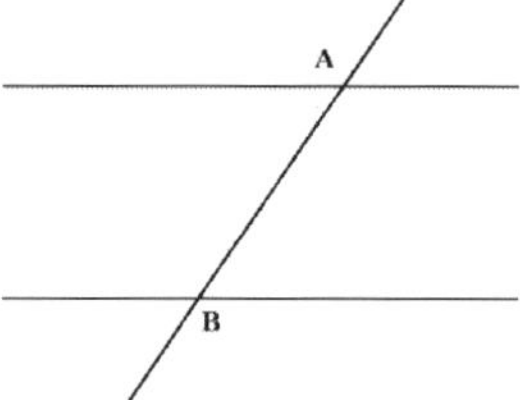

A) -5
B) -3
C) 3
D) 21

5) A nautical mile is 6,000 feet, while a standard mile is 5,280 feet. If a distance of 8 nautical miles is covered on land, what is the distance in standard miles, rounded to the nearest tenth?

A) 9.1 miles
B) 9.0 miles
C) 7.1 miles
D) 7.0 miles

6) If three-fifths of x is 12, what is one-third of x?

A) $\frac{12}{5}$
B) $\frac{20}{3}$
C) 15
D) 20

7) Which of the following functions has a single value of x for which $f(x) = 0$?

A) $f(x) = x^2 + 3$
B) $f(x) = -2x^2 - 3$
C) $f(x) = 3x^2 - 3$
D) $f(x) = 12x^2$

Questions 8 and 9 are based on the chart below, showing median weekly income in dollars by education level. This data is from the Bureau of Labor Statistics, 2014.

	Males	Females	Total
Total, All Education Levels	922	752	839
Less than a high school diploma	517	409	488
High school graduates, no college	751	578	668
Some college or associate degree	872	661	761
Bachelor's Degree Only	1249	965	1101
Bachelor's Degree and Higher	1385	1049	1193
Advanced Degree	1630	1185	1386

8) Which of the following groups has the lowest standard deviation?

A) Advanced degrees, male and female
B) Less than high school diploma, male and female
C) All male incomes
D) All female incomes

9) In terms of percentage, how much larger is overall income with a bachelor's degree only compared to a high school graduate with no college?

A) 39%
B) 61%
C) 65%
D) 164%

10) A sales firm has a certain number of leads, which are distributed equally to its employees. If each employee is given three leads, there are three leads leftover. If each employee is given five leads, then the firm is nine leads short. How many employees work for the company?

A) 5
B) 6
C) 10
D) 15

11) Anush is buying a laptop for school. A refurbished laptop is 20% off the full price, and Anush has a coupon for an additional 10% off. If the MacBook costs $748.80 after the two discounts, what was the original price?

A) $539.14
B) $973.44
C) $1040.00
D) 1069.71

12) A survey of pet owners finds that 27 seniors have a pet dog, 35 seniors have a pet cat, and 9 seniors have both a dog and cat, how many seniors participated in the survey?

A) 53
B) 62
C) 71
D) The answer cannot be determined

Questions 13-15 are answered by the chart below.

	Height	Burn Time	Max. Payload
Space Shuttle	56 m	124 s	24,400 kg
Ares I	94 m	150 s	25,000 kg
Saturn V	116 m	165 s	118,000 kg
Ares V	116 m	-	188,000 kg

13) Which rocket can move the most payload per meter of height?

A) Space Shuttle
B) Ares I
C) Saturn V
D) Ares V

14) If the Ares V rocket requires 30% more burn time than the Ares I per meter of height than the Ares I, what would be the best estimate for the Ares V's burn time?

A) 129 s
B) 239 s
C) 240 s
D) 262 s

15) What is the best description of the relationship between burn time and maximum payload?

A) Increases exponentially
B) Increases linearly
C) Increases logarithmically
D) Decreases exponentially

16) A model rocket is fired upward from an initial height of 60 feet, where the trajectory for the rocket is approximately modeled by $f(x) = -5x^2 + 10x + 120$. If $f(x)$ corresponds with the distance of the rocket from the ground and x corresponds with the time of flight in seconds, how long after launch will the rocket land?

A) 4 seconds
B) 6 seconds
C) 20 seconds
D) 30 seconds

17) A circle with a radius of $\frac{5}{\pi}$ inches has an arc of 72° What is length of the arc in inches?

A) 6.3 inches
B) $\frac{5}{2}$ inches
C) 2 inches
D) 1.26 inches

18) If $\frac{3+i}{3-i}$ is put into $a + bi$ form, what is the value of a?

A) 3
B) 1
C) $\frac{4}{5}$
D) $\frac{3}{5}$

19) After taking a survey of incomes within a particular neighborhood, the research team found that the median income was $40,000 and the average income was $55,000. Which of the following inferences can be made from the survey?

A) Each of the incomes are close to $55,000.
B) A few people in the survey make far more money than the others.
C) The majority of people in the survey make below the median income.
D) Most people make between $40,000 and $55,000

20) If $f(x) = \frac{3}{2}x + 8$ and $g(x) = 5 - x^2$, how many points of intersection will the two functions have?

A) None
B) One
C) Two
D) Three

21) Which interval gives the range of answers for $\sqrt{4-x} + 3 \leq 5$, if x is an integer?

A) $x \leq 0$
B) $x \geq 0$
C) $x \leq 4$
D) $4 \geq x \geq 0$

22) If the cosine of a certain angle in a right triangle is .6, and the length of the side adjacent to the angle is 3, how long is the hypotenuse?

A) 2
B) 4
C) 5
D) 6

23) Which function has a maximum in the fourth quadrant?

A) $y = -5 - 2(x-3)^2$
B) $y = 2(x-3)^2 - 2$
C) $y = (x+5)(x-7)$
D) $y = -4x + 6$

24) The arithmetic mean of $3x$ and 8 is m, the arithmetic mean of $4x$ and 10 is n, and the arithmetic mean of $5x$ and 6 is z, what is the arithmetic mean of m, n, and z?

A) $2x + 4$
B) $3x + 6$
C) $3x + 12$
D) $6x + 12$

25) Allain makes three times as much money as Bhav, and Bhav makes 1/3 as much money as Charles. If their average hourly rate is $28, how much money does Bhav make per hour?

A) $9.30
B) $12
C) $28
D) $35

The chart below shows per capita income according to the Bureau of Labor Statistics in five year intervals.

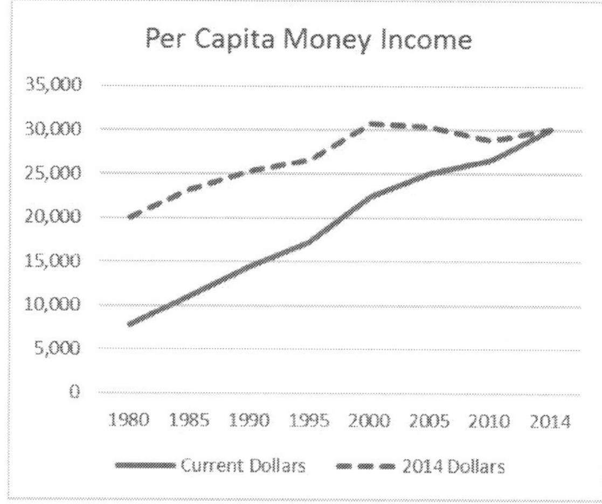

26) Which interval had the greatest percentage change in income in 2014 dollars?

A) 1995-2005
B) 1990-2000
C) 1985-1995
D) 1980-1990

27) What inference is supported by this data?

A) When measured in 2014 dollars, per capita income has had a constant increase from 2000 - 2010.
B) The formula to convert base dollars to 2014 dollars is based on a linear equation.
C) While income increased from 2005 to 2010, the value of this money did not.
D) In 2020, per capita income can be expected to be over 60 thousand 2014 dollars.

28) The speed of a Bugatti Veyron is 267 miles per hour after thirty seconds of warmup, and the speed of an Atlas V rocket is 600 miles per hour after an initial launch sequence of twenty minutes when the rocket is not moving. If the rocket begins the countdown as the Bugatti reaches top speed, how many minutes will the rocket need to catch up to the car?

A) 36 minutes
B) 52 minutes
C) 54 minutes
D) 134 minutes

29) A linear equation has a negative slope and is charted by the equation $x + y = a(x - y)$. What must be true about the value of a?

A) $-1 < a < 1$
B) $a > 0$
C) $a \neq 0$
D) $a < -1$

30) An isosceles triangle has side lengths of 18, 3x+6, and 4x. What is a possible value of x?

A) 3.5
B) 4.5
C) 5
D) 18

GRID-IN

31) Two thirds of a class of 576 freshmen at Duquesne University are in-state students. How many more out of state students must enroll to reach a 50% enrollment?

32) A right triangle has two sides measuring 24 and 7. What is a possible integer length for the 3rd side?

33) A cone and cylinder have the same height, but the cylinder holds twelve times as much liquid. What is the ratio of the radius of the cylinder compared to the cone?

34) What is the slope of a line that is perpendicular to a line passing through the origin and (0,4)?

35) If the polynomial $x^3 - 4x^2 - 4x - 1$ is divided by $(x - 1)$, the result is a binomial equivalent to $ax^2 + bx + c$. What is the value of $|c|$?

36) A cubic equation is modeled by the function $f(x)$ shown below. If $g(x)$ is a modeled by a linear function with in $y = mx + b$ form that has a slope of 0 and three shared solutions with $f(x)$, what is the value of b?

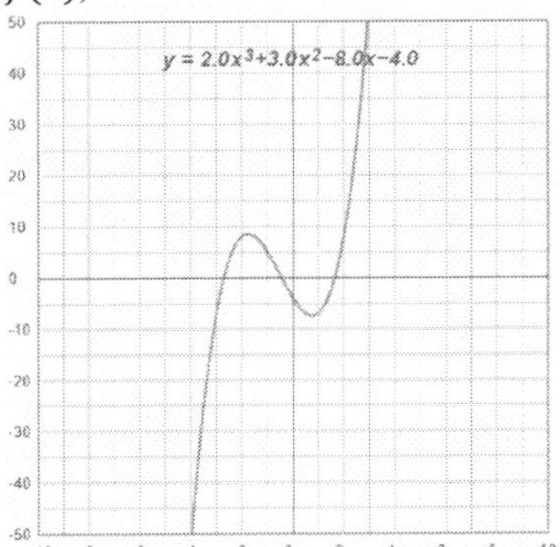

37) The interest generated by a bank account is made at a 7% annual rate for the first year, and 5% for every year after the first. What will be the total profit of a $1,000 investment, rounded to the nearest dollar, after six years?

38) What percent increase would the account have made after the six years in the previous question?

End of Exam

Refer to Pittsburgh Prep's SAT Practice Exam 1 *Answer Explanations* to review and score this exam

SAT PRACTICE TEST #1

Answer Explanations

Proper methods of review:

1. **Always read every single word in this packet. Make sure to not skim, and always try to thoroughly understand the correct as well as the incorrect choices.**
2. **Reason out the "why" – as in, why is this answer correct? And why did I get this question wrong? Or why is this not the correct choice?**
3. **Make certain you can identify your particular issue at hand – did you miss a factual question? Was a deduction question? If so, how can you make sure you can improve on these question types in the future?**
4. **Review this packet for all question, including the questions that you answered correctly on test day.**
5. **Stay positive! SAT scores ain't nuthin but a number dawg. Keep your head up and maintain positive thoughts. You can do this.**

Section 1: Reading Test

QUESTION 1.

Choice D is the best answer. We can identify the recovery as miraculous since the mother states Lise has "healed completely, merely by praying over her last Thursday" (line 20-22) and a Dr. Herzenstube admits he "is amazed; I can make nothing of it" (line 37-38). Further, Lise is more interested in giving the message to Alyosha, starting from line 41 onwards, where we see that Alyosha is constantly surprised through it all, since he is "flush crimsoning his cheeks" (lines 50-51), exclaiming in disbelief that "she wants me to see her? Me?" in "great astonishment."

Choice A is wrong because Lise does not ask anything of the elder. Choice B and C are incorrect since the author does not focus on the elder as the main purpose of the passage.

QUESTION 2.

Choice B is the best answer because the visitor, who we find out is Lise's mother, "sheds silent tears" (line 3) that turns out to be from "genuinely good disposition" (line 5). In other words, we find that Lise's mother's tears are honest tears shed from a true appreciation of the elder's blessings.

Choice A, C and D are incorrect because there is no false acknowledgment, not a contrast established between the visitor and the elder. Further, there is no connection the author establishes between the elder's actions and the mother's beliefs.

QUESTION 3.

Choice A is the best answer because Lise wants to relay the important message from Katerina to Alyosha. At this point, we should note that Alyosha and Alexey are the same people, with different nicknames. Lise attempts to be serious only because her mother told her to "thank" the elder. However, even though Lise "clasped her hands before" the elder to thank him, she cannot contain the joy she has, in anticipation of relaying Katerina's message to Alyosha.

Choice B is incorrect because Lise is not smiling uncontrollably due to her recovery, but rather, over her excitement upon seeing Alexey. Choice C is irrelevant. And Choice D is incorrect since Lise does care about her illness – the author never mentions nor hints that this is not the case.

QUESTION 4.

Choice B is the best answer. Lines 46-48 shows that her "pointing" at Alyosha and not being able to "repress her mirth" provides the best evidence that Lise is more excited about giving Alyosha the message than about her medical recovery.

Choice A is incorrect because this shows that Lise is attempting to be serious about thanking the elder. Choice C and D are incorrect since Alyosha turning "crimson" does not provide the correct justification for Lise's joy upon seeing Alexey, nor does the Elder's act of turing to see Alyosha provide the proper evidence.

QUESTION 5.

Choice A is the best answer. Lise's mother states that it is his "Christian duty" (lines 73-74) to do so. Further, Katerina is "suffering" (lines 76-80) lending credence to the idea that a man of faith such as Alexey is obligated to visit Katerina.

Choice B is incorrect because Alexey does not have the desire to visit Katerina. In fact, he is "perplexed" (line 76) throughout the entire conversation. Choice C is incorrect because it is not Lise, but her mom, who seems to know the real reason for the visit. Choice D is incorrect because we do not know if Katerina is in danger – all we are given is that she is "suffering" (line 77), though it is unclear as to why.

QUESTION 6.

Choice B is the correct answer. In lines 53-54 we learn Alexey's last name is Fyodorovitch, which is the same as the person responsible for Katerina's "suffering" (line 78) named Dimitri Fyodorovitch. Hence, we can make the inference that Alexey and Dimitri are related in some way. (In fact, they are brothers, but this is not germane to this question).

Choice A is incorrect because Alyosha visited Katerina "only once" (line 75) in the past, and the author clearly states that her suffering has everything to "do with Dmitri" (line 68). Choice C directs the issue improperly to Lise's medical condition. Choice D incorrectly present a mystery that is never mentioned in the passage itself.

QUESTION 7.

Choice D is the best answer. The primary support for this answer comes from lines 95-96 where Lise's mother states that Lise is "never happy except with you." Logic dictates that Lise cares less about her recovery than about being with Alyosha. Further evidence is found when Lise gives thanks to the elder only momentarily, but proceeds to talk to Alyosha excitedly.

Choice A, B and C are all incorrect because there is no evidence that Lise's mother is overbearing, or that Lise will look to marry Alexey, or that anyone should regard the urgent note with a sense of merry or joy.

QUESTION 8.

Choice D is the best answer. The statement that the mother provides gives us the best evidence for Lise's true source of happiness – to be with Alyosha.

Choice A, B and C are incorrect because they do not provide the right reference for Lise's happiness.

QUESTION 9.

Choice C is the best answer. We can derive the definition in context since Alexey is filled with "perplexity" (line 77) and the note was given "without any sort of explanation" (lines 83-84).

Choice A, B and D are incorrect because they lack the contextual evidence within the passage in describing the word "enigma".

QUESTION 10.

Choice C is the best answer. The author's main contention is that the banking industry only "did take steps to reform… after it became obvious tougher regulations were eventually coming down the pike" (line 58-60) and the reason is that this "inefficient equilibrium" (line 86) delayed the law from taking effect earlier than, well, now.

Choices A, B and D are incorrect because they do not accurately point to the main purpose, but aspects of the passage that were discussed in some minor or detailed fashion.

QUESTION 11.

Choice A is the best answer because it most accurately describes the progression of the argument implemented by the author. The first paragraph presents us with the legislative action that was delayed "five years" (line 13). The second presents us with the problem of this delay, and the overarching question "why didn't the banks put stronger rules in place long ago?" in paragraph 3. Paragraphs 4-6 then carefully breaks down the psychology behind the answer to the question, aka "inefficient equilibrium."

Choice B is incorrect because the author does not argue the law is inefficient. Choice C is incorrect because it calls for an amendment to the legislative action that the author never proposes. Choice D is incorrect because it states the law should not be enacted at all, something the author never proposes.

QUESTION 12.

Choice D is the best answer because the author clearly states that "some might reflexively answer that bankers are greedy bastards who don't care what happens to their companies in the long run" on lines 44-46.

Choice A, B and C are incorrect since the author never mentions laws are not effective, or that the threat of a law is more powerful than the law itself. Speed of implementation was also not a point of contention.

QUESTION 13.

Choice C is the best answer. The key words "some might" already anticipates a criticism against enacting laws such as the 2010 Dodd Frank. Indeed, the contention that bankers are "greedy bastards" (line 45) anyway seems to make the law a moot legislative action.

Choice A, B and D are all incorrect due to improper assertions or justifications.

QUESTION 14.

Choice B is the best answer. The author begins by stating, "the delay means… the impact … will be less significant" (line 18-29), yet presents a balanced viewpoint by stating "still, the regulations should make a difference" (line 25-26).

Choice A is incorrect because the creation of the law was not discussed. Choice C is incorrect because this approach to regulating banks was not presented as a new, or novel, way. And finally, choice D is incorrect since the approach is not shown to be ineffective, merely not as impactful as it might have been.

QUESTION 15.

Choice B is the best answer. Many students will get this question confused since choice C may also look interchangeable. However, the answer lies in the context. Bankers who risk everything for selfish reasons, without regard to the public shareholders or directors, have a negative connotation associated with their behaviors. As such, choice B is the best choice to make, since careless means "irresponsible".

Choice C is incorrect because carefree means "without anxiety, relaxed," which does not have a negative connotation associated with the definition. Choice A and D are both incorrect because they connote a positive attitude.

QUESTION 16.

Choice D is the best answer. The author clearly states in the beginning of the paragraph: "to understand both why banks didn't go further on their own ... it worth consulting a famous essay from 1973" by a social scientist who studied similar effects within the National Hockey League.

Choice A, B and C are all incorrect since there are no analogies presented in each of these paragraphs.

QUESTION 17.

Choice D is the best answer because the sentence prior indicates that it "took five years for the six responsible agencies to put together a reasonable proposal" after 2010 Dodd-Frank legislation had passed. Therefore, we can reasonably infer that the "months" (line 15) the author indicates will most likely be even be longer.

Choice A, B and C are incorrect because the timeline of "months" is not strict, nor is it stated with the intention to criticize, and certainly not to show confidence in the regulatory bodies.

QUESTION 18.

Choice A is the best answer because the author states when "individually rational choices" (lines 86-87) are made, they can make "a collectively irrational outcome" (lines 88-89) in the world of hockey. The author's argument, therefore, would apply in the same way in the world of banking.

Choice B, C and D are incorrect because the author never mentions banks and regulatory agencies not agreeing with each other, nor does the author say the threat of the law is more powerful (just that the threat was enough to enact certain changes in banks themselves prior to the enactment of the Dodd-Frank), and finally, he never contends that all laws in banking will always be delayed.

QUESTION 19.

Choice D is the best answer because it is the strongest assertion the author makes in the entire passage. Since Schelling's point is that once a law is enacted (in the NHL) everyone will follow through with the law, we can reasonably argue that the 2010 Dodd-Frank law will also have similar effects.

Choice A looks promising, however, the author qualifies his statement with an "if" clause and the words "at least on the margin" (line 31-32) that does not have as much strength as the last sentence of this passage. Choice B and C are incorrect because they do not assert any positive changes will occur as a result of the legislative action.

QUESTION 20.

Choice C is the best answer because the general outline of the article hinges on the idea that there is a "conflict of interest" between patient and "drug seller" (line 18) aka. pharmacies.

Choice A is a commonplace act that some sellers may engage in improperly that provides justification for the main purpose. Choice B is irrelevant to the article itself. And choice D incorrectly states that the patients are unfairly treated. Nowhere in the passage does the articles state that the patient is unfairly treated.

QUESTION 21.

Choice A is the best answer. Unprincipled is closest in meaning to what the author wants to convey, in that salesmen invite patients to try to take "advantage of their friendship and shared illness to try to woo the business" (line 7-9). A mercenary is a profiteer who is usually associated with times of war, however, any person hired for a job can be described as such.

Choice B and C are incorrect because they convey an entirely different meaning than intended. Choice D may have confused some readers, however, salesmen do not have to be aggressive to be unprincipled (or mercenary). These sorts of associations should be approached with caution.

QUESTION 22.

Choice A is the best answer. Do not fall prey to "tips & tricks" that advise against extreme answer choices. The evidence shows that the mother is concerned that the drug sellers view her son as a "cash cow" (line 12) rather than a patient to care for.

Choice B is incorrect because the Austin being a "cash cow" has little to do with, nor does the author mention that, the pharmacological industry has a cavalier attitude. Choice C is incorrect because the mother is not making a blanket statement about the drug makers. And Choice D is incorrect because it would be a stretch to assume that the statement "cash cow" would mean that all parents share a hatred for all drug sellers.

QUESTION 23.

Choice B is the best answer because the author states that it may be due to "fierce competition among specialty pharmacies…. and the lingering distrust of drug companies" (line 57-63) by patients who have been afflicted negatively in the past.

Choices A, C and D are incorrect because drug sellers were not always looked upon as untrustworthy, parents with hemophiliac children sometimes act unethically, and the author never mentions anything about the criminal justice system.

QUESTION 24.

Choice D is the best answer. This question has been specifically answered above. Always remember to justify your answers via direct evidence from the passage.

Choices A, B and C are inaccurate evidences for this question.

QUESTION 25.

Choice B is the best answer. This is the only paragraph where the argument FOR the patient advocates is made. The rest of the passage then devotes itself to the underlying issues facing drug sellers and patients.

Choices A, C and D are incorrect. A may seem correct, however, we are never given the author's position. C is inaccurate since a single paragraph hardly will be effective in leveling the playing field. And D is incorrect since this passage is not a persuasive argument to sway anyone. **Note that the tone of the passage is more analytical.*

QUESTION 26.

Choice C is the best answer because the author states that Austin's "treatments cost more than $1 million a year" (line 10). Further, the author also states patients care can cost "over $1 million, whose antibodies produce "inhibitors" (line 87). We can therefore deduce that Austin suffers from this particular condition.

Choice A is incorrect because it was never discussed in the passage. Choice B and D are also incorrect since there are no compromises, nor a singular reliance on the mom that the author points to.

QUESTION 27.

Choice A is the best answer. See above for the proper evidence and reasoning.

Choices B, C and D all point to inaccurate evidence to justify the question properly.

QUESTION 28.

Choice B is the best answer. Author states in line 91 "the global market for hemophilia is now worth about $10 billion a year." Many suppliers have been "spun off" to be "bought" by other giants in the industry. Hence, these divisions are simply put, profitable enough to be sold to more lucratively seeking drug companies.

Choices A, C and D are incorrect because the market isn't putting pressure on the companies to sell off their divisions, economic theory be damned, and gene therapy may or may not replace drug makers – no one knows for sure, and the author never hints at anything like this at all.

QUESTION 29.

Choice D is the best answer because we can deduce that a "$10 billion a year" industry is the reason for why smaller drug companies are selling off their hemophiliac divisions to larger drug makers.

Choices A, B and C are all incorrect because they all point to inaccurate evidence as justification for the previous question.

QUESTION 30.

Choice B is the best answer. The author provides the last two paragraphs to assert that continued growth in the hemophiliac drug industry is strong, and, therefore, the ethical issue facing patient advocates will also continue as pharmacies look to hire patients as drug sellers.

Choices A, C and D are incorrect because the author never mentions policy will resolve this issue completely, or that drug companies will fail after selling their hemophiliac divisions, or that Austin has tougher choices to make than other hemophiliac patients.

QUESTION 31.

Choice B is the best answer because the passage states Lewis et al.'s "results falsify Gould's hypothesis that Morton manipulated his data to conform with" (line 14-16) his views. In other words, Lewis denies Gould's assertion that Morton had exhibited racial bias.

Choices A, C and D are all incorrect. Lewis et al. do not agree with Morton's findings, per se, but that his measures were not racial biased. Note the difference here. Further, there is no mention of the text *The Mismeasure of Man* as seen from the perspective of Lewis et al. Lastly, both Morton and Gould cannot be wrong at the same time.

QUESTION 32.

Choice D is the best answer because this is where the author discusses Lewis et al.'s published critique that denies Gould's hypothesis that "Morton's measurements were biased by his racism" (lines 13-14).

Choices A, B and C all incorrectly point to wrong evidence. These sentences serve as the basis for the author's overarching argument re: Morton's original findings.

QUESTION 33.

Choice A is the best answer. In the third paragraph, the author describes Morton's second method that he used in 1844 using BB shots as having "superiority" over peppers, and "objective, accurate, repeatable" (lines 51-53). In other words, not flawed.

Choices B, C and D are all incorrect. They confuse the new method as either being flawed or unrepeatable.

QUESTION 34.

Choice A is the best answer because the author states that the re-measured skulls in 1844 "did not change by the same amounts" (lines 60-61). Hence, Gould believes the "best explanation for the more dramatic change in African mean was unconscious manipulation on Morton's part in 1839" (lines 67-69).

Choices B, C and D are incorrect because Lewis was not right, BB shots themselves do not provide evidence for Morton's racial bias, and Lewis et al. only measured "half the skulls" (line 74) not Gould.

QUESTION 35.

Choice B is the best answer. Since we do not have any other data except between African, American, and Caucasian groups, the only assertion to be made is choice B. A quick visual survey identifies Americans as the lowest difference in measures out of the three groups.

Choices A, C and D are incorrect because the Caucasian group is the median measure, and the African group held the largest difference amongst all the groups.

QUESTION 36.

Choice C is the best answer. Since we know that the CAT measures are greater than the CAM measures, we can make the proper deduction that the CAT measures were conducted on 1844 with the BB shots, and the CAM measures were conducted in 1839 with the pepper seeds.

Choices A, B and D are incorrect either because of improper timeline, or due to improper portrayal of the accuracy of the CAT/CAM measures.

QUESTION 37.

Choice C is the best answer. It is the only answer choice that discusses the author's point that Morton may have held an "unconscious racial bias" (lines 40-41) due the greater difference in measure within the African group.

Choices A and D are wrong because they discuss intellect, which is a topic that is purposely not discussed in the passage. Choice B is incorrect because CAM measures are the BB shot measures that were seen as more accurate and "repeatable" (line 53).

QUESTION 38.

Choice A is the best answer. The author of Passage two furthers the argument that Lewis et al.'s conclusion is incorrect, however, leaves open the possibility there may be other factors involved they may not be considering. "Perhaps there are other explanations" on line 109 best provide evidence for this viewpoint.

Choices B and D are incorrect because the author does not argue for an inherent flaw within Gould's research, nor does the author of Passage 2 emphasize actually measuring Morton's original skulls. Choice C may or may not be true, but is irrelevant to the question at hand.

QUESTION 39.

Choice A is the best answer. Remember that rhetorical questions do not need an answer because they are merely statements posed as if they are questions. Lewis et al. pose the question to state that objective accounts are not attainable, agreeing with Gould's general statement above that "studies of human variation are inevitably biased" (line 120).

Choices B and C are not correct because the author isn't presenting an age-old mystery, nor is the question itself opposing Gould's belief about studies of human variation; Choice D is wrong because the question does serve a purpose in that it is trying to pose some doubt into Gould's conclusion regarding Morton's measurements.

QUESTION 40.

Choice A is the best answer because the author is arguing that given all the measures are correctly conducted by Morton, Gould is pointing to the one major discrepancy within African group – an obvious and glaring difference that shows unconscious racial bias.

Choice B, C and D are incorrect. They do not make sense.

QUESTION 41.

Choice C is the best answer. Passage 1 details Morton, Gould and Lewis et al.'s overarching viewpoints, whereas Passage 2 goes into specific depth on the various points that Gould has made, in addition to the "prima facia" (line 116) evidence of unconscious racial bias. These are highlighted on 3rd, 4th and 5th paragraphs in Passage 2.

Choices A, B and D are incorrect. Choice A inaccurately portrays the relation between the passages. Choices B and D do not correctly represent the proper relationship between the two passages.

QUESTION 42.

Choice C is the best answer because it is the only one that is logically evident in both passages. Passage 1 presents us with the scientific underpinnings of Morton, Gould and Lewis et al. where the main premise lies in the fact that the differences in measures from peppers to shots "did not change by the same amounts" (lines 60-61) in the African group. Along with Passage 2's contention that "Lewis et al.'s remeasurements shed no light" (line 112) to Gould's conclusion that Morton poses unconscious racial bias, we can conclude that choice C is the only reasonable answer choice.

Choice A is incorrect because the authors do not call for remeasurements of the skulls. Choice B is wrong because Morton's measures are in question, as Gould points out. And choice D is incorrect because Gould and Lewis et al.'s roles are switched improperly.

QUESTION 43.

Choice A is the best answer. The author states that the quote "has proved so offensive to Judge Douglas" (lines 6-7) because Lincoln agrees that "variety in domestic institutions of different states is necessary and indispensable" (lines 8-10) such as "cranberry laws in Illinois" (line 12) but not in Indiana.

Choice B, C and D are incorrect because the Passage does not mention a war on Slavery, nor does it state that all States should share same laws, nor is there ever a comparison between commerce vs. Slavery.

QUESTION 44.

Choice B is the best answer because Lincoln points out that Douglas takes offense at the quote (line 7), and explains further in line 8 that "variety" is both necessary and indispensable.

Choice A, C and D are incorrect because these sentences provide improper evidence for Douglas' viewpoint.

QUESTION 45.

Choice B is the best answer because Lincoln states that he does "not mean to produce a conflict" but rather, "a most peaceful tendency" (lines 1-5). Therefore, tendency in this instance must closely mean something that produces, or consequence.

Choice A, C and D are incorrect because these definitions are not supported by the context within the Passage.

QUESTION 46.

Choice B is the best answer. Lincoln, without as much mentioning Slaves, allows the reader to infer that if you are a free slave, or "surplus population" (line 49), who moved to the territories, it would be unfair for that free slave to find that slaves are no longer free simply because someone who moved from a Slave State resides there and exercised their rights. Further evidence is given in the following paragraph where Lincoln states that the "real issue" is of racism.

Choices A, C and D are inept answers to provide the best inference since the Passage does not provide sufficient evidence to make such inferences.

QUESTION 47.

Choice A is the best answer because the "cancer" (line 69) that Lincoln describes is the issue of slavery. In effect, he states that you may "not be able to cut it out lest you bleed to death, but surely it is no way to cure it to graft it and spread it over your body" (lines 69-72). In other words, the issue of slavery cannot be solved by allowing it to spread unfettered into the territories of the United States. The government should intervene and prevent this from happening so.

Answer choice B, C and D all miss the mark. Lincoln does not take issue with income or gender gaps, nor does he take issue with rights afforded to free vs. indentured slaves. This point is strictly about slavery within the territories of the US.

QUESTION 48.

Choice D is the best answer because Lincoln states that he "think(s) that as white men we have" (line 48) interest in providing an "outlet for our surplus population" (line 49) or slaves, that is clear as "right and wrong" (lines 78-79) to afford slaves their "common right of humanity" (line 82).

Choices A, B and C are incorrect because they do not justly identify the main purpose of the entire passage.

QUESTION 49.

Choice A is the best answer. Lincoln admits that "I agree with him very readily that the different states have the right" (lines 35-36) but "our controversy with him is in regard to the new territories" (lines 36-38) only. This is to mean that states with laws allowing slavery are not to be interfered with by both Douglas and Lincoln.

Choice B and D are unsupported by the passage on whether Judge Douglas would agree with these statements. Choice C is something that is never discussed within the passage, not alluded to, to make a proper logical decision on whether Lincoln and Douglas would both agree wholeheartedly.

QUESTION 50.

Choice D is the best answer. See above for the full explanation.

Choice A, B and C are incorrect because they do not provide sufficient evidence for justifying the answer for question 49.

QUESTION 51.

Choice A is the best answer because Lincoln makes a parallel and powerful argument that "it is the eternal struggle between these two principles, right and wrong" (lines 77-79) involving the common right of humanity and the other is the divine right of kings" (lines 82-83). Therefore, Lincoln believes that the effect of the principle that "You work and toil and earn bread and I'll eat it" (lines 84-85) is plainly wrong.

Choice B, C and D are incorrect because it is not about royal families, per se, nor does Lincoln guarantee that slavery will end after Lincoln takes office, nor does the principle establish that tyranny will rule the day.

QUESTION 52.

Choice C is the best answer. No other words work in this sentence since the "mouth of a king who seeks to" dominate the "people of his nation and live by the fruits of their labor" (line 87-89) is the only meaning that makes sense here.

Choices A, B and D are incorrect. Harbor and aid share similar definitions, whereas relegate means to send to a lower class which does not quite fit the bill here since the people of his nation are already at a lower class.

SECTION 2: Writing and Language Test 1

QUESTION 1.

Choice B is the best answer because "findings" is the proper noun to complete this clause.

Choices A, C and D are all incorrect because "founds" is not a proper noun, and "determinants" and "resolutions" are improper diction.

QUESTION 2.

Choice D is the best answer because there is no need for a transitional word here. The participial phrase that begins with "Located approximately 7800 light-years away" is sufficient to continue the logical argument of the author concisely.

Choices A, B and C all add needless words or transitional adverbs that does not identify the relationship between the phrase and the corresponding clause.

QUESTION 3.

Choice A is the best answer because it states the reason for why Kimura led a team of his peers to observe the phenomenon. Without this phrase added, readers are only left to wonder who these 26 astronomers may be.

Choices B, C and D are incorrect because they all do not provide good reason for why Kimura led a team of peers, misconstruing and misinterpreting the actual reason for doing so.

QUESTION 4.

Choice B is the best answer because the verb "noted" agrees in conjugation and tense with the proper singular subject, "the team."

Choices A, C, and D are incorrect because there is no need for a perfect tense construction, nor would usage of the present participle be appropriate.

QUESTION 5.

Choice A is the best answer because the infinitive phrase "to observe" is the correct idiomatic phrasing.

Choices B, C and D are incorrect because they utilize incorrect prepositions with either a present participle or noun.

QUESTION 6.

Choice A is the best answer because the verb "validated" in its simple past tense is correct and parallel with the prior two verbs "identified" and "controlled".

All other choices are incorrect because they act to interrupt the parallel structure established by all other verbs.

QUESTION 7.

Choice B is the best answer because the relationship between the dependent clause and the independent clause is properly attained.

Choices A, C and D are incorrect for various reasons: improper use of the pronoun "their", lacking references to the budget cuts, or creating an improper relationship between science and the news itself.

QUESTION 8.

Choice B is the best answer because it is consistent with the tone and diction employed by the author in the formal way language is used.

Choices A, C and D are incorrect since language employed is much too colloquial, not academic enough, or points to the wrong purpose, such as "relationship with the cosmos" which is not appropriate.

QUESTION 9.

Choice D is the best answer because there is no need for a conjunction to combine the two clauses together. The subordinate conjunction "even though" serves to create a proper comparison between the two clauses.

Choices A, B and C are incorrect because they contain conjunctions that are unnecessary.

QUESTION 10.

Choice D is the best answer because the conjunctive adverb "however" properly connects the relationship between research projects that do not capture the imagination to how they are, in fact, relevant and meaningful.

QUESTION 11.

Choice C is the best answer because the statement is a clear and concise restatement of the author's primary argument. The first paragraph gives us a strong indicator when it states that the study was important for "scientific research itself."

Choices A, B and D are incorrect because it is not concise as written, the black hole phenomenon does not provide a summary, nor has the project's entire focus been on providing scientific research in and of itself.

QUESTION 12.

Choice A is the best answer because the notion that the author did not understand Calypso music becomes resolved by the use of the phrase "that is". The author now understands Calypso music because she visited her homeland of Trinidad.

Choices B, C and D are all incorrect because are transitional words, or conjunctive adverbs, that do not logically connect the prior sentence to why the author visited Trinidad.

QUESTION 13.

Choice D is the best answer because the possessive noun does not require any further punctuation for the underlined phrase.

Choice A is incorrect because the sentence creates two possessive nouns incorrectly. Choices B and C are incorrect because the use of punctuation (commas) leads to an awkward and incorrect clausal structure.

QUESTION 14.

Choice D is the best answer because the pronoun "it" is somewhat ambiguous. The clear referent should be Calypso.

Choices A, B and C are all incorrect because the pronouns used are ambiguous or denote something else different entirely.

QUESTION 15.

Choice C is the best answer because the historical development of the slave trades in other locations is unnecessary to the passage.

Choices A and B are incorrect because there is no value associated with an irrelevant statement. Choice D is incorrect because the comparative value of the slave trade among locations, again, has no value at all, implied or not.

QUESTION 16.

Choice C is the best answer because the coordinating conjunction "and" is used properly to connect the two possessive pronoun objects "their slave masters" with "their brutalies" correctly.

Choices A, B and D are incorrect because they lack a coordinating conjunction or incorrectly utilizes punctuations between two objects.

QUESTION 17.

Choice B is the best answer because it is an exemplification of another language, "creole", along with "patwa", that satisfies the question.

Choice A is incorrect because a second example is missing. Choices C and D are incorrect because they do not provide a specific second example.

QUESTION 18.

Choice D is the best answer because it transforms two independent clauses into one independent clause with a corresponding participial phrase.

Choices A, B and C all utilize prepositions incorrectly, creating an awkward sentence overall.

QUESTION 19.

Choice A is the best answer because it follows the prior phrases in parallel form. Each of what Calypso provides is contrasts with something else, utilizing contrasting cues such as, "against" and "despite."

Choice B lacks this contrast, using the word "within" incorrectly. And Choices C and D flip-flops the contrasted object, "destitute living conditions" to the "listeners."

QUESTION 20.

Choice B is the best answer because the pronoun that should be used is the objective pronoun "me".

Answer choice A utilizes an unnecessary reflexive pronoun. Choice C utilizes both an incorrect preposition and reflexive pronoun. And finally choice D uses the subject pronoun "I" incorrectly.

QUESTION 21.

Choice C is the best answer because it places the (past) participial phrase "Created with more…" correctly with the corresponding noun "Calypso".

Choices A, B, and D all suffer from misplaced modifiers, since the location of the noun Calypso does not correspond to the participial phrase correctly.

QUESTION 22.

Choice B is the best answer. Both the third paragraph and fourth paragraph indicate that the author now understand Calypso deeper as a result of her visit to Trinidad. Also, consider the questions at the end of the paragraph about the origin of Calypso, and that we get an explanation for these inquiries in paragraph two.

QUESTION 23.

Choice C is the best answer because the use of the colon creates the correct relationship between the first clause and exemplification in the second. Further, the transitional word "namely" is also used correctly to convey an example that follows.

Choices A, B and D are incorrect because of either incorrect punctuation usage or utilizing incorrect adverbs that do not convey the proper relationship between how evangelists have proposed detoxing to the example that follows.

QUESTION 24.

Choice A is the best answer because the transitional word "however" provides the correct relationship between the prior clause and the current clause.

Choices B, C and D are all incorrect due to the improper logic conveyed in the conjunctive adverbs.

QUESTION 25.

Choice B is the best answer because the chart's data clearly shows that the greatest change in perception occurred within the farmer population during the thirty-year period, as opposed to all other groups.

Choices A, C and D are incorrect because the information within the chart does not support these assertions.

QUESTION 26.

Choice B is the best answer because the additional information usefully connects the data given within the chart to the logical reason for why the data cultivated the general population's beliefs about detox.

Choices A, C and D are incorrect because each of these misinterprets the information from the chart to the reason why detox and its myths are so prevalent today.

QUESTION 27.

Choice D is the best answer because the that-clause is used correctly after the verb "writes". Note that these that-clauses are entirely different from relative nouns. Both, however, do not utilize commas.

Choices A, B and C are incorrect because of wrong punctuation usages or improper prepositional usage.

QUESTION 28.

Choice A is the best answer since we already know that Dr. Merrell's book was met with mixed reviews, and Dr. Sadler says with exasperation that his statement has no meaning – "What's it even mean?"

Choice B is incorrect because innocence has nothing to do the words that Dr. Merrell uses. Choice C and D are incorrect because these common vocab words are not logical in context.

QUESTION 29.

Choice C is the best answer because the subjective pronoun "our" reflects the proper antecedent – humans.

Choice A and D are incorrect because the wrong pronoun case is used. Choice B is incorrect because it utilizes a contraction.

QUESTION 30.

Choice C is the best answer because the structure of the sentence is kept parallel. Furthermore, the phrase "vitamin A in large doses" is kept in the same tone of the overall passage.

Choices A, B and D are incorrect because they are not parallel with the general structure of the entire clause. Furthermore, there is no need to state that people ingest them too much when a more concise way can be found in choice C.

QUESTION 31.

Choice D is the best answer because it presents clear, concise and correct wording that is consistent with the general tone of the passage.

Choices A, B and C are incorrect because they are either too verbose or illogical.

QUESTION 32.

Choice D is the best answer because it is parallel with the overall structure of the clause.

Choices A, B and C are incorrect because the proper noun "athletes" is not the main object. Instead, the noun "testimonials" is used incorrectly.

QUESTION 33.

Choice D is the best answer because the comma is utilized correctly to clearly denote that a "fallacy" should be defined as a "grave mistake."

Choices A, B and C are incorrect due to incorrect punctuation usage.

Government policies and entrepreneurship

QUESTION 34.

Choice A is the best answer because it is the correct diction that conveys the main point the author is trying to make.

Choices B, C and D are incorrect because these words do not correctly convey the proper purpose that the author is trying to make. In choice B, the word "chance" may be the right word, but it creates an awkward clause – perhaps if it was accompanied by the preposition "due to chance" the clause would work. Choices C and D are wrong word choices altogether.

QUESTION 35.

Choice D is the best answer because the usage of the comma correctly creates an appositive phrase to begin the sentence. In other words, the appositive phrase ends with a proper comma that serves to describe the American policy further.

Choices A, B and C are incorrect because a dash, semi-colon, and colon are all improper punctuations.

QUESTION 36.

Choice C is the best answer because the addition would serve to take away the focus of the author, who is indeed developing the particulars of governmental policies of that era.

Choices A, B are incorrect because there is no value added to the main point of the author. Choice D is incorrect because the author is not focused on the distinction between immigrants and non-immigrants.

QUESTION 37.

Choice A is the best answer because the wording corresponds with the author's structure of the sentence.

Choices B, C and D are incorrect because they each contain language that are either vague or improper in context.

QUESTION 38.

Choice B is the best answer because the coordinating conjunction "and" sufficiently combines the two prepositional phrases that begin this sentence, without the need for commas. In fact, adding the two commas or any comma at all creates a needless appositive phrase-hybrid scenario that is incorrect.

Choices A, C and D are all incorrect for this reason.

QUESTION 39.

Choice C is the best answer because the use of "from…to…" is the correct idiomatic phrase and the gerund "focusing" is consistent with the style and structure of the sentence that the author employs.

Choices A, B and D are incorrect because of improper idiomatic usage or inconsistent structure.

QUESTION 40.

Choice D is the best answer because the adverb "diversely" is needed here to describe the "woven growth" that is consistent with the other adverb "intricately".

Choices A, B and C are incorrect because an adverb is needed. All other constructions are nouns or adjectives.

QUESTION 41.

Choice A is the best answer because the present participle "creating" that sets up the participial phrase properly describes the consequence of how big businesses vie for the talents of the few.

Choices B and C are incorrect because that and which are relative pronouns used improperly here. Choice D is incorrect because "having created" is not consistent with the present tense "vying" in the previous phrase.

QUESTION 42.

Choice A is the best answer because the adverb "hence" accurately conveys the final point the author is trying to make about government policies today.

Choices B, C and D are improper transitional words that do not logically convey the author's argument overall.

QUESTION 43.

Choice B is the best answer because the third person plural simple past tense form of to be ("were") most accurately conveys the author's argument about government policies from the middle of the 20th century to now.

Choice A is incorrect because the singular verb conjugation does not agree with the plural subject. Choice C is incorrect because the present perfect tense improperly conveys policies that were shaped in the past. Choice D is incorrect because both the perfect tense and the redundant use of the adverb "thus" is unnecessary.

QUESTION 44.

Choice A is the best answer because the paragraphs then all move chronologically. That is, each paragraph describes the changing policies in step with the progression of time from the 18th century to the 19th century to the 20th century to current timeframe.

Choices B, C and D are all incorrect because displacing the final paragraph would result in a confusing progression of ideas and logic to the overall passage.

SECTION 3
Math No Calculator Test

QUESTION 1.

Choice D is the best answer because the minimum of any absolute value function is zero. Therefore, $|x - 5|$ must have a value of zero for the function to be at its lowest value. If we substitute 5 for x, we now have $|5 - 5| + 3$, giving us $0 + 3$ and a minimum value of 3 for $f(x)$.

Choices A, B, and C are incorrect because each value of x will give us a nonzero value for $|x - 5|$, ensuring an absolute value that is not the minimum.

QUESTION 2.

Choice B is the best answer. This is a straightforward system of equations, which we can solve with combination easily, since y in the first equation and $-y$ in the second equation will cancel each other without any coefficients. We can add $x + y = 9 + (x - y = 15)$ to get $2x = 24$, and then divide by 2 to get $x = 12$. Now that we know that, we can substitute 12 for x with either equation to find y: start with $12 + y = 9$, subtract 12 from both sides, and we get $y = -3$.

Choices A and C are common mistakes resulting from not paying attention to signs during the combination; take extra care with negative signs, since a small mistake is very costly and usually hard to catch later in the problem.

QUESTION 3.

Choice C is the best answer because it modifies the number of sales made as (s-7) before multiplying by the $5 made per sale. If not sure about how the formula works, we could choose a number of sales to substitute and plug in answers. With 7 sales, for example, Diego would get no extra money, so plugging in 7 for s ought to turn up only $64 for an answer.

While A may seem to be a valid option, the given formula simply subtracts 7 from the result of 5s. Choices B and D both ignore a piece of necessary information, making them bad choices.

QUESTION 4.

Choice D is the best answer. First, let's note that we aren't washing the six walls of a box; we are only washing four walls, not the top or bottom. This affects the dimensions that we use! The four walls being washed are made up of two 15×20 walls and two 20×20 walls. Since $Area = Length \times Width$, we can find the area of the four walls with $A = 2(15 \times 20) + 2(20 \times 20)$, and dividing by $200\frac{ft^2}{hr}$ will give us the 7 hours we need.

Choice B is a very compelling answer, especially if we do not take care to note which walls need to be washed. It is still wrong, however! The same goes for choice D, which is what would be needed to wash all six sides of the structure.

QUESTION 5.

Choice D is the best answer because of the fact that we are comparing area, in which radius is squared. If $Area = \pi r^2$ and we double the radius, remember that $2r$ is the new radius and our new area is now $\pi(2r)^2$, simplifying to $4\pi r^2$, which is 4 times the initial area.

Choice B ignores the fact that we are comparing area and not radius, while choice C mistakes the order we are looking at- remember that we are comparing NEW to OLD, so our ration should be NEW:OLD. Choice A mistakes the order as well as the comparison.

QUESTION 6.

Choice D is the best answer. Let's look at the given chart first; remember, a chart is only helpful if it helps us organize data! We should recognize that the days in the incubator act as an independent variable and population is acting as dependent, and we can then recognize the information given is exponential because exponential growth by definition happens when the slope (or change in dependent variable) is increases or decreases. Since we can see the change by days (2000 on Day 2, 3000 on Day 3, 4000 on Day 4), we can estimate that on Day 5 the increase will be 5000 and Day 6 will be 6000, giving us a total gain of $11{,}000$ and D for a correct answer.

Choices A and B assume linear growth, but since we know the increase is not constant, the choices must be wrong. Choice C notes exponential growth, but has too small of a growth for two days.

QUESTION 7.

Choice C is the best answer when we simplify. First, distribute the 3i and 2i to get $15i + 3i^2 - 8i + 2i^2$, taking care with the distribution of the negative 2i. From there, remember that i^2 simplifies to -1, so we have $15i - 3 - 8i - 2$. After simplifying again to $7i - 5$, we can move the terms to match up with C, our correct answer. A simple way to keep imaginary numbers from becoming overwhelming is to save conversion for the final simplification, and using exponent rules to reduce to i^2 and i^4 to -1 and 1, respectively.

Choices A, B, and D all come from the same mistake- not keeping track of signs while distributing. Remember, if you're distributing $-2i$, the negative sign comes along as well!

QUESTION 8.

Choice B is the best answer. The first thing we should do is assess our ratios. Since the ratio of Onions to Carrots to Celery is $2:1:1$, we know that we have four total parts in our ratio $(2 + 1 + 1)$.
We know that two of these four parts must be onions, so we can make a ratio of $2:4$ for Onions to Total, reduce it to $1:2$, and realize that if we need 38 grams total, we would multiply 2 by 19 to get 38, and so we must multiply our 1 part onion by 19 to get 19 grams. Alternatively, once we know we have a $2:4$ ratio, we can convert it to the fraction $\frac{2}{4}$, reduce $\frac{2}{4}$ to $\frac{1}{2}$, and realize that half of 38 is 19.

Choice C is incorrect because it does not account for all four parts, A is a common answer if a mistake was made in building the ratio, and B is a common error resulting from miscalculation.

QUESTION 9.

Choice A is the best answer because the perpendicular slope is always the negative reciprocal of the original slope. First, we need the slope, which is change in y over change in x. By plugging our coordinates into a slope expression ($\frac{y_2-y_1}{x_2-x_1}=\frac{13-8}{3-0}=\frac{5}{3}$), so we can find the negative reciprocal of this slope, which is $-\frac{3}{5}$.

Choices B, C, and D all are incorrect for either inverting

QUESTION 10.

Choice D is the best answer. We can solve this problem graphically or logically. Since our quadratic has roots of 5 and -2, we know that $x=5$ and $x=-2$, and that $(x-5)(x+2)=0$. Plugging this function into a calculator should show that all four quadrants are filled.

Alternatively, since we know one root is positive and one root is negative, we know that our function crosses the y- axis. Since it is positive and has two roots, we can also assume that our function opens upward, and has a vertex below the x-axis. The only way a function can cross both y and x with is if all four quadrants are covered.

QUESTION 11.

Choice B is the best answer. Since we have a system of equations, we can either solve by combination or substitution. If we choose combination, we rewrite the second equation as $-x+2y=19$ and multiply both sides by 4 to get $-4x+8y=76$, and add both equations to cancel x and get $5y=40$ and $y=8$. We can plug y back into the second equation to find that $2(8)-x=19$, so x must equal -3. Adding those results gives $x+y=5$.

Alternatively, substitution would take one of the equations, solve for a single variable, and solve. The second equation, for example, easily becomes $2y-19=x$, and we can plug $2y-19$ in for x in the first equation to get $4(2y-19)-3y=-36$. Distribute to get $8y-72-3y=-36$, combine like terms to get $5y-72=-36$, move 72 to get

QUESTION 12.

Choice D is the best answer. Since the SAT does not test logarithms, we should always try to convert any expression with a variable in the exponent into values with like bases. Since $2^3=8$, we can substitute 2^3 for 8 to change the numerator to $2^{3^y}=2^{3y}$ and because we are given $y=x-5$, we can plug in $x-5$ for y to find that $2^{3(x-5)}=2^{3x-15}$. The whole left side of the equation is now $\frac{2^{3x-15}}{2^{x+3}}$. Since dividing values with the same base allows us to subtract their exponents, $\frac{2^{3x-15}}{2^{x+3}}=2^{(3x-15)-(x+3)}$and $2^{3x-15-(x+3)}=2^{3x-x-15-3}=2^{2x-18}$. Now that the left side is simplified, we should try to reduce the right side; since we have a base of 2 on the left side, we should try to match that on the right side. We can convert the right side to a base of 2 to yield $2^{2x-18}=2^4$. When we have an equation where both sides have the same base, the exponents must be equal, so $2x-18=4$, simplifying to $x=11$.

Choice A comes from a mistake in signs, and choices B and C might happen if we mistook the nature of the problem; remember, when performing exponent operations, the base stays the same!

QUESTION 13.

Choice D is the best answer, which becomes clearer when we realize that equations cross the x-axis at their x-intercept. The major issue here is that our equation has a strange fraction for a term. To get rid of it, we will set $f(x) = 0$ (since we want an x-intercept, and at the x intercept $y = 0$) and multiply both sides of the equation by $x - 3$ (the fraction's denominator). We end up distributing all across the polynomial to end up with $0 = (x + 5) + (x^2 - 3x) + (5x - 15)$, which simplifies to $0 = x^2 + 3x - 10$. Since this is quadratic (form of $ax^2 + bx + c$), it can be factored to $0 = (x + 5)(x - 2)$. Since either binomial could be zero, we can say that $0 = x + 5$ or $0 = x - 2$, and the roots for this equation are now clear as -5 and 2.

Remember though, that according to our original equation, $x \neq 3$, because x-3 was the denominator of our original fraction; this would make our fraction undefined!

Choices C and B have an incorrect root, but choice A is tempting; however, just because a number appear in the original question does not guarantee any logical answer!

QUESTION 14.

Choice D is the best answer. We have two scenarios here, so there are a few approaches we can take. One way is substitution: we plug in the new values in terms of the old ones. We know the object has triple the velocity $3v$ and half the mass $\frac{m}{2}$ of the original, so we plug in those values and get $K = \frac{1}{2}\left(\frac{m}{2}\right)(3v)^2$, and simplify that to $K = \frac{m}{4}9v^2$. If we put the new formula in a ratio with the original formula, we get $\frac{\frac{9}{4}mv^2}{\frac{1}{2}mv^2}$, and once the variables cancel out we get $\frac{9}{2}$.
Alternatively, we can plug in values. Let's assume that the first scenario has a velocity of 1 and a mass of 2 (units won't matter here since they will cancel), and the second scenario has a velocity of 3 and a mass of 1. So, $\frac{1}{2}(1)(3)^2$ and $\frac{1}{2}(2)(1)^2$. We simplify to get 4.5 and 1, which is equivalent to a ratio of $\frac{9}{2}$

QUESTION 15.

Choice B is the best answer after we build the function and complete the square. The steps to solve this problem may be a bit involved:

- Since we know the intercepts, we know our quadratic looks like $f(x) = (x - 4)(x - 10)$. We can FOIL to get $f(x) = x^2 - 14x + 40$.
- We should recognize that the answer choices are in vertex form, which we can find by completing the square on our equation. Half of -14 is -7, and $(-7)^2 = 49$, so we need our quadratic to have 49 for a c term ($f(x) = x^2 - 14x + 49$).
- Our current equation ends in 40, but we can fix that: since $49 - 9 = 40$ we can substitute $49 - 9$ and end up with $f(x) = x^2 - 14x + 49 - 9$, or $f(x) = (x - 7)^2 - 9$.

Alternatively, we know that the x-intercepts are (4,0) and (10,0), so the correct answer should be the function with an output of 0 when both 4 and 10 are plugged in for x.

Options A, C, and D all fail to yield a single acceptable zero. Completing the square is a sure skill here but unnecessary; if you feel comfortable with the intercepts, plug in values!

QUESTION 16.

12 is the correct answer. Start by building an equation: the square of a number (x^2), one-third of that ($\frac{1}{3}x^2$) is equal to 48 ($\frac{1}{3}x^2 = 48$). Solve to find that the square of the number is 144, leaving us with 12.

QUESTION 17.

15 is the correct answer. We should realize that if $\overline{BC}$ and $\overline{DE}$ are parallel in these triangles, and if $\angle CAB$ is the same as $\angle EAD$, we have similar triangles. We can use this to build a proportion: $\frac{AB}{BC} = \frac{AD}{DE}$. We fill in what we know to find that $\frac{4}{3} = \frac{20}{DE}$, cross-multiply to find that $60 = 4(\overline{DE})$, and thusly that $\overline{DE} = 15$.

QUESTION 18.

2011 is the correct answer. We can use number sense to notice while some values double and triple, the greatest increase seems to be going from 8k to 39k. Percent change is modeled by $\frac{Diffence\ in\ Values}{Actual\ Values} \times 100\%$, but… the answer is merely asking for the year! Clearly Apple had a good year in 2011, so that is the best choice. Don't be confused by excess information!

QUESTION 19.

6 is the correct answer. Starting with the cone formula, $V = \frac{1}{3}\pi r^2 h$, and filling in our values gives us $V = \frac{1}{3}\pi 9^2 \frac{8}{\pi}$. The π cancels, leaving us with $\frac{1}{3} \times 81 \times 8$, and 216 for a volume. That volume is now going into a cube; since the measure of the volume of a cube is $V = L \times W \times H$,

QUESTION 20.

.5 is the correct answer. Don't panic when trigonometry problems appear; they are simply testing ratios and triangles! Use SOHCAHTOA (Sine=$\frac{Opposite}{Hypotenuse}$,Cosine=$\frac{Adjacent}{Hypotenuse}$, Tangent=$\frac{Opposite}{Adjacent}$). Since cosine is adjacent $\frac{Adjacent}{Hypotenuse}$, we know that we could have a right triangle with a hypotenuse of 2 and an adjacent side of $\sqrt{3}$. Since we know two sides of a right triangle, we can find the third using the Pythagorean Theorem. Since $a^2 + \sqrt{3}^2 = 2^2$, we can deduce that a is a side of 1, and therefore the sine must be $\frac{1}{2}$.

SECTION 4
Math Calculator Test

QUESTION 1.

Choice A is the best answer. This problem is best solved with simple word translation. Following the sentence, we know that nine more (9 +) than three times x ($3x$) is (=) fifteen (15), leaving $3x = 6$ and $x = 2$. Okay, on to more challenging problems!

Choices B and D are incorrect, and usually caused by translating the question improperly. If you got choice C, just be careful with your operations – did you add nine to fifteen instead of subtracting?

QUESTION 2.

Choice B is the best answer. We need to use the formula to find the area of a triangle, $A = \frac{1}{2}bh$, and recognize that a height that is four times the base will translate to $h = 4b$, so $50 = \frac{1}{2}b \times 4b$ and $50 = 2b^2$. We can divide both sides by 2 to get $25 = b^2$, and take the square root of 25 to get an answer of 5.

Choices B and C are probably the result of incorrectly building our equation, and choice D is the result of a not remembering to divide by 2 or forgetting the $\frac{1}{2}$ in the triangle formula.

QUESTION 3.

Choice D is the best answer. We have two discounts here (\$899 → 30% off → 10% off → Answer), so we will need two equations. For the second discount we know that 10% *off* is 90% *of* the price. So, 90% of a price is \$899 is the same as $\frac{90}{100}p = 899$. If we divide by $.9$, we find that $p = 998.89$. Now for the first 30% discount. If 30% off means that we pay 70% of the price, we know that $.7p = 998.89$, so we can solve for p and get $p = \$1{,}427$.

QUESTION 4.

Choice B is the best answer. If the parallel lines are transected by a third line, we know that certain angles are equal; vertical angles, interior angles, and exterior angles all have the same measure. We do not have a measure, but we do know that $a = 5x + 9$ and $b = 3x + 3$. We also know that if they are exterior angles, then $5x + 9 = 3x + 3$. We only need to simplify to $x = -3$.

Choice C is the result of losing track of negative signs, which is a common folly. Choice D would happen if we mistook the angles as supplementary ($5x + 9 + 3x + 3 = 180$) instead of setting the two angles equal.

QUESTION 5.

Choice A is the best answer. This problem is dependent on the concept of unit conversion. Since 1 nautical mile is equivalent to 6000 feet, and 1 standard mile is equivalent to 5280 feet, we can do a simple conversion. The 8 listed nautical miles are really 48,000 feet. We also can say that since 1 mile and 5,280 feet are the same measure, multiplying by $\frac{1\ mile}{5{,}280\ feet}$ is really multiplying by 1. We can multiply this fraction by our 48,000 feet to get 9.09 miles, which rounds up to 9.1

In this case, choices C and D could be caused by mistaking information in the problem and multiplying by 5,280 and dividing by 6,000 instead of vice versa. Choice B is the result of not paying attention while rounding; we must take care to be precise!

QUESTION 6.

Choice B is the best answer. The most important thing to do with a problem that gives a relationship between values is to map it as an equation. Our problem really reads $\frac{3}{5}x = 12$. We can multiply both sides of our equation by $\frac{5}{3}$ to find $x = 20$, so $\frac{1}{3}$ of x must be $\frac{20}{3}$.

Choice A would be the result of multiplying 12 by $\frac{3}{5}$ instead of its reciprocal, and choices C and D are bad estimates.

QUESTION 7.

Choice D is the best answer. There are two basic strategies here: graphing and logic. We could put each function into a graphing calculator and decide which point only touches the X axis once.
We could also use logic. Most quadratics $f(x) = ax^2 + bx + c$ will have two zeroes/roots. However, any quadratic with a positive a value positive c value will have no y-intercepts, just like any quadratic with negative a and c value.
For a quadratic to have only one root/zero, it can either be a perfect square, or have no b or c term. The only time these functions will have a root is at the vertex. Choice D is not a perfect square, but since it has no b or c term, it is the only choice.

Choice A has no roots, while choices B and C have two roots.

QUESTION 8.

Choice B is the best answer. Remember that standard deviation is the average distance of each value from the overall average. This would take a long time to find, so an estimation is in order. For each of the four answer choices, we should infer that choices with a broader range (difference between highest and lowest values) will have a greater distance from the average. To estimate which group will have the smallest standard deviation, we can look for the smallest range. (NOTE: While the College Board does not expect you to calculate standard deviation, they do expect you to understand the concept)

For options C and D, there is a vast range between the highest and lowest values (because education is valuable). Between A and B, notice that the range for All Education Levels is about 200. Where the range for people with less than a high school diploma is barely 100; we can infer that these values will have a lower average, range, and more importantly, standard deviation.

QUESTION 9.

Choice C is the best answer. The only issue in this problem is finding overall income with a bachelor degree ($1101), income with diploma only ($668), and remembering that since we are looking for percent increase, we should subtract the two to use the difference $(1101 - 668 = 443)$ for the percentage change. Plug the difference in for our percentage formula, taking care to use our original total $\frac{443}{668} \times 100\%$ to get a percentage increase of 65%.

Choice A would be the result of mixing up values in the equation – if you got this, use more caution when assembling your equations! Choice D is caused by not paying attention to the wording of the problem; while it is true that the bachelor's degree only

QUESTION 10.

Choice B is the best answer. First and foremost, we should recognize that there are two scenarios in this problem with similar variables: in each case we have the same number of employees (x) and leads (y). In the first case, we have three leads per employee $(3x)$, and three extra leads means that we should add three to our previous value $(3x + 3)$. We also know that the same number of leads will be nine short (-9) when five leads $(5x)$ are distributed $(5x - 9)$. Since the 'certain number of leads' is the same in both scenarios, we can set the two values equal! Once

we do, $3x + 3 = 5x - 9$ can be simplified by adding nine to both sides, then subtracting $3x$ from $3x + 12 = 5x$ to get $2x = 12$ and $x = 6$.

Choices A, B, and D are all the product of not translating the equation properly.

QUESTION 11.

Choice C is the best answer. This problem is the opposite of the earlier percentage problem, since we are given the price after discount and need to work our way back to the original price. When dealing with series of discounts (which is a common problem type), a major consideration is that the 'original value' is constantly changing. In this case, we have the final price rather than the original price. Consider the 10% discount first, since we are working our way backwards. Since 10% off of our original price is the same as paying 90% of our original price, we can state that $Original \times 90\% = 748.80$, and now we know that we can divide our sales price by .9 to find $\frac{748.80}{.9} = 832$. We can then take our \$832 as the new sale price for the 20% discount and perform the same operation as before with 80% (or $.80$) instead of $.9$. $\frac{832}{.8} = 1040$, giving us C as our choice.

Keep in mind with any problem with multiple percentages that *taking two percent discounts is never the same as the sum*!

Choice A is 70% of the final price, which is incorrect. Choice B is usually reached by mixing up percentages and percent off. Choice D is reached with the proper method, but by using 30% instead of 20% & 10%.

QUESTION 12.

Choice A is the best answer. This problem is testing our knowledge of sets and unions. Since the survey is only of pet owners, we don't have to be worried about anyone outside of our three populations (which would make D a valid answer). Keep in mind that the nine seniors that have both a dog and cate are counted in both the dog numbers and cat numbers. If this is true, adding the dog and cat groups ($27 + 35 = 62$) counts the both category twice, so we must subtract ($62 - 9 = 53$). Just think about the groups as a Venn diagram: if you count both circles, you have counted the middle section twice!

Choice B is reached by not subtracting the 9 seniors with both a dog and cat, and choice C is reached by adding 9 instead of subtracting. Cho

QUESTION 13.

Choice D is the best answer. The first thing that we can quickly do here is eliminate options making no sense. Looking at Saturn V and Ares V, they have the same height, but since Ares V holds more payload with the same height, Saturn V is a bad option. Also, the Ares I holds nearly the same payload with twice the height, eliminating it as a viable option.
Mathematically, are looking at payload per meter of height, acknowledging that per means 'for'. The operation for this problem then would be $\frac{Max.Payload}{Height}$. The space shuttle's $\frac{24{,}400\ kg}{56\ m} = 435.7\frac{kg}{m}$ is far lower than Ares V's $\frac{188{,}000\ kg}{116\ m} = 1{,}620\frac{kg}{m}$, leaving Ares V as the best answer.

QUESTION 14.

Choice C is the best answer. Let's start with the first obstacle: what is the Ares I's burn time per meter of height? Since we aren't given the burn time in this case, we can find $\frac{seconds}{meter}$ with some quick division. The burn time per meter for the Ares I is $\frac{150}{94} = 1.596\frac{s}{m}$, and to get 30% more we can multiply by 1.3. So, the efficiency is now $2.07\frac{s}{m}$, and since we know the height of Ares I is 116 m, multiplying the efficiency by the height will give us $2.07\frac{s}{m} \times 116\ m = 240.12\ s$.

Choice A is reached by multiplying the burn time per meter by .7 instead of 1.3, giving us 30% *less* burn time. If you reached Choice B, you may have cut a digit off during your math, and we should never round until we reach our final answer! Choice D is the result of baldly guessing a large number, which is not a reliable strategy.

QUESTION 15.

Choice A is the best answer. This answer is based on the key difference between linear and exponential functions; *linear functions will always increase at the same rate, where exponential functions increase at a changing rate.* Logarithmic growth is not tested by the SAT I; it typically has a short burst of growth, but the rate slows quite quickly.

Choice B is incorrect because there is no constant multiple for the relationship between burn time and payload ($\frac{24400}{124} = 196.8$ for the shuttle, $\frac{25000}{150} = 166.7$ for Ares I). Choice C is not a tested concept (we should only guess on an unknown if everything else is eliminated; as Sherlock Holmes says, once we eliminate the impossible, whatever remains, no matter how improbable, must be the truth). Choice D is incorrect as the relationship is increasing: as payload increases, burn time increases).

QUESTION 16.

Choice B is the best answer. We should notice that the trajectory is modeled as a quadratic equation. This matters because when the rocket lands, it will be 0 feet from the ground; we want to know when $f(x) = 0$. Since quadratics are an area we should know, we should realize that we are looking for the zeroes of the function. Since each term is divisible by -5, we can factor out a -5 to get $0 = -5(x^2 - 2x - 24)$, and then factor $x^2 - 2x - 24$ down to $(x - 6)(x + 4)$. With zeroes at 6 and -4, we can confidently say that the rocket will land in 6 seconds since -4 is an illogical answer (rockets have yet to move backwards in time).

Choice A might seem reasonable since $(x + 4)$ was a factor of our equation, but remember that this would be a zero $(x + 4 = 0)$, and would really be -4. Choices C and D are the result of multiplying a zero by 5. This may seem reasonable since we factored out -5, but we don't need to multiply zeroes by anything; if we substitute 6 for x in our equation we get $-5(2)(0)$, which will still multiply to zero.

QUESTION 17.

Choice C is the best answer. To find an arc, we should recognize that the arc is part of the circumference of the circle (just like a sector is proportional to the area of the circle). If we know that a 360° arc is really just the circumference ($2\pi r$), we can set that ratio as equal to 72° and the unknown arc. We can build a proportion ($\frac{Circumference}{360°} = \frac{Arc\ Length}{Arc\ Angle}$and fill in $\frac{5}{\pi}$ for the radius, giving us $\frac{2\pi\frac{5}{\pi}}{360} = \frac{x}{72}$ (or something similar), and letting us cross-multiply and simplify to $720 = 360x$, and finally giving us $x = 2$.

Choice A would be the result of ignoring π in the denominator radius (which actually makes the calculation trickier, since it cancels the π in the circumference formula). Choice B might look correct as well, but it is just a variation on presented information. If you reached choice D, check your proportion; the 360° should be paired with the circumference and the 72° should be paired with the arc.

QUESTION 18.

Choice C is the best answer. The standard form for imaginary numbers is $a + bi$, where a is the real term and b is the coefficient for any i value. Getting this expression into standard form first means getting rid of the complex fraction. Because of the imaginary number (i) in the denominator, we should multiply both the numerator and denominator by the conjugate of the numerator ($3 + i$, which is the denominator with the sign of i switched). Now that we know we need $\frac{3+i}{3-i} \times \frac{3+i}{3+i}$, we can simplify to $\frac{9+6i+i^2}{9-i^2}$ (taking care to FOIL since we are multiplying

binomials), simplify i^2 to -1, and get $\frac{8+6i}{10}$. We could also write this expression as $\frac{8}{10}+\frac{6}{10}i$, making $\frac{4}{5}$ our simplified a term.
With imaginary numbers, the simplest strategy is to treat i like any other variable, only reducing at the end of the problem.

Choices A and B are common results of not understanding how to approach the problem. The 3 in $3+i$ is not the same as the a term because we have a complex denominator, and simply dividing 3 by 3 to get the 1for choice B disregards one of our fraction rules (we can break up a complex numerator, but not a complex denominator). Choice D is the result of not taking care of signs when simplifying.

QUESTION 19.

Choice B is the best answer. This problem is focused on knowing the definitions of median and mean. We should recognize that the median is the middle-most value in the frequency, and the average is the sum of all the values divided by the total of values. One difference is that median values are not changed by an outlier value, which is far outside of the expected range. A small outlier would have a strong decrease on the average, where a large outlier would increase the average. In a perfect, normalized distribution, the mean and median would be the same. Since the mean is larger, we can infer that some large values are skewing the measurement, and that B is the best choice.

Choice A is an inference that cannot be supported; while this could be true, we need evidence to support this that isn't given. Choice C might be tempting, but by definition the median of a set of values is the middle value; we couldn't have more than 50% of people below the median. Choice D also fits the explanation of choice A: with no evidence, there is no inference!

QUESTION 20.

Choice A is the best answer. Many people would assume that if a quadratic equation has two zeroes, it has two arms and the answer would be two. Our quadratic has undergone some shifts, though. If rewritten as $g(x) = -x^2 + 5$, we should note that we have a negative transformation (since $a = -1$) flipping our parabola downwards and a vertical translation of +5 (since $c = 5$) pushing our vertex to (5,0). Our $g(x)$ has a maximum of 5, which is at $x = 0$. At the same x value, $f(x) = 8$. Our $f(x)$ also has a relatively small slope, so there is not a chance of an intersection. Despite both being functions with domains of all real numbers, these functions will never touch.

Alternatively, we could set both functions equal to find a common x value of intersection. If $\frac{3}{2}x + 8 = 5 - x^2$, then we can combine like terms to $x^2 + \frac{3}{2}x + 3 = 0$. This quadratic won't factor nicely, but we can put it in the quadratic formula $\frac{-b\pm\sqrt{b^2-4ac}}{2a}$ to get $\frac{-\frac{3}{2}\pm\sqrt{\frac{9}{4}-4(1)(3)}}{2(1)}$, but since $\frac{9}{4} - 4(1)(3)$ is negative, we won't get a real answer.

QUESTION 21.

Choice D is the best answer. While this problem might appear intimidating at first, we use algebra to make this a straightforward process. Start by simplifying: subtracting three from both sides gives us $\sqrt{4-x} \leq 2$. After this, we square both sides of the inequality to get $4 - x \leq 4$ (Since we have a positive square root, we don't need to worry about changing the direction of our inequality). We now subtract four to get $-x \leq 0$ and multiply both sides by -1 (remembering to invert our sign) to yield $x \geq 0$.
We aren't done yet, though! Because we have a square root with a variable in it, we must find the **radicand**, which ensures that a square root must not be negative. Since we have $\sqrt{4-x}$, we know that $4 - x \geq 0$, so x must also be less than or equal to 4.

Choice A ignores the radicand, but also has not changed the inequality's direction (an easy mistake to make, but a serious issue!). Choices B and C are both partially right, but also ignore a portion of the inequality. We have to remember that solving inequalities requires precision and diligence!

QUESTION 22.

Choice C is the best answer. Because this problem only gives us one length to go on, we can use the definition of cosine ($\frac{Adjacent}{Hypotenuse}$) to find sides that will fit. We can fill in the adjacent side length, set the hypotenuse equal to x, and make this ratio equal to the 0.6 cosine. With $\frac{3}{x} = 0.6$, we can solve for x by multiplying both sides by x and dividing both sides by $.6$. This leads us to $x = \frac{3}{0.6}$, and $x = 5$.

The issue with choices A, B, and D is that there are triangles that have a hypotenuse of 2, 4, or 6 as well as a cosine of 0.6, but once we specify an adjacent length of three, there really is only one correct answer.

QUESTION 23.

Choice A is the best answer. If we're looking for the maximum of a function, we should realize first that only functions with an even degree have maximums, making D a bad option (linear equations go into infinity). Next, remember that a quadratic function only has a maximum if it opens downward, making B and C illogical choices as well. Notice that A will have not only a negative vertex $(3, -5)$ but also a downward chute, making it the ideal choice.

Logic aside, graphing would be another efficient way to find the proper function, but the time needed to enter the four functions into a calculator is significantly longer than the time needed to use logic and elimination.

QUESTION 24.

Choice B is the best answer. The most straightforward way to tackle this problem is to remember that a mean is the sum of values divided by the number of values. For example, we know that since m is composed of two values ($3x$ and 8, $m = \frac{3x+8}{2}$. We can make similar equations for n and z. While they all have the same denominator, note that we are looking for the *mean* of these three values, meaning that we must divide $\frac{3x+8+4x+10+5x+6}{2}$ by 3, which simplifies to $2x + 4$.

Choice D may have been tempting, but this is the result of not dividing the sum of our three values by three. Choices A and C are usually the result of not adding our values carefully.

QUESTION 25.

Choice B is the best answer. A few things are notable in this problem: first, it's quite handy that each person's name begins with a different letter (since we need to assign variables to each person). Second, both Allain and Charles have incomes that are given in terms of Bhav! That means that we can build a system of equations and substitute variables until we can solve for one equation. We can say that the average of the three incomes would look like $\frac{A+B+C}{3} = 28$, and we also are given $A = 3B$ and $B = \frac{1}{3}C$ (or $3B = C$). Now we can substitute $A = 3B$ and $3B = C$ into our original equation to get $\frac{3B+B+3B}{3} = 28$, combine B and multiply both sides by 3 to get $7B = 84$, and divide by 7 to get $B = 12$.

Choice C is a very distracting one, since one value is in terms of being tripled and another is in decreased to a third. It would be easy to assume Bhav makes the average value. We have to be vigilant, though, to read carefully and prove the problem out algebraically. If you reached choice A, you probably didn't translate the relationship between the three values properly.

QUESTION 26.

Choice D is the best answer. Finding the data points to put into the percent change formula ($\frac{New-Old}{Old} \times 100\%$) should be our first priority. Keep in mind that the lower the initial data point, the greater a change becomes.

Many people will look to choice A because it is the highest dollar amount, but the percentage actually ends up a bit lower (37% vs 40%)

QUESTION 27.

Choice C is the best answer. With regards to C, we can infer that measuring in terms of 2014 dollars is a more consistent measure than base dollars because of the constant point of reference. Looking between 2005 and 2010, while base dollars had a mild increase, the same period had no increase with a consistent reference point.

With A, we can clearly see the lack of positive slope from 2005-2010. B may be a tempting choice as a linear equation; a best-fit line may work but the word linear is clearly a misnomer since there is no constant slope. Choice D is not the most logical extrapolation because of the slowed growth from 2000 – 2010; while there may be an increase, it is not certain.

QUESTION 28.

Choice A is the best answer. This problem starts with realizing that when the rocket 'catches up,' the distance traveled by both the rocket and car is equal. Since distance is equal and the rate of speed for both vehicles is given, we can use $d = rt$ to calculate the distance traveled by both, and set them equal. Notice though that our time is in minutes, so we can convert both rates by multiplying by $\frac{1\ hour}{60\ minutes}$ to get $\frac{600\ miles}{60\ minutes}(t-20) = \frac{267\ miles}{60\ minutes}(t)$. We use $t - 20$ for the rocket since the rocket only starts after the Bugatti has driven for 20 minutes.

Choices C and D are the result of not carefully setting up the conversions, and choice B would be the result of not using $t - 20$ as the rocket's launch time.

QUESTION 29.

Choice A is the best answer. Treat this problem like any other algebra problem; it can be manipulated until it has a form that fits. Since we are looking for slope, we should solve for y. That cannot happen until we distribute the a, though. We get $x + y = ax - ay$, and we can put each y on the same side ($ay + y = ax - x$). Factor out like terms $y(a + 1) = x(a - 1)$, divide by $a + 1$, and we now have $y = \frac{a-1}{a+1}x$. We know that $\frac{a-1}{a+1}$ must be negative, but because of the opposing operations, D is not a valid option; only A will keep the negative slope.

Option C is incorrect since setting a equal to zero actually would give a negative slope in our initial equation.

QUESTION 30.

4, 4.5 or 6 is the correct answer. We have an interesting scenario here, where any of the two sides could equal each other. We have three possible pairs of equal sides here: $18 = 3x + 6$, $18 = 4x$, and $4x = 3x + 6$. Any of these values could be true; without further information on the triangle, any of the three options should suffice:

- Subtract 6 from both sides of $18 = 3x + 6$ to get $12 = 3x$, and divide by 3 to get $x = 4$.
- Divide both sides of $18 = 4x$ by 4 to get 4.5,
- Subtract $3x$ from both sides of $4x = 3x + 6$ to get $x = 6$

QUESTION 31

192 is the correct answer. The first piece of data that we are given is the most important: since we have 576 freshmen, and $\frac{2}{3}$ of 576 ($\frac{2}{3} \times 576$) are in-state, we have 384 in-state students, which we can subtract to get 192 (or one-third) of our students from out of state. Since we can't un-enroll students, we need to ask ourselves how many out of state students we need to add to reach an even number of enrollees. If we take 192 away from 384, we should see that we need 192 more out of state students.

QUESTION 32.

25 is the correct answer. This problem uses a rare Pythagorean triple. Since we know we need an integer length for the third side, there are two possibilities:

- 24 is the hypotenuse, and $24^2 - 7^2$ is a perfect square (it isn't), or
- $24^2 + 7^2 = c^2$ and the hypotenuse is the missing third side. $576 + 49 = 625$, and 625 is 25 squared, giving us an answer of 25.

QUESTION 33.

5 or $\frac{1}{2}$ is the correct answer. Let's start the problem by setting an equation: since we know the cylinder holds five times the cone, $12(Cone) = Cylinder$ would balance the equation. We can substitute in the formulas for the cylinder and cone to get $12\left(\frac{1}{3}\pi r^2 h\right) = \pi r^2 h$. Since the radii are different, though, we should use different variables, like $12\left(\frac{1}{3}\pi x^2 h\right) = \pi y^2 h$. We can simplify the left side of the equation to get $4\pi x^2 h = \pi y^2 h$. Since we know π is constant and the height is the same, we can divide both sides by πh to get $4x^2 = y^2$. Since each term is a perfect square, we can take the square root of both sides to get $2x = y$. Since y was our cylinder radius, we have a radius of $1:2$, or $\frac{1}{2}$.

QUESTION 34.

5 or $\frac{1}{2}$ is the correct answer. We know enough about the original line to realize that if the origin (0,0) and (0,4) share a vertical line, we won't need the true definition of a perpendicular line (negative reciprocal). The only line that would be perpendicular here

QUESTION 35.

1 is the correct answer. Barring the fact that polynomial division is not explicitly tested on the SAT, we could use synthetic division to solve this problem, but there is a far more efficient and elegant method: notice that there is no remainder when our cubic equation is divided by a binomial. That fact assures us that $\frac{1}{-1} = c$, and that $c = -1$. This in turn gives us an absolute value of 1. In cases like this, rely on the fact that the exam only tests a known set of variables!

QUESTION 36.

$-7.4 < b < 8.4$ is the correct answer. This question is asking for a line with a slope of zero, which we should recognize as a horizontal line. We should also recognize that to have three solutions shared with $f(x)$, then $g(x)$ should be between the relative minimum and maximum of $f(x)$. We could find the maximum of 8.4 and minimum of -7.4 graphically, or even by using calculus, but it is unnecessary at this point! Just use a value like 0 that we know will fit.

QUESTION 37.

366 is the correct answer. The first step to solving this problem is to break the interest up into two periods based on the differing rates. Finding the first year's interest is not particularly difficult: $1000 \times 1.07 = 1070$. For the remaining five years, though, we will need to use the compound interest formula to find the remaining five years. Keep in mind that we are using 1070, the amount after one year, as a principal. If we calculate $1070(1.05)^5$, we will get 1365.62, but the question wants the interest only, so subtract the original 1000 to get 365.62, or 366 rounded to the nearest dollar.

QUESTION 38.

36.6 is the correct answer. We can use our previous interest to find the percentage increase here quite easily. Using our percentage formula ($\frac{Part}{Whole} \times 100\%$), we should remember that we always use our original value as the 'whole' here, giving us $\frac{1366}{1000} \times 100\% = 136.6\%$. We want percent increase, though, so don't count the original 100%. Once we subtract, we get a clear 36.6%

SAT Practice Test #2
Pittsburgh Prep

Version 2.0
8.5.2016

This Page is Intentionally Left Blank

READING TEST 2: Section 1

65 MINUTES, 52 QUESTIONS

Turn to section 1 of your answer sheet to answer the questions in this section.

Directions

Each passage or pair of passages is followed by a set of questions. After reading each passage or pair, choose the best choice based on the what is stated or implied in the passage(s) and in any other graphics.

Questions 1-11 are based on the following passage.

This passage is adapted from the novel *Caleb Williams,* written by William Godwin in 1794. The main character Caleb spends his life evading imprisonment, from Squire Falkland, his master, and Falkland's bounty hunter Gines.

It is as I foreboded. The presage with which I was visited was prophetic. I am now to record a new and terrible revolution of my fortune and my mind. Having made experiment of various situations with one uniform result, I at length determined to remove myself, if possible, from the reach of my persecutor, by going into voluntary banishment from my native soil. This was my last resource for tranquility, for honest fame, for those privileges to which human life is indebted for the whole of its value. "In some distant climate," said I, "surely I may find that security which is necessary to persevering pursuit; surely I may lift my head erect, associate with men upon the footing of a man, acquire connections, and preserve them!" It is inconceivable with what ardent Teachings of the soul I aspired to this termination.

This last consolation was denied me by the inexorable Falkland. At the time the project was formed I was at no great distance from the east coast of the island, and I resolved to take ship at Harwich, and pass immediately into Holland. I accordingly repaired to that place, and went, almost as soon as I arrived, to the port. But there was no vessel perfectly ready to sail. I left the port, and withdrew to an inn, where, after some time, I retired to a chamber. I was scarcely there before the door of the room was opened, and the man whose countenance was the most hateful to my eyes, Gines, entered the apartment. He shut the door as soon as he entered.

"Youngster," said he, "I have a little private intelligence to communicate to you. I come as a friend, and that I may save you a labor-in-vain trouble. If you consider what I have to say in that light, it will be the better for you. It is my business now, do you see, for want of a better, to see that you do not break out of bounds. Not that I much matter having one man for my employer, or dancing attendance after another's heels; but I have special kindness for you, for some good turns that you wot of, and therefore I do not stand upon ceremonies! You have led me a very pretty round already; and, out of the love I bear you, you shall lead me as much further, if you will. But beware the salt seas! They are out of my orders. You are a prisoner at present, and I believe all your life will remain so. Thanks to the milk-and-water softness of your former master! If I had the ordering of these things, it should go with you in another fashion. As long as you think proper, you are a prisoner within the rules; and the rules with which the soft-hearted squire indulges you, are all England, Scotland, and Wales. But you are not to go out of these climates.

The Squire is determined you shall never pass the reach of his disposal. He has therefore given orders that, whenever you attempt so to do, you shall be converted from a prisoner at large to a prisoner in good earnest. A friend of mine followed you just now to the harbour; I was within call; and, if there had been any appearance of your setting your foot from land, we should have been with you in a trice, and laid you fast by the heels. I would advise you, for the future, to keep at a proper distance from the sea, for fear of the worst. You see I tell you all this for your good. For my part, I should be better satisfied if you were in limbo, with a rope about your neck, and a comfortable bird's eye prospect to the gallows: but I do as I am directed; and so good night to you!"

The intelligence thus conveyed to me occasioned an instantaneous revolution in both my intellectual and animal system. I disdained to answer, or take the smallest notice of the fiend by

whom it was delivered. It is now three days since I received it, and from that moment to the present my blood has been in a perpetual ferment. My thoughts wander from one idea of horror to another, with incredible rapidity. I have had no sleep

1) What "private intelligence" (30-31) does Gines offer Caleb?

A) Caleb must stay on the mainland or face serious consequences.
B) Prisoners do not have the right to leave the mainland.
C) Gines needs Caleb's help in capturing a runaway convict.
D) Gines lacks the power to stop Caleb, though he wants to.

2) What evidence from the passage best supports this?

A) Lines 38-40 ("I …ceremonies!")
B) Lines 44-48 ("You… fashion.")
C) Lines 49-52 ("You…climates.")
D) Lines 64-66 ("I…gallows.")

3) What is Caleb's reaction after Gines leaves?

A) Caleb is ignorant.
B) Caleb disdains Gines' warning.
C) Caleb decides to move to Holland.
D) Caleb is shocked.

4) Which choice provides the best answer to the previous question?

A) Lines 69-71 ("The intelligence…animal system.")
B) Lines 71-73 ("I disdained…it was delivered.")
C) Lines 73-75 ("It is now three days…in a perpetual ferment.")
D) Lines 76-78 ("I have had no sleep.")

5) Gines addresses Caleb in a(n) ______________ manner.

A) cautionary and well-intentioned
B) hostile and violent
C) friendly and nostalgic
D) inquisitive and curious

6) In line 1, the word "presage" most nearly means

A) omen.
B) denial.
C) assurance.
D) report.

7) The function of the second paragraph is to

A) establish a setting for the main passage.
B) reveal surprising information to Caleb.
C) develop a dialogue between two characters.
D) provide insight into the inner workings of Squire Falkland

8) As used in Line 18, the word "inexorable" most nearly means

A) inescapable.
B) sympathetic.
C) mutable.
D) purposeful.

9) Which choice best describes the central point of the passage?

A) One character is banished to Holland.
B) One character physically assaults another character.
C) One character warns another of possible danger.
D) One character wishes another character to die.

10) What does Caleb's old master Squire Falkland desire?

A) Falkland wishes Caleb's safe return.
B) Falkland wants Caleb's immediate death.
C) Falkland requests Caleb to repay his debt.
D) Falkland seeks to warn Caleb of the consequences of leaving the mainland.

11) What do lines 15-16 ("It…termination") indicate about Caleb's attitude?

A) He is worried.
B) He is content.
C) He is inspired by God.
D) He is determined.

12) Which choice best describes the development of the passage?

A) A response to an anecdote.
B) An appeal to the reader's emotions.
C) An important meeting of two characters.
D) An analysis of England's justice system

Questions 13-22 are based on the following passages

The following passages are taken from the 1944 U.S. Supreme Court Case "Korematsu v. United States". This landmark case concerned the constitutionality of the internment of Japanese-Americans during World War II. The first article, given by Justice Black, upholds the Court's final decision. The second article is a dissenting opinion given by Justice Roberts.

Passage 1*: Concurring Opinion, the Opinion of the Court, delivered by Justice Black*

"It is said that we are dealing here with the case of imprisonment of a citizen in a concentration camp solely because of his ancestry, without evidence or inquiry concerning his loyalty and good disposition towards the United States. Our task would be simple, our duty clear, were this a case involving the imprisonment of a loyal citizen in a concentration camp because of racial prejudice. Regardless of the true nature of the assembly and relocation centers -- and we deem it unjustifiable to call them concentration camps, with all the ugly connotations that term implies -- we are dealing specifically with nothing but an exclusion order. To cast this case into outlines of racial prejudice, without reference to the real military dangers which were presented, merely confuses the issue. Korematsu was not excluded from the Military Area because of hostility to him or his race. He was excluded because we are at war with the Japanese Empire, because the properly constituted military authorities feared an invasion of our West Coast and felt constrained to take proper security measures, because they decided that the military urgency of the situation demanded that all citizens of Japanese ancestry be segregated from the West Coast temporarily, and, finally, because Congress, reposing its confidence in this time of war in our military leaders -- as inevitably it must -- determined that they should have the power to do just this. There was evidence of disloyalty on the part of some, the military authorities considered that the need for action was great, and time was short. We cannot -- by availing ourselves of the calm perspective of hindsight -- now say that, at that time, these actions were unjustified.

Passage 2*: Dissenting Opinion, delivered by Justice Roberts.*

"I dissent, because I think the indisputable facts exhibit a clear violation of Constitutional rights.

This is not a case of keeping people off the streets at night, as was *Hirabayashi v. United States,* nor a case of temporary exclusion of a citizen from an area for his own safety or that of the community, nor a case of offering him an opportunity to go temporarily out of an area where his presence might cause danger to himself or to his fellows. On the contrary, it is the case of convicting a citizen as a punishment for not submitting to imprisonment in a concentration camp, based on his ancestry, and solely because of his ancestry, without evidence or inquiry concerning his loyalty and good disposition towards the United States. If this be a correct statement of the facts disclosed by this record, and facts of which we take judicial notice, I need hardly labor the conclusion that Constitutional rights have been violated.

The Government's argument, and the opinion of the court, in my judgment, erroneously divide that which is single and indivisible, and thus make the case appear as if the petitioner violated a Military Order, sanctioned by Act of Congress, which excluded him from his home by refusing voluntarily to leave, and so knowingly and intentionally defying the order and the Act of Congress.

The petitioner, a resident of San Leandro, Alameda County, California, is a native of the United States of Japanese ancestry who, according to the uncontradicted evidence, is a loyal citizen of the nation."

13) Justice Black, in passage 1, believes that the internment of Japanese-Americans serves what greater purpose?

A) To enforce a separate but equal segregation ruling
B) To stop Japanese culture from corrupting American culture.
C) To create more jobs and opportunities for White-Americans.
D) To help protect the U.S. West Coast from Japanese Invasion during war.

14) Which choice provides the best evidence for the answer to the previous question?

A) Lines 9-12 ("Our…prejudice.")
B) Lines 17-20 ("To…issue.")
C) Lines 20-22 ("Korematsu…race.")
D) Lines 22-25 ("we…Coast")

15) In line 30 in passage 1, "reposing" most nearly means

A) reaffirming.
B) calming.
C) enlivening.
D) questioning.

16) Justice Black, in passage 1, attempts to dissuade which of the following ideas?

A) The Court decision was based on fear of spies.
B) There is a conspiracy within the government
C) Racial prejudice decided the Court ruling.
D) Some members of the military were disloyal.

17) In the third paragraph of passage 2 (lines 61-69), Justice Roberts refutes which of the Court's claims?

A) Korematsu has rights a U.S. citizen.
B) Korematsu purposefully violated military orders.
C) Congress sanctioned the Japanese-American internment camps.
D) The U.S. should not be afraid of invasion of the West Coast.

18) What criterion does Justice Roberts establish in Passage 2 for the case to be deemed unconstitutional?

A) The defendant was charged mainly due to his immediate and extended family
B) The evidence in the case is circumstantial
C) The ruling of the case contradicts the ruling set by *Hirabayashi v. United States*
D) The defendant was targeted because of race

19) Which of the following can be best inferred from the author's use of the phrase "single and indivisible" in Line 63 of Passage 2?

A) He believes that the country must stay united during times of war.
B) He believes that rights are universal and can't be denied to any one individual.
C) He believes that the Constitution is flawed in its role towards immigration.
D) He believes that the majority opinion must be enforced despite its problems.

20) In passage 2, *Irabayashi v. United States* is mentioned to mainly emphasize what point?

A) To further justify the internment of Japanese-Americans.
B) To contrast a previous case with the case at hand.
C) To show the past harms of prejudice in the legal system
D) To identify the first racial case in recent US history

21) What is the main point of contention between these two authors?

A) The role of the defendant's race in the trial.
B) The militarization of urban neighborhoods.
C) The threat of espionage to the state.
D) The evidence, or lack thereof, for an informed decision to be made.

22) What would the two justices most likely agree to?

A) The Constitutionality of the charges.
B) Korematsu violated an exclusion order
C) The necessity of internment camps
D) Japanese-American citizens pose a threat to America

Questions 22-31 are based on the following passage

*This passage is adapted from Brandon Atkins and Wilson Huang, "**A Study of Social Engineering in Online Frauds**" © 2013.*

Social engineers are able to exploit human weaknesses to obtain desired behaviors and privilege information via psychologically constructed communications. These fraudsters can skillfully manipulate victims into an emotionally vulnerable state with just a disguised, attractive e-mail. The variation and extent of social engineering attacks are only limited by the creativity of the hacker. These attacks prove to be effective because they target the most vulnerable link of any organization, its people. Social engineering attacks have the potential to bypass the best technical security and expose an organization's critical information.

There are numerous types of social engineering attacks; a few include Trojan e-mail and phishing messages, advance-fee fraud, impersonation, persuasion, bribery, shoulder surfing, and dumpster diving. Among them, Trojan e-mail and phishing messages are two of the most common examples of social engineering attacks. They are technical attacks in nature, but they actually rely on strategically constructed messages to lure victims to open attachments or click on embedded hyperlinks. This makes these classic examples, which assist technical exploits, a very common feature in many social engineering attacks. These attacks serve as stepping stones to the attacker's ultimate goal, which could be, for example, complete control of an organization's network servers. Phishing e-mails or Trojan attacks can be employed to collect private information or system credentials, or potentially to compromise the security of the user's operating system by installing malicious software that allows the attacker full access to the system. In 2007, phishing attacks accounted for more than a quarter of all reported computer crimes.

Another common technique employed by social engineers is the use of fake credentials. This can be a simple ploy executed by printing fake business cards, or a more elaborate tactic such as creating counterfeit identification cards or security badges. The use of contemporary technology has made it easy to create hard-to-detect duplicates of identification cards. With that in mind, attackers do not always need to create the most realistic looking fake credentials as they are able to sell a good story to go with it. In one vulnerability assessment, an attacker created a very simple green plastic badge with a commonly seen recycling symbol. When caught going through the dumpsters by the organization's security personnel, the attacker assumed the role of a recycling coordinator doing a compliance inspection. The attacker claimed that, because the organization was not sorting its recyclable waste aside, the company leadership could be subject to a large fine from the government. As a result of this simple trick, supervisors from the organization personally ensured all paper products were separated off to the side for the remainder of the assessment. Each day the social engineer returned to collect presorted paper products and sorted through them at leisure to look for any information of value. This attacker was so successful at this trick that he was given a tour of the organization later in the week and was able to come and go at will once personnel got used to seeing him on a daily basis.

Social Engineers can utilize various techniques to impersonate a person. Attackers will often conduct impersonation attacks by calling personnel in the target organization on the telephone, pretending to be coworkers from a different department, reporters, or even students doing research. Social engineers will even carry out impersonation attacks in person by walking into a selected organization utilizing fake credentials or a good story to elude security. Additional techniques frequently employed by social engineers are persuasion attacks. Persuasion attacks consist of the social engineer tricking a person into giving critical information or to assist the attack in a different way. Oftentimes the victim is persuaded into believing the attacker is doing him/her a favor in some way. The victim, then, feels obligated to assist the attacker even when organizational policies may be violated. In a variation of this attack, the social engineer uses persuasion techniques to have the employee bypass company procedures in order to hurry up the process or bypass the problem altogether.

Social engineering attacks are easy to commit and very difficult to defend against because they focus on the human factors. Since most people are usually helpful in attitude and tend to believe that this type of attack will not happen to them, they are often fooled without even knowing they have been a victim of an online fraud. The natural human tendency to take people at their word continues to leave users vulnerable to social engineering attacks

Persuasions used in phishing e-mails (N = 100).

Types of Persuasions	% Yes
Authority	100%
Urgency	71%
Fear/Threat	41%
Politeness	74%
Formality	55%

Table 1: The table above showcases the frequency of the various styles of phishing emails.

23) Which of the following is among the most prevalent form of social engineering attacks?

A) Bribery
B) Impersonation
C) Trojan Emails
D) Intimidation

24) As used in line 44, what does the word "contemporary" most nearly mean?

A) antiquated
B) modern
C) elementary
D) complicated

25) As used in line 52, a "compliance inspection" would be most similar to which of the following situations?

A) An employer ranks workers on productivity.
B) Workers self-evaluate their efficiency.
C) An outside firm optimizes operations at a company.
D) An examiner determines if a company is following the rules.

26) The most effective social engineering attacks target what aspect of human emotions?

A) Frailty
B) Anxiety
C) Infirmity
D) Gullibility

27) Which choice provides the best evidence for the answer to the previous question?

A) Lines 81-84 ("Persuasion … way")
B) Lines 39-40 ("Another…credentials")
C) Lines 99-101("The…attacks")
D) Lines 23-25 ("They…hyperlinks")

28) Which of the following scenarios occurred in the passage?

A) An attacker compromised a corporation's infrastructure by posing as an authority figure.
B) An attacker collected valuable information through the use of fake credentials.
C) An attacker extorted money from thousands of people from phishing e-mails.
D) An attacker gathered classified materials by impersonating a coworker.

29) The main point of this passage is to

A) Warn the reader of the dangers of social engineering attacks
B) Inform the reader of the prevalence of social engineering attacks
C) Discuss the variations used in social engineering attacks
D) Pitch possible countermeasures to social engineering attacks to the reader

30) Based on the passage, what would be the best series of events which an attacker utilizing fake credentials would use?

I. Ask for assistance from an employee
II. Complete a rudimentary task
III. Glean information from target

A) I, II, III
B) II, I, III
C) III, I, II
D) III, II, I.

31) Based on the data collected in Table 1, which phishing email would you most expect to receive?

A) A man claiming to be your boss cordially asks for your social security number.
B) A man claiming to be a prince seeks your help for an imperative diplomatic matter.
C) A man claiming to be a member of the FBI threatens to arrest you.
D) A man claiming to be a store representative will give you a brand new TV if you respond immediately.

32) Does the information in the table support the author's claims from the passage?

A) Yes, because the percentages brought up in the article match those in the table.
B) Yes, because the prevalence of authority and politeness in phishing is discussed through the examples in the passage.
C) No, because the article is about social engineering attacks while the table is about phishing.
D) No, because it contradicts the idea that fake credentials are hard to detect.

Questions 33-42 are based on the following passages

This passage is adapted from Matthew Campbell et. al, "Computer animations stimulate contagious yawning in chimpanzees" © 2009 by the Royal Society Publishing.

Empathy in humans is so highly developed that humans empathize with fictitious depictions of human behavior (e.g. theatre in its many live and recorded forms), and even non-living representations of humans and animals, such as puppets, cartoons and computer animations. Our emotional engagement with the characters in the various media is why we experience suspense at their predicaments and happiness, sadness or other emotions that ensue. The perception–action model (PAM) proposes that our emotional connection derives from an activation of neural representations associated with our own experiences. Recently, imitation of computer-generated animations has been put to clinical use in children with autism spectrum disorder and has also been a cause for concern over violent video games.

Three-dimensional computer animation is of potential interest for studying the cognition, emotion and behavior of non-human animals. Presentation of video images of real behavior has several limitations. Different examples of the same behavior may be highly variable owing to factors outside of the experimenter's control (e.g. individuals present/absent, intensity and duration of behaviors, lighting, background composition etc.). Rare behaviors pose additional challenges, since recording multiple examples requires either extraordinary luck or a large and uncertain time investment. Videos of 'impossible' behaviors (i.e. behaviors not in the repertoire of the subjects or species) are by definition impossible to obtain. All of these obstacles can be overcome using computer animation, and the creation of impossible behaviors is one application of animation that has already been exploited with pigeons. The disadvantage to computer animation is that the stimuli may not look like real conspecifics; they are inherently artificial. Before the advantages of animations can be exploited, two critical questions need to be answered. (i) Do non-human animals view or process animated images the same way they do real images of conspecifics? (ii) Will non-human animals identify or empathize with animations? We know humans both process and empathize with animations in a way similar to the way they do real humans, and if other animals do as well, then computer animations represent a new and flexible tool in the study of animal behavior.

The first question above was recently answered by Parr (2008), who tested how chimpanzees (*Pan troglodytes*) categorize facial expressions using virtual chimpanzees created with Poser 6.0. Chimpanzee facial expressions are graded signals, and the computer program allowed for a precise, standardized library of images impossible to collect through photography. Chimpanzees discriminated between different expressions, and inversion of the animated faces disrupted performance, as it does with photographs of actual chimpanzee faces. The inversion effect demonstrates configurative processing of animations, the same way chimpanzees process faces, rather than feature-based processing. If the animations were not processed as whole faces but rather as a collection of shapes and colors, no inversion effect would have been seen.

The next step is to determine whether chimpanzees identify with animations, thus addressing the second question above. We tested whether chimpanzees show contagious yawning in response to animated chimpanzee yawns.

Contagious yawning is well suited for this type of test for several reasons. Because yawning is involuntary, contagion would indicate subconscious identification with the animations rather than deliberate imitation (which may result in opening of the mouth but not an actual yawn). Physiological measurements of emotional arousal might also indicate identification, but these methods are not currently feasible with awake, behaving, adult chimpanzees. Hence, there is a need for purely behavioral measures. Whether considered a part of affect or not, contagious yawning and emotional responses are both involuntary psychophysiological responses. Hence, they provide complementary measures of an empathic connection to a stimulus. Although the methods, results and conclusion vary, evidence for contagious yawning has been observed in chimpanzees, stumptail macaques, and domestic dogs, so our experiment may generalize to other species.

Anderson (2004) found that two of six chimpanzees yawned more in response to videos of chimpanzees yawning than to control videos. The population-level statistic was non-significant, which is not surprising given the small sample size. We presented 24 chimpanzees with three-dimensional

computer-animated chimpanzees yawning or displaying control mouth movements. We hypothesized that if the chimpanzees identified with the animations, then they would yawn more in response to the yawn animations than the control animations.

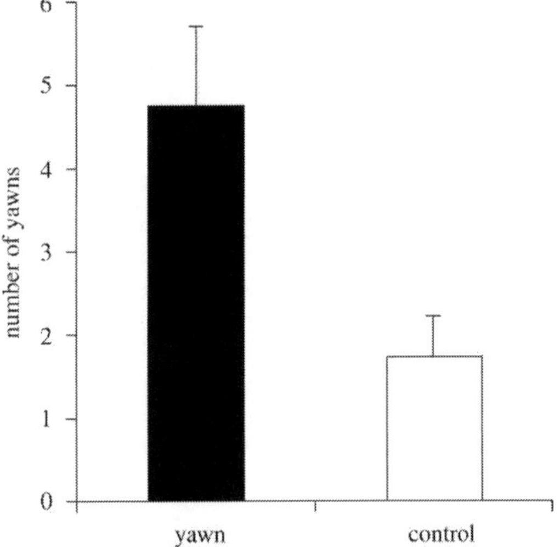

Figure 1: Mean (+standard error of mean) number of yawns per subject during the yawn and the control sessions

33) The author uses the word *repertoire* in Line 30 to signify

A) the set of all possible behaviors an animal can exhibit
B) the set of normal behaviors an animal exhibits
C) the set of all impossible behaviors an animal can exhibit
D) the set of all rare behaviors an animal can exhibit

34) What conclusions about the experiment can we draw from the chart and passage?

A) The chimpanzees identified with the animations, because of a significant difference between the yawn and control group.
B) The chimpanzees did not identify with the animations, because of a significant difference between the yawn and control group.
C) The chimpanzees identified with the animations, because of an insignificant difference between the yawn and control group.
D) The chimpanzees did not identify with the animations, because of an insignificant difference between the yawn and control group.

35) What is a central question the experiment is attempting to answer?

A) Do animals interpret artificial stimuli differently than natural stimuli?
B) How do animals sympathize with artificial renderings?
C) Is yawning contagious to animals?
D) What effect does three-dimensional computer animation have on modern science?

36) As used in line 43, what does conspecific most nearly mean?

A) Parallel objects
B) Similar actions
C) Unique stimuli
D) Same species

37) If the notion that non-human animals behave the same way that humans do towards artificial stimuli is true, then what applications could this have for the scientific community?

A) 3-D animations can be used to study the activity levels of humans
B) Yawning could be used to invoke emotional responses
C) Fabricated simulations can be designed to investigate animal behavior
D) POSER 6.0 can be used to discriminate between a multitude of human facial expressions

38) What was the primary finding of Anderson's study?

A) There is no significant difference in induced yawning with artificial stimuli.
B) The sample size was not representative of a population.
C) Stumptail macaques are less responsive to animations than chimpanzees
D) Chimpanzees respond better to artificial stimuli than control videos.

39) What element of 3-D computer animations make them better than videos of real-behavior?

A) Elimination of control variables
B) Additional control over behavior length
C) Ability to simulate actions not found in the natural world
D) Capability of producing multiple actions in a desired succession

40) How was the question "Do non-human animals view or process animated images the same way they do real images of conspecifics?" (lines 41-43) answered?

A) Determine willingness of animals to play games with simulated conspecifics
B) Check if animals react to artificial sounds differently than natural sounds
C) Compare images of animals and heterospecifics utilizing POSER 6.0
D) Have animals discriminate images collected from a digital library

41) What is the drawback in anatomical tests for this behavioral study?

A) More inaccurate than behavioral measures
B) Risk of harm to test subjects' neural networks
C) Restraining active test subjects
D) Animal research testing regulations

42) The data in the table best supports which of the following conclusions from the passage?

A) Computer animations are a flexible tool in the study of animal behavior
B) The inversion effect would not have been seen with a lower standard error.
C) Chimpanzees were caused to yawn by viewing the yawn animations.
D) Chimpanzees naturally yawned five times, but when forced to yawn, only yawned twice.

Questions 43-52 are based on the following passage

This passage is adapted from Michael Laver, "Most Exquisite Curiosities of Nature and Art: The Dutch East India Company, Objets d'Art and Gift Giving in Early Modern Japan". © 2013 by World History Connected.

In July 1654, the president of the Dutch factory on the island of Deshima noted in his diary that the Governor of Nagasaki was pleased with the presents that were liberally bestowed upon him by the Dutch East India Company (VOC) for that year. He continued on, in what can plausibly be construed as a piece of advice for his successors who would no doubt look back at the diary, stating, "You can see how one could capture and retain favors here with trifles." In a similar piece of advice offered a few years earlier, the chief merchant on Deshima noted in a tone of political calculation, "I think that this stratagem should be pursued in future, for it only costs the company a handful of spectacles, some telescopes, butter, tent wine, almonds, cheese, and other such trifles." The chief merchant might have included in this list a number of other luxury goods that were used as gifts for the influential ruling elite in Tokugawa Japan, some indeed mere trifles, but others anything but. Throughout the centuries, company servants recorded the shipment to Japan of such large animals as elephants, camels, Persian horses, and water buffalo, surely no mean logistical feat. Other goods were less bulky (and certainly less odorous), yet just as valuable. Included in this group are objects that could broadly be defined as art, items such as gilt timepieces, decorative globes with luxurious stands made of such material as ebony and silver, jewelry cases, mirrors, metal "lanterns," telescopes with elaborately crafted tubes, a variety of carpets, and more conventional art such as paintings and engravings. There is no doubt that these objects were given as gifts simply because they were exotic, but their value lay also in the fact that they were examples of the finest European craftsmanship of the time, characteristics that helped the Dutch to "capture and retain favor" with the ruling elite of early modern Japan.

Since 1609 the Dutch East India Company had been trading in western Japan, and from 1640 they were the only Europeans allowed to live and work in the country, albeit separated from the great majority of Japanese by their forced removal to the man made island of Deshima, separated from the city of Nagasaki by a bridge that was constantly guarded by a contingent of guards whose sole duty it was to ensure that the Dutch remained relatively isolated. The only Japanese allowed access to the island other than officials and merchants were prostitutes who were euphemistically referred to as "house keepers," and whom Englebert Kaempfer referred to uncharitably as "none of the best and handsomest." VOC trade was particularly profitable in Japan throughout the middle decades of the seventeenth century, largely because in return for silk and other Asian luxury goods, the company was able to procure exceedingly large amounts of precious metals: silver at first, and later gold and copper when silver exports were banned. In this context, it became important for company servants to maintain cordial relations with a whole host of officials, both in Nagasaki and at the shogun's court in Edo. The bestowal of lavish gifts on Japanese officialdom was a prime method of maintaining a good working relationship as well as currying favor with influential members of the shogunal government.

43) As used in line 10, what does "trifle" most nearly mean?

A) An item of little importance
B) A delicious dessert
C) An act of good faith
D) An intriguing secret

44) What would a visiting 17th century government representative likely present to a diplomat to improve relations?

A) A selection of exquisite pastries native to the diplomat's country.
B) A common replica of an ancient artifact
C) A letter of intent to domesticate the native inhabitants
D) An authentic work of art from the representative's nation

45) Who was NOT permitted access to Deshima?

A) Merchants
B) Government officials
C) Tailors
D) Prostitutes

46) As used in line 51, what does "euphemistically" most nearly mean?

A) Negatively
B) Politely
C) Insightfully
D) Bluntly

47) Who was the VOC trying to win over?

A) The Dutch government
B) The Deshima government
C) The Nagasaki government
D) The Shoguns of Japan

48) What was the primary purpose of gift-giving for the VOC?

A) The Japanese would overlook illegal operations
B) The Japanese would supply prostitutes and merchants
C) The VOC could open up trade networks with Japan
D) The VOC could use Japan's extensive natural resources

49) Which of the following exports were embargoed from Japan?

A) A precious metal
B) Silk
C) British Tea
D) European cheeses

50) Which choice best describes the main function of the passage?

A) A discussion of the intricacies of a company
B) An instructional guide on how to internationally trade
C) A list and explanation of the most valuable goods in Asia
D) An analysis of a historical interaction

51) When was the Dutch East India Company trade in Japan most successful?

A) 1600s
B) 1650s
C) 1750s
D) 1850s

52) What evidence from the passage best supports your answer above?

A) Lines 1-6 ("July 1654…year")
B) Lines 40-43 ("Since 1609…country")
C) Lines 54-56 ("VOC trade…century)
D) Lines 61-64 ("It became…Edo")

WRITING AND LANGUAGE: TEST 2: Section 2

35 MINUTES 44 QUESTIONS

Turn to section 2 of your answer sheet to answer the questions in this section.

Directions:

Each passage that follows require you to utilize your skillset in recognizing errors in proper sentence structure, rhetorical usage, and/or punctuation. Some may contain charts or graphs for you to decipher or revise.

Answer each carefully, as best as you can. If there are no errors, choose NO CHANGE.

Questions 1-11 refer to the following passage.

The Dept. of Motor Vehicles

It has come to my attention that the myriad rules that form the comprehensive legal framework within the Department of Motor Vehicles in most States are both chaotic and confusing all at once. The department handles all new license-seeking registrants and potential drivers, [1] <u>who in turn take exams showing</u> their proficiency as it pertains to the rules of the road. [2] <u>In any event</u>, the department manages registration and titles for all vehicles according to the individual State's laws. Finally, to add to the complexity of the department, and in no less importance, the department [3] <u>tracked</u> all tickets and motor vehicle violations under an arbitrary system that makes no sense at all.

1)

A) NO CHANGE
B) who, in turn, take exams to show
C) which, in turn, take exams to show
D) who in turn taking exams showing

2)

A) NO CHANGE
B) Without a doubt
C) Although
D) Furthermore

3)

A) NO CHANGE
B) tracks
C) had tracked
D) had been tracking

[4] The biggest gripe many residents have with the DMV is their points system where motor vehicle violations supposedly award points to drivers based on the severity of the violations themselves. Complicating things further, the DMV has two separate categories under moving violations and [5] violations where your vehicle is not moving, yet points accumulate under a single unified track. Some special violations incur the full wrath of the DMV in the form of an immediate suspension or revocation of a driver's license without possibility of an appeal.

Fail to stop for a stop sign? 3 points. Illegal U-turn? 3 points. Drive 10 miles over the speed limit? 2 points. Accumulate your first 6 points, your license gets suspended for 30 days automatically. Drive past a school bus with flashing red lights? 5 points plus an automatic 60-day suspension. All of [6] this violations incur severe fines. Fail to pay your fine on a timely basis? Automatic suspension of your license for one full year. Plus additional fines. And more points. With possible jail time, arbitrarily based upon the Judge's decision at the time of your hearing. Oh, I'm sorry, you didn't make it to the hearing? You are now found in contempt of court and will carry a criminal misdemeanor charge against you for the rest of your life. More serious crimes such as driving under the influence (DUI) will cost you a hefty fine, points against your license, jail time, and automatic suspension of your license for a year or more all at once. [7] Residents would like to see some changes in reforming the DMV.

4) Which of the following choices best represents a continuity in thought from the previous paragraph?

A) NO CHANGE
B) The best system the DMV is proud of
C) What the law enforcement agencies find most confusing
D) Laws seem to have no effect on one thing, and that

5)

A) NO CHANGE
B) sedentary violations
C) non-moving violations
D) egregious violations

6)

A) NO CHANGE
B) such
C) those
D) these

7)

At this point, the author would like to add the following sentence:

> Serious moving violations such as hit-and-run that causes bodily harm to another automatically incur a felony charge in most States with massive fines, imprisonment, and immediate revocation of your license.

A) Yes, because it lays the foundation for the reforms needed in the DMV.
B) Yes, because it is an example of a complication in the system.
C) No, because the claim is inaccurate according to previous statements in the passage.
D) No, because the information is redundant.

Since the 1950's, the DMV has long held the position of educator, disseminator, and adjudicator for drivers of automobiles. Unfortunately, times have changed. Drivers include not only cyclists and mopeds, [8] but Lyft and Uber drivers who work commercially on their own time. Manuals and information [9] has essentially remain unchanged during all this time period. This is not good and has caused many of the functions within the DMV to become even slower than they already were.

For the DMV to remain relevant and efficient, it must adapt to the changing circumstances of the modern day. I propose a total overhaul of the DMV's rules, [10] that currently are almost impossible for the common person to decipher. While a certain degree of pedantry is inevitable in any bureaucratic institution, it ought to be our goal to make life as easy as possible for the working people of our nation to do something as simple as getting their license renewed. [11]

8)

A) NO CHANGE
B) yet
C) but also
D) however, also include

9)

A) NO CHANGE
B) have essentially remain unchanged
C) has essentially remained unchanging
D) have essentially remained unchanged

10)

A) NO CHANGE
B) which
C) these rules
D) those rules

11)

Which sentence most logically concludes the passage?

A) The rulebook of the DMV is confusing and excessively long, so it must be shortened and simplified.
B) Modern problems require modern solutions, and the DMV's procedures don't account for modern technologies that comprise our daily lives.
C) The point system is the main problem that should be reformed in this new system.
D) Making the DMV just a little bit less annoying and arbitrary than everyone seems to find it is thus a worthwhile and necessary endeavor.

Questions 12-22 refer to the following passage.

Goodbye Yellow Brick Road

"So goodbye, yellow brick road, where the dogs of society howl. You can't lock me in a penthouse; I'm going back to my trough." The path to fame and success is much like Dorothy's yellow brick road from the Wizard of Oz. Seeming to never end, [12] <u>artists are expected to follow the road</u> to some lofty goal of better entertaining the world. However, after a long career riddled with hardships, the road loses some of its shine to artists. Even though Elton John wrote "Goodbye Yellow Brick Road" when he was 36, the 71-year-old's decision to hang up his microphone and piano [13] <u>bring</u> to mind the old verse.

(1) Anyone alive during Elton's rise to fame would find his music to be as ground-breaking now as [14] <u>then</u>. (2) His music was fun and family-friendly, while being as glamorous as he was. (3) Even more influential than his music was his presence as a performer. (4) Heart-shaped glasses, feathered jackets, and tight pants were certainly popular in that age of Bowie and [15] <u>Mercury, thus, they</u> only served to boost Elton John's popularity as a public figure. (5) The Elton John hit machine was unprecedented, producing songs like the glitzy "Benny and the Jets" to the soulful "Rocket Man." [16]

12)

A) NO CHANGE
B) artists' lives have been planned out in order
C) the road that artists must travel leads
D) one must understand the hardship of traveling a road

13)

A) NO CHANGE
B) brings
C) will bring
D) had brought

14)

A) NO CHANGE
B) was then
C) used to be
D) it was then

15)

A) NO CHANGE
B) Mercury; thus, they
C) Mercury so they
D) Mercury and thus, they

16)

To make the paragraph most logical, sentence 5 should be moved to

A) before sentence 1.
B) after sentence 2.
C) after sentence 3.
D) where it is now.

Even Elton's most loyal fans might be surprised to learn of his success as a composer. His career was prolific, [17] it provided the music for Disney's *The Lion King* and its Broadway adaptation along with the West End production *Billy Elliot the Musical*. He even forayed into the hip-hop industry after a performance with Eminem at the 2001 Grammys. [18] A recent cover of Khalid's *Young, Dumb, and Broke* was recorded by Elton for Spotify, where the hip-hop phenom Khalid made a surprise feature.

Despite his recent activity, Elton John has finally decided that it's time for him to give it up. In a recent interview, Elton—citing concerns about his [19] voice, stated his intention to retire. Elton John's farewell tour is already getting sold out at its events a year from now and is slated to be larger than [20] any other retiring star. Vendors love the tour because [21] they provide the concert scene with an injection of revenue from old-timers wanting to see Elton one last time. His most ardent fans, of course, maintain that he should stay in the industry. After all the music he has given us, Elton John is more than entitled to feel [22] complacent with his legacy.

17)

A) NO CHANGE
B) providing
C) it serving to provide
D) having been provided

18)

The author is considering deleting the underlined sentence. Should the sentence be kept or deleted?

A) Kept, because it provides a contrast with Elton's performance at the Grammys.
B) Kept, because it exemplifies the foray mentioned in the previous sentence.
C) Deleted, because it blurs the focus of the paragraph by introducing an unrelated detail that goes unexplained.
D) Deleted, because it doesn't provide an effective transition to the next paragraph.

19)

A) NO CHANGE
B) voice
C) voice—
D) voice, he

20)

A) NO CHANGE
B) has been any
C) that of any
D) those of any

21)

A) NO CHANGE
B) those provide
C) their events provide
D) it provides

22)

A) NO CHANGE
B) smug
C) gratified
D) conceited

Questions 23-33 refer to the following passage.

How the Other Half Lived

While one must be careful to not consider poverty a [23] forgone problem (as it still exists), few remember how bad it was just 100 years ago. Even at the time, few in the upper half of society realized the impact that low wages had on the quality of life of the working poor. The Progressive Party was formed primarily to deal with issues of workers, but it subsequently [24] became difficult to get anyone to care.
[25] In fact, the public consciousness was convinced that the poor could rise to the top through the hard work displayed in dime novels. One new technology and one inspired individual worked to change that perception: the camera was powerful in the hands of Jacob Riis.

The Danish-American was described by his opponents as a "muckraker." [26] Riis went where other journalists were unwilling to go. The tenement houses of New York housed [27] laborers, who made the city tick, in its walls. Riis captured undeniable evidence of the abject conditions of these laborers in his article *How the Other Half Lives*.

23)

A) NO CHANGE
B) inevitable
C) bygone
D) untenable

24)

A) NO CHANGE
B) had become
C) had been
D) would have been

25)

A) NO CHANGE
B) In addition
C) However
D) Therefore

26)

At this point the author is considering adding the following sentence:

"He and his contemporaries certainly dug up plenty of dirt on the corrupt institutions of the time."

Should the author make this addition?

A) Yes, because it expands on the main focus of the passage.
B) Yes, because it clarifies the meaning of the term introduced in the previous sentence.
C) No, because it introduces a loosely related detail that blurs the focus of the paragraph.
D) No, because it doesn't adhere to the formal tone established by the author.

27)

A) NO CHANGE
B) laborers who
C) laborers that
D) the laborers that

The article contained photographs of the poor packed like sardines into tenement rooms. [28] The article was first published in the Christmas edition of Scribner's magazine. Famously, Theodore Roosevelt, concerned that a number of hidden issues [29] were plaguing the city, consulted with Riis, calling him "the most useful citizen of New York." The article was less well-received [30] in powerful political figures interested in maintaining status quo conditions.

Both major parties had dominant factions looking to silence figures like Riis and his fellow muckrakers like Upton Sinclair. The public, meanwhile, was extremely dissatisfied with the conditions the parties were trying to protect; [31] however, support for both Democrats and Republicans dwindled. The photographs taken by Riis ended up indirectly causing the [32] surprising rise of a new political party: the Progressives. Leaving a lasting mark on the public consciousness, their members eventually expanded to include politicians like Roosevelt. Roosevelt, as well as his compatriots, [33] have muckrakers like Riis to thank for exposing the truth behind *How the Other Half Lives*.

28)

Which choice best sets up the information that follows in the next part of the paragraph?

A) NO CHANGE
B) The poor were quite unmoved by the contents of the book, which were part of their everyday existence.
C) The article reached the eyes of influential people and spurred social change.
D) Riis peppered the article with his salient wit, critiquing the ignorance exhibited by society up to that point.

29)

A) NO CHANGE
B) was plaguing
C) were being plagued by
D) plague

30)

A) NO CHANGE
B) by
C) for
D) amongst

31)

A) NO CHANGE
B) instead
C) so
D) thus

32)

The writer wants to emphasize how the dominant two-party system experienced its first major challenge in American history. Which choice most effectively accomplishes this goal?

A) NO CHANGE
B) unprecedented
C) shocking
D) flabbergasting

33)

A) NO CHANGE
B) has
C) will have
D) have had

Questions 34-44 refer to the following passage.

Manipulation of Memory

When a witness swears solemnly to "tell the truth, the whole truth, and nothing but the truth, juries are typically instructed to take their testimony to be [34] bona fide. Taking a closer look at the way that memory functions, which has required new [35] technology. Researchers have found evidence that suggests memory is as about as reliable as video. This is not to say that it's trustworthy, but rather that it can be easily altered by someone with the right skills.

This issue [36] had not been so problematic if it weren't for pre-trial "coaching." Lawyers will go over the sequence of events with a witness to make sure they "remember" what happened. Due to the phenomenon of neuroplasticity, or the ability of our brain cells to change, this altered sequence of events or other details "slipped" into pre-trial discussions sometimes [37] plants information into the mind of the witness. Largely treated as conjecture, recent research has shown how "coaching" can harm the sanctity of the criminal justice system.

34)

Which choice best maintains the style and tone of the passage?

A) NO CHANGE
B) hunky-dory
C) accurate
D) spot-on

35)

A) NO CHANGE
B) technology, researchers
C) technology, and researchers
D) technology; researchers

36)

A) NO CHANGE
B) has not been
C) would not be
D) will not be

37)

A) NO CHANGE
B) plant
C) has planted
D) will be planted

[38] Interested in participating, researchers showed subjects a short video just moments before giving them a short quiz on its events. In between the video and the quiz, the subjects were given a short written summary of events. Half of the subjects were [39] randomly, by chance given false descriptions of certain events, while the rest were given normal ones. The ones who received the false descriptions scored significantly worse on the quiz. [40] Even more alarming to researchers, however, was the type of people most affected by this deception.

Researchers mostly believe that the problem with coaching is not its inherent flaws, but the groups that it targets. Most susceptible to having their memory affected [41] were the very old, the very young, and those who had recently experienced a trauma. The criminal justice system is certainly not meant to target the weak, but rather [42] for helping them. Allowing lawyers to alter the testimony of a witness, especially of those who are already preyed on the most, is surely unethical.

38)

A) NO CHANGE
B) Consisting of a short cartoon
C) Containing true or false questions
D) Testing the ability to affect memory

39)

A) NO CHANGE
B) randomly, contingently
C) randomly, they were by chance
D) randomly

40)

Which choice provides the most effective transition to the next paragraph?

A) NO CHANGE
B) Researchers were concerned that coaching is used in not only civil trials, but also criminal ones.
C) Coaching as a practice was, however, seen as largely beneficial by these same researchers.
D) This general result was the main factor that concerned researchers.

41)

A) NO CHANGE
B) was
C) DELETE the underlined section and replace with a comma and appropriate spacing.
D) DELETE the underlined section, END the previous sentence with a period, and START the new sentence with a capital letter.

42)

A) NO CHANGE
B) so as to help
C) to help
D) to have helped

The million-dollar question remains how to reform the criminal justice system to avoid this type of exploitation. Even more pressingly, [43] who do we look to that can lead this reform? Until the USCJS finds a reformer worthy of his or her title, any reform is unlikely. In the meantime, if you ever get jury duty, be sure to take everything [44] they tell you with a grain of salt.

43)

A) NO CHANGE
B) whose do we look to
C) to whom do we look
D) to whom do we look to

44)

A) NO CHANGE
B) we
C) researchers
D) witnesses

MATHEMATICS TEST 2, NO CALCULATOR: Section 3

25 MINUTES, 20 QUESTIONS

Turn to section 3 of your answer sheet to answer the questions in this section.

Directions

For questions 1-15, solve each problem, choose the best answer from the choices provided, and fill in the corresponding circle on your answer sheet. For questions 16-20, solve the problem and enter your answer in the grid on the answer sheet. You may use any available space in your test booklet for scratch work.

Notes

1. The use of a calculator is permitted.
2. All variables and expressions represent real numbers unless otherwise indicated.
3. Figures provided are drawn to scale unless indicated.
4. All figures lie in a plane unless indicated.
5. Unless indicated, the domain for each function is all real numbers.

Reference Formulas and Shapes

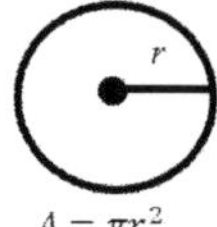

$A = \pi r^2$

$C = \pi d$ or $2\pi r$

$A = l \times w$

$P = 2(l + w)$

$A = \frac{1}{2}(b \times h)$

Pythagorean Theorem

$a^2 + b^2 = c^2$

1, 2, $\sqrt{3}$, 60°, 30°

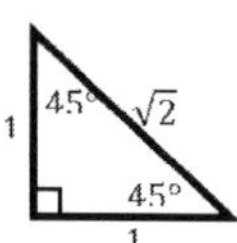

Common Right Triangles

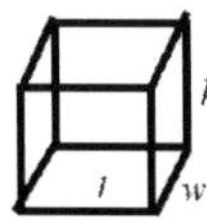

$V = l \times w \times h$

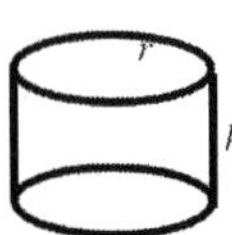

$V = \pi r^2 h$

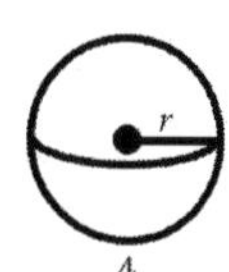

$V = \frac{4}{3}\pi r^3$

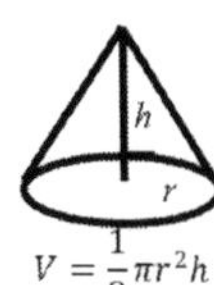

$V = \frac{1}{3}\pi r^2 h$

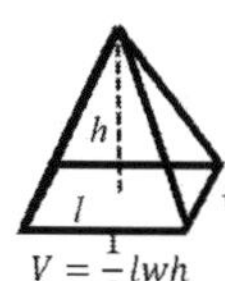

$V = \frac{1}{3}lwh$

A circle contains 360 degrees and 2π radians.
The sum of the angles of a triangle is 180.

---

1) If $\frac{k+3}{k} = 7$, what is the value of k?

A) $\frac{3}{8}$
B) $\frac{1}{2}$
C) 2
D) 4

2) What is the simplified expression of $(x^2 + 7x)x - (3x^2 - 3y + 9x)$?

A) $3x^2 + 3y - 2x$
B) $2x^2 + 3y + 16x$
C) $x^3 + 4x^2 + 3y - 9x$
D) $3x^3 + 3y + 16x$

3) If $\frac{1}{5}x + \frac{3}{4}y = 10$, what is the value of 4x + 15y?

A) 20
B) 50
C) 200
D) 300

4)
$$3x + 2y = 14$$
$$x + y = 4$$

Given the system of equations above, what is the value of 2xy?

A) -24
B) 3
C) 6
D) 12

5) The quadratic $x^2 + 7x + c$ has real roots at -5 and -2. What is the value of c?

A) -7
B) 3
C) 10
D) 14

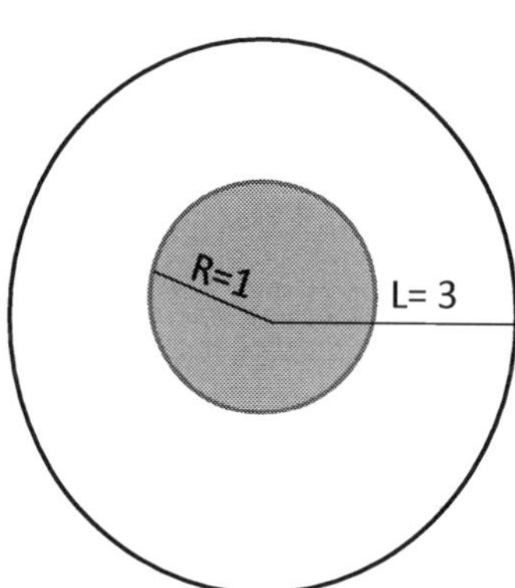

6) Based on the figure above, what is the area of the non-shaded region if R is the radius from the center of the inner circle to the end of the inner circle, and L is the radius from the center of the inner circle to the end of the outer circle?

A) π
B) 3π
C) 4π
D) 8π

7) Laura is a grocer at the local supermarket. She helps a certain number of customers, c, each hour. If Laura assists 5,200 customers in a year (52 weeks), and works every weekday from 9AM to 5PM with no break, then what is the value of 8c?

A) 4
B) 15
C) 20
D) 30

8) On a Friday night, John drives at 20 mph down a 5-mile stretch of road. Arman drives down that same road, but at 33 mph. Approximately how much longer does it take John to reach the end of the road than Arman?

A) 0.1 hrs.
B) 0.15 hrs.
C) 0.25 hrs.
D) 0.5 hrs.

9) Ashley goes to the bank to take out a loan. The bank gives Ashley a $5000 loan with 8% interest compounded monthly. Which expression represents the amount of money Ashley owes the bank after t years?

A) $5000(1.08)^t$
B) $(5000)(12t)(0.08)$
C) $5000e^{0.08t}$
D) $5000\left(1+\frac{0.08}{12}\right)^{12t}$

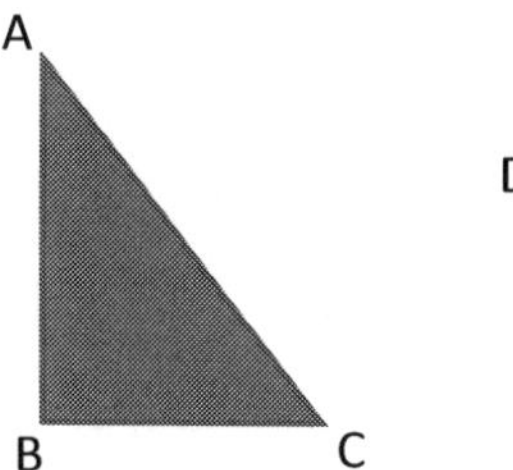

10) Given similar right triangles ΔABC and ΔEFD above, the length of segment BC is 6 and the length of segment FD is 3. If FE is 4, then what is the length of the hypotenuse AC?

A) 5
B) 7
C) 8
D) 10

11) Solve for x in the equation $x^2 + 7x + 14 = 0$.

A) -2
B) -1
C) 1
D) No real solutions

12) What ordered pair (x,y) satisfies the inequality $2x + y < xy$?

A) (0,4)
B) (1,3)
C) (2,5)
D) (0,0)

13) What is a possible solution to the equation $\frac{32x+64}{x^2-4} - \frac{16}{x-2} = 4$?

A) 2
B) 6
C) 14
D) None of the above

14) A guest list for a party contains 15 guests whose average age is exactly 20. If Max and the Wilson twins (3 people) are added to the list and the average age jumps to exactly 21, what is the average age of the 3 people added?

A) 25
B) 26
C) 27
D) 28

15) Hayley is conducting a biology project where she wants to understand the nature of bacteria growth. Her data is shown below. What graph best represents the growth of her bacteria qualitatively?

Day	Amount of Bacterium (Hundreds)
0 (Initial)	12
1	23
2	49
3	99
4	213
5	409
6	836

A) 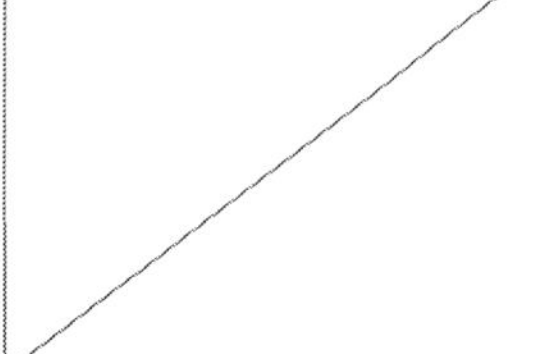

B) 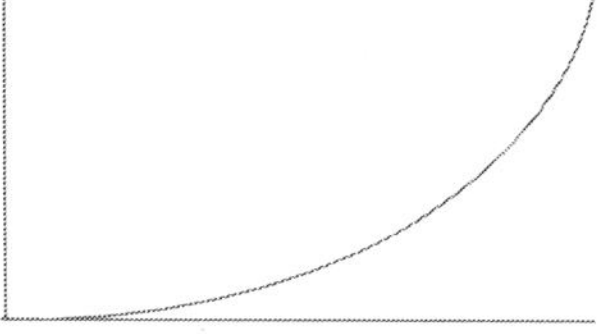

C) 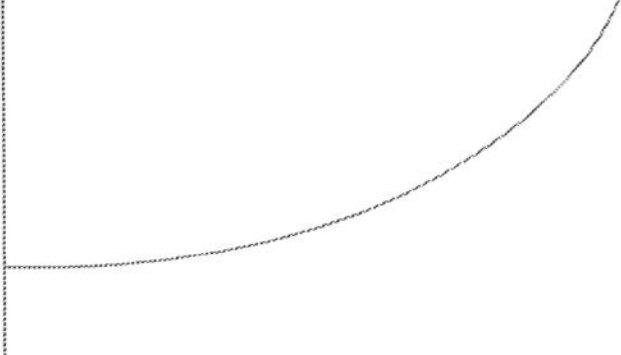

D) 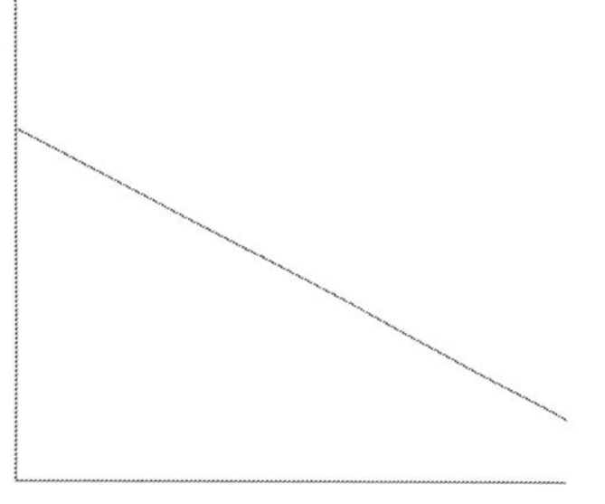

PITTSBURGH PREP

GRID-IN

16) Rachel, a world traveler, has $52 to spend on food on a trip to Germany. If she only has two options available to her, sandwiches at $3 each and salads at $7 each, what is the largest number of sandwiches Rachel can get if she wants a salad with every sandwich?

17) Rachel makes her trip to Germany every month for an entire year. The usual cost for the trip is $1500. But, because of her frequent flyer discount, she gets every fourth trip 10% off. How much, in dollars, does Rachel save in a year from her frequent flyer discount?
(12 months in a year auxiliary?)

18) What is a possible real solution to the following quadratic equation $3x^2 - 15x + 12 = 0$?

19) If $\sin^2(x) = \frac{16}{25}$ and $-\frac{\pi}{2} \leq x \leq \frac{\pi}{2}$. then what is the value of 2cos(x)?

20) What is the slope of the line perpendicular to the line which has points (1,4) and (-3,6)?

PITTSBURGH PREP

MATHEMATICS TEST 2, CALCULATOR: Section 4

55 MINUTES, 38 QUESTIONS

Turn to section 4 of your answer sheet to answer the questions in this section.

Directions

For questions 1-29, solve each problem, choose the best answer from the choices provided, and fill in the corresponding circle on your answer sheet. For questions 30-38, solve the problem and enter your answer in the grid on the answer sheet. You may use any available space in your test booklet for scratch work.

Notes

1. The use of a calculator is permitted.
2. All variables and expressions represent real numbers unless otherwise indicated.
3. Figures provided are drawn to scale unless indicated.
4. All figures lie in a plane unless indicated.
5. Unless indicated, the domain for each function is all real numbers.

Reference Formulas and Shapes

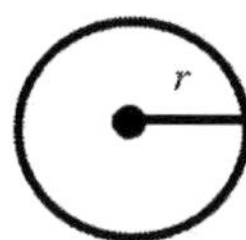

$A = \pi r^2$

$C = \pi d \text{ or } 2\pi r$

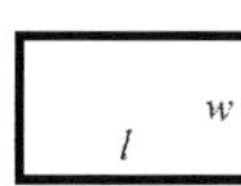

$A = l \times w$

$P = 2(l + w)$

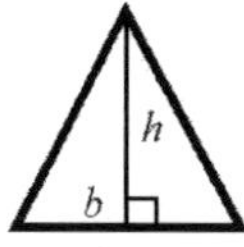

$A = \frac{1}{2}(b \times h)$

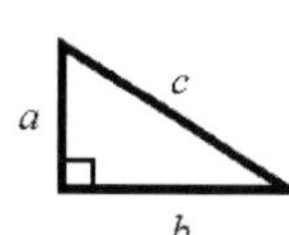

Pythagorean Theorem

$a^2 + b^2 = c^2$

1, 2, 60°, 30°, $\sqrt{3}$

1, 45°, $\sqrt{2}$, 45°, 1

Common Right Triangles

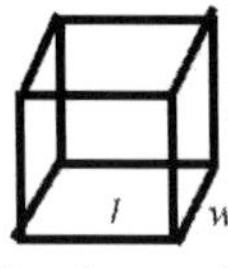

$V = l \times w \times h$

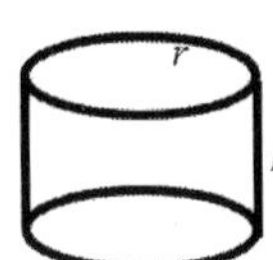

$V = \pi r^2 h$

$V = \frac{4}{3}\pi r^3$

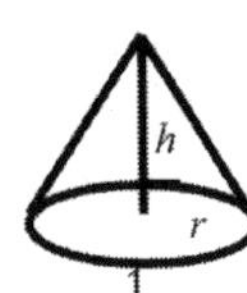

$V = \frac{1}{3}\pi r^2 h$

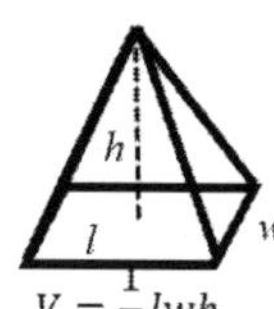

$V = \frac{1}{3}lwh$

A circle contains 360 degrees and 2π radians.
The sum of the angles of a triangle is 180.

---

1) What is the value of the function $f(x) = |x - 3| - 5$ at x=2

A) 4
B) -4
C) -1
D) -6

2) Joey, Paul, and Adam all take a test. The teacher states that the average among the three students is an 87%. What is the new average, to the nearest whole percent, if Chris's score of 78% is factored in?

   A) 80%
   B) 82%
   C) 84%
   D) 85%

3) The number of cars bought from a dealership in a day is represented with the following equation: C=32+5t, where C is the number of cars bought and t is the time elapsed in hours. Which of the following could the value of 32 best represent?

   A) The number of cars bought online from the dealership, where purchases are updated daily.
   B) The number of cars sold per hour by the dealership
   C) The number of cars the dealership has available to sell
   D) The number of cars the dealership sold the day before

4) The amount of time that it takes Josh to run is directly proportional to the distance that he runs. If Josh runs three miles in twenty minutes, then how long in **hours** does it take Josh to run 10 miles?

   A) 0.9 hours
   B) 1.1 hours
   C) 6 hours
   D) 66.7 hours

5) Bart works at a sub shop, where he makes several sandwiches each day. Last Friday, Bart made 6 more sandwiches than he did on Thursday. If Bart made 15% more sandwiches on Friday than Thursday, then how many sandwiches did he make on Friday?

   A) 24
   B) 40
   C) 46
   D) 90

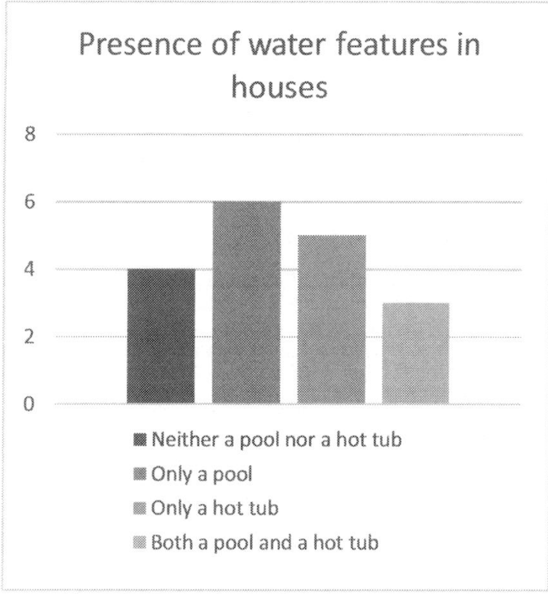

6) Within a neighborhood, a survey was conducted on all of the houses to find out how many houses had pools, hot tubs, or both. What is the ratio of houses that have a pool to the total houses in the neighborhood?

A) 1:1
B) 1:2
C) 1:3
D) 11:18

7) Susan enjoys cross-training. Each morning, Susan runs at 8 miles an hour and bikes at 15 miles an hour. Susan wants to log at least 30 miles in at most three hours. If x is how many miles she runs and y is how many miles Susan bikes, which of the following systems of inequalities represents Susan's activity?

A) $\begin{gathered}15x + 8y \geq 30 \\ x + y \geq 3\end{gathered}$

B) $\begin{gathered}8x + 15y \geq 30 \\ x + y \geq 3\end{gathered}$

C) $\begin{gathered}\frac{1}{8}x + \frac{1}{15}y \geq 30 \\ x + y \geq 3\end{gathered}$

D) $\begin{gathered}8x + 15y \geq 30 \\ x + y \leq 3\end{gathered}$

8) Miriam has a block of fudge. She gives half of her fudge to Enrique, gives one quarter of the rest of the fudge to Marta, eats two-thirds of what's left, and throws the rest away. If she threw away 15 grams of fudge, how much did she start with?

A) 30
B) 60
C) 120
D) 180

9) What is the equation of Circle C, containing point P, as shown below?

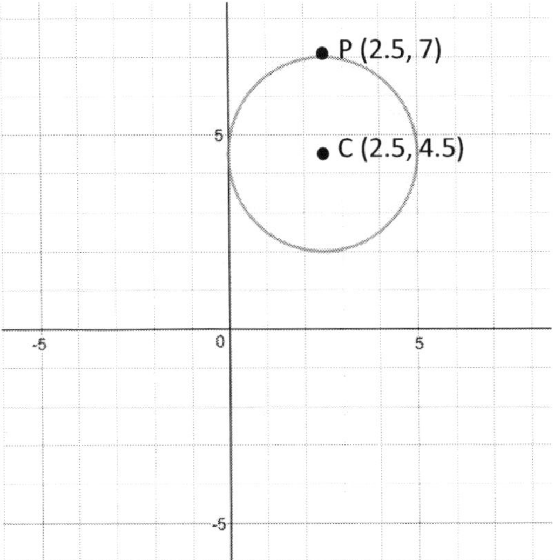

A) $(x+2.5)^2+y^2=2.5^2$
B) $(x-5)^2+(y-4.5)^2=2.5^2$
C) $(x+2.5)^2+(y+4.5)^2 \ =2.5^2$
D) $(x-2.5)^2+(y-4.5)^2=2.5^2$

10) Jesse and Julia are collecting data on velocity of a skateboard on a ramp. Initially, the skateboard is moving at 4 meters/second (m/s). At t=1 second, the skateboard is moving at 9 m/s. At t=2 seconds, the skateboard is moving at 14 m/s. At t=4 seconds, the skateboard is moving at 24 m/s. What equation best describes the skateboard's velocity with time as the independent variable and acceleration as the dependent variable?

A) $v(t)=5t+4$
B) $v(t)=25t^2+16$
C) $v(t)=7t^2+4$
D) $v(t)=4t+5$

11) For a more conventional SAT fractions/percentages question, an alternative might be: Aziz donates one-fourth of his baseball card collection to Chris, whose card collection increases by 50%. If Chris has 12 cards in his collection after the donation, how many cards did Aziz originally have?

A) 12
B) 16
C) 24
D) 48

12) Justin goes to the gym every day. He increases the amount of weight he lifts each day by the same amount. He starts off lifting 10lbs., and at the end of two weeks, he is lifting 80 lbs. What equation best describes the amount of weight, W, Justin is lifting after t days?

A) W=35t+10
B) W=70
C) W=5t
D) W=5t+10

13) Greg, who works in a high-end pizzeria, earns a base pay of $23.50 an hour plus a certain amount of tips. Greg works on average 45 hours in a week and made $7025 in the first six weeks of the year. What percent of his money earned was from tips?

A) 9.7
B) 12
C) 36
D) 40

14) If $-\frac{49}{11} < -3z + 6 < -\frac{17}{7}$ for an integer z, what is the greatest possible value of 9z-18?

A) -9
B) -1
C) 3
D) 9

15) $(x-2)^2 + y^2 = 16$
$x + y = 4$

The equations above represent the graph of a circle and a line that intersects the circle at two points. What two quadrants are the points of intersection located in?

A) II and III
B) I and III
C) II and IV
D) I and IV

16) Line m contains points (9,3) and (4,8). If line m is parallel to line n, then which of the following set of points could be on line n?

A) (5,3) and (7,1)
B) (11,2) and (9,3)
C) (4,8) and (5,7)
D) (9,1) and (10,11)

17) Consider f(x)=$x^2 2^x$ for all real numbers. If f(a)=72, a must be

A) 3
B) 4
C) 5
D) 7

18) What is the difference between the median and mode of the following set of integers?

S: {17, 92, 23, 55, 84, 84, 12, 17, 10, 67, 17}

A) 6
B) 14
C) 17
D) 55

19) Suppose f(x)=x^2+7x and g(x)=x^3+3. What is $(f \circ g)$ (3)?

A) 900
B) 27,000
C) 963
D) $3x^5 + 21x^4 + 9x^2 + 63x$

20) The data shown below represents the relationship between height and weight of professional wrestlers, with its line of best fit. Based on the data, height and weight have a

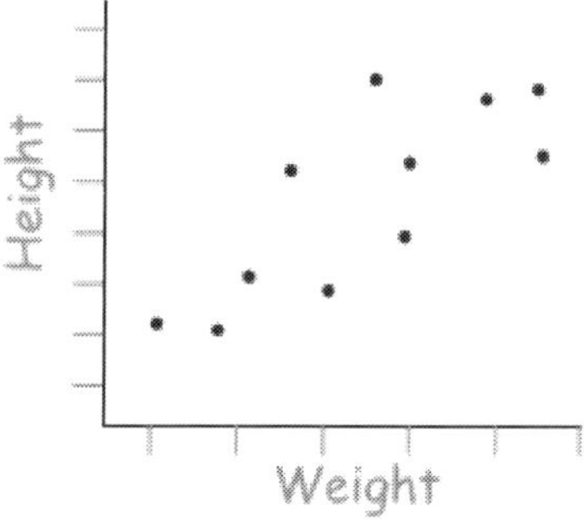

A) weak positive association.
B) strong positive association.
C) weak negative association.
D) strong negative association.

21) Rob drinks a can of soda with every meal that he eats in a day. A soda costs Rob 2$, and the rest of the meal costs him, on average, 15$. How many extra cans of soda can Rob get after a full day (three meals), if he has a daily budget of 60$.

A) 9
B) 5
C) 4
D) 15

22) Janice goes to the bank, looking to take out a loan. The bank agrees and determines an expression for the amount of money that Janice has to pay back in t years: $P=1500(1.50)^t$. How much does Janice owe the bank after a year, in dollars?

A) 2250
B) 1500
C) 750
D) 2000

23) The straight-line distance between Washington, D.C. and New York is 204 miles, and that between New York and Montreal is 332 miles. Which of the following could be the straight-line distance between Washington, D.C. and Montreal, in miles?

A) 105
B) 490
C) 540
D) 605

24) Given that $i = \sqrt{-1}$, what is the value of the expression $(x + i)(x - i)$ when x=3?

A) 8
B) 9i
C) 10
D) 9-6i-1

25) sin(60-x) = cos(x^2 +18), where all angle measures are in degrees and x is a positive angle. Which of the following could be the value of x?

A) 3
B) 4
C) 5
D) 6

26) A certain high school Biology curriculum offers the option of practice tests prior to every test. Before the year-end final exam, 37 out of the 240 students opted to take the practice test. Students in the two groups are shown to have approximately the same skill level as shown by pretest scores. when it comes to Biology. Out of these 37 students, 23 students scored in the first quartile range of the test. 30 kids who did not take the practice test scored in the first quartile range of the test. What is an appropriate conclusion you can make from this information?

A) Taking practice tests leads to poorer performance on the actual test.
B) There is no benefit to taking practice tests.
C) Taking practice tests leads to greater performances on the actual test.
D) There is not enough information to support any of the choices.

27) A survey was conducted to determine the most popular types of cereals in a local supermarket. The manager of the supermarket asks that each customer fill out the survey on a certain day. The data from the survey is shown below.

Types of Cereal	Adults purchasing cereal for kids	Adults purchasing cereal for themselves
Low Sugar Content	238	393
High Sugar Content	413	456

If a random customer purchases a cereal, what is the probability that he or she purchasing low sugar content cereal for his or her kids?

A) 15.8%
B) 18.9%
C) 42.1%
D) 43.4%

28) How many solutions are there to the systems of equations shown below?

$$3x + 12y = 4$$
$$18x = 24 - 72y$$
$$x + 4y = \frac{4}{3}$$

A) Zero
B) One
C) Two
D) Infinite

29) Line L intersects Line M at the point (4,3). If Line L contains the point (6, -1) and the two lines are perpendicular, which of the following could be a point on Line M?

A) (1, 9)
B) (2, 4)
C) (5, 5)
D) (6, 4)

30) What is the remainder when the function f(x) = x^4 – x^2 + 7x – 10 is divided by x+1?

A) -19
B) -17
C) -3
D) 0

GRID-IN

31) In the xy-plane, the function $f(x)=4x^2-3$ and the function $g(x)=2x-3$ intersect at two points. How far apart are these points?

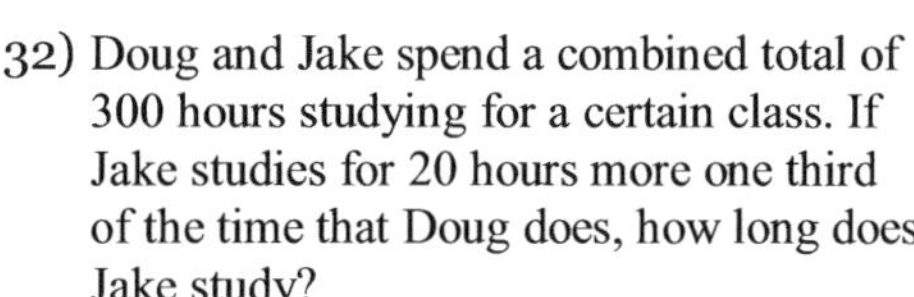

32) Doug and Jake spend a combined total of 300 hours studying for a certain class. If Jake studies for 20 hours more one third of the time that Doug does, how long does Jake study?

33) Given the circle O below, the radius OA=5 and the chord AB has a shortest distance of 3 from the center of the circle. The arc AB is 12 units. What is the measure of angle AOB, in radians?

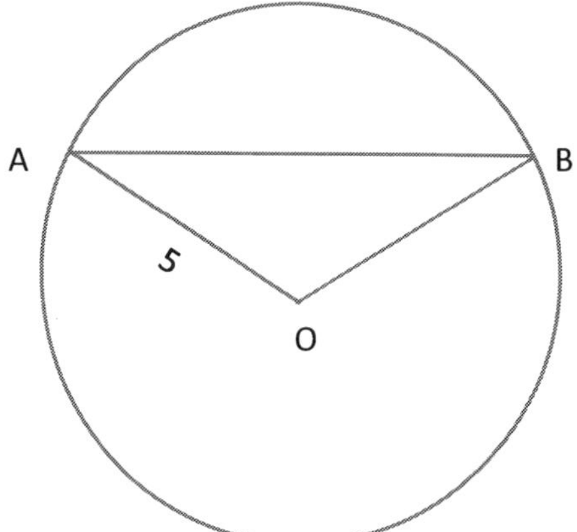

34) A triangle is transformed by a height increase of x percent and a base decrease of 12 percent. If the area of the triangle decreased by 10%, what is the value of x to the nearest whole percent?

35) A Spanish class took a quiz with scores ranging from 65-100. The average score of the first thirty students who took the exam was an 83. What is the highest possible score the thirty first student can get if the new average is 81 with thirty-five students accounted for?

36) Carbon-14 has a half life of 5730 years, meaning it exponentially decays to half of its initial mass every 5730 years. If a 1000-year old sample is 50 grams, what was the initial mass of the sample to the nearest gram?

37)

$$2x - y = 44$$
$$5x - by = 110$$

The system of equations above has infinite solutions. Find the value of b.

38) A high-school cross country team took varying amounts of time to finish a 5K. The times are recorded below. If the mean time taken to complete the race was exactly 20 minutes, then what is the value of x to the nearest minute?

Number of Runners	Time Taken (minutes)
1	17
2	18
3	X
4	22
5	19

End of Exam

Refer to Pittsburgh Prep's SAT Practice Exam 2 *Answer Explanations* to review and score this exam

PITTSBURGH
PREP

SAT PRACTICE TEST #2

Answer Explanations

Proper methods of review:

1. **Always read every single word in this packet. Make sure to not skim, and thoroughly understand the correct as well as the incorrect choices.**
2. **Reason out the "why" – as in, why is this answer correct? And why did I get this question wrong? Or why is this not the correct choice?**
3. **Make certain you can identify your particular issue at hand – did you miss a factual question? Was a deduction question? If so, how can you make sure you can improve on these question types in the future?**
4. **Review this packet for all question, including the questions that you answered correctly on test day.**
5. **Stay positive! SAT scores ain't nuthin but a numba, dawg. Keep your head up and maintain bro.**

Section 1: Reading Test

QUESTION 1

Choice A is the best answer. This is a factual question. Gines approaches Caleb to inform him that "the rules with which the soft-hearted squire indulges [him], are all England, Scotland, and Wales. But [he is] not to go out of these climates." (lines 49-52). Thus, Gines will be forced to find and bring Caleb in immediately if he even attempts to leave England via shop.

Choice B is wrong since Gines makes no mention of prisoner rights. Choice C is incorrect because there is no mention or evidence of a third convict in England in the passage. Choice D is incorrect because there is no evidence suggesting the lack of authority Gines has in this case.

QUESTION 2

Choice C is the best answer. This is an evidence question. B is the only choice which supports the fact that Caleb cannot leave the U.K. Gines warns Caleb to "not to go out of these climates", (line 52) meaning the U.K. The fact that "the soft-hearted squire indulges you, are all England, Scotland, and Wales" (line 51) goes to show that Caleb is currently able to roam the mainland discreetly, albeit in a confined state.

Choices A, C, and D are wrong, as they provide no evidence or correlate to Caleb's predicament of being trapped in the U.K under Falkland's careful watch.

QUESTION 3

Choice D is the best answer. This is an analysis question. Caleb is best described as shocked, based on the repeated description of him as surprised and restless, his thoughts wandering as to why this warning could have come and what may come next.

Choice A incorrectly states that Caleb ignores the warning, Choice B incorrectly identifies the warning as the source of disdain rather than Gines himself, and Choice C is incorrect because no mention is made of Holland.

QUESTION 4

Choice C is the best answer. This is a justification question. Choice C is correct because the line "my blood has been in a perpetual ferment [...] I have had no sleep" indicates the classic symptoms of someone in shock.

Choices A, B, and D are incorrect because they do not support the answer from the previous question.

QUESTION 5

Choice A is the best answer. This is a tone question. Gines addresses Caleb in a cautionary manner, as is evidenced by his constant warnings: "but beware the salt seas!" (line 43) and "you are not to go out of these climates."(line 52). Gines also addresses Caleb in a well-intentioned manner, as is seen when Gines first introduces the dilemma: "I come as a friend, and that I may save you a labor-in-vain trouble." (31-33). and "If you consider what I have to say in that light, it will be the better for you." (33-34). Gines wants to help Caleb, and so his intentions are pure.

Choice B is incorrect since at no point in the passage does Gines threaten or act hostile towards Caleb. Choice C is incorrect because Gina never fondly remembers his relationship with Caleb, and there is no mention of them having a friendship. Choice D is incorrect because Gines never asks Caleb a question, nor is he curious about any of Caleb's affairs.

QUESTION 6

Choice A is the best answer. This is a vocab-in-context question. The correct answer is "omen" since a "presage" (line 1) is a sign that something bad will happen. Even if the word is unfamiliar, the modifier "prophetic" (line 2) implies a vision of the future. This should indicate that the "presage" relates to a sign of things to come, and so the only answer choice which fits this is choice C.

A, B, and D are incorrect answers because their meanings do not correlate to the meaning in the context. A good strategy to answering these types of questions is to replace your choices back into the sentence to verify that your choice is correct.

QUESTION 7

Choice A is the best answer. This is an organization question. Choice A is correct because the second paragraph establishes Caleb's location "on the east coast of the island" and his subsequent journey to the inn near the port.

Choice B is incorrect because Caleb receives no information whatsoever in the second paragraph. Choice C is incorrect because there is no mention of Caleb speaking to anyone in the second paragraph. Finally, Choice D is incorrect because Squire Falkland's inner workings are not mentioned in the passage.

QUESTION 8

Choice A is the best answer. This is a vocab-in-context question. The correct answer is "inescapable." The word inexorable means inevitable. In the context of the passage, Falkland, the narrator's master, continues to search for him as he changes his location. The narrator would thus describe Falkland as inescapable, or inexorable.

Choices B, C, and D all contain incorrect ideas that don't make sense in the context of the passage. The narrator would not describe his master (at least at this point in the passage) as sympathetic, mutable (flexible), or purposeful. These questions often are related more closely to your ability to use language precisely based on the passage than your knowledge of the vocab word in question (inexorable).

QUESTION 9

Choice C is the best answer. This is a main idea question. The central takeaway from the whole passage is that one character (Gines) warns the main character (Caleb) that he will face grave consequences if he boards a ship to Holland. Gines' master Falkland orders Gines to tell Caleb that he will have him brought in if he attempts to leave the U.K., or even lingers near the ocean for too long.

Choice A is incorrect because Caleb chooses "voluntary banishment" from England; he is never banished by another person to Holland. Choice B is incorrect because Gines is not necessarily aggressive, and no true "conversation" occurs between the two men since Caleb never responds. Choice D is incorrect because Gines does not want to kill Caleb, which is why he warns Caleb "out of the love" he has for him, not hatred.

QUESTION 10

Choice D is the best answer. This is an inference question. D is the correct answer since Falkland commands Gines to warn Caleb at the inn. Gines does as he is "directed" and tells Caleb that Falkland is "determined you shall never pass the reach of his disposal" (lines 53-54).

Choice A is incorrect since Gines never asks Caleb to return to Falkland. Choice B is incorrect because Gines could kill Caleb immediately at the inn, but those are not Falkland's orders. Finally, choice C cannot be correct as there is no mention of Caleb owing Falkland any money or debt.

QUESTION 11

Choice D is the best answer. This is a tonal question. Choice D is correct because the "ardent Teachings of the soul" indicates an enthusiastic and avid determination. This most nearly correlates to determined.

Choice A is incorrect because the line makes no mention of Caleb's anxiousness. Choice B is also incorrect because Caleb's happiness is not mentioned in the line. Choice C is incorrect because there is no mention of a divine entity in the line.

QUESTION 12

Choice C is the best answer. This is an organization question. C is the correct choice since one character (Gines) encounters another (Caleb) to inform him of impending danger.

Choice A is not the correct answer because there is no mention of an anecdote. Choice B is incorrect because the author, Caleb, does not necessarily intend to persuade readers. Choice D is incorrect because the author never mentions England's official justice system.

QUESTION 13

Choice D is the best answer. This is a factual question. "Military authorities feared an invasion of our West Coast" is directly stated in lines 22-24. In the context of the passage, Justice Black shows that the primary reason for the internment is safety from a homeland attack.

Choice A, B, and C are all incorrect because there is no evidence in the passage to support any of these choices.

QUESTION 14

Choice D is the best answer. This is a justification question. The evidence which best supports the answer in the previous question is found in lines 22-24, specifically "military authorities feared an invasion of our West Coast". This line shows that the internment of Japanese-Americans was done primarily to protect against a military attack.

Choices A, B, and C are incorrect because they do not support the answer from the previous question.

QUESTION 15

Choice A is the best answer. This is a vocab-in-context question. Reposing, broken down into its parts, literally means to position again. This most nearly correlates to reaffirming, or to place confidence in something again.

Choice B, C, and D are incorrect because they are not what reposing means.

QUESTION 16

Choice C is the best answer. This is an analysis question. Justice Roberts argues that racial prejudice does not play a role in the court's decision, as seen in lines 20-21. He states "Korematsu was not excluded from the Military Area because of hostility to him or his race".

Choices A, B, and D are incorrect because Justice Black does dissuade any of those notions.

QUESTION 17

Choice B is the best answer. This is an analysis question. Justice Roberts states in lines 60-68 that the government made it "appear as if petitioner violated a military order". This strongly implies the contrary to be true, in Justice Roberts' opinion.

Choice A is incorrect because Justice Roberts does not refute this claim, but rather affirms Korematsu's rights. Choice C and D are incorrect because Justice Roberts does not make mention of these.

QUESTION 18

Choice D is the best answer. This is a factual question. Justice Roberts states in lines 50-52 ("case…ancestry) and lines 57-59 ("I…violated") that if the decision to convict a citizen is based on his/her race, then his/her constitutional rights have been violated.

Choice A is incorrect because the ancestry mentioned is not used literally, but instead references a race at large. Choice B is incorrect because the evidence in the case is not open for interpretation. Choice C is wrong because Justice Roberts does not mention a ruling in *Hirabayashi v. United States.*

QUESTION 19

Choice B is the best answer. This is an inference question. Justice Roberts refers to the rights of citizens when he discusses "that which is single and indivisible" (line 63). This can be seen by looking at the context of the passage, where Roberts affirms that Korematsu is a citizen and so is entitled to certain rights that were not granted to him.

Choice A is incorrect because there is no mention of the executive branch in Robert's argument. Choice C is incorrect because certain Constitutional rights have been violated, but not the Constitution itself as a whole. Choice D is incorrect because there is no mention of a national identity.

QUESTION 20

Choice B is the best answer. This is an analysis question. If we look at the language used in Lines 43-45, Roberts clearly says "This is not a case of keeping people off the streets at night, as was Hirabayashi v. United States". The key word here is NOT, showing a contrast between the two cases.

Choices A is incorrect because Roberts is not trying to justify the internment camps. Choice C is incorrect because the impacts of the case are not stated. Choice D is incorrect because there is no mention of it being the first racial case.

QUESTION 21

Choice A is the best answer. This is a comparison question. Justice Black's main point in the first passage is to dissuade any claims of the role of racial prejudice in the court's decision, as seen in lines 20-21. Justice Roberts' main point in the second passage is to affirm that racial prejudice did play a major role in the court's decision, as seen in lines 50-52. Thus, there contention falls under this issue of race.

Choice B, C, and D are all incorrect because the Justices do not argue any of these issues.

QUESTION 22

Choice B is the best answer. This is an application question. Justice Black claims that this case is a matter of an "exclusion order", in lines 15-16. Justice Roberts states that the main point of the trial is "not a case of temporary exclusion" (line 45), but he does not deny that Korematsu did violate this order. Instead, Justice Roberts stance is one of the morality behind the exclusion order. Thus, the two would agree on the exclusion order being violated.

Choice A, C and D are all incorrect because the Justices disagreed on the underlying concepts of all these choices.

QUESTION 23

Choice B is the best answer. This is a data analysis question. Realize that N universally represents sample size. As seen at the top of the table, N is set to the value of 100, so this makes B the correct choice. Even if you did not know what N represented, you could use the process of elimination to get choice B as the correct answer.

Choice A is incorrect because the sum of the percent values is not equivalent to the sample size. Choice C and D are incorrect because the sample size is not one of the percent values.

QUESTION 24

Choice C is the best answer. This is a factual question. Lines 20-21 detail which type of attack is the most common: "Among them, Trojan e-mail and phishing messages are two of the most common examples of social engineering attacks". Since Phishing messages were not an answer choice, we should default onto Trojan emails.

Choice A and B are incorrect because, although they are stated to be types of social engineering attacks, there is no evidence supporting that they are among the most common. Choice D is incorrect because intimidation is not a type of social engineering attack.

QUESTION 25

Choice B is the best answer. This is a vocabulary-in-context question. Contemporary, broken down in to its separate parts, means with (con) the times (temporary). Thus, contemporary translates to up-to-date or modern.

Choices A, C, and D are incorrect because contemporary does not correspond with any one of those choices. Also, Choices A and D would not make sense in the context of the passage.

QUESTION 26

Choice A is the best answer. This is a vocabulary-in-context question. Within the context of the passage, a compliance inspection refers to an inspection checking whether a system is up-to-code. Thus, a compliance inspection is a satisfactory inspection so answer choice A is correct.

Choice B may be tempting, as compliance inspections may be mandatory. However, the compliance part of does not intrinsically correlate to the mandatory nature of the inspection. Answer choices C and D are incorrect because compliance does not mean either one of these definitions.

QUESTION 27

Choice D is the best answer. This is an analysis question. As is evidenced in lines 99-101, "the natural human tendency to take people at their word continues to leave users vulnerable". This most nearly means that people are gullible.

Answer choices A, B, and C are all incorrect because there is no evidence for any of these choices. Frailty, anxiety, and infirmity are not mentioned in the passage.

QUESTION 28

Choice C is the best answer. This is an evidence question. Lines 99-101 showcases the factor naiveté plays in social engineering attacks: "the natural human tendency to take people at their word continues to leave users vulnerable". This supports the idea that humans are gullible.

Choices A, B, and D are incorrect because they do not support the correct answer in the previous question. Choice A does discuss the overall goal of social engineering attacks, but it is too general to be used as evidence for the previous question. Choices B and D do not contain any evidence to support the answer in the previous question.

QUESTION 29

Choice B is the best answer. This is a factual question. This specific example occurs in lines 50-65. The attacker used fake credentials be "creating a very simple green plastic badge" (line 50). This allowed him to gain access to the company's recycled papers and so, glean valuable information.

Choices A, C, and D are all incorrect because they did not actually happen in the passage. These choices may be tempting because their base themes are referenced in the passage, but the actual implementation of these tactics is not used.

QUESTION 30

Choice C is the best answer. This is a purpose question. The entire passage revolves around the different types of social engineering attacks. The main essence of the passage is captured in lines 15-16: "There are numerous types of social engineering attacks". This sets up the rest of the passage for a discussion of the various styles of attacks.

Choice A is incorrect because the passage is more informative than cautionary, and does not focus on the consequences of these attacks. Choice B is incorrect because the focus of the passage is not centered on the prevalence with which these attacks are made. There is little mention of the overall frequency of these attacks, except for line 36-38. However, these lines are more of a side-fact than a main point. Choice D is incorrect because there is no mention as to safety measures when it comes to social engineering attacks.

QUESTION 31

Choice B is the best answer. This is an analysis question. The choice corresponds to a scenario in which an attacker completes a rudimentary task, then asks for assistance from the individual, and then finally obtains the goal i.e. information. Using the example provided in lines 50-65 as a guideline, the social engineer first completes the rudimentary task of pretending to rummage through a company's waste. Next, he asks for assistance by requesting they separate the recyclable material from the trash. Then finally, as his third step, the engineer sifts through the recycled material to glean information from the target.

Choices A, C, and D are incorrect because they do not follow the flow provided by the example used in the passage.

QUESTION 32

Choice A is the best answer. This is an application question. Choice A combines elements of authority (boss) and politeness (cordially) to create an enticing email. These two persuasions have the highest frequency in the table, 100% and 74% respectively.

Choice B is incorrect because, although it uses the authority element (prince), it only uses the third most common persuasion tactic: urgency. Urgency has an occurrence rate of 71%, which is less than politeness so choice B is incorrect. Choice C is incorrect because it combines the elements of authority (FBI) and fear, which is the lowest frequency persuasion tactic. Choice D is incorrect because it uses the urgency persuasion tactic, which is not the most common.

QUESTION 33

Choice A is the best answer. This is a vocab-in-context question. To answer this question correctly, we must look to lines 30-32: "Videos of 'impossible' behaviors (i.e. behaviors not in the repertoire of the subjects or species)". This line defines what it means by impossible behaviors, and in doing so, defines a repertoire as any behavior that is not impossible, or rather possible.

Choice B is incorrect because the lines do not restrict the repertoire to strictly common behaviors. Choice C is incorrect because line 32 contradicts this, by saying impossible behaviors are not in the repertoire. Choice D is incorrect because there is no evidence which restricts the repertoire to strictly uncommon behaviors.

QUESTION 34

Choice B is the best answer. This is a data analysis question. Looking at the graph, the line above each of the bars represents the standard error of mean, as referenced in the table description. Between the two bars, the greatest margin of error is in the yawn group which is approximately 1 yawn.

Choice A is incorrect because the control group does not have the highest margin of error. Choice C is incorrect because 5.8 is the possible number of yawns with the margin of error added. Choice D is incorrect because there is a margin of error.

QUESTION 35

Choice A is the best answer. This is a data-analysis question. As stated in the fifth paragraph: "If the chimpanzees identified with the animations, then they would yawn more in response to the yawn animations than the control animations" (lines 101-104). Because the yawn group is more than double that of the control group, there is a significant difference between the two. Therefore, we can conclude that the chimpanzees must have identified with the animations.

Choice B is incorrect because it contradicts the statement in the fifth paragraph. Choice C and D are incorrect because there is a significant difference between the two groups.

QUESTION 36

Choice A is the best answer. This is a main idea question. Lines 41-43 pose the question "Do non-human animals view or process animated images the same way they do real images of conspecifics?" This question essentially asks if animated, or artificial, stimuli have the same effect as real world stimuli. The experiment answers this by stimulating yawning in chimpanzees through artificial yawning and natural yawning.

Choice B, C, and D are incorrect because these questions are not answered by the experiment, or posed at all in the passage.

QUESTION 37

Choice D is the best answer. This is a vocab-in-context question. To answer this question correctly, we must first realize that experiment conducted utilized chimpanzee artificial yawns to stimulate chimpanzees. Because these were the same species, and the question asks about conspecific stimuli, conspecific most nearly means same species.

Choice A, B, and C are incorrect because they are not what conspecific means.

QUESTION 38

Choice C is the best answer. This is an application question. Lines 47-49 show that, if the notion is true, "then computer animations represent a new and flexible tool in the study of animal behavior". The only choice which studies animal behavior via computer simulations is choice C.

Choices A, B, and D are incorrect because they do not use computer animations to study animal behavior.

QUESTION 39

Choice A is the best answer. This is a factual question. Anderson's study found that "the population-level statistic was non-significant" (line 96). The population-statistic, as seen in the previous lines, is a reference to the number of "chimpanzees who yawned more in response to videos of chimpanzees yawning than to control videos" (lines 94-95).

Choice B is incorrect because it is a possible fault of the experiment, but not the primary conclusion. Choice C is incorrect because there is no reference to the relation between stumptail macaques and chimpanzees. Choice D is incorrect because this was the finding of Campbell's research, not Anderson's.

QUESTION 40

Choice C is the best answer. This is an analysis question. As seen in the second paragraph, "Videos of 'impossible behaviors are by definition impossible to obtain. All of these obstacles can be overcome using computer animations." (lines 30-33). Thus, it is stated here that computer animations can produce impossible behaviors and so simulate actions not found in the natural world.

Choice A is incorrect because only undesirable variables can be eliminated, not control variables. Choice B is incorrect because behavior length does not have an impact on the quality of the experiment and is not referenced in the passage. Choice D is incorrect because it is not mentioned in the passage.

QUESTION 41

Choice D is the best answer. This is an analysis question. In the third paragraph, it is stated that "the first question was recently answered by Parr, who tested how chimpanzees categorize facial expressions using virtual chimpanzees" (lines 50-54). Having the chimpanzees categorize the facial expressions most nearly correlates to having the animals discriminate between images.

Choice A is incorrect because there is no mention of the test subjects playing games in the passage. Choice B is incorrect because this test answered the second question, not the first. Choice C is incorrect because there were no images of heterospecifics (of a different species) in the test with POSER 6.0

QUESTION 42

Choice C is the best answer. This is a factual question. In the fourth paragraph of the passage, it is stated that "[Physiological methods] are not currently feasible with awake, behaving, adult chimpanzees." (lines 80-82). This indicates that conscious, aware animals will not submit to a physiological test willingly, making the test rather difficult.

Choice A, B, and D are all incorrect because there is no mention of them in the passage

QUESTION 43

Choice A is the best answer. This is a vocab-in context question. The evidence can be found through a list of instances of "trifles" found in lines 14-16: "handful of spectacles, some telescopes, butter, tent wine, almonds, cheese, and other such trifles". All of these items fall under the first category option.

Choice B is incorrect because each of these items is not a dessert. Although a trifle may mean a cold desert, in this context, it would not make sense. Choice C and D are incorrect because they are not what trifles mean.

QUESTION 44

Choice D is the best answer. This is an application question. There are two pieces of evidence to look for in this passage. First, "these objects were given as gifts simply because they were exotic" (lines 34-35). This mandates that the gift should be from a different culture than the recipient's. Second, "Included in this group are objects that could broadly be defined as art" (lines 26-27). This evidence shows that the gift could fall under the category of art work. Therefore, an authentic work of art would be the best choice.

Choice A is incorrect because it is not exotic. Choice B is incorrect because it is not valuable. Choice C is incorrect because it would have a harmful impact on the relations.

QUESTION 45

Choice C is the best answer. This is a factual question. "The only Japanese allowed access to [Deshima] other than officials and merchants were prostitutes" (lines 49-51). The only category not mentioned was tailors.

Choice A, B, and D are all incorrect because they are mentioned in the passage.

QUESTION 46

Choice B is the best answer. This is a vocab-in-context question. The word "euphemistic" directly means polite or inoffensive. In this context, the offensive term "prostitutes" was substituted for a politer expression of "house keepers".

Choice A, C, and D are all incorrect because they are not what euphemistically means.

QUESTION 47

Choice C is the best answer. This is an analysis question. The entire passage revolves around the VOC's involvement with the city of Nagasaki. In the first sentence, it is stated that "the Governor of Nagasaki was pleased with the presents bestowed upon him by the VOC" (lines 3-5). This makes the Nagasaki government the target of the VOC's attempted flattery.

Choice A, B, and D are incorrect because they are not referenced in the passage.

QUESTION 48

Choice C is the best answer. This is a main point question. As seen in the second paragraph, "the Dutch East India Company had been trading in western Japan, and from 1640 they were the only Europeans allowed to live and work in the country" (lines 40-43). This was a direct result of the VOC's exchange of gifts with the governor of Nagasaki.

Choice A, B, and D are incorrect because they are not mentioned in the passage.

QUESTION 49

Choice A is the best answer. This is a factual question. The evidence is found in the second paragraph: "large amounts of precious metals: silver at first, and later gold and copper when silver exports were banned". Because embargo means to ban or prohibit, this makes silver, a precious metal, the best option.

Choices B, C, and D are all incorrect because they are not banned in the passage.

QUESTION 50

Choice D is the best answer. This is a main point question. The entire passage revolves around the interaction between the VOC and the Japanese government in Nagasaki. It explores the role of gift-giving, and in doing so, analyzes different aspects of the interaction.

Choice A is incorrect because the primary focus is not on the various inner workings of the VOC. Choice B is incorrect because this passage is not an instructional guide. Choice C is incorrect because the list of valuable items is only a consequence of the main point, not the primary focus itself.

QUESTION 51

Choice B is the best answer. This is a factual question. As seen in paragraph 2, the "VOC trade was particularly profitable in Japan throughout the middle decades of the seventeenth century" (lines 54-55). The middle decades of the seventeenth century would be the 1650s.

Choice A, C, and D are incorrect because they are not the middle decade of the seventeenth century.

QUESTION 52

Choice C is the best answer. This is an evidence question. As seen in paragraph 2, the "VOC trade was particularly profitable in Japan throughout the middle decades of the seventeenth century" (lines 54-55). The middle decades of the seventeenth century would be the 1650s and so this supports the answer from the previous question.

Choice A and B are incorrect because they do not make mention of any financial success. Choice D is incorrect because it makes no mention of a time frame.

SECTION 2: Writing and Language: Test 2

QUESTION 1.

Choice B is the best answer because the dependent relative clause "who in turn… the road" correctly utilizes the parenthetical interrupter "in turn" with surrounding commas. Generally, non-essential interrupters like "in turn" or "in fact" (among others) necessitate proper punctuation like commas, dashes or parenthesis.

Choice A is incorrect because the parenthetical interrupter "in turn" does not utilize proper punctuation and the use of participial phrase "showing their proficiency" is not as proper as the infinitive phrase "to show their proficiency". Choice C is incorrect because the relative pronoun "which" refers only to non-living things. Choice D is incorrect due to awkward phrasing.

QUESTION 2.

Choice D is the best answer because "furthermore" continues the logical progression of the passage. The author is conveying another responsibility of the DMV in this sentence so the transitional adverb "furthermore" is the best choice here.

Choices A, B and C are all incorrect because they all retain inappropriate transitions – such as contrasts or summary declaratives – that are not warranted.

QUESTION 3.

Choice B is the best answer because the previous sentences all utilize the present simple tense/aspect in parallel form. To keep this consistent, this sentence must also use the present simple tense/aspect as "the department tracks…" or "subject + present simple tense verb" form.

Choices A, C and D are incorrect because past simple, past perfect, and past perfect progressive forms of the verb are not parallel with the previous two sentences presented in the paragraph.

QUESTION 4.

Choice A is the best answer. Note that in the previous paragraph, the author ended with a statement that traffic violations are handled in a manner that makes "no sense at all." Therefore, a logical way to continue this train of thought would be to introduce some of the issues that drivers may have against the DMV. In this instance, it's the dreaded points system.

Choice B confuses the logic the author is trying to convey by asserting that the points system is something DMV is proud of. Choices C and D are incorrect because "their" points system is an ambiguous one for both cases. Further, the author is not talking about law enforcement agencies or the legislature in the previous paragraph so these choices can be safely eliminated.

QUESTION 5.

Choice C is the best answer because it correctly distinguishes between the two separate categories of "moving" vs. "non-moving" violations.

Choice A is incorrect because the sentence is words and not parallel in construction. Choices B and D use incorrect diction.

QUESTION 6.

Choice D is the best answer because the proper pronoun to be used here points to many violations, not just one. Therefore, the demonstrative pronoun "these" is the best choice. Further, the pronoun "these" is best suited when referring to specific ideas that were mentioned in previous sentences.

Choice A, B and C are all incorrect because all of these pronouns do not correctly point to the many violations referred to by the author.

QUESTION 7.

Choice D is the best answer because the information has already been exemplified in the previous sentence when the author claims that "more serious crimes..." will land the driver in hot water, resulting in various amount of punishments. There is no need to exemplify another crime here.

Choice A, B and C are incorrect because they provide inaccurate interpretations or incorrect viewpoints to be added to the paragraph.

QUESTION 8.

Choice C is the best answer because "not only . . . but also" is the correct idiomatic phrase.

Choices A and C are incorrect because they utilize the wrong phrase in conjunction with the leading "not only," as does choice D, which further uses the wrong parallel structure.

QUESTION 9.

Choice D is the best answer because the subject of the clause is "manuals and information," which is plural, and the verb is in the present perfect tense. Thus, the verb "to have" must be conjugated as *have* and the participle of "to remain," *remained*, must be used.

Choices A and C are incorrect because they use the singular form of "to have." Choice B is incorrect because it doesn't use the participle *remained.*

QUESTION 10.

Choice B is the best answer because it correctly uses a relative clause. Led by a comma and referring to a thing, the relative clause should be headed by the relative pronoun *which.*

Choice A is incorrect because the relative pronoun *that* is not led by a comma. Choices C and D are incorrect because they incorrectly join two independent clauses.

QUESTION 11.

Choice D is the best answer because it references the important ideas of the passage in a conclusive tone. Referring generally to the problems with the DMV and prescribing a solution in a way that ties up the passage, D is the best option.

Choices A and C are incorrect because they focus on minutia in specific paragraphs of the passage. Choice B is incorrect because it uses phrasing that leaves the reader expecting another sentence to elaborate/conclude.

QUESTION 12

Choice C is the best answer. The modifier "seeming never to end" refers to the road; hence, *road* must be the subject of the sentence.

Choices A, B, and D are incorrect because "seeming never to end" doesn't modify *artists*, *lives* (hopefully not), or *one*.

QUESTION 13

Choice B is the best answer. The subject, *decision*, is singular and the action takes place in the present tense, so the correct form of the verb is *brings*.

Choice A is incorrect because the subject is singular, not plural. Choices C and D are incorrect because the action of bringing to mind is happening now, rather than in the past or future.

QUESTION 14

Choice D is the best answer. '*It was*' is the only option containing a subject and a verb, which is necessary as the answer is parallel to a subject and a verb in *music* and *to be*.

Choices A, B, and C either contain neither a subject nor a verb or just a verb.

QUESTION 15

Choice B is the best answer. '*Mercury; thus, they*' correctly joins two independent clauses using a semicolon, conjunctive adverb, and a comma.

Choice A is a comma splice (joining two independent clauses with a comma). Choices C and D incorrectly use a coordinating conjunction (FANBOYS) without a comma to join two independent clauses.

QUESTION 16

Choice B is the best answer. In sentence 3, the paragraph transitions from a discussion of Elton John's music to his persona. Sentence 5 discusses his music, elaborating on the points brought up in sentences 1 and 2, so it should go after sentence 2.

Choice A is incorrect because it talks about John's music career before introducing it. Choices C and D place the sentence in a part of the paragraph that has already moved on from talking about John's music.

QUESTION 17

Choice B is the best answer. It uses a participial phrase to avoid incorrectly joining two independent clauses while still maintaining the original meaning of the author.

Choices A and C incorrectly join two independent clauses with a comma. Choice D is incorrect because it indicates that John had been provided the music rather than having provided it.

QUESTION 18

Choice B is the best answer. The sentence provides an example of John's foray into hip-hop.

Choice A is incorrect because the sentence exemplifies rather than contrasts with the intent of the Grammys performance. Choices C and D are incorrect because the sentence fits in with the main idea of the paragraph and provides an example of the 'recent activity' used to transition into the next paragraph.

QUESTION 19

Choice C is the best answer. The phrase is led by a dash, so it must be closed by a dash.

Choices A, B, and D are incorrect because they do not close the phrase with a dash.

QUESTION 20

Choice C is the best answer. The phrase is in parallel with Elton's tour, so it should be compared to a tour, which in this case, can be replaced by the pronoun *that* in the phrase *that of any other retiring star.*

Choices A and B incorrectly compare a tour to a star, or the verb phrase *has been.* Choice D incorrectly uses a plural pronoun to refer to the singular *tour.*

QUESTION 21

Choice D is the best answer. The antecedent is tour, so the singular pronoun *it* must be used.

Choices A, B, and C are wrong because they use plural pronouns or refer to the vendors' events instead of the tour.

QUESTION 22

Choice C is the best answer. *Gratified* best conveys the author's meaning that Elton John should be satisfied for all the good work that he has produced and is entitled to a break.

Choices A. B, and D are incorrect because they are negatively connoted words that distort the author's meaning.

QUESTION 23

Choice C is the best answer. *Bygone* best conveys the author's meaning that poverty is not a problem of the past.

Choices A, B, and D convey different meanings. Respectively, they denote that poverty shouldn't be considered predetermined, unavoidable, or unreachable. Emphasizing that poverty still exists, the author clearly doesn't want to convey any of these things.

QUESTION 24

Choice A is the best answer. The first clause is in the past tense, so the second clause, which occurred chronologically after, should also be in the past tense, as *became* correctly is.

Choices B, C, and D are incorrect because they incorrectly use the past perfect and conditional perfect tenses.

QUESTION 25

Choice A is the best answer. '*In fact*' expands on an already stated idea that it was difficult to get people to care.

Choice B incorrectly implies the addition of a new point rather than elaboration on a previous one. Choice C incorrectly implies contrast. Choice D incorrectly assumes a logical conclusion made from an idea, rather than a factual support for it.

QUESTION 26

Choice B is the best answer. The sentence clears up why journalists were called muckrakers.

Choice A is incorrect because the main focus of the passage is not the word muckraker. Choices C and D are incorrect because the sentence relates to the paragraph and the author uses a semi-informal, conversational tone.

QUESTION 27

Choice A is the best answer. Even though it sounds terrible, the author chose to make the relative clause *who made the city tick* non-essential by ending it with a comma, so it must be started with a comma.

Choice B is incorrect because it doesn't surround the relative clause with commas. Choices C and D incorrectly use a clause led by *that*, which doesn't carry a trailing comma.

QUESTION 28

Choice C is the best answer. By introducing the idea of the article being seen by influential people, choice C sets up the information that follows about Theodore Roosevelt (he hated being called Teddy, so don't call him that).

Choices A, B, and D all contain pertinent information related to the main idea of the passage, but don't set up the information about Theodore.

QUESTION 29

Choice A is the best answer. The phrase 'a number' followed by a prepositional phrase containing a quantifiable noun is conjugated in the plural.

Choice B incorrectly uses the singular conjugation. Choice C distorts the author's meaning, as the issues were plaguing the city, not being plagued by the city. Choice D incorrectly uses the present tense.'

QUESTION 30

Choice B is the best answer. The correct pronoun is *by*, as it shows that the figures were the actors who did not receive the article well.

Choices A and D are incorrect because they imply that the article was not actively received by the figures, but rather describe a condition of being. Choice C would incorrectly imply that someone else received the ideas on behalf of the figures.

QUESTION 31

Choice D is the best answer. *Thus* is the best suited conjunctive adverb to connect the idea of the parties engaging in unpopular action to its logical consequent, their support dwindling.

Choices A and B incorrectly imply contrast. Choice C is incorrect because it is a FANBOYS (coordinating) conjunction. *So* can only be used to join two sentences with a comma, not with a semicolon.

QUESTION 32

Choice B is the best answer. *Unprecedented* is the word that best conveys that the change had never been seen before.

Choices A, C, and D all imply surprise, but stop short of addressing the events that have happened before this particular one (or its precedent).

QUESTION 33

Choice B is the best answer. The phrase led by *as well as* is prepositional, so it can't contain the simple subject, which is *Roosevelt*. A singular subject should take the singular present tense 'has.'

Choices A and D are incorrect because they are conjugated in the plural. Choice C is incorrect because it implies a future action rather than a general statement in the present (which is fine to use even though Roosevelt is dead, as the credit is a general idea that continues into the present).

QUESTION 34

Choice C is the best answer. *Accurate* has the correct meaning of absolutely true and the correct tone.

Choices A, B, and D all use slang or informal terminology. Choices A and B further have a meaning closer to genuine than true.

QUESTION 35

Choice B is the best answer. The first "sentence" is in fact just a participial phrase, containing no independent clause. To join a participial phrase to an independent clause, just use a comma.

Choices A, B, and D are incorrect because they treat the phrase led by *taking* as an independent clause. Since it isn't, it can't be concluded by a period, or joined using comma + FANBOYS or a semicolon.

QUESTION 36

Choice C is the best answer. The conditional best expresses a hypothetical state of being that would exist if something else were to happen.

Choices A, B, and D are incorrect because they assume a true event that happened, has happened, or will happen, as opposed to a hypothetical one.

QUESTION 37

Choice B is the best answer. The rule of OR dictates that the closest noun to the verb conjugates it. In this case, the plural *details* should conjugate "to plant" as the plural *plant*.

Choices A and C incorrectly conjugate "to plant" in the singular. Choice D incorrectly switches the verb from active to passive, changing the meaning of the sentence.

QUESTION 38

Choice D is the best answer. *Testing the ability to affect memory* is the only modifier that describes the subject of the sentence, *researchers*.

Choices A, B, and C are incorrect because rather than describing *researchers*, they describe *subjects*, *video*, and *quiz*.

QUESTION 39

Choice D is the best answer. *Randomly* is a strong enough word to imply something happens by chance, so the most stylistically correct and non-repetitive option is to leave it by itself.

Choices A, B, and C unnecessarily add description that adds no meaning to the sentence and detracts from style. Choice C is also a comma splice.

QUESTION 40

Choice A is the best answer. This sentence best connects the results that the researchers found to their broader concerns that coaching targets the weak.

Choice B incorrectly implies that researchers were worried about which trials coaching is used in. Choice C incorrectly introduces the idea that coaching is generally good. Choice D incorrectly states that the general trend, rather than the specific groups affected by the problem, was the main concern of researchers.

QUESTION 41

Choice A is the best answer. The simple subject of the sentence, *old, young,* and *those*, is plural, so the use of the plural verb *were* is correct.

Choice B is incorrect because it is conjugated for a singular subject. Choices C and D delete the main verb of the independent clause, turning the sentence into a fragment or two fragments, respectively.

QUESTION 42

Choice C is the best answer. In parallel with *to target*, the phrase *to help*, a plain infinitive phrase, makes the most sense.

Choices A and B incorrectly put prepositional phrases in parallel to an infinitive. Choice D incorrectly puts a perfect infinitive phrase in parallel to an infinitive.

QUESTION 43

Choice C is the best answer. It doesn't really matter where you put the preposition 'to,' but the pronoun is correctly stated as *whom* in answer choice C, as it is the object of the preposition.

Choices A and B are incorrect because they don't use the objective form of the pronoun. Choice D incorrectly repeats the preposition *to*.

QUESTION 44

Choice D is the best answer. The pronoun has no antecedent, so the author must clarify that he is referring to the witnesses.

Choices A and B have no antecedent, leaving it unclear as to who *they* or *we* are. Choice C incorrectly indicates that you shouldn't believe researchers, rather than witnesses.

SECTION 3
Math No Calculator Test

QUESTION 1

Choice B is the best answer. This is an algebra question. First multiply both sides of the equation by k, eliminating the denominator, and making it equivalent to $k + 3 = 7k$. From here, subtract k from both sides to obtain $6k = 3$. Divide both sides by 6 to get $= \frac{1}{2}$.

Choice A is incorrect because the equation cannot be manipulated to get that result. Choice C is incorrect because we do not divide 6 by 3, but 3 by 6. Choice D is incorrect for the same reason as A.

QUESTION 2

Choice C is the best answer. This is a Heart of Algebra question with an emphasis on foiling/factoring. The first step to take is multiplying $x^2 + 7x$ by x. This gives us $x^3 + 7x^2$. Combining like-terms with the second part of the expression, we get $x^3 + (7x^2 - 3x^2) + 3y - 9x$. Evaluating this expression will yield $x^3 + 4x^2 + 3y - 9x$.

Choices A, B, and D are all incorrect because the expression cannot be manipulated into any of those forms.

QUESTION 3

Choice C is the best answer. This is an algebra question with an emphasis on fractions. Get rid of the denominators in the equation by multiplying both sides of the equation by their least common multiple. In this case, the least common multiple of 5 and 4 is 20. So, multiplying both sides by 20 will produce 4x+15y=200.

Choices A, B, and D are wrong because $20 * 10 \neq 50, 10, \text{or } 300$.

QUESTION 4

Choice A is the best answer. This is a algebra question with an emphasis on system of linear equations. There are multiple methods to solving this problem. The idea is to eliminate a variable in both of the equations by manipulating each independently to obtain the same term. For example, multiplying the bottom equation by 3 on both sides will yield the system of linear equation $\begin{matrix} 3x + 2y = 14 \\ 3x + 3y = 12 \end{matrix}$. Subtract the bottom equation from the top equation and get the new equation: $-y = 2$. Thus, $y = -2$. If we substitute this value for y back into either equation, we get the $x = 6$. Plugging these values back into 2xy, $2(6)(-2) = -24$.

Choice B, C, and D are incorrect because they are not the values of 2xy. Choice C might be tempting, since we found the value of x, but remember the question does not ask for the specific value of x, but rather an expression which contains the value of x as a component.

QUESTION 5

Choice C is the best answer. This is an algebra question with an emphasis on quadratics and foiling/factoring. A root is a solution to the quadratic when set to 0. Thus, $x^2 + 7x + c = 0$ must have -5 and -2 as solutions. Rewrite the quadratic as $(x + 5)(x + 2) = 0$. Foil this to get the result $x^2 + 7x + 10 = 0 = x^2 + 7x + c$. Simplify to 10=c.

Choices A, B, and D are all incorrect because these values of c do not allow -5 and -2 to be real solutions.

QUESTION 6

Choice D is the best answer. This is a geometry question focusing on areas of circles and word translation. First, find the area of the whole circle, with radius L, and then subtract the area of the inner circle, with radius R. Since the area of a circle is πr^2, the area of the whole circle is $\pi(3^2)$=9π. Subtract the inner circle, of area $\pi(1^2)$, the correct answer is 8 π.

Choice A is incorrect because this value is the area of the shaded region. Choice B is incorrect because it is not the area of the non-shaded region. Choice C is incorrect because we do not subtract the radii and then substitute that value in for πr^2.

QUESTION 7

Choice C is the best answer. This is a word translation problem involving unit conversion. Break down the year into weeks, and the weeks into how many days Laura works. Since Laura works 52 weeks at 5 days a week, she works 260 days. We do not have to worry about her hours worked, because we are finding the value of 8C and she works 8 hours, so those values cancel out. If we divide 5,200 by 260, we get 20 as the answer for 8C.

Choices A, B, and D are all incorrect as they are not the correct values of 8C.

QUESTION 8

Choice A is the best choice. This is a word translation problem. Determine the amount of time it takes John and Paul to drive down the road, then find the difference. Divide the distance by John's speed, $\frac{5\ miles}{20\ mph}$, and find that John takes 0.25 hours to get to the end of the road. Divide that same distance by Paul's speed, $\frac{5\ miles}{33\ mph}$ and find that Paul takes 0.1515 hours to get to the end of the road. The difference is about 0.1 hours.

Choices B and C are incorrect because the question does not ask for either of the individuals' time. Choice D is incorrect because the difference between the times for John and Paul is not 0.5 hours.

QUESTION 9

Choice D is the best answer. This is an interest problem. Identifying the correct expression for compound interest is key to this problem. Compound interest can be expressed as $P\left(1 + \frac{r}{n}\right)^{nt}$ where P is the initial amount, r is the rate of interest, and n is how often the interest is compounded in a year. Then, just plugging in the values from the problem will give us answer choice D.

Choice A, B, and C are all incorrect because they are not the right expressions for compound interest rate.

QUESTION 10

Choice D is the best choice. This is a similar triangles problem. We know the ratio of the two triangles, as it is given by AB: EF is 6:3, or 2:1. Then, we can deduce that, since FD is proportional to BC and FD is 4, BC must be 8. We

have the lengths of ABC as AB=6, BC=8 and so, by the Pythagorean theorem, the hypotenuse must be 10. Alternatively, recognize that ABC is a 3-4-5 triangle and so the hypotenuse must be in similar proportions.

Choice A and B are both incorrect because the length of the hypotenuse cannot be shorter than either of the other lengths. Choice C is incorrect because we are not trying to find the length of BC.

QUESTION 11

Choice D is the best answer. This is a quadratic question. The quadratic formula is $x = \frac{-b\pm\sqrt{b^2-4ac}}{2a}$ for any equation of the form $ax^2 + bx + c = 0$. By using this formula to solve for x, $x = \frac{-7\pm\sqrt{49-56}}{2}$. Since the value under the radical is not positive, the only solutions are imaginary (square root of a negative number). Thus, there are no real solutions.

Choice A, B, and C are all incorrect because none of those values satisfy the equation.

QUESTION 12

Choice C is the best answer. This is an inequality question. Substitute each ordered pair in for the x and y values. The only choice which satisfies the inequality is (2,5), because 9 < 10.

Choices A and B are incorrect because their values make the left side of the inequality greater than the right side. Choice D is incorrect because the inequality is not less than or equal, ≤, but rather strictly less than <.

QUESTION 13

Choice B is the best answer. This is a factoring and fractions problem. Factor out the 32 from 32x+64 to get x+2 in the numerator. If we factor the denominator of the first term, we get x^2-4=(x+2)(x-2). So, after manipulating the term, we get $\frac{32(x+2)}{(x+2)(x-2)}$ and we can eliminate the x+2 from the top and bottom. So, we are left with $\frac{32}{x-2} - \frac{16}{x-2} = 4$. Since we have a common denominator, this equals $\frac{16}{x-2} = 4$. Multiplying both sides by x-2 yields the equation 16=4x-8, and after adding 8 to both sides and dividing by 4, x=6.

Choice A and C are both incorrect because they are not solutions to the equation. Choice D is incorrect because there is a correct choice.

QUESTION 14

Choice B is the correct answer. This is an average problem. The average of the initial 15 guests is 20, meaning the sum of their ages is 15*20=300. The new average is equal to the new sum over the new total, so (where the sum of the three new guests' age is s) $\frac{300+s}{15+3} = 21$. Multiplying both sides by 18, one finds that 300 + s = 378, meaning the new guests have a sum age of 78. Dividing that by the number of new guests (3) gets that the average age of the new guest is exactly 26.
Choices A, B, and C are all incorrect because they don't result in an exact average age of 21.

QUESTION 15

Choice C is the best answer. This is a data analysis question. Looking at the data presented in the table, it is clear that at each day the value approximately doubles from the previous day. This is representative of an exponential function, not a linear one. Since there is an initial amount of bacteria, the y-intercept must be positive. The only graph that has these characteristics is choice C.

Choice A is incorrect because the growth is not linear. Choice B is incorrect because the initial value is not 0. Choice D is incorrect because the growth is neither negative nor linear.

QUESTION 16

5 is the correct answer. This is a word translation problem. Since Rachel wants a salad with every sandwhich, the number of salads and sandwiches she can buy are the same. So, 3x+7x=52, or 10x=52. Then, dividing both sides by 10, x=5.2. Because you cannot purchase 0.2 sandwiches, we round down to 5.

QUESTION 17

450 is the correct answer. This is a percent problem. Realize that 10% off a 1500$ trip is 150$. Since Rachel gets this discount every four months, and there are twelve months in a year, Rachel receives this discount 3 times. Multiply 150$ by 3 to get 450$.

QUESTION 18

4 or 1 are both correct answers. The first step is to factor out the three from the equation, to get $3(x^2 - 5x + 4) = 0$. Now, factor the remaining quadratic to get $3(x - 4)(x - 1) = 0$. The only values for x which would satisfy this equation are 4 and 1.

QUESTION 19

6/5 or 1.2 are both correct answers. This is a trigonometry question, with an emphasis on identities. The most important identity to this problem is $\sin^2(x) + \cos^2(x) = 1$. Since $\sin^2(x)$ is $\frac{16}{25}$, $\cos^2(x)$ must be $\frac{9}{25}$. Finding the square root of $\cos^2(x)$ gives us $\frac{3}{5}$. Multiplying that value by 2 gives us $\frac{6}{5}$ or in decimal form, 1.2.

QUESTION 20

2 is the correct answer. This is a coordinate plane question. The slope of a perpendicular line is the negative reciprocal of the slope of the original line. So, to find the slope of the original line, use the equation $m = \frac{y_2 - y_1}{x_2 - x_1}$. Plugging in the two points given will yield the slope of $-\frac{1}{2}$. Taking the negative reciprocal of that value will give us 2.

SECTION 4
Math Calculator Test

QUESTION 1

Choice B is the best answer. This is an absolute value question. Substituting 2 in for x makes the value |2-3|-5 which is 1-5=4.

Choice A is incorrect because there is no absolute value sign over the whole function. Choice C is incorrect because it is just the number inside the absolute value sign. Choice D is incorrect because the absolute value sign cannot be ignored.

QUESTION 2

Choice D is the best answer. This is an average problem. Assume that, since the average is 87 for three students, each student got an 87. Then factor Chris into the new average with rest of the scores: $\frac{87+87+87+78}{4} = 84.75$. Rounding up gives 85%.

Choice A, B, and C are incorrect because they are not the new average.

QUESTION 3

Choice A is the best answer. This is a data analysis problem. Since the equation represents the number of cars bought daily, 32 must be a number that resets each day. The only choice where this is true is when the purchases are updated daily when bought online.

Choice B is incorrect because that is what the value of 5 represents. Choice C is incorrect because the equation as a whole represents the total cars sold, not the cars available to sell. Choice D is incorrect because the number of cars bought the day before has no impact on the number of cars sold on the current day.

QUESTION 4

Choice B is the best answer. This is a proportion problem. Since Josh's time is directly proportional to the distance he runs, set up an equation: $T = aD$ where T is time and D is distance with some constant a. There is already an ordered pair for this equation, 0.33 hours=a(3 miles). Solving for a yields the value 0.11 hours for a mile. Multiply this by 10 miles and get 1.1 hours.

Choice A is incorrect since 0.33 hours is divided by miles, not miles divided by hours. Choice C is incorrect because Josh does not take that long to run 10 miles. Choice D is incorrect because the measurement is in hours, not minutes.

QUESTION 5

Choice C is the best answer. This is a word translation problem. Since Bart made 15% more sandwiches on Friday, and that is the same as 6 sandwiches, then $0.15x = 6$ where x is the number of sandwiches made on Thursday. Solving this equation makes $x = 40$. Since Bart made 6 more sandwiches on Friday, he made 46 sandwiches.

Choice A is incorrect because Bart did not make 24 sandwiches on Friday. Choice B is incorrect because that is the amount of sandwiches made on Thursday. Choice D is incorrect because it multiplied 6 by 0.15.

QUESTION 6

Choice B is the best answer. This is a ratio problem. The correct way to solve this problem is count the number of houses with a pool and then compare it to the total number of houses surveyed. There are 6 houses with only a pool and 3 houses with both a pool and a hot tub, so 9 houses have a pool. There are 4+6+5+3 = 18 houses in total. The ratio 9:18 reduces due to the common factor of 9 to 1:2.

Choice A is incorrect not all houses have a pool. Choice C is incorrect because it doesn't include the houses that have both a pool and a hot tub. Choice D is incorrect because it finds the proportion of houses that only have one water feature.

QUESTION 7

Choice D is the best answer. This is a word translation problem. Because Susan wants to run at least 30 miles in total in at most 3 hours, have x and y signify amount of time running and biking, respectively. Since she wants to run at most 3 three hours, then the combined times of x and y must be equal to or less than 3: $x + y \leq 3$. Since Susan wants to run at least 30 miles, $8x + 15y \geq 30$.

Choice A is incorrect because the first equation has swapped variables. Choice B is incorrect because the time should be at MOST 3 hours, not at least 3 hours. Susan does not want to exceed this time frame. Choice C is incorrect because the reciprocals is not the speed.

QUESTION 8

Choice C is the best answer. This is a fraction problem. Working backwards, if Miriam threw away 1/3 of the fudge she had left, she had 15 * 3 = 45 grams after giving fudge to Marta. If she gave 1/4 of her fudge to Marta, then 3/4 of her fudge before that point is 45 grams, meaning she had 45 * 4/3 = 60 grams of fudge before Marta. Considering she gave half to Enrique and kept half, she must have had 120 grams of fudge at the beginning of the problem.

Choice A is incorrect because it assumes 15 grams were given to Enrique. Choice B is incorrect because it assumes 15 grams is the amount eaten by Miriam. Choice D is incorrect because it assumes that 1/4 of the original amount of fudge was given to Marta, instead of 1/4 of the 1/2 that was left.

QUESTION 9

Choice D is the best answer. This is a circle problem. The general equation of a circle in the coordinate plane is $(x - a)^2 + (y - b)^2 = r^2$ with a being the horizontal shift and b being the vertical shift. Since the circle is shifted 2.5 units to the right and 4.5 units up, these are the values of a and b respectively.

Choice A is incorrect because it does not account for the vertical shift. Choice B is incorrect because the circle is not shifted over 5 units. Remember that the shift is measured from the center of the circle from the origin. Choice C is incorrect because the equation is of the incorrect form $(x + a)^2 + (y + b)^2 = r^2$.

QUESTION 10

Choice A is the best answer. This is a word translation problem. The equation 5t+4 is the only model which fits each data point precisely.

Choices B and C are incorrect because there is the growth is linear. Choice D is incorrect because it does not fit the first point (t=0).

QUESTION 11

Choice B is the best answer. This is a percentages problem. Similar to question 5, we must work backwards. If Chris's collection increased by 50% to its current size of 12, then the original amount x increased by 0.5*x, meaning x+0.5x=12. Thus, 1.5x = 12 and x = 8. The donation was thus of size 4. The 4 cards Aziz donated constituted 25% of his original collection, meaning he started with 16 cards.

Choice A incorrectly provides the number of cards Aziz has after the donation. Choice C

QUESTION 12

Choice D is the best answer. This is a word translation problem. Since there are 14 days in 2 weeks, divide the total change in weight by 14 to get the daily increment in weight. $\frac{70}{14} = 5$, so 5 is the slope. Since Justin starts off with 10 pounds, it must be the y intercept. Therefore, W=5t+10 is the best equation. Choice A is incorrect because we are not looking for the time in t weeks, but t days. Choice B is incorrect because it only shows an overall change in weight. Choice C is incorrect because it does not include Justin's starting amount.

QUESTION 13

Choice A is the best answer. This is a word translation problem. Since Greg works 45 hours a week at $23.50 an hour, for 6 weeks, he earns a total of $6345 from wage alone. The rest of the money comes from tips. Subtract the wage salary from the total amount to get $680 made from tips. Divide this by the total amount of money earned to get 9.7 percent as a final answer.

Choice B, C, and D are incorrect because they are not the percent earned from tips. Each of these answers can be obtained through common errors.

QUESTION 14

Choice D is the best answer. This is an inequality problem. The only possible value of z that would satisfy the inequality would be 3. Plug this into 9z-18 to get 9.

Choice A is incorrect because it is the value of -3z. Choice B is incorrect because it would require z to be a non-integer value. Choice C is incorrect because it is the value of z.

QUESTION 15

Choice D is the best answer. This is a coordinate plane problem. Solve this problem by graphing it in your calculator. Look for the points of intersections and find that they are located in the first and fourth quadrants. Alternatively, use algebra to solve this by substituting y=4-x into the equation of the circle, and finding what values of x satisfy the equation. After that, plug the values of x back into x+y=4 to get the y-coordinate and then deduce the quadrants from that information.

Choices A, B, and D are all incorrect because they are not where the line intersects the circle.

QUESTION 16

Choice A is the best answer. This is a parallel lines question. Remember that parallel lines have the same slope, but do not intersect. The slope of line m is -1, as can be found using the formula $m = \frac{y_2 - y_1}{x_2 - x_1}$. Only two of the options have the same slope: the pair (5,3) and (7,1) and the pair (4,8) and (5,7). The latter pair intersects with line m, so it cannot be parallel. That leaves the former.

Choice B is incorrect because it does not have the same slope and it intersects line m. Choice C is incorrect because it intersects line m. Choice D is incorrect because it does not have the same slope as line m.

QUESTION 17

Choice A is the best answer. This is an algebra problem. Since f(x) is 72, set the equation equal to that value: 72=$x^2 2^x$. The only value which satisfies this equation is 3.
Choices B, C, and D are all incorrect because those values all make the function exceed 72.

QUESTION 18

Choice A is the best answer. This is a median and mode question. The first step is to sort the elements of S in numerical order. S:{10, 12, 17, 17, 17, 23, 55, 67, 84, 84, 92}. The median, or middle value, is 23. The mode, or the most frequent element, is 17. The difference between the two is 6.

Choice B is incorrect because it is not the difference between the median and mode. Choice C is incorrect because it is the mode. Choice D is incorrect because it is just an element of the set, not the difference between the median and mode.

QUESTION 19

Choice C is the best answer. This is a composition problem. The notation $f \circ g$ is the same as writing f(g(x)). So, take the value of g(x) at x=3, and then plug that in for the input value for f(x). This produces the value of 963.

Choice A is incorrect because it is the value of each function evaluated at 3 and multiplied. Choice B is incorrect because f(3) is not the input for g(x), but vice versa. Choice D is incorrect because the functions are multiplied together and by 3.

QUESTION 20

Choice C is the best answer. This is a data-analysis problem. Realize that the temperature of each day has no bearing on the number of milkshakes purchased on that day. Both values are random relative to each other, and so there is no correlation.

Choice A is incorrect because the number of milkshakes purchased does not increase with the temperature. Choice B is incorrect because the number of milkshakes purchased does not decrease as the temperature increases. Choice D is incorrect because there is no such thing as a quadratic correlation.

QUESTION 21

Choice C is the best answer. This is a word translation problem. Since a soda costs Rob 2$ and a meal costs Rob 15$, the combo costs him 17$. Since Rob has three of these combos in a day, he has 60$-3*$17=9$. Rob can afford 4 cans at 2$ a piece with this budget.

Choice A is incorrect because it isthe amount of money left over. Choice B is incorrect because he cannot afford the fifth can. Choice D is incorrect because Rob cannot afford 15 extra cans of soda.

QUESTION 22

Choice A is the best answer. This is an exponential problem. Since there is only a year span, substitute 1 in for the value of t. This makes the amount of money that Janice has to pay back $1500(1.5)^1$=2250.

Choice B is incorrect because it does not account for interest. Choice C is incorrect because it does not account for the initial loan. Choice D is incorrect because this is not the amount of money that Janice owes the bank.

QUESTION 23

Choice B is the best answer. This is a geometry problem. Washington, New York, and Montreal form a triangle. By the triangle inequality theorem, no side of a triangle can be greater than the sum of the other two sides or less than the difference between them. The distance between Washington and Montreal must be greater than 128 miles and less than 536 miles. Only 490 miles is in this range.

Choice A, C, and D are all incorrect because they do not fall in the range of possible side lengths.

QUESTION 24

Choice C is the best answer. This is an imaginary problem. FOIL the two factors. This will yield the expression $x^2 + ix - ix - i^2 = x^2 - i^2$. Since i^2 is -1, the expression can further be simplified to x^2+1. Substituting 3 in for x gives us the result 10.

Choice A is incorrect because we do not subtract one, but add one at the end. Choice B is incorrect because the expression does not simplify to ix^2. Choice D is incorrect because the middle term cancels itself out.

QUESTION 25

Choice B is the best answer. This is a trigonometry question. If sin(x) = cos(y), x + y = 90°. The equation becomes a quadratic when 90 is subtracted from both sides, leaving $x^2 - x - 12 = 0$, factoring into (x-4)(x+3) = 0. x is a positive angle, so its measure must be 4 degrees. Plug and chug is also an option, but less fun.

Choices A, C, and D are incorrect because they do not result in the angles 60-x and x^2 +18 being complementary.

QUESTION 26

Choice C is the best answer. The correct answer is C. This is a data analysis question. 62% of kids who took the practice test scored in the top fourth compared to the 15% of kids who did not take the practice test and scored in the top fourth shows that there is a significant advantage to taking the practice test.

Choice A, B, and D are all inappropriate conclusions.

QUESTION 27

Choice A is the best answer. This is a ratio question. Use the data from the table to extrapolate a probability. There are 238 customers that purchased low sugar content cereal for kids. Divide this by the total number of customers, 1499, to get a probability of 15.8%.

Choice B is incorrect because it divides by the sum of the other categories, not the total amount of people. Choice D is incorrect because it focuses solely on the cereal for kids, not the low-sugar cereal overlap. Choice C is incorrect because it focuses solely on the low-sugar cereal, not the kids' cereal overlap.

QUESTION 28

Choice D is the best answer. This is a system of linear equations problem. Each of the equations are just manipulations of the same base equation. Divide the second equation by 6 and bring the y-term over to the left side to obtain the same equation as the first. Multiply the third equation by 3 to find that it is the same as the first equation. Thus they are all the same line and there is an infinite amount of solutions.

Choice A and B are both incorrect because the lines are not parallel nor do they intersect solely once. Choice C will always be incorrect for lines because a line cannot intersect another line just twice.

QUESTION 29

Choice D is the best answer. This is a lines problem. Calculate the slope of Line L using m = $\frac{\Delta y}{\Delta x}$, yielding a slope of -2. The slope of the line perpendicular to L must be its opposite reciprocal, which is $\frac{1}{2}$. The only point which forms a line with (4, 3) that has a slope of $\frac{1}{2}$ is D, (6, 4).

Choice A is incorrect because it's a point on Line L. Choice B is incorrect because it would make the slope of the perpendicular line $-\frac{1}{2}$ (the reciprocal). Choice C is incorrect because it would make the slope of the perpendicular line 2 (the opposite).

QUESTION 30

Choice B is the best answer. This is a polynomial division problem. Use the remainder theorem for a shortcut, knowing that f(x)/(x-c) must have a remainder of f(c), in this case f(-1) = -17. Otherwise use synthetic or long division to get the answer.

Choice A is incorrect answer obtained by omitting the $0x^3$ term in division. Choice C is the result of incorrectly using 1 as the test zero in synthetic division or x-1 as the divisor in long division. Choice D is incorrect because (x+1) is not a factor of the function f(x).

QUESTION 31

1.12 is the correct answer. This is a function problem. To find the points of intersection, set the two functions equal to each other: $f(x) = g(x) \rightarrow 4x^2 - 3 = 2x - 3$. Bring everything to one side to obtain $4x^2 - 2x = 0$. The only solutions are x=0 and x=0.5. Now plug this into either equation to find the y-coordinates. So g(0)=-3 and g(0.5)=-2. Now that there are two points, (0,-3) and (0.5, -2), find the distance between them using the distance formula: $d = \sqrt{(x_2 - x_1)^2 + (y_2 - y_1)^2} = \sqrt{(0.5 - 0)^2 + (-2 + 3)^2} = \sqrt{1.25} = 1.12$.

QUESTION 32

90 hours is the correct answer. This is a combined work problem. Use a system of equations. Define D to be the amount of time Doug studies and J the amount of time Jake studies. Since combined, they both study 300 hours, one of the equations will be D+J=300. Also, since Doug studies 3 times as much as 20 hours less than Jake studies, the other equation will be D=3(J-20). Substitute the second equation into the first to get 3(J-20)+J=300. Solve for J and get 90 hours.

QUESTION 33

2.4 is the correct answer. The arclength on a circle can be calculated by multiplying the measure of the central angle theta times the radius r ($s = \theta r$). Solving for the angle theta entails dividing both sides by the measure of the radius. The angle measures 12/5 = 2.4 radians.

QUESTION 34

2 is the correct answer. This is a percentage problem. The area of a triangle is $A = \frac{1}{2}bh$. Since the height is increased by x percent, the base decreased by 12 percent, and the total area decreased by 10 percent, set up the new equation for

the area as $(1 - 0.10)A = \frac{1}{2}(1 + 0.x)b(1 - 0.12)h$. Because this is a general problem, substitute values in for the base and height and then find an area. For the simplicity of calculations, use b=1, h=1, and A=0.5. Then manipulate the equation to get $0.9(0.5) = \frac{1}{2}(1.x)(0.88)$. Solving this, get 1.x=1.02. Thus, x is 2.

QUESTION 35

85 is the correct answer. This is an average problem. Since the first thirty kids got an 83, assume that each of them got an 83. Because the overall average goes down by 2 percent, the next five kids have to have averages below 81. For the 31st kid to have the highest score, the other students must have the smallest score possible. So, using 65 as each of the other four kids new scores, set up a new equation to determine the 31st kid's score: $\frac{(83*30)+(65*4)+x}{35} = 81$, with x as the 31st kids score. Solving for x, x=85.

QUESTION 36

56 is the correct answer. This is an exponential problem. There are a number of ways to solve any exponential problem, but the most efficient uses the data given. We know that every 5730 years, the function will half in size, which following an exponential relationship yields $m(t) = I\left(\frac{1}{2}\right)^{\frac{t}{5730}}$ where I is the initial mass. The only unknown is I, so simple plug and chug gets the initial mass to be approximately 56 grams.

QUESTION 37

2.5 is the correct answer. This is a system of equations problem. Multiply the top equation by -5 and the bottom one by 2 and combine. This yields that (5-2b)x = 0. For this to always be true (for any value of x), 5-2b must equal 0, meaning b = 2.5. An alternate solution would be to recognize that systems of linear equations with infinite solutions have the same slope. Slope = 2/1 = 5/b. b= 2.5.

QUESTION 38

21 is the correct answer. This is a data analysis problem. Since it took everybody an average of 20 minutes to finish the race, write an average equation as: $\frac{(17+2(19)+3x+4(22)+5(18))}{15} = 20$. Solving this for x, x=21.33. Rounding this to the nearest whole number, 21 is the final answer.

#win

Made in the USA
Lexington, KY
25 March 2019